AS & A2 Psychology

A-Level Psychology is seriously tricky — no question about that.
To do well, you're going to need to revise properly and practise hard.

This book has thorough notes on everything you need to know for the AQA A specification, plus plenty of detailed psychological studies.

There are also warm-up and exam-style practice questions for every topic, with a separate section of advice on how to do well in the exams.

And of course, we've done our best to make the whole thing vaguely entertaining for you.

Complete Revision and Practice

Exam Board: AQA A

AS-Level Contents

Introduction — What is Psychology?

Section One — Cognitive Psychology

Section Two — Developmental Psychology

Section Three — Research Methods

Section Four — Biological Psychology

Section Five — Social Psychology

Section Six — Individual Differences

Do Well in Your Exam

We deliberately haven't put any answers in this book, because they'd just be saying what's already in the book. So instead, we've included sections on how to write answers and do well in the exam.

A2-Level Contents

Published by CGP

Editors:
Katie Braid, Polly Cotterill, Katherine Craig, Ali Palin, Kate Redmond, Jane Sawers

Contributors:
Radha Bellur, Lauren Burns, Richard Carciofo, Dr Karen Goodall, Elisa M Gray, Nigel Holt, Christine Johnson, Tracey Jones, Kate Robson, Denise Say, Stuart Wilson.

ISBN 978 1 84762 422 2

With thanks to Glenn Rogers and Hayley Thompson for the proofreading.

Groovy website: www.cgpbooks.co.uk

Jolly bits of clipart from CorelDRAW®
Printed by Elanders, Newcastle upon Tyne.

Based on the classic CGP style created by Richard Parsons.

AS-Level Psychology

Exam Board: AQA A

What is Psychology?

These two pages give you a very quick intro to psychology. Don't spend ages learning this cos it's really just an overview of stuff you'll cover in detail later on.

Psychology is a Science with **Lots of Theories** and **Few Facts**

Psychology is "**the scientific study of experience and behaviour**."
This basically means that psychologists look at what people and animals do, why they do it, and how they feel.

A lot of psychology sounds like **common sense**, but it's a science, so everything's got to be investigated.
You've got to come up with a **theory** about something and then **scientifically test** it.

It's difficult to prove things in psychology, so there are loads of disagreements and a lot of theories that sound rubbish. But you can't just say they're rubbish in your exam — that'd be too easy. No, you've got to use other theories and experiments to support your answer.

The different schools of thought are called **approaches**. Each approach has its own explanation for why we do what we do. You'll be looking at the **cognitive**, **biological**, **developmental**, **social**, and **psychodynamic** approaches. Fortunately for you, they're split up into handy little sections.

The **Cognitive Approach** Focuses on **Internal Processes**

This section is part of **Unit 1**.

The brain is a complex information processor.

1) Cognitive psychologists focus on **internal processes** to understand behaviour, such as how we perceive or remember things.
2) They compare the human mind to a **computer** system, so they use **computer models** to try to understand human cognition (thinking).
3) Using concepts from information processing, cognitive psychologists describe the brain as a **processor** — it receives **input**, **processes** it, and produces an **output**. Obviously it's ridiculously more complicated, but the general idea is the same.
4) Cognitive psychology studies are often laboratory-based and **artificial**, so they can lack **validity** in the **real world**. This is known as '**ecological validity**' (see page 6).

Developmental Psychology is About How Humans **Develop**... Obviously...

This bit's also part of **Unit 1**. It's a bit of a jumble of ideas from different approaches...

1) Developmental psychologists look at how people **develop** and **change** over their lifetime. They place emphasis on the importance of **early experiences** in shaping the rest of a person's life.
2) The approach focuses on the importance of **attachment** — the **emotional bond** that **infants** form with their **caregivers**.
3) Some researchers, like **Bowlby**, believe that the attachment has to be with the **mother**. This is known as **monotropy**. Others have shown that infants will attach to their **primary caregiver**, even if that's not their biological mother.
4) A big area of research looks at what can happen if attachments are broken (**deprivation**) or never form in the first place (**privation**). It ranges from studying things like the effect of being put into **day care**, where an infant is away from its caregiver for a few hours, to research on children who've had hardly any human contact their **entire lives**.

Because a lot of the research is done on **children**, one of the main **research methods** is **observational research**. This ensures that the children's behaviour is **natural**. Researchers have to be really careful about **ethics**, because people under 18 can't give **informed consent**. They have to get consent from the child's parents instead, and make sure that they use the **least stressful** procedure possible.

Alan won't be able to start growing until the nurse loosens her grip.

What is Psychology?

The **Biological Approach** Explains Behaviour as a Product of **Nature**

This approach is covered in **Unit 2**.
There are three **key assumptions**:

Human behaviour can be explained by looking at internal, biological stuff, like hormones and the nervous system.

Experimental research that uses **animals** can tell us about **human behaviour** because we have similar biological make-ups.

Unwanted behaviour can sometimes be changed for the better using **biological treatments** — e.g. medication for mental illness.

So, as far as this approach is concerned, it's what's inside that counts...

1) Researchers look at **genetics**, the **brain**, **hormones** and the **nervous system** to explain behaviour.
2) It's very scientific — research is mostly carried out in **laboratory experiments**.
3) Common research techniques include **brain scans** and **correlational studies**.

Social Psychologists Look at How We **Interact** with Each Other

This bit is also in **Unit 2**.

1) This approach is all about how we **influence** each other.
2) Major areas of research include **conformity** and **obedience**.
3) Society needs people to conform and be obedient in order to function properly — e.g. if drivers didn't abide by the rules of the road there would be chaos.
4) This can be a problem though, because people might be more likely to do something they think is wrong if they feel pressured by others.

Probably the most famous experiment in social psychology is **Milgram's Behavioural Study of Obedience** (1963). In the experiment he tested people's obedience by asking participants to give someone electric shocks. Most of his participants carried on giving the shocks, even when they thought they were causing harm. He concluded that most people will follow orders even if it means doing something they don't think is right. Pretty scary stuff. You can find this study on page 76.

Individual Differences is About **Differences** Between... erm... **Individuals**

Last one, hurrah. This section is part of **Unit 2**. It's another one that's made up of bits from loads of approaches. The main thing that researchers want to find out is **how** and **why** we're all **different** from each other. You might think it's pretty obvious that we're all different, but psychologists have got to find something to fill the day.

We all have different interests.

1) Other areas of psychology tend to assume that people are broadly the same — e.g. developmental psychologists assume that we all go through the same basic stages of development.
2) A big area of research is **abnormality**. Deviation from the norm is okay to a point, but societies have difficulties dealing with people who are considered to be very abnormal.
3) Because of this, an important issue to bear in mind is how **normality** is **defined**, and whether anyone has the right to decide that someone else is **abnormal**.

It's psychology, Jim, but not as we know it...

There are so many different types of psychology that it can get quite confusing Some of them are like biology, some are more like computing, and some seem to be about pretty much everything else in between. But they all have the same aim — to explain human thoughts and actions. That's why it's so interesting, cos everyone likes talking about themselves...

The Scientific Process

'How Science Works' is all about the scientific process — how we develop and test scientific ideas. It's what scientists do all day, every day. Well, except at coffee time. Never come between scientists and their coffee.

Science Answers Real-life Questions

Science tries to explain **how** and **why** things happen — it **answers questions**. It's all about seeking and gaining **knowledge** about the world around us. Scientists do this by **asking** questions and **suggesting** answers and then **testing** them, to see if they're correct — this is the **scientific process**.

The evidence supported Quentin's Theory of Flammable Burps.

1) **Ask** a question — make an **observation** and ask **why or how** it happens.
2) **Suggest** an answer, or part of an answer, by forming a **theory** (a possible explanation of the observations).
3) Make a **prediction** or **hypothesis** — a **specific testable statement**, based on the theory, about what will happen in a test situation.
4) Carry out a **test** — to provide **evidence** that will support the prediction (or help to disprove it).

Suggesting explanations is all very well and good, but if there's **no way to test** them then it just ain't science. A theory is **only scientific** if it can be tested.

Science is All About Testing Theories

It starts off with one experiment backing up a prediction and theory. It ends up with all the scientists in the world **agreeing** with it and you **learning** it. Stirring stuff. This is how the magical process takes place:

1) The results are **published** — scientists need to let others know about their work, so they try to get their results published in **scientific journals**. These are just like normal magazines, only they contain **scientific reports** (called papers) instead of celebrity gossip. All work must undergo **peer review** before it's published.

   - **Peer review** is a process used to **ensure the integrity** of published scientific work. Before publication, scientific work is sent to **experts** in that field (**peers**) so they can assess the **quality** of the work.
   - This process helps to keep scientists **honest** — e.g. you can't '**sex-up**' your conclusions if the data doesn't support it, because it **won't pass** peer review.
   - Peer review helps to **validate conclusions** — it means published theories, data and conclusions are more trustworthy. But it **can't guarantee** that the conclusions are 100% right. More **rounds** of predicting and testing are needed before they can be taken as '**fact**'.
   - Sometimes **mistakes** are made and bad science is published. Peer review **isn't perfect** but it's probably the best way for scientists to **self-regulate** their work and to ensure **reliable** scientific work is **published**.

2) Other scientists read the published theories and results, and try to **repeat them** — this involves repeating the **exact experiments**, and using the theory to make **new predictions** that are tested by **new experiments**.
3) If all the experiments in all the world provide evidence to back it up, the theory is thought of as scientific 'fact' (**for now**).
4) If **new evidence** comes to light that **conflicts** with the current evidence the theory is questioned all over again. More rounds of **testing** will be carried out to see which evidence, and so which theory, **prevails**.

If the Evidence Supports a Theory, It's Accepted — For Now

Our currently accepted theories have survived this '**trial by evidence**'. They've been tested **over and over and over** and each time the results have backed them up. **BUT**, and this is a big but (teehee), they never become totally undisputable fact. Scientific **breakthroughs or advances** could provide new ways to question and test a theory, which could lead to **changes and challenges** to it. Then the testing starts all over again...

And this, my friend, is the **tentative nature of scientific knowledge** — it's always **changing** and **evolving**.

The Role of Science

Science is all about the search for truth and knowledge. But why bother? We want to know as much as possible so we can use it to try to improve our lives (and because we're nosy).

Science Helps Us Make **Better Decisions**

Lots of scientific work eventually leads to **important discoveries** that could **benefit humankind**. Oh yes. These results are **used by society** (that's you, me and everyone else) to **make decisions** about the way we live. All sections of society use scientific evidence to make decisions:

1) **Politicians** use science to devise policy. E.g. **cognitive behavioural therapy** is available on the NHS because there's evidence to show it can help people with **depression**.
2) **Private organisations** use science to determine what to make or develop — e.g. evidence has shown that the number of people being diagnosed with **depression** is increasing, so drugs companies might put **more money** into this area of research.
3) **Individuals** also use science to make decisions about their **own lives** — e.g. evidence suggests that we should exercise and eat healthily, but it's up to individuals to **decide** whether they take that advice or not.

Other **Factors** Can **Influence** Decision Making

Other factors can influence decisions about science or the way science is used:

Economic factors

- Society has to consider the **cost** of implementing changes based on scientific conclusions — e.g. the **NHS** can't afford the most expensive drugs without **sacrificing** something else.
- Scientific research is **expensive** so companies won't always develop new ideas — e.g. developing new drugs is costly, so pharmaceutical companies often only invest in drugs that are likely to make **money**.

Social factors

- **Decisions** affect **people's lives**. How psychologists decide what's **normal** and what's **abnormal** affects how people are treated — e.g. homosexuality was defined as an **abnormal behaviour** until 1987.

Environmental factors

- Scientists believe **unexplored regions**, like parts of rainforests, might contain **untapped drug** resources. But some people think we shouldn't **exploit** these regions because any interesting finds might lead to **deforestation, reduced biodiversity** and **more CO_2** in the atmosphere.

Science Has **Responsibilities**

Yes, you've guessed it — **ethics.** Science has to be **responsible** in many ways. Scientists aren't allowed to test something just because they can. They have to think about the **ethical considerations** surrounding the experiment design and how the results could affect society.

1) **Design** — e.g. experiments involving **animals** are tightly controlled and monitored. **Studies** are checked to ensure they aren't placing individuals in **unnecessary danger**. If a study shows a drug has a highly **beneficial effect**, it's stopped and those in the **placebo** (negative) group are given the drug too.
2) **Results** — e.g. scientists' understanding of some **genetic disorders** could lead to tests to detect members of the population that carry the genes for them. But would people want to know?

Society does have a say in what experiments take place. **Controversial experiments** involving ethical issues have to be approved by scientific and **ethics councils** before they are allowed to be carried out.

So there you have it — how science works...

Hopefully these pages have given you a nice intro to how science works — what scientists do to provide you with 'facts'. You need to understand this, as you're expected to use it to evaluate evidence for yourselves — in the exam and in life.

The Cognitive Approach

Welcome to the cognitive approach. A fine approach if ever I saw one. A real rollicking riotous romp of an approach — full of mystery and intrigue, with a few exciting twists and turns along the way. So get comfy on your bedroom floor, line up your miniature highlighters, and saddle up the revision pony, cos the next stop's Examsville, Arizona...

Cognitive Psychology Looks at How We **Interpret** the World

1) Cognitive psychology is all about **how** we think.
2) Cognitive psychologists try to **explain behaviour** by looking at our **perception**, **language**, **attention** and **memory**.
3) **Computers** and computer models are often used to explain how we think and behave. Humans are treated as **information processors** (computers) and behaviour is explained in terms of **information processing** (how computers deal with information). Cognitive psychology is sometimes called the **information processing** approach.
4) But cognitive psychology has **limitations**. Research is often carried out in artificial situations (laboratories, using computer models) and the role of emotion and influence from other people is often ignored. For these reasons some argue that the results aren't valid in the real world.
5) A second criticism is that cognitive psychology fails to take **individual differences** into account by assuming that all of us process stuff in exactly the same way.

Cognitive Psychology Developed as the **Computer Age Developed**

1) People began to see similarities in how computers and humans make sense of information.
2) Computer terms are often used in cognitive psychology:
The brain is described as a **processor** (the thing that makes things happen) — it has data **input** into it, and **output** from it. Some parts of the brain form **networks** (connections of bits). Other parts work in **serial** (info travels along just one path) or in **parallel** (info travels to and fro along lots of paths at the same time).
3) Cognitive psychologists use computers to create **computational models** of the human mind.

Cognitive Psychologists Use **Four** Main Research Methods

Here's a snappy little phrase for you to learn before you read on: '**ecological validity**' — it's the measure of how much the result of an experiment reflects what would happen in **natural settings**. If a result has **low** ecological validity, it might work fine in the lab. But try and use it to explain real life behaviour, and you'll find yourself up the creek without a paddle. And no-one wants that.

1 — Laboratory Experiments

A lot of research in cognitive psychology happens in **laboratories**. This is very **scientific** and reliable as it is possible to have great control over variables in a lab. However, often this type of research doesn't tell us much about the real world — it has **low ecological validity**.

2 — Field Experiments

Field experiments take place in a **natural** situation (e.g. studies of memory or attention in a school environment), so they have more ecological validity, but there's less control of other variables.

3 — Natural Experiments

Natural experiments involve making observations of a **naturally occurring situation**. The experimenter has little control of the variables, and participants can't be randomly assigned to conditions. Natural experiments have **high ecological validity**, but they're **not massively reliable**, as **uncontrolled** (or **confounding**) variables can affect the results.

4 — Brain Imaging

Brain imaging can now be carried out during a cognitive task. For example, MRI scans have been used to show the blood flow in different brain areas for different types of memory tasks.

The Cognitive Approach

Case Studies *Provide Support for the Cognitive Approach*

Case studies use patients' behaviour to test a theory. **Brain damaged** patients are often studied — the damaged parts of the brain are linked to observed differences in behaviour. However, it's hard to make **generalisations** from the study of subjects with brain damage to 'normal' individuals. Also, **individual differences** between people mean that one subject may respond in a way that is totally different from someone else. Hmmm, tricky.

Cognitive psychologists believe that the different types of memory are **separate systems** in the brain. The case study of HM supported this by showing that short- and long-term memory must be based in different brain structures.

Milner et al (1957) — case study of HM

Diagnosis: HM was a patient with severe and frequent epilepsy. His seizures were based in a brain structure called the hippocampus. In 1953, doctors decided to surgically remove part of the brain round this area.

Results: The operation reduced his epilepsy, but led to him suffering memory loss.
He could still form short-term memories (STMs), but was unable to form new long-term memories (LTMs). For example, he could read something over and over without realising that he had read it before. He also moved house and had difficulty recalling the new route to his house. However, he could still talk and show previous skills (**procedural memory**). From tests, they found HM's **episodic memory** (for past events) and **semantic memory** (for knowledge, e.g. word meanings) was affected more than his **procedural memory**.

Cognitive Psychologists Apply ***Animal Research*** *to Humans*

The results of **non-human** studies can be **applied** to human cognitive abilities. For example, discovering whether chimpanzees can learn language helps psychologists develop theories about how humans learn language.

However, there are so many **differences** between humans and animals that results can be explained wrongly. For example, you might conclude that chimpanzees can't learn a **spoken** language because they lack the **cognitive** abilities. But it's actually more likely to be because they lack the **physiological** attributes, like a voice box.

Gardner and Gardner (1969) — teaching ASL to a chimp

Method: Washoe, a chimpanzee, was raised like a human child and taught American Sign Language (ASL).

Results: By the end of the 22nd month of the project, Washoe had learnt at least 34 signs.

Conclusion: The development of language in the chimpanzee appeared to follow the **same patterns** as language development in children (both speaking children, and those using ASL). Washoe learnt language at similar rates to children of the same age. Additionally, language acquisition seemed to require **interaction** with caregivers and communication in everyday situations. However, she did not learn **grammar**.

Evaluation: There are **ethical** considerations, in that Washoe was taken from the wild and deprived of other chimpanzees for companionship. There are also issues of **external validity** — it is not possible to accurately generalise results from a chimp to human children.

Practice Questions

Q1 Why is cognitive psychology sometimes called the information processing approach?

Q2 Why are laboratory experiments more reliable than field experiments?

Q3 How is brain imaging useful in cognitive psychology?

Exam Questions

Q1 Explain how the study of HM provided support for cognitive psychological thinking. [4 marks]

Q2 Explain why animal studies have been criticised as lacking validity. [3 marks]

Syntax error. Funny line does not compute. Insert file 'humour for books'.

If your brain goes wrong just turn it off and on again. That normally works for me. One day we'll probably know enough about the brain to be able to build computer people. Then you could make a computerised version of yourself and amaze your friends and family by projecting illegally downloaded TV out of your own face. Imagine that. They'd be so proud...

Short-Term and Long-Term Memory

I used to worry that I could remember where I was in, say, May '98, but I couldn't recall why I'd just walked into a room. But it's due to the difference between short-term and long-term memory. Or something... I forget the exact reason.

Memory is a **Process** in Which Information is **Retained** About the Past

Memories are thought to have a physical basis or '**trace**'. Most psychologists agree that there are three types of memory — **sensory memory (SM)**, **short-term memory (STM)** and **long-term memory (LTM)**.

SM is visual and auditory information that passes through our senses very briefly. SM disappears quickly through **spontaneous decay** — the trace just fades. SM isn't around for very long, so most studies are on LTM and STM.

STM and LTM differ in terms of:

1) **Duration** — How long a memory lasts.
2) **Capacity** — How much can be held in the memory.
3) **Encoding** — Transferring information into code, creating a 'trace'.

STM has a **limited capacity** and a **limited duration** (i.e. we can remember a little information for a short time).

LTM has a pretty much **unlimited capacity** and is theoretically **permanent** (i.e. lots of information forever).

Research Has Been Carried Out into the Nature of **STM and LTM**

Peterson and Peterson (1959) Investigated STM Using Trigrams

Peterson and Peterson (1959) investigated the duration of STM.

Method: Participants were shown **nonsense trigrams** (3 random consonants, e.g. CVM) and asked to recall them after either 3, 6, 9, 12, 15 or 18 seconds. During the pause, they were asked to count backwards in threes from a given number. This was an **'interference task'** — it prevented them from repeating the letters to themselves.

Results: After **3 seconds**, participants could recall about **80%** of trigrams correctly.
After **18 seconds**, only about **10%** were recalled correctly.

Conclusion: When rehearsal is prevented, **very little** can stay in STM for longer than about **18 seconds**.

Evaluation: The results are likely to be reliable — it's a **laboratory experiment** where the variables can be tightly controlled. However, nonsense trigrams are artificial, so the study lacks **ecological validity** (see page 37 for more about reliability and validity). Meaningful or 'real-life' memories may last longer in STM. Only one type of **stimulus** was used — the duration of STM may depend on the type of stimulus. Also, each participant saw **many different trigrams**. This could have led to confusion, meaning that the first trigram was the only realistic trial.

Bahrick et al (1975) Investigated LTM in a Natural Setting

Bahrick et al (1975) studied very long-term memories (VLTMs).

Method: 392 people were asked to list the names of their ex-classmates. (This is called a **'free-recall test'**.)
They were then shown photos and asked to recall the names of the people shown (**photo-recognition test**) or given names and asked to match them to a photo of the classmate (**name-recognition test**).

Results: Within 15 years of leaving school, participants could **recognise** about **90%** of names and faces. They were about **60%** accurate on **free recall**. After 30 years, **free recall** had declined to about **30%** accuracy.
After 48 years, name-recognition was about **80%** accurate, and photo-recognition about **40%** accurate.

Conclusion: The study shows evidence of **VLTMs** in a **'real-life'** setting. Recognition is better than recall, so there may be a huge store of information, but it's not always easy to **access** all of it — you just need help to get to it.

Evaluation: This was a field experiment and so had **high ecological validity**. However in a 'real-life' study like this, it's hard to **control** all the variables, making these findings less reliable — there's no way of knowing exactly **why** information was recalled well. It showed better recall than other studies on LTM, but this may be because **meaningful** information is stored better. This type of information could be rehearsed (if you're still in touch with classmates, or if you talk to friends about memories of classmates), increasing the rate of recall.
This means that the results can't be generalised to other types of information held in LTM.

Short-Term and Long-Term Memory

STM and LTM Have Very **Different Capacities**

Jacobs (1887) studied the capacity of STM.

Method: Participants were presented with a string of letters or digits. They had to repeat them back in the same order. The number of digits or letters increased until the participant failed to recall the sequence correctly.

Results: The majority of the time, participants recalled about **9 digits** and about **7 letters**. This capacity increased with **age** during childhood.

Conclusion: Based on the range of results, Jacobs concluded that STM has a **limited storage capacity** of **5-9 items**. Individual differences were found, such as STM increasing with age, possibly due to increased brain capacity or use of memory techniques, such as **chunking** (see below). Digits may have been easier to recall as there were only 10 different digits to remember, compared to 26 letters.

Evaluation: Jacobs' research is **artificial** and **lacks ecological validity** — it's not something you'd do in real life. More meaningful information may be recalled better, perhaps showing STM to have an even greater capacity. Also, the previous sequences recalled by the participants might have confused them on future trials.

Miller (1956) reviewed research into the capacity of STM. He found that people can remember about seven items. He argued that the capacity of STM is **seven, plus or minus two** — 'Miller's magic number'. He suggested that we use '**chunking**' to combine individual letters or numbers into larger more meaningful units. So 2,0,0,3,1,9,8,7 is about all the digits STM can hold. 'Chunked' into the meaningful recent years of 2003 and 1987, it's much easier to remember. STM could probably hold about seven such pieces of chunked information, increasing STM's capacity.

Encoding is About the Way Information is Stored in Memory

In **STM**, we sometimes try to keep information active by repeating it to ourselves. This means it generally involves **acoustic** coding. In **LTM**, encoding is generally **semantic** — it's more useful to code words in terms of their meaning, rather than what they sound or look like (although encoding in LTM **can** also be visual or acoustic).

Encoding can be visual (pictures), acoustic (sounds, e.g. 'chunky' and 'monkey' are acoustically similar) or semantic (meanings, e.g. 'chunky' and 'beefy' are semantically similar).

Baddeley (1966) investigated encoding in STM and LTM.

Method: Participants were given four sets of words that were either **acoustically similar** (e.g. man, mad, mat), **acoustically dissimilar** (e.g. pit, cow, bar), **semantically similar** (e.g. big, large, huge) and **semantically dissimilar** (e.g. good, hot, pig). The experiment used an **independent groups** design (see page 36) — participants were asked to recall the words either immediately or following a 20-minute task.

Results: Participants had problems recalling acoustically similar words when recalling the word list immediately (from **STM**). If recalling after an interval (from **LTM**), they had problems with semantically similar words.

Conclusion: The patterns of confusion between similar words suggest that **LTM** is more likely to rely on **semantic** encoding and **STM** on **acoustic** encoding.

Evaluation: This is another study that **lacks ecological validity**. Also, there are **other types** of LTM (e.g. episodic memory, procedural memory) and **other methods** of encoding (e.g. visual) which this experiment doesn't consider. The experiment used an **independent groups** design, so there wasn't any control over participant variables.

Practice Questions

Q1 What is meant by encoding?

Q2 What is chunking?

Exam Question

Q1 Identify one flaw in the design of a study into the duration of STM.
How could this flaw have been overcome? [4 marks]

Remember the days when you didn't have to remember stuff like this...

Whether you're going to remember something depends a lot on how much it means to you personally. So trivial things that have no bearing on your life whatsoever are forgotten pretty quickly. But more important things like the Hollyoaks theme tune tend to go round and round in your head forever. Or is that just because you've got it on in the background...

Models of Memory

This page is all about why you can't remember the last page. Maybe you didn't rehearse it enough, or maybe you only looked at the letters instead of trying to understand the facts. Or maybe you spilt tea on it and couldn't read the words...

Atkinson and Shiffrin (1968) Created the **Multi-Store Model**

1) The multi-store model proposes that memory consists of three stores — a **sensory store**, a **short-term store** and a **long-term store**.
2) Information from our environment (e.g. visual or auditory) initially goes into **sensory memory**. You don't really notice much of this stuff. However, if you pay attention to it, or think about it, the information will be encoded and will pass into **short-term memory**.
3) Short-term memory has a **finite** capacity and duration. But if information is processed further (rehearsed) then it can be transferred to **long-term memory**. In theory, the information can then remain there forever. Unless you really really need to remember it, in which case it'll probably stay there until something more interesting comes along, like a bee or a cloud.

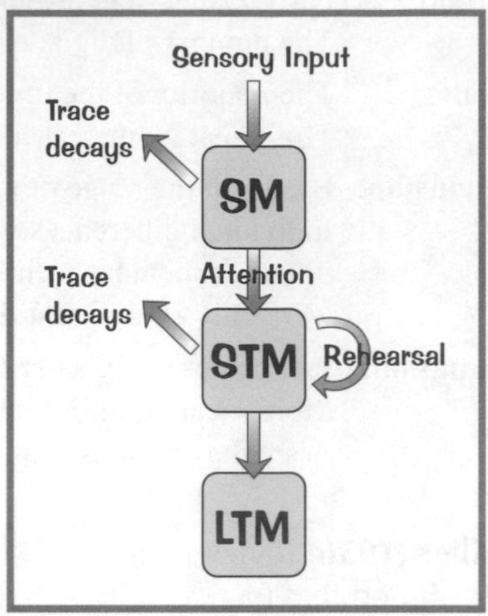

Many Studies **Support** the Multi-Store Model...

Several studies have been carried out that show that memory is made up of separate stores.

1) The **Primacy Effect** — Research shows that participants are able to recall the first few items of a list better than those from the middle. The multi-store model explains this because **earlier** items will have been **rehearsed** better and transferred to **LTM**. If rehearsal is prevented by an interference task, the effect disappears, as the model predicts.

2) The **Recency Effect** — Participants also tend to remember the last few items better than those from the middle of the list. Earlier items are rehearsed, so transfer to LTM, whilst **later** items are recalled because they're still in **STM**.

3) People with **Korsakoff's Syndrome** (amnesia that's mostly caused by chronic alcoholism) provide support for the model. They can recall the **last** items in a list (unimpaired recency effect), suggesting an unaffected **STM**. However, their **LTM** is very poor. This supports the model by showing that STM and LTM are **separate stores**.

...But There Are Also Many **Limitations** of the Model

Although there's lots of support for the model, there's plenty of criticism too.

1) In the model, information is transferred from the STM to LTM through **rehearsal**. But in **real life** people don't always spend time rehearsing, yet they still transfer information into LTM. Rehearsal is not always needed for information to be stored and some items can't be rehearsed, e.g. smells.

2) The model is **oversimplified**. It assumes there is only one long-term store and one short-term store. This has been disproved by evidence from **brain damaged** patients, suggesting several **different** short-term stores, and other evidence suggesting different long-term stores.

Models of Memory

Baddeley and Hitch (1974) Developed the **Working Memory Model**

Baddeley and Hitch developed a multi-store model of STM called the 'working memory model'. Their model proposed that STM is made up of several different stores.

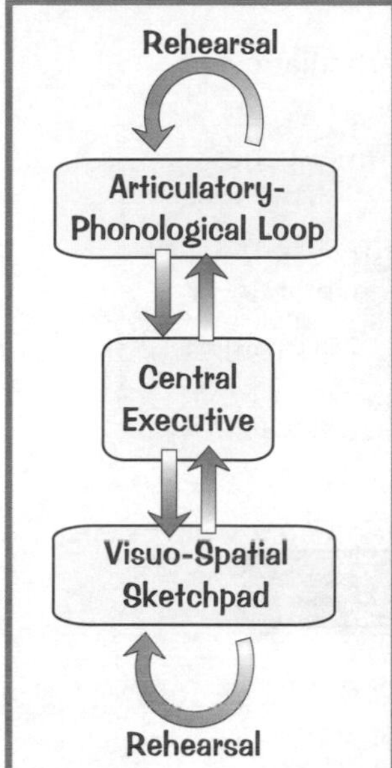

The **central executive** is the key component and can be described as attention. It has a **limited capacity** and controls two 'slave' systems that also have **limited capacity**:

1) The **articulatory-phonological loop** holds speech-based information. It contains a **phonological store** (the inner ear) and an **articulatory process** (the inner voice).
2) The **visuo-spatial sketchpad** deals with the temporary storage of visual and spatial information.

Baddeley and Hitch based their model on results from studies that used '**interference tasks**':

1) If participants are asked to perform two tasks simultaneously that use the same system, their performance will be affected — e.g. saying 'the the the' while silently reading something is very difficult.
2) According to the working memory model, both these tasks use the articulatory-phonological loop. This has limited capacity so it can't cope with both tasks. Performance on one, or both tasks, will be affected.
3) However, if the two tasks involve different systems, performance isn't affected on either task (e.g. saying 'the the the' whilst tracking a moving object).

As Usual the Model has **Strengths** and **Weaknesses**

Shallice and Warrington (1974) found **support** for the working memory model through their case study of KF.

KF was a brain damaged patient who had an impaired STM. His problem was with immediate recall of words presented **verbally**, but not with visual information. This suggested he had an impaired **articulatory loop**, therefore providing evidence for the working memory model's view of STM.

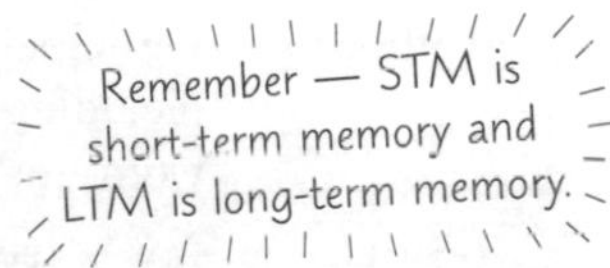

However, many psychologists have **criticised** this model — they think that Baddeley and Hitch's idea of a central executive is **simplistic** and **vague**. Their model doesn't really explain exactly what the central executive is, apart from being involved in attention.

Practice Questions

Q1 What is the primacy effect?

Q2 Name the components of the multi-store model of memory.

Q3 Who came up with the working memory model?

Q4 How did the study of KF provide support for the working memory model?

Q5 What have I drawn on my visuo-spatial sketchpad? That's right, it's a house.

Exam Questions

Q1 Evaluate Atkinson and Shiffrin's multi-store model of memory. [8 marks]

Q2 How did Baddeley and Hitch use the results from studies involving interference tasks to develop their model? [4 marks]

Memory, all alone in the moonlight... something about the moon... la la la...

I don't know about you, but I find these pages pretty boring. Kind of learnable, but still boring enough that you find yourself face-down on your desk in a pool of dribble, with a biscuit stuck to your forehead. Don't fret though — it's not long before you can start learning about the gory experiments with electric shocks and nastiness. Much better than this stuff...

Eyewitness Testimony

If you witness a crime or an accident, you might have to report what you saw, and your version of events could be crucial in prosecuting someone... But your memory isn't as accurate as you might think...

Eyewitness Testimony Can Be **Inaccurate** and **Distorted**

1) **Eyewitness testimony** (EWT) is the **evidence** provided by people who **witnessed** a particular event or crime. It relies on **recall** from memory.
2) EWT includes, for example, **descriptions** of criminals (e.g. hair colour, height) and crime scenes (e.g. time, date, location).
3) Witnesses are often **inaccurate** in their recollection of events and the people involved. As you can probably imagine, this has important implications when it comes to police interviews.
4) Many cognitive psychologists focus on working out what **factors** affect the accuracy of eyewitness testimony, and how accuracy can be **improved** in interviews.

Eyewitness Testimony Can Be Affected by **Misleading Information**

Loftus and Palmer (1974) investigated how EWT can be **distorted**.
They used **leading questions**, where a certain answer is subtly implied in the question:

Loftus and Palmer (1974) studied eyewitness testimony.

Loftus and Palmer carried out two experiments in their study.

Experiment 1:

Method: Participants were shown a film of a multiple car crash. They were then asked a series of questions including 'How fast do you think the cars were going when they **hit**?' In different conditions, the word 'hit' was replaced with **'smashed'**, **'collided'**, **'bumped'** or **'contacted'**.

Results: It was seen that participants given the word **'smashed'** estimated the **highest speed** (an average of 41 mph), and those given the word **'contacted'** gave the **lowest** estimate (an average of 32 mph).

Experiment 2:

Method: The participants were split into three groups. One group was given the verb 'smashed', another 'hit', and the third, control group wasn't given any indication of the vehicles' speed. A week later, the participants were asked **'Did you see any broken glass?'**.

Results: Although there was no broken glass in the film, participants were more likely to say that they'd seen broken glass in the **'smashed'** condition than any other.

Conclusion: **Leading questions** can affect the **accuracy** of people's memories of an event.

Evaluation: This has implications for questions in **police interviews**. However, this was an artificial experiment — watching a video is not as **emotionally arousing** as a real-life event, which potentially affects recall. In fact, a later study found that participants who thought they'd witnessed a **real** robbery gave a more **accurate** description of the robber. The experimental design might lead to **demand characteristics**, where the results are skewed because of the participants' expectations about the purposes of the experiment. For example, the leading questions might have given participants **clues** about the nature of the experiment (e.g. they could have realised that the experiment was about susceptibility to leading questions), and so participants might have acted accordingly. This would have reduced the **validity** and **reliability** of the experiment.

Eyewitness Testimony

Loftus and Zanni (1975) also Looked at Leading Questions

Loftus and Zanni (1975) showed participants a film of a car accident, then asked them either 'Did you see **the** broken headlight?' or 'Did you see **a** broken headlight?' There was no broken headlight, but **7%** of those asked about '**a**' broken headlight claimed they saw one, compared to **17%** in the group asked about '**the**' broken headlight. So, the simple use of the word 'the' is enough to affect the accuracy of people's memories of an event.

The Accuracy of Eyewitness Testimony is Affected by Many Factors

As well as leading questions, there are other factors that can affect the accuracy of eyewitness testimony.

The Age of the Witness can Affect the Accuracy of Recall

Studies have shown that the **age** of the witness can have an effect on the accuracy of eyewitness testimony.

	Valentine and Coxon (1997) studied the effect of age on EWT.
Method:	3 groups of participants (children, young adults and elderly people) watched a video of a kidnapping. They were then asked a series of leading and non-leading questions about what they had seen.
Results:	Both the elderly people and the children gave more incorrect answers to non-leading questions. Children were misled more by leading questions than adults or the elderly.
Conclusion:	Age has an effect on the accuracy of eyewitness testimony.
Evaluation:	This has **implications** in law when children or elderly people are questioned. However, the experiment was **artificial** and so wasn't as emotionally arousing as the same situation would have been in real life — the study **lacks external validity**. The study could have seemed like an experiment into how well people remember things from TV, which isn't the same as real life.

Anxiety can Affect Focus

Psychologists tend to believe that **small increases** in anxiety and arousal may **increase the accuracy** of memory, but **high levels** have a **negative effect** on accuracy. In **violent crimes** (where anxiety and arousal are likely to be high), the witness may focus on **central details** (e.g. a weapon) and neglect other peripheral details.

	Loftus (1979) studied weapon focus in EWT.
Method:	In a study with an **independent groups** design (see page 36), participants heard a discussion in a nearby room. In one condition, a man came out of the room with a pen and grease on his hands. In the second condition, the man came out carrying a knife covered in blood. Participants were asked to identify the man from 50 photographs.
Results:	Participants in condition 1 were 49% accurate. Only 33% of the participants in condition 2 were correct.
Conclusion:	When anxious and aroused, witnesses focus on a weapon at the expense of other details.
Evaluation:	The study has **high ecological validity**, as the participants weren't aware that the study was staged. However, this means that there are also **ethical** considerations, as participants could have been very stressed at the sight of the man with the knife.

Eyewitness Testimony

The **Cognitive Interview** was Developed to **Increase Accuracy**

Cognitive psychologists have played a big part in helping to **increase the accuracy** of eyewitness testimony. As you've seen, research shows that the accuracy of eyewitness testimony is affected by many factors. The **cognitive interview technique** was developed by **Geiselman et al (1984)** to try to increase the accuracy of witnesses' recall of events during police questioning.

Here's basically what happens in cognitive interviews:

1) The interviewer tries to make the witness **relaxed** and tailors his/her **language** to suit the witness.
2) The witness recreates the environmental and internal (e.g. mood) **context** of the crime scene.
3) The witness reports absolutely **everything** that they can remember about the crime.
4) The witness is asked to recall details of the crime in **different orders**.
5) The witness is asked to recall the event from various **different perspectives**, e.g. from the eyes of other witnesses.
6) The interviewer avoids any **judgemental** and **personal comments**.

There is **Research** to **Support** the Cognitive Interview

Research has shown that people interviewed with the cognitive interview technique are much more **accurate** in their recall of events. For example:

Geiselman et al (1986) studied the effect of the cognitive interview.

Method:	In a staged situation, an intruder carrying a **blue** rucksack entered a classroom and stole a slide projector. Two days later, participants were questioned about the event. The study used an **independent groups** design — participants were either questioned using a standard interview procedure or the cognitive interview technique. Early in the questioning, participants were asked 'Was the guy with the **green** backpack nervous?'. Later in the interview, participants were asked what colour the man's rucksack was.
Results:	Participants in the cognitive interview condition were less likely to recall the rucksack as being green than those in the standard interview condition.
Conclusion:	The cognitive interview technique **enhances memory recall** and **reduces the effect of leading questions**.
Evaluation:	The experiment was conducted as though a real crime had taken place in the classroom — it had **high ecological validity**. The experiment used an **independent groups** design. The disadvantage of this is that the participants in the cognitive interview condition could have been naturally less susceptible to leading questions than the other group.

Practice Questions

Q1 What is eyewitness testimony?

Q2 What are leading questions?

Q3 Give two factors that can affect the accuracy of eyewitness testimony.

Exam Questions

Q1 Outline and evaluate one study into the effect of misleading information on eyewitness testimony. [8 marks]

Q2 Outline the techniques used in the cognitive interview. [4 marks]

A tall thin man, quite short, with black, fair hair — great fat bloke she was...

Well, now I haven't a clue what I've really experienced in my life. Did that man I saw shoplifting really have stubble, scars, a pierced chin and a ripped leather jacket, or is that just my shoplifter stereotype kicking in? In fact, come to think of it, I couldn't actually tell you whether my granny has a hairy chin or not. I think she does, but then I think all grannies do...

Strategies for Memory Improvement

This stuff might actually come in handy when you're revising for your exams. You can't say we never try to help you...

Mnemonics are Internal Memory Strategies

We often avoid having to remember things by making **notes** and **lists**. However, sometimes this isn't possible — say, when you're learning stuff for an **exam**. This is where **mnemonics** come in useful. These use things like **visual imagery** and **associations** to **cue** your recall.

There are Loads of Different Mnemonics

Here are just a few...

Organising Material Makes it Easier to Remember

Research has shown that when we're learning something, we often automatically **organise** the material in a way that makes it easier to remember.

For example, **Jenkins and Russell** (1952) studied the recall of **word lists**. The word lists contained words that were **highly associated** (e.g. knife and fork). They found that participants tended to **group** the associated words together in recall even though they'd been **separated** in the original presentation. So, if 'knife' and 'fork' had been separated by other words in the original list, they'd be recalled together.

Tulving (1962) repeatedly gave his participants a list of words to learn. He found that the **order** of the participants' recall became increasingly **consistent** — they were **organising** and **chunking** the material to be learnt into easily remembered groups. E.g. if the word list contained cat, daisy, sock, giraffe, shoe, scarf, dog and rose, it's likely that no matter what order they were presented in, the words would be grouped together into categories for recall — animals, clothes and flowers.

The Method of Loci is a Strategy that Uses Imagery

Method of Loci

It's useful for remembering a **list of words or objects**, e.g. the items on a shopping list.
The items to be remembered are associated with **locations** (**loci**) in a **well-known place**, e.g. your house:

1) So, for example, say the shopping list contains **milk**, **chocolate**, **apples**, **bananas** and **bread**.

2) You'd take a **mental tour** around your house, **visually placing each object** at a **specific place**.

3) You could place the bottle of milk at your front door, put the chocolate on a table in the hall, put the apples on the sofa in the living room, put the bananas in the kitchen sink and, finally, put the bread on the stairs.

4) When you get to the supermarket, all you'd need to do is **mentally repeat the tour** around your house, remembering which items were placed where.

Wait — wasn't the bread supposed to be on the stairs...

Strategies for Memory Improvement

The Peg-Word Technique Uses Imagery Too...

Peg-Word Technique

This is another technique that uses imagery to remember a set of objects or words.
Take the shopping list example again — milk, chocolate, apples, bananas and bread.

The peg-words rhyme with the numbers — this helps you to remember them.

1) First of all, you use a set of peg-words which are **already stored in memory**.
2) So, for this list of five objects, you'd need five peg-words:

One is a bun | Two is a shoe | Three is a tree | Four is a door | Five is a hive

3) Then, **each item** on the shopping list is **linked to a number**. So, you could imagine a bar of chocolate inside a bun, bananas poking out of a shoe, apples hanging on a tree, and so on...
4) In the supermarket, you'd just need to remember each peg-word and picture the item associated with it.

The First Letter Mnemonic Helps with Learning Something's Order

The trick here is to use the **first letter** of each word to create a new sentence.
Say you're trying to learn the order of the **planets**:

Mercury, **V**enus, **E**arth, **M**ars, **J**upiter, **S**aturn, **U**ranus, **N**eptune

You could turn this into...

My **V**olkswagen **E**ats **M**ouldy **J**am **S**andwiches **U**ntil **N**oon

(...or something even funnier, cos I'm not that funny).

Mnemonic Verses are Little Poems that Help you Remember Facts

Mnemonic verses help you remember information by encoding it **acoustically** (by **sound**, see page 9).
There are loads of really famous ones...

...like the one to help you remember how many days there are in each month...

Thirty days has **September**,
April, June, and **November**,
All the rest have thirty-**one**,
Except February **alone**,
Which has twenty-eight days **clear**,
And twenty-nine each leap **year**.

...the one to help you remember what happened to Henry VIII's six wives...

Divorced, beheaded, died,
Divorced, beheaded, survived.

...and the one to help you remember how to spell words like **tie** and **cei**ling...

'**i**' before '**e**', except after '**c**'.

(...although unfortunately this one is less useful with words like w**ei**gh and sc**ie**nce).

Strategies for Memory Improvement

Narrative Stories Link Words Together

This method involves **linking** together all the items that need remembering. This is done by putting them into a **story**. So, say the list of words to be learnt is **bicycle**, **duck**, **ice cream**, **tree** and **house** — you could turn this into...

> Bob got onto his **bicycle** and rode down to the **duck** pond at the park. He bought an **ice cream** and sat under a **tree** to eat it. After a while, he cycled back to his **house**. That's Bob for you — he lives on the edge. He's a crazy guy.

Bower and Clark (1969) studied narrative stories.

Method: The study used an independent groups design — participants were split into two conditions. Each group was given 12 lists, each containing 10 words. In one condition, the participants were advised to come up with stories to link the 10 words together. The second group of participants was a control group — they were simply asked to learn the word lists.

Results: Both groups recalled the lists equally well immediately after learning each one. However, when it came to recalling all 12 lists at the end of the session, recall was much better in the group that had created stories with the words.

Conclusion: Creating narrative stories aids recall from long-term memory.

Evaluation: This links to the **multi-store model** — the words are moving into long-term memory because they are being **rehearsed** during the creation of stories. The study used a **control condition**, which meant that the effect of the independent variable (the stories) could be measured. However, it **lacks ecological validity** — learning word lists isn't something that you'd normally do in real life.

Mnemonic Strategies have *Limitations*

1) The above strategies work best when you're learning a list, or trying to learn the order of something. This isn't much use if it's equally important to **understand** something whilst you're learning it.
2) You've still got to be able to **remember** the mnemonic — e.g. the **peg-words**. If you forget those, you've got **no link** to the stuff you were trying to remember.

Practice Questions

Q1 What are mnemonics?

Q2 How does the method of loci work?

Q3 What is a peg-word?

Q4 Describe the narrative story strategy.

Q5 Why not try to come up with a mnemonic to help you spell the word mnemonic? Something like Mike Never Eats Meat Or Nibbles Into Cheese...

Exam Questions

Q1 Evaluate two strategies that could be used to improve the recall of a list of words. [6 marks]

Q2 Describe two limitations of mnemonic strategies. [4 marks]

Mnemonics — I can't even say the damn word...

Just make sure that you don't wander around the supermarket claiming that there's a banana in your shoe — or you might have some explaining to do once security have finished strip-searching you. Oh, and don't get too engrossed in trying to turn this whole book into bizarre sentences. It might be amusing, but it won't be so funny when it comes to your exam...

The Developmental Approach

*Developmental psychologists focus on how we change and develop throughout our lives. Describing **how** we change isn't enough though — they also try to explain **why** the changes take place. Show-offs.*

*Different **Research Methods** Are Used **Depending** On What's Being Studied*

(There's more general stuff on research methods on pages 32-33, for those of you who can't get enough of 'em...)

Observational Studies Can Be Naturalistic or Controlled

1) **Naturalistic observation** takes place in the child's own environment and none of the variables are manipulated — e.g. a parent might note down their child's behaviour in a diary.

Advantage

Ecological validity — behaviour will be natural because the subject is in a real-life, familiar setting.

Disadvantage

Extraneous variables — there's no control over the variables, so you can't be sure what caused your results.

2) With **controlled observation** the child is observed by a researcher, usually in a laboratory setting. Some of the variables are controlled — e.g. a child might be given a certain toy to play with and observed through a one-way mirror.

Advantage

Control — the effect of **extraneous variables** is minimised, so you're more likely to be able to establish cause and effect.

Disadvantage

Observer bias — the observer's expectations may affect what they focus on and record, so the reliability of the results might be a problem. Another observer might have come up with very different results.

Correlational Studies Look for Relationships Between Variables

Variables often rise and fall together — e.g. height and weight usually rise together as a child grows. But this doesn't mean that one variable **causes** the other to change — that's pretty important to remember. The data for correlational studies often comes from surveys, questionnaires and interviews.

Advantage

Ethical — you can study variables that would be unethical to manipulate, e.g. whether there's a relationship between smoking during pregnancy and low birthweight.

Disadvantage

Causal relationships — these can't be assumed from a correlation. Results may be caused by a third, unknown variable.

Case Studies Are Detailed Descriptions of One Person

Case studies allow researchers to analyse unusual cases in lots of detail — e.g. the study of **Genie** (page 27).

Advantage

Rich data — researchers have the opportunity to study rare phenomena in a lot of detail.

Disadvantage

Generalisation — only using a single case makes generalising the results extremely difficult.

Interviews Are like Conversations

1) **Clinical interviews** are used loads in developmental psychology. They're **semi-structured**, meaning that the researcher asks some specific questions, but also lets the participant ramble on about stuff.
2) Participants could be children, or their carers, teachers or parents.
3) Face-to-face interviews can include **open-ended** (non-specific) or **fixed** (specific) questions.

Advantage

Rich data — especially from open-ended questions.

Disadvantage

Participants — children can have implicit knowledge but be unable to verbalise it, so their skills can be underestimated.

The Developmental Approach

Experiments Can Have a *Longitudinal* or *Cross-Sectional Design*

Two main kinds of experimental design are used to work out how behaviour changes with age — **longitudinal** and **cross-sectional**. These are used **alongside** the **research method**.

1) A **longitudinal design** tests the **same people** repeatedly as they get older and wrinklier.
2) This means you can plot the **group average** as a function of age. It also allows you to look at the development of **individuals** within the group.
3) Researchers can then look at whether the data shows a **gradual change**, or a more sudden shift that suggests **stage-like development**.
4) Longitudinal designs can be **retrospective**. This involves looking back over a period of time — e.g. looking at a child's medical history.

Advantage — you get detailed data about the same people, and individual differences are taken into account.

Disadvantage — studying the development of the same people can take years, so it's time-consuming and costly.

1) A **cross-sectional design** tests different people of **different ages**. For example, if you wanted to look at how vocabulary increases with age, you could measure the vocabulary of children in different year groups.
2) Their performance is then **averaged** over different individuals at each age.

Advantage — they provide a quick estimate of developmental changes, and are much less time-consuming than a longitudinal design.

Disadvantage — they don't take individual differences into account. Different people are measured at each age, so you can't be sure they all developed in the same way.

Researchers Have to Think About *Ethics*

Psychologists have to be extra careful when they're conducting research with children.

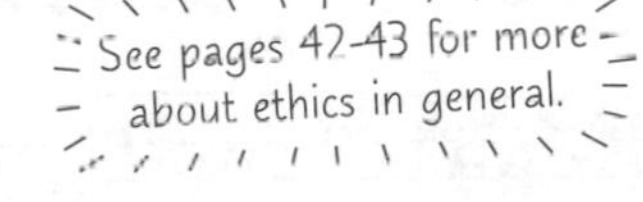

1) Under-18s might not understand the implications of participating in a study, so researchers have to get **informed consent** from their parents or guardians.
2) It's important that researchers get the **power balance** right because children generally view adults as more powerful than them. Extra care has to be taken to inform children of their rights — e.g. the right to **withdraw**.
3) Researchers need to make sure that a study won't cause the participants physical or psychological **harm**. They have to use the **least stressful** procedure possible, and **abandon** the study if the child seems distressed.

Animal studies have provided **valuable information** for developmental research. But there's debate about whether they're ethical or not.

Advantage — Some **research designs** couldn't have been conducted on humans ethically — e.g. Harlow's study of attachment, where young monkeys were separated from their mothers (see page 20).

Disadvantages — Some see it as **unethical** to inflict suffering on animals, especially when they can't give consent. Animals and humans are different, so you can't **generalise** results from one species to the other.

Practice Questions

Q1 Give one advantage of correlational studies.

Q2 Give one disadvantage of longitudinal designs.

Q3 What ethical considerations are important when children are involved in a study?

Exam Question

Q1 A researcher conducts a study to find out how children in different stages of development play with a particular toy.

a) Identify a research method and an experimental design that could be used for this study. [2 marks]

b) Evaluate the experimental design you identified in part a). [4 marks]

*I once did an experiment on my luggage...**

Basically there are loads of different ways to test your theory, so all you need to do is pick the one that best fits whatever you're studying. Or you could just shut your eyes, point at the page, and see what comes up. A word of advice though — if you end up trying to do clinical interviews on babies, then maybe have a rethink. Or try monkeys instead...

* It was a case study.

Explanations of Attachment

These pages deal with the different psychological explanations for how and why attachments develop between infants and their carers. Simple eh — you'd think, but this is psychology...

Attachment** is a Strong **Emotional Bond

Attachment is a close emotional relationship between infants and their caregivers.
'Attached' infants will show a desire to be **close** to their **primary caregiver** (usually their biological mother).
They'll show **distress** when they're **separated**, and **pleasure** when they're **reunited**.

Learning Theory** Links **Attachment** to **Pleasure

This is also known as **behaviourist theory**, and focuses on the baby wanting its needs fulfilled.
Conditioning is given as an explanation for how attachments form.

Classical Conditioning. This is about learning **associations** between different things in our environment. Getting food naturally gives the baby **pleasure**. The baby's desire for food is fulfilled whenever its mother is around to feed it. So an **association is formed between mother and food**. So, whenever its mother is around, the baby will feel pleasure — i.e. 'attachment'.

Operant Conditioning. **Dollard and Miller (1950)** claimed that babies feel discomfort when they're hungry and so have a desire to get food to **remove the discomfort**. They find that if they cry, their mother will come and feed them — so the discomfort is removed (this is '**negative reinforcement**'). An easy life. The mother is therefore associated with food and the baby will want to be close to her. This produces 'attachment behaviour' (distress when separated from the mother, etc.).

Harlow** Showed That **Comfort** is Important in **Attachment

Just because babies spend most of their time either eating or sleeping, it doesn't mean they automatically attach to the person who feeds them. **Schaffer and Emerson (1964)** found that many babies didn't have strong attachments with their mother, even though she fed them. **Good quality interaction with the baby seemed more important** — the baby will attach to whoever is the most sensitive and loving. This is also shown in **Harlow's** study, **'Love in Infant Monkeys'**.

Harlow (1959) showed the need for 'contact comfort'.

Method: Harlow aimed to find out whether baby monkeys would prefer a source of **food** or a source of **comfort** and **protection** as an attachment figure. In **laboratory experiments** rhesus monkeys were raised in isolation. They had two 'surrogate' mothers. One was made of wire mesh and contained a feeding bottle, the other was made of cloth but didn't contain a feeding bottle.

Results: The monkeys spent most of their time clinging to the cloth surrogate and only used the wire surrogate to feed. The cloth surrogate seemed to give them **comfort** in new situations. When the monkeys grew up they showed signs of **social** and **emotional disturbance**. The females were bad mothers who were often violent towards their offspring.

Conclusion: Infant monkeys formed more of an attachment with a figure that provided comfort and protection. Growing up in isolation affected their development.

Evaluation: This was a **laboratory experiment**, so there was strict control of the variables. This means that it's unlikely the results were affected by an unknown variable. The findings of this study were **applied to real life**. They led to a change in hospital procedure — human babies in incubators are now given soft blankets. However, it can be argued that you can't **generalise** the results of this study to human beings, because humans and monkeys are **qualitatively different**. There were also **ethical problems** with this study — the monkeys were put in a stressful situation, and later they showed signs of being psychologically damaged by the experiment. Monkeys are social animals, so it was unfair to keep them in isolation. The fact that they were in isolation also means that the study lacked **ecological validity** — the monkeys weren't in their natural environment, so the results can't be reliably applied to real life. Laboratory experiments can usually be **replicated**, but ethical guidelines now in place mean that you couldn't repeat this study today to see whether you'd get the same results.

Explanations of Attachment

We're Not Done Yet — There's the **Ethological Approach...**

Lorenz wasn't an experienced father, but his geese loved him.

1) Ethology is the study of animals in their natural environment. **Konrad Lorenz (1935)** found that geese automatically 'attach' to the first moving thing they see after hatching, and follow it everywhere (I bet this gets quite annoying). This is called **imprinting**.
2) Normally the geese would imprint onto their mother, but Lorenz managed to get them to attach to him because he was the first thing they saw.
3) Imprinting seems to occur during a **'critical period'** — in this case, the first few hours after hatching. It's a **fast**, **automatic** process.
4) It's unlikely to occur in humans. Our attachments take a **longer** time to develop and we don't automatically attach to particular things — quality care seems more important in human attachment formation.

...and **John Bowlby's Evolutionary** Theory...

Bowlby (1951) argued that something like imprinting occurs in humans. He developed several main claims:

1) We have **evolved** a biological need to attach to our main caregiver — usually our biological mother. Having one special attachment is called **monotropy**. Forming this attachment has survival value as staying close to the mother ensures food and protection.
2) A strong attachment provides a **'safe base'**, giving us confidence to explore our environment.
3) It also gives us a **'template'** for all future relationships — we learn to trust and care for others.
4) The first 3 years of life are the **critical period** for this attachment to develop — otherwise it might never do so.
5) If the attachment doesn't develop (e.g. because of separation or death), or if it's broken, it might seriously damage the child's social and emotional development (see pages 24-29).

Comments on Bowlby's theory:

1) There is some **evidence** for his claims. **Harlow's** study supports the idea that we have evolved a need to attach. It also suggests that social and emotional development might be damaged if an attachment isn't formed. See pages 24 and 25 for more studies that support Bowlby's theory.
2) **Schaffer and Emerson (1964)** provided evidence against Bowlby's claims about monotropy. They found that many children form **multiple attachments**, and may not attach to their mother.
3) **Harlow's** study of monkeys raised in isolation also goes against the idea of **monotropy**. Other monkeys who didn't have a mother, but who grew up together, didn't show signs of social and emotional disturbance in later life. They didn't have a primary caregiver, but seemed to attach to each other instead.
4) There is **mixed evidence** for claims of a **critical period** for attachments to develop (pages 27-29).
5) The effect of attachment not developing, or being broken, may not be as bad as Bowlby claimed (pages 24-29).

Practice Questions

Q1 What is 'attachment'?

Q2 What is meant by 'imprinting'?

Q3 What is 'monotropy'?

Exam Questions

Q1 a) Outline one theory of attachment. [6 marks]

b) Explain two criticisms of the theory outlined in part a). [4 marks]

Monkey lovin'...

Hanging around a pond waiting for the geese to hatch always seems like a nice idea at the time. We'd all love to have some instant gosling children following us round. But a word of warning — it's not quite so much fun when you're having to regurgitate worms into their beaks at four in the morning. And then they break your arm with their big wings. Or is that swans...

Types of Attachment

If you enjoyed the last two pages, then you're gonna love these ones. As you know, an 'attachment' is a strong, emotional bond between two people. Psychologists are interested in how our first attachments form and what influences them.

Attachments Can Be Secure or Insecure

Secure Attachments

In a secure attachment, there's a **strong bond** between the child and its caregiver. If they're separated, the infant becomes **distressed**. However, when they're reunited, the child is **easily comforted** by the caregiver. The majority of attachments are of this type. Secure attachments are associated with a healthy cognitive and emotional development.

Insecure Attachments

Attachments can also be insecure. Here, the bond between child and caregiver is **weaker**. Ainsworth et al came up with **two types** of insecure attachment:

Insecure-avoidant

If they're separated from their caregiver, the child **doesn't** become particularly distressed, and can usually be comforted by a **stranger**. This type of insecure attachment is shown by children who generally **avoid** social interaction and intimacy with others.

Insecure-resistant

The child is often **uneasy** around their caregiver, but becomes **upset** if they're separated. Comfort can't be given by strangers, and it's also often **resisted** from the caregiver. Children who show this style of attachment both **accept** and **reject** social interaction and intimacy.

There are many ways to form a strong attachment with your child.

An Infant's **Reaction** in a **Strange Situation** Shows if It's **Securely** Attached

Ainsworth came up with the concept of the **strange situation**. She used it to assess how children react under conditions of **stress** (by separation from the caregiver and the presence of a stranger) and also to **new situations**.

Ainsworth et al (1978) — The Strange Situation

Method: In a **controlled observation**, 12-18 month old infants were left in a room with their mother. Eight different scenarios occurred, including being approached by a stranger, the infant being left alone, the mother returning, etc. The infant's reactions were constantly observed.

Results: About 15% of infants were **'insecure-avoidant' (type A)** — they ignored their mother and didn't mind if she left. A stranger could comfort them.
About 70% were **'securely attached' (type B)** — content with their mother, upset when she left, happy when she returned and avoided strangers.
About 15% were **'insecure-resistant' (type C)** — uneasy around their mother and upset if she left. They resisted strangers and were also hard to comfort when their mother returned.

Conclusion: Infants showing different reactions to their carers have different types of attachment.

Evaluation: The research method used allowed control of the variables, making the results reliable. However, the laboratory-type situation made the study artificial, reducing the ecological validity. The parents may have changed their behaviour, as they knew that they were being observed. This could have had an effect on the children's behaviour. Also, the new situation in the experiment may have had an effect on the children's behaviour — the study might not accurately represent their behaviour in real life. Another problem is that the mother may not have been the child's **main attachment figure**.

Types of Attachment

Similar Studies Have Taken Place in **Different Cultures**

Ainsworth et al's (1978) findings have been shown many times in the **USA**, but it wasn't then known whether they could be applied to other **cultures**. **Cross-cultural studies** have since taken place:

Van Ijzendoorn and Kroonenberg (1988) — cross-cultural studies

Method:	Van Ijzendoorn and Kroonenberg carried out a meta-analysis of 32 studies of 'the strange situation' in different countries (e.g. Japan, Britain, Sweden, etc.). They were analysed to find any overall patterns.
Results:	The percentages of children classified as secure or insecure were very **similar** across the countries tested. Secure attachments were the most common type of attachment in the countries studied. Some differences were found in the distribution of insecure attachments. In Western cultures, it was seen that the dominant type of insecure attachment was avoidant. However, in non-Western cultures, the dominant type was resistant.
Conclusion:	There are cross-cultural similarities in raising children, producing common reactions to the 'strange situation'.
Evaluation:	Children are brought up in different ways in different cultures. This might result in different types of attachment in different cultures. Because of this, the 'strange situation' might not be a suitable method for studying cross-cultural attachment. Using a **different type** of study may have revealed different patterns or types of attachment in different cultures. Also, the study assumes that different **countries** are the same thing as different **cultures**. One problem with the research method is that meta-analyses can **hide** individual results that show an unusual trend.

There are Important **Findings** from Strange Situation Research

1) **Some cultural differences are found. Grossman et al (1985)** claimed that more 'avoidant' infants may be found in Germany because of the value Germans put on independence — so 'avoidance' is seen as a good thing.
2) **The causes of different attachment types are debatable.**
The causes may be the sensitivity of their carers and/or their inborn temperament.
3) **The strange situation experiment doesn't show a characteristic of the child.** The experiment only shows the child's relationship with a specific person, so they might react differently with different carers, or later in life.

Attachment type may influence later behaviours. Securely attached children may be more confident in school and form strong, trusting adult relationships. 'Avoidant' children may have behaviour problems in school and find it hard to form close, trusting adult relationships. 'Resistant' children may be insecure and attention-seeking in school and, as adults, their strong feelings of dependency may be stressful for partners.

Practice Questions

Q1 What is a secure attachment?

Q2 What are the two types of insecure attachment?

Q3 Who came up with the 'strange situation'?

Q4 What have cross-cultural studies shown about attachments?

Exam Questions

Q1 Outline and evaluate Ainsworth's (1978) 'strange situation' study. [12 marks]

Q2 Explain two disadvantages of using the 'stange situation' in a study of attachment. [4 marks]

Try to get all these ideas firmly attached to the inside of your head...

Next time you're in trouble at school and your parents are called in to 'discuss your behaviour', try sobbing gently under your breath, 'I think it's all my anxious-resistant attachment formation, it's left me insecure and needy of attention'. It's a desperate attempt, but it might just make your parents feel bad enough to let you off. This holds no guarantees though...

Disruption of Attachment

The attachments we form are pretty important — there can be serious consequences if they're broken...

Attachment Can be Disrupted by **Separation** or **Deprivation**

Separation is where a child is away from a **caregiver** they're attached to (such as their mother). The term's used when it's a **relatively short** time, just hours or days — not a longer or permanent separation.

Deprivation describes the loss of something that is **wanted or needed**. So, 'maternal deprivation' is the loss of the mother (or other attachment figure). A more **long-term** or even **permanent** loss is implied.

Separation Can Have **Major Effects**

According to several studies, infants or children who have been separated from their carer may react through the following stages.
The stages are referred to as the **'PDD model' — Protest, Despair, Detachment**:

1) **Protest** — During the first few hours, the child will **protest** a lot at being **separated** from its mother (or other attachment figure), by crying, panicking, calling for its mother, etc.

2) **Despair**

After a day or two, the child will start to lose interest in its surroundings, becoming more and more **withdrawn**, with occasional crying. They may also eat and sleep less.

3) **Detachment**

After a few days, the child will start to become more **alert** and interested again in its surroundings. It will cry less and may seem to have '**recovered**' from its bad reaction to the separation. However, its previous attachment with its carer may now be permanently **damaged** — the trust and security may be lost.

Robertson and Robertson's (1968) Study **Supports** the **PDD Model**

	Robertson and Robertson (1968) — evidence for the PDD model
Method:	In a naturalistic observation, several children who experienced short separations from their carers were observed and filmed. For example, a boy called John aged around 18 months stayed in a residential nursery for nine days while his mother had another baby.
Results:	John showed the signs of passing through '**protest**' for the first day or two. Then he showed **despair** — he tried to get attention from the nurses but they were busy with other children so he 'gave up' trying. Then he showed **detachment** — he was more active and content. However, when his mother came to collect him, he was reluctant to be affectionate.
Conclusion:	The short-term separation had very **bad effects** on John, including possible **permanent damage** to his attachment with his mother.
Evaluation:	John's reaction might not have been due to separation — it could have been down to his new environment or the fact that he was getting much less attention than he was used to. There will have been little control of **variables**, and it would be difficult to replicate each **individual situation**. However, as the study took place in a natural setting, the results will have **ecological validity** but will be less **reliable**.

Disruption of Attachment

The **PDD Model** has **Strengths and Weaknesses**

Some comments on the PDD model include...

1) Findings suggest that **separating a child from its carers should be avoided** whenever possible. This has important implications for childcare practice, e.g. children should be allowed to visit, or remain with, their mothers during a stay in hospital. Sounds fair enough to me.

2) Studies have shown that children who receive **foster care** do better than those placed in an **institutionalised setting**. It would seem that children manage to cope with the separation as long as they still receive **one-on-one emotional support**, even though it's not from their primary caregiver.

3) **Many factors** influence how a child reacts to a separation. These include age (older children will cope better), the quality of the care received during the separation, the individual temperament of the child, and how often it has experienced separations. So, **separations do not necessarily produce the PDD effects**. They may even be good for the child (see pages 30-31).

John Bowlby (1953) Studied Longer-Term Maternal **Deprivation**

Even if short-term separation may not necessarily be bad for a child, **John Bowlby** argued that long-term **deprivation** from an attachment figure could be harmful. He produced his **maternal deprivation hypothesis**:

1) Deprivation from the main carer during the **critical period** (the first 3-5 years), will have harmful effects on a child's emotional, social, intellectual and even physical development. Not so good.
2) Long-term effects of deprivation may include **separation anxiety** (the fear of another separation from the carer). This may lead to problem behaviour, e.g. being very clingy, and avoiding going to school. Future relationships may be affected by this emotional insecurity. Bowlby's research showed evidence for this.

	Bowlby (1944) — The 44 Juvenile Thieves
Method:	**Case studies** were completed on the backgrounds of 44 adolescents who had been referred to the clinic where Bowlby worked because they'd been stealing. There was a **control group** of 44 'emotionally disturbed' adolescents who didn't steal.
Results:	17 of the thieves had experienced frequent separations from their mothers before the age of two, compared with 2 in the control group. 14 of the thieves were diagnosed as 'affectionless psychopaths' (they didn't care about how their actions affected others). 12 of these 14 had experienced separation from their mothers.
Conclusion:	Deprivation of the child from its main carer early in life can have very **harmful long-term consequences**.
Evaluation:	The results indicate a link between deprivation and criminal behaviour. However, it can't be said that one **causes** the other. There may be **other factors** that caused the criminal behaviour. Although case studies provide a lot of **detailed information**, the study relied on **retrospective data**, which may be unreliable.

Disruption of Attachment

Studies** Have Suggested **Long-Term Effects** of **Separation

Bowlby's study of the 44 Juvenile Thieves, and others on institutionalisation and hospitalisation, suggested that long-term effects of separation included:

1) **Affectionless psychopathology** (as seen in the 44 Juvenile Thieves study).
2) **Anaclitic depression** — involving appetite loss, sleeplessness and impaired social and intellectual development.
3) **Deprivation dwarfism** — infants are physically underdeveloped due to emotional deprivation.

*Bowlby's **Maternal Deprivation Hypothesis** has **Strengths and Weaknesses***

Strength:

Other evidence **supports** Bowlby's claims. **Goldfarb (1943)** found that orphanage children who were socially and maternally deprived were later less intellectually and socially developed.

Weaknesses:

The **evidence** can be criticised: Bowlby linked the thieves' behaviour to maternal deprivation, but **other things were not considered**, e.g. whether the poverty they grew up in led them to steal. The children in Goldfarb's study may have been most harmed by the **social deprivation** in the orphanage rather than the maternal deprivation.

*The **Effects** of **Disruption of Attachment** can be **Reversed***

Even when deprivation has harmful effects, these may be reversed with appropriate, **good quality care**.

Skeels and Dye (1939) found that children who had been socially deprived (in an orphanage) during their first two years of life quickly **improved** their **IQ scores** if they were transferred to a school where they got one-to-one care.

Practice Questions

Q1 What is the PDD model?

Q2 Outline the results of Robertson and Robertson's (1968) study.

Q3 What are the strengths and weaknesses of the PDD model?

Q4 What does Bowlby's maternal deprivation hypothesis propose?

Q5 How might the effects of disruption of attachment be reversed?

Exam Questions

Q1 Evaluate one study into the effects of separation. [4 marks]

Q2 Outline research into the long-term effects of disruption of attachment. [8 marks]

The PDD model can also be applied as a reaction to excessive study...

So, if your mum leaves you alone for a while when you're little you might well become a bank robber — sounds like a pretty poor excuse to me, but there you go. It's certainly interesting stuff. Even if you don't agree, the bottom line is you have to learn the theories, who came up with them, and what their pros and cons are — it's a world of pain.

Failure to Form Attachments — Privation

Maternal privation *is when a child has* ***never*** *had an attachment to its mother or another caregiver. (In contrast to deprivation where an attachment has formed but is broken.)*

Privation *Means* ***Never*** *Forming a* ***Bond*** *with a* ***Caregiver***

Rutter (1981) claimed that the effects of **maternal privation** are more likely to be **serious** than the effects of **maternal deprivation**. Evidence for this comes from **case studies** of children who have suffered difficult conditions or cruel treatment. Some nasty stuff coming up...

Some ***Case Studies*** *of* ***Privation*** *Include:*

Curtiss (1977) — The Case of Genie

This reported the case of a girl who suffered **extreme cruelty** from her parents, and never formed any attachments. Her father kept her strapped to a high chair with a potty in the seat for most of her childhood. She was beaten if she made any sounds, and didn't have the chance to play with toys or with other children.

She was finally discovered when she was 13 years old. She was **physically underdeveloped** and could only speak with **animal-like sounds**.

After a lot of help she later learned some language but her **social and intellectual skills never seemed to fully develop**.

Koluchova (1976) — The Case of the Czech twin boys

This is the case of **twin boys** whose mother died soon after they were born. Their father remarried and their stepmother treated them very cruelly. They were often kept locked in a cellar, beaten, and had no toys.

They were found when they were seven with rickets (a bone development disease caused by a lack of vitamin D), and **very little social or intellectual development**.

They were later adopted and made lots of progress. By adulthood they had above average intelligence and had normal social relationships.

There are ***Differences*** *Between these Cases*

Differences between the cases might explain why the Czech twins **recovered** better than Genie. We should consider...

1) The **length** of privation and how **old** the children were when they were discovered — the Czech twins were much younger than Genie, so still had time to develop once they were in a better environment.
2) Their **experiences** during the isolation — the twins were kept together, so they may have attached to each other.
3) The **quality of care** they received after the isolation — the twins were adopted, but Genie was passed between psychologists and eventually put in an institution.
4) **Individual differences**, including ability to recover.

The evidence suggests that **recovery from privation is possible**. However, because of the lack of information about what had happened to the children, we can't know for sure exactly what they experienced, e.g. whether they had ever had even a brief attachment. So we can't ever be sure **why** the twins recovered more than Genie.

Failure to Form Attachments — Privation

*There are a Number of **Limitations** to this Evidence*

1) The children didn't just suffer **maternal privation** — they also had very little **social** and **intellectual stimulation**, and were generally treated horribly. So all of these factors have to be taken into account when we're looking at their development.

2) There are problems with **generalising** the findings because they only focus on individual cases (see page 18, and also have a look at page 33 for more general stuff on case studies).

3) The case studies show **mixed results** for how much children can **recover** from privation early in life. The Czech twins recovered well, but Genie didn't.

4) **More controlled, scientific evidence is needed**, but it would be **ethically wrong** to actually put children in situations of privation to see what might happen. Some studies of children raised in institutions have provided evidence of the effects of privation, although we still can't be precisely **sure** of the **reasons** behind these effects.

Hodges and Tizard (1989) Studied Early Institutional Care

Studies of children raised in **institutions** (e.g. orphanages) may provide **more accurate records** of what the children experienced, seeing as they can be properly scientifically observed over a long period of time.

	Hodges and Tizard (1989) studied children raised in institutions.
Method:	This was a **longitudinal** (long-term) study of 65 children who had been placed in a residential nursery before they were four months old. They hadn't had the opportunity to form close attachments with any of their caregivers. By the age of four, some of the children had returned to their birth mothers, some had been adopted, and some stayed in the nursery.
Results:	At 16 years old, the **adopted** group had **strong** family relationships, although compared to a control group of children from a 'normal' home environment, they had weaker peer relationships. Those who stayed in the **nursery** or who returned to their **mothers** showed **poorer** relationships with family and peers than those who were adopted.
Conclusion:	Children can **recover** from early maternal privation if they are in a good **quality**, **loving** environment, although their social development may not be as good as children who have never suffered privation.
Evaluation:	This was a **natural experiment**, so it had **high ecological validity**. However, the sample was quite **small** and more than 20 of the children couldn't be found at the end of the study, so it's hard to **generalise** the results. The results are supported by other studies, such as **Rutter et al (1998)**, who studied 111 Romanian orphans **adopted** by British families before they were two years old. Their development was compared to a control group of British children. They were initially below normal development, but by four years of age their **development** had **caught up**. This supports Hodges and Tizard's findings that children can **recover** from **deprivation** if they have good quality **care**.

Failure to Form Attachments — Privation

Research Suggests Two **Long-Term Effects** of **Privation**

Privation of attachments early in life will **damage** a child's development, although how much it's damaged depends on several factors, such as **age**. Children can **recover** to some extent, but some of the effects of privation might be **permanent**:

Reactive Attachment Disorder — Parker and Forrest (1993)

Parker and Forrest (1993) outlined this rare but serious condition, which occurs in children who have been **permanently damaged** by early experiences such as **privation** of attachment.

Symptoms include:
1) an inability to give or receive affection
2) poor social relationships
3) dishonesty
4) involvement in crime

The **Cycle of Privation**

Some studies suggest that children who experience privation go on to have difficulties caring for their own children:

Quinton et al (1985) compared 50 women who had experienced institutional care as children, with 50 women who hadn't. They found that the women who had been raised in institutions were more likely to have parenting difficulties later in life. This suggests that there is a **cycle of privation** — children who have experienced privation later go on to become less caring parents. Therefore their children are deprived of a strong maternal attachment and may then be less caring to their children, and so on.

The cycle of privation — even worse than the roller skate of neglect.

Practice Questions

Q1 Explain the difference between deprivation and privation.
Q2 Explain a limitation of case study evidence.
Q3 Why might the Czech twins have recovered better than Genie?
Q4 Outline the strengths and weaknesses of Hodges and Tizard's (1989) study.
Q5 What is reactive attachment disorder?
Q6 What is meant by a cycle of privation?

Exam Questions

Q1 Define the terms deprivation and privation. [2 marks]

Q2 Outline the results of one study on the effects of privation. [4 marks]

Developmental problems — enough to make you develop mental problems

There are some pretty grisly case studies of seriously abused children on these pages. Not the nicest of topics, though it is interesting to see how these theories of severe privation fit in with the earlier ones about children separated from their carers. My advice would be to get the theories and case studies in your head quickly and move on to the next bit.

The Effects of Day Care on Child Development

*'**Day care**' refers to any **temporary care** for a child provided by someone other than the parents or guardians they live with. It can include **day nurseries, childminders** and **nannies**, but doesn't include residential nurseries or fostering.*

Day Care** Might Affect **Social Development

It may be necessary for children to form a strong attachment with their main carer before they can learn social skills and have relationships with others (see pages 24-29). Here are some studies that explore the impact of day care on attachment, peer relations and aggression.

Clarke-Stewart et al (1994) — positive effects of day care

Method: This study was made up of a series of separate **observations**, to examine the effects of day care. One experiment looked at the **peer relationships** of 150 children aged 2-3 years, who came from different social backgrounds. In another experiment, the **strength of attachment** in a group of 18-month-old children was studied. These children had at least 30 hours of day care per week. The 'strange situation' was used. The results were compared with those of children who had 'low intensity' day care (less than 10 hours per week).

Results: The 2-3 year olds who had experienced day care were good at coping with social situations and negotiating with each other. In the 'strange situation' experiment, the 18-month-olds who had high intensity day care were just as distressed when separated from their mothers as those who had low intensity day care.

Conclusion: Day care can have a positive effect on the development of peer relationships in 2-3 year olds. Attachment in 18-month-olds is not affected by temporary separation.

Evaluation: The observations were **controlled**, so the study could easily be replicated. However, because the situation was artificial, the study lacks **ecological validity** and the results can't be **generalised** to other children.

Shea (1981) — positive effects of day care

Method: Infants aged between 3 and 4 were videotaped in the playground during their first 10 weeks at nursery school. Their behaviour was assessed in terms of **rough-and-tumble play, aggression, frequency of peer interaction, distance from the teacher** and **distance from the nearest child**.

Results: Over the 10 weeks the children's peer interaction increased and their distance from the teacher decreased. There was a decrease in aggression and an increase in rough-and-tumble play. The increase in sociability was more evident in children who attended day care 5 days a week than in those who went 2 days a week.

Conclusion: Day care causes children to become more sociable and less aggressive.

Evaluation: This was a **naturalistic observation**, meaning that the study has high **ecological validity** because none of the behaviour was manipulated. However, it means that the results could have been affected by **extraneous variables**. The behaviour was open to interpretation, so the findings could be biased — e.g. it could be difficult to differentiate between 'aggression' and 'rough-and-tumble play'.

Belsky and Rovine (1988) — negative effects of day care

Method: Infants were placed in the '**strange situation**' to assess how secure their attachments with their mothers were (see page 22). One group had experienced no day care and one had experienced at least 20 hours of day care per week before their first birthday.

Results: The infants who had received day care were more likely to have an **insecure** attachment type. They were either **'insecure-avoidant' (type A)** — ignored their mother and didn't mind if she left, or **'insecure-resistant' (type C)** — uneasy around their mother and upset if she left. Those who hadn't had day care were more likely to be **securely attached** (type B).

Conclusion: Day care has a **negative** effect on an infant's social development.

Evaluation: The 'strange situation' is a **controlled observation**, so there was **good control** of the variables. However, this means that the study lacks **ecological validity**, because it creates an artificial situation. **DiLalla (1998)** also found negative effects on children's **peer relationships** — the more day care children had, the **less prosocially** they behaved, i.e. the less they helped, shared, etc.

The Effects of Day Care on Child Development

Research into How Day Care Affects Development **Varies Widely**

All these different studies and still nobody can decide whether day care is good or bad for children. They might as well not have bothered... But they did, which means more for you to learn. Hurrah. Here are some of the reasons why the findings vary so much:

1) The studies focus on slightly different things (e.g. quality of care, age of child), and use different **samples**.
2) There are **methodological problems** with the studies that might lead to inconsistent results. E.g. Clarke-Stewart has admitted that the '**strange situation**' isn't a good way of assessing attachment in infants who have day care (despite using it in her study). They're used to temporary separation so might respond indifferently and be wrongly classed as '**insecure**'.
3) All of these studies rely on **correlations**, so it's not possible to establish **cause and effect**.
4) The studies don't take **individual differences** like temperament into account.

Research Has Affected **Day Care Practices**

Research into child development and day care has influenced decisions about what might be best for children in day care. **Scarr (1998)** identified several factors that make for good day care:

1) Good **staff training**
2) Adequate **space**
3) Appropriate **toys** and **activities**
4) A good **ratio of staff to children**
5) **Minimising staff turnover** so that children can form **stable attachments** with carers

Arnold had made lots of friends since being in day care.

Vandell et al (1988) found that children who had **good quality** day care were more likely to have **friendly interactions** with others compared to those receiving **lower quality** day care.

Scarr (1998) and Vandell et al's (1988) studies show that **high quality day care** can have a **positive effect** on **social development**.

Practice Questions

Q1 Why might day care affect a child's social development?

Q2 Evaluate a study that shows the negative effects of day care on social development.

Q3 Why might the results from studies into the effects of day care differ from each other?

Q4 So, how do you make a great day care centre?

Exam Questions

Q1 Outline research findings on the effects of day care on social development. [6 marks]

Q2 Evaluate research findings on the effects of day care on social development. [6 marks]

If this is all getting too difficult you can always blame it on your day care...

Let me see if I've got this — if a child is stuck in poor quality day care their social skills won't develop very well. But if the day care is good and stimulating, it can have positive effects on the child's development. I don't mean to knock these guys' hard work — but it's not exactly rocket science. Anyway, no complaints — it makes it all easier to learn...

Research Methods

*This is everything you could ever want to know (and probably a bit more too...) about **how** psychologists go about testing their theories. Have a look at pages 42-43 for more on the **ethical issues** surrounding different research methods.*

Laboratory Experiments *are Controlled and Scientific*

1) An **experiment** is a way of conducting research in a **controlled** way.
2) The aim is to **control** all relevant variables except for **one key variable**, which is altered to see what the effect is. The variable that you alter is called the **independent variable** (see page 35).
3) Laboratory experiments are conducted in an **artificial setting**, e.g. Milgram's study (see page 76).

Advantages

Control — the effects of confounding variables (those that have an effect in addition to the variable of interest — see page 35) are minimised.
Replication — strict controls mean you can run the study again to check the findings.
Causal relationships — ideally it's possible to establish whether one variable actually causes change in another.

Disadvantages

Artificial — experiments might not measure real-life behaviour (i.e. they may lack ecological validity).
Demand characteristics — participants may respond according to what they think is being investigated, which can bias the results.
Ethics — deception is often used, making informed consent difficult.

Field Experiments *are Conducted* ***Outside*** *the Laboratory*

In **field experiments** behaviour is measured in a **natural environment** like a school, the street or on a train. A **key variable** is still altered so that its effect can be measured.

Advantages

Causal relationships — you can still establish causal relationships by manipulating the key variable and measuring its effect, although it's very difficult to do in a field experiment.
Ecological validity — field experiments are less artificial than those done in a laboratory, so they relate to real life better.
Demand characteristics (participants trying to guess what the researcher expects from them and performing differently because of it) — these can be avoided if participants don't know they're in a study.

Disadvantages

Less control — confounding variables may be more likely in a natural environment.
Ethics — participants who didn't agree to take part might experience distress and often can't be debriefed. Observation must respect privacy.

Natural Experiments *Measure but* ***Don't Control*** *Variables*

A **natural experiment** is a study that measures variables that **aren't** directly manipulated by the experimenter. For example, comparing behaviour in a single-sex school and a mixed school.

Advantages

Ethical — it's possible to study variables that it would be unethical to manipulate, e.g. you can compare a community that has TV with a community that doesn't to see which is more aggressive.

Disadvantages

Participant allocation — you can't randomly allocate participants to each condition, and so confounding variables (e.g. what area the participants live in) may affect results. Let's face it — you've got no control over the variables so it's ridiculously hard to say what's caused by what.
Rare events — some groups of interest are hard to find, e.g. a community that doesn't have TV.
Ethics — deception is often used, making informed consent difficult. Also, confidentiality may be compromised if the community is identifiable.

Naturalistic Observation — Observing *but NOT Interfering*

Naturalistic observation involves observing subjects in their natural environment. Researchers take great care not to interfere in any way with the subjects they're studying.

Advantages

Ecological validity — behaviour is natural and there are no demand characteristics, as the participant is unaware of being observed.
Theory development — can be a useful way of developing ideas about behaviour that could be tested in more controlled conditions later.

Disadvantages

Extraneous variables — can't control variables that may affect behaviour.
Observer bias — observers' expectations may affect what they focus on and record. This means the reliability of the results may be a problem — another observer may have come up with very different results.
Ethics — you should only conduct observations where people might expect to be observed by strangers. This limits the situations where you can do a naturalistic observation. Debriefing is difficult. Observation must respect privacy. Getting informed consent can be tricky.

Research Methods

Correlational Research Looks for Relationships Between Variables

Correlation means that two variables rise and fall together, or that one rises as the other falls — but **not** always that one variable **causes** a change in the other, e.g. as age increases so might intelligence, but ageing doesn't **cause** intelligence.

Advantages

Causal relationships — these can be ruled out if no correlation exists.
Ethics — can study variables that would be unethical to manipulate, e.g. is there a relationship between the number of cigarettes smoked and incidences of ill health?

Disadvantages

Causal relationships — these cannot be assumed from a correlation, which may be caused by a third, unknown variable.
Ethics — misinterpretation can be an issue. Sometimes the media (and researchers) infer causality from a correlation.

Questionnaires — Written, Face-to-Face, on the Phone, or via the Internet

Advantages

Practical — can collect a large amount of information quickly and relatively cheaply.

Disadvantages

Bad questions — leading questions (questions that suggest a desired answer) or unclear questions can be a problem.
Biased samples — some people are more likely to respond to a questionnaire, which might make a sample unrepresentative.
Self report — people sometimes want to present themselves in a good light (social desirability bias — see page 41). What they say and what they actually think could be different, making any results unreliable.
Ethics — confidentiality can be a problem, especially around sensitive issues.

Interviews — More Like a Conversation than a Face-to-Face Questionnaire

Structured interviews follow a fixed set of questions that are the same for all participants.
Unstructured interviews may have a set of discussion topics, but are less constrained about how the conversation goes.

Advantages

Rich data — can get detailed information, as there are fewer constraints than with a questionnaire. Unstructured interviews provide richer information than structured interviews.
Pilot study — interviews are a useful way to get information before a study.

Disadvantages

Self report — can be unreliable and affected by social desirability bias (see questionnaires).
Impractical — conducting interviews can be time-consuming and requires skilled researchers.
Ethics — confidentiality can be a problem, especially around sensitive issues.

Case Studies are Intensive Descriptions of a Single Individual or Case

Case studies allow researchers to analyse unusual cases in a lot of detail, e.g. Milner et al's study of **HM** (page 7).

Advantages

Rich data — researchers have the opportunity to study rare phenomena in a lot of detail.
Unique cases — can challenge existing ideas and theories, and suggest ideas for future research.

Disadvantages

Causal relationships — the researcher has very little control over variables.
Generalisation — only using a single case makes generalising the results extremely difficult.
Ethics — informed consent can be difficult to obtain if the subject has a rare disorder.

Practice Questions

Q1 What are the main advantages of laboratory experiments?
Q2 Outline one disadvantage of using correlational research.
Q3 Why might you get an unrepresentative sample when carrying out questionnaire-based research?

Exam Questions

Q1 Describe what a field experiment is and outline its main advantages and disadvantages. [4 marks]

Q2 Describe the two types of interview a researcher might conduct.
Outline the main differences between them. [8 marks]

Aims and Hypotheses

*When research is conducted, the idea is to carry out an **objective test** of something, i.e. to obtain a scientific measurement of how people behave — not just someone's opinion. Well that's what I reckon...*

***Research Aims** are Important*

An **aim** is a statement of a study's purpose — for example Asch's aim might have been: 'To study majority influence in an unambiguous task'. (See page 70 for the detail of Asch's study.)

Research should state its aim **beforehand** so that it's **clear** what the study intends to investigate.

***Hypotheses** are Theories Tested by Research*

Although the **aim** states the **purpose** of a study, it isn't usually **precise** enough to **test**. What is needed are clear statements of what's actually being tested — the **hypotheses**.

1) **RESEARCH HYPOTHESIS**

The **research hypothesis** is proposed at the beginning of a piece of research and is often generated from a theory. For example — Bowlby's research hypothesis was that maternal deprivation causes delinquency. (See page 25 for the details of Bowlby's study.)

2) **NULL HYPOTHESIS**

The **null hypothesis** is what you're going to **assume is true** during the study. Any data you collect will either back this assumption up, or it won't. If the data **doesn't support** your null hypothesis, you **reject** it and go with your **alternative hypothesis** instead.

Very often, the null hypothesis is a prediction that there will be **no relationship** between key variables in a study — and any correlation is due to **chance**. (An example might be that there is no difference in exam grades between students who use a revision guide and students who don't.)

(Note: It's quite usual to have something you **don't actually believe** as your null hypothesis. You assume it **is** true for the duration of the study, then if your results lead you to reject this null hypothesis, you've **proved** it **wasn't true** after all.)

3) **EXPERIMENTAL HYPOTHESIS** (or **ALTERNATIVE HYPOTHESIS**)

If the data forces you to **reject** your null hypothesis, then you accept your **experimental (alternative) hypothesis** instead.

So if your null hypothesis was that two variables **aren't** linked, then your alternative hypothesis would be that they **are** linked. Or you can be more specific, and be a bit more precise about **how** they are linked, using **directional** hypotheses (see below).

4) **DIRECTIONAL HYPOTHESIS**

A hypothesis might predict a difference between the exam results obtained by two groups of students — a group that uses a revision guide and another group that doesn't.

If the hypothesis states which group will do better, it is making a **directional prediction**.

For example, you might say that students who use a revision guide will get **higher** exam grades than students who don't — this is a directional hypothesis.

Directional hypotheses are often used when **previous research findings** suggest which way the results will go.

5) **NON-DIRECTIONAL HYPOTHESIS**

A **non-directional hypothesis** would predict a difference, but wouldn't say which group would do better.

For example, you might just say that there will be a **difference** in exam grades between students who use a revision guide and students who don't — this is a **non-directional** hypothesis, since you're not saying which group will do better.

Non-directional hypotheses can be used when there is **little previous research** in the area under investigation, or when previous research findings are **mixed** and **inconclusive**.

Aims and Hypotheses

Some Variables are Manipulated by the Researcher — Others Aren't

A **variable** is a quantity whose **value** can **change** — for example, the time taken to do a task, anxiety levels, or exam results. There are various different kinds of variable.

The Independent Variable is Directly Manipulated

1) An **independent variable** (**IV**) is a variable **directly manipulated** by the researcher.
2) In the example on the previous page about students, exams and revision guides, there are two variables. One is 'whether or not a revision guide is used' (so this variable has only two possible values: yes or no). The other is the 'exam grade' (and this could have lots of possible values: e.g. A, B, C, D, E, N, U).
3) In this case, the **independent variable** is 'whether or not a revision guide is used' — since this is **directly** under the control of the researcher.

The Dependent Variable is Only Affected Indirectly

1) The **dependent variable** (**DV**) is the variable that you think is **affected** by changes in the independent variable. (So the DV is **dependent on** the **IV**.)
2) In the exam grades example, the dependent variable is the 'exam grade'. The exam grade is dependent on whether a revision guide was used (or at least, that's what's being **investigated**).

Ideally in a study the *only* thing that would influence the **DV** (the thing you're measuring) would be the **IV** (the thing you're manipulating). Usually though, there are other things that will have an effect.

An **extraneous variable** is any variable (other than the **IV**) that **could** affect what you're trying to measure. If these things **are** actually **influencing** the DV then they're called **confounding variables**.

Operationalisation is Showing How the Variables Will Be Measured

1) Variables must be **operationalised**. This means describing the **process** by which the variable is **measured**.
2) Some things are easy to operationalise (e.g. **height** might be operationalised as 'the distance in centimetres from the bottom of an object to the top'). Other things are difficult to operationalise (e.g. a mother's love for her newborn baby).
3) **Operationalisation** allows others to see exactly how you're going to define and measure your variables. It also has 18 letters, which is the same as soporiferousnesses, or yaaaaaaawwwwwwwwwn.

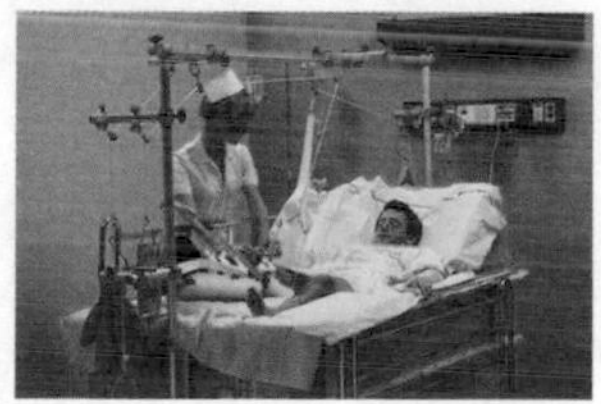

"Don't worry, sir — once we get your variable operationalised you'll be right as rain."

Practice Questions

Q1 When would you reject the null hypothesis?

Q2 What is the difference between a directional and non-directional hypothesis?

Q3 What is an independent variable?

Exam Question

Q1 Bruno is interested in whether taking fish oil supplements every day for a month can improve memory performance.

a) What would an appropriate experimental hypothesis be for his study? [2 marks]

b) Identify the dependent variable in Bruno's study. [1 mark]

Aim to learn this page — I hypothesise you'll need it...

Remember, you assume the null hypothesis is true unless your data suggests otherwise — if it does then you quickly switch allegiance to the alternative hypothesis instead. And remember, the IV is deliberately manipulated by the researcher. This might lead to an effect on the DV, but it's often a kind of indirect, knock-on effect. Yep, I agree — that's enough.

Research Design

Once you've got a theory, this is how you'd actually go about researching it...

The Research Design Must Make the Hypothesis ***Testable***

Research example — does the presence of an audience help or hinder people doing the 'wiggly wire' task (moving a loop along a wire without touching it and setting off the buzzer)? Based on previous research, we expect people to do this better without anyone watching them.

1) The IV (the variable being manipulated) is the presence or absence of an audience.
2) The DV (the variable being measured) is 'how well' the participants do on the task — but it must be testable. You need a **precisely defined** (or **operationalised**) DV, which should be **quantitative** wherever possible. An operationalised DV for this experiment might be 'the time taken to move the loop from one end of the wire to the other without setting off the buzzer'.

There are Three ***Research Designs*** that are Used Loads

1) An **independent groups design** means there are **different participants** in each group. Here, for example, one group does the task **with** an audience and another group does it **alone**. This avoids the problem that if all the participants did the test in both conditions, any improvement in performance might be due to them having two goes at the task (which would be a confounding variable).

Advantages

No **order effects** — no one gets better through practice (**learning effect**) or gets worse through being bored or tired (**fatigue effect**).

Disadvantages

Participant variables — differences between the **people** in each group might affect the results (e.g. the 'without audience' group may just have people who are better at the task — so we can't safely compare groups).

Number of participants — **twice as many** participants are needed to get the same amount of data, compared to having everyone do both conditions.

2) A **repeated measures design** is where, e.g., all participants do the task both **with** an audience and then **without**. You can compare the performances in each condition, knowing the differences weren't due to participant variables.

Advantages

Participant variables — now the same people do the test in both conditions, so any differences between individuals shouldn't affect the results.

Number of participants — **fewer** participants are needed to get the same amount of data.

Disadvantages

Order effects — if all participants did the 'with audience' condition first, any improvements in the second condition could be due to **practice**, not the audience's absence. (But see **counterbalancing** on the next page.)

3) A **matched pairs design** means there are different participants in each condition, but they're **matched** on important variables (like age, sex and personality). Some studies use **control groups**. These groups have not experienced any of the manipulations of the **IV** that an experimental group might have. This allows the researcher to make a direct comparison between them. In the example above the group that didn't have an audience would be the control group.

Advantages

No order effects — there are **different people** in each condition.

Participant variables — important differences are minimised through **matching**.

Disadvantages

Number of participants — need twice as many people compared to repeated measures.

Practicalities — **time-consuming** and difficult to find participants who **match**.

It's Sometimes Good to Run a Small ***Pilot Study*** First

1) No piece of research is perfect. To help foresee any problems, a small-scale **pilot study** can be run first.
2) This should establish whether the **design** works, whether **participants** understand the wording in **instructions**, or whether something important has been **missed out**.
3) Problems can be tackled before running the **main study**, which could save wasting a lot of **time** and **money**.

Research Design

Variables Can Be *'Controlled'* so Their Unwanted Effects are *Minimised*

Counterbalancing (mixing up the order of the tasks) can solve **order effects** in **repeated measures** designs. Half the participants do the task **with** an audience **first** and **then without**. The others do the conditions **the other way round**. Any order effects would then be equal across conditions.

Random allocation (e.g. by drawing names out of a hat) means everyone has an **equal chance** of doing **either** condition. An **independent measures** study with, for example, more men in one group than the other could have a confounding variable. Any difference in performance may be due to **sex** rather than the real IV. Random allocation should ensure groups are **not biased** on key variables.

Extraneous variables can be controlled by: (i) keeping them **constant** for all participants (e.g. everyone does the task in the same place so distractions are similar),
(ii) eliminating them altogether (e.g. everyone does the task somewhere with no noise distractions — shhhh...).

Standardised instructions should ensure the **experimenters** act in a similar way with all participants. Everything should be **as similar as possible** for all the participants, including each participant's **experience** in such studies.

Researchers have to Consider *Reliability* and *Validity*

Reliability

- If a test is consistent within itself, it has **internal reliability**. The **split-half technique** assesses this. A questionnaire is randomly split in two — if all participants score similarly on both halves, the questions measure the same thing.
- If the measure is stable over time or between people, then it has **external reliability**. This can be assessed by measuring **test-retest reliability** (does the same person always score similarly on the test?) or **inter-rater reliability** (do different assessors agree, i.e. do they both give the same score?).

Validity

- If an experiment shows that the results were caused by the manipulation of the **variables**, rather than the effect of something else, then it has **internal validity**.
- If the findings can be **generalised** beyond the experimental setting (e.g. to different groups of people or different settings), then the experiment has **external validity**.

Research Should be Designed with *Ethical Issues* in Mind

Ethical guidelines assist researchers who have **ethical dilemmas,** and should ensure that research is **acceptable** and participants are **protected**.

Ethical guidelines are discussed on pages 42-43.

Practice Questions

Q1 Give one disadvantage of an independent groups design.

Q2 Give one design that overcomes the disadvantage you identified in Q1.

Q3 What are the main benefits of running a pilot study?

Exam Questions

Q1 Why might a researcher choose to use a repeated measures design instead of an independent groups design? What could the researcher do to minimise any order effects that might influence the results? [6 marks]

Q2 Choose an example of a famous piece of psychological research and identify the design used in the study. Outline any control issues that the researchers would have had to consider before conducting the study. [4 marks]

Inter-test validity, no... split-rater ethics, no... oh sod it.... zzzzzzzzz...

There are a lot of details here, but they're all really important. If you're not really careful when you design a piece of research, the results you get might not be worth the paper you end up writing them down on. And that'd be no good. Spending a little bit of time thinking at the design stage will make it all worth it in the end — trust me.

Observations, Questionnaires and Interviews

*This page will tell you everything you could ever wish to know about **naturalistic observation** — the collection of data by observing participants in their natural environments.*

Researchers** can use **Participant** or **Non-Participant Observation

1) **Participant observation** is when the researcher **participates** in the activity under study in an **overt** way (their presence is obvious to the other participants).
   Advantages — The researcher develops a relationship with the group under study, so they can gain a greater understanding of the group's behaviour.
   Disadvantages — The researcher loses objectivity by becoming part of the group.
   — The participants may act differently if they know a researcher is amongst them.
2) **Non-participant observation** is when the researcher observes the activity without getting involved in it. This is a **covert** technique (their presence is unknown to the participants).
   Advantages — The researcher can remain objective throughout the study.
   Disadvantages — The researcher loses a sense of the group dynamics by staying separate from the group.

Sometimes researchers undertake **structured observations.** This is where the behaviour categories that are going to be used are defined in **advance**.
Advantages — It's easier to gather relevant data because you already know what you're looking for.
Disadvantages — Interesting behaviours could go unrecorded because they haven't been pre-defined as important.

Naturalistic Observation** Involves Making **Design Decisions

There are various ways of organising **structured observations** to make sure no behaviours are missed.

Recording Data	If you want **qualitative data** you could just make **written notes**. But **video** or **audio recording** means that you have a more accurate permanent record.
Categorising Behaviour	You must **define** the behaviours you aim to observe. For example, if you were going to observe children in a school playground to see how many behave aggressively, you'd have to decide **what counts as aggression**. This involves giving an **operationalised definition** (i.e. some **specific**, **observable** behaviours). For example, you might say that *'aggression is any physical act made with the intention to harm another person — such as punching, kicking, etc.'* But you have to be careful not to **miss out** anything important otherwise your definition may not be valid, e.g. aggression can also be verbal.
Rating Behaviour	The behaviours that you're interested in may be things that are a matter of **degree**, so you might need to use a rating scale to classify behaviour. You could put each participant's behaviour into one of several **categories**, e.g. *not aggressive*, *mildly aggressive* or *very aggressive*. Or you could use a **coding system** where each participant is given a **number** (e.g. between 1 and 10) to represent how aggressive they are, where a **higher score** indicates **more aggression**. However, you still have to **define** what kinds of behaviour are included for each number on the scale (e.g. 5 = *pushing* and 10 = *kicking or punching more than once*). Behaviour rated in this way provides **quantitative data** (data in the form of **numbers**).
Sampling Behaviour	You have to decide **how often** and for **how long** you're going to observe the participants. **Event sampling** — this is when you only record particular events that you're interested in (e.g. aggression shown by the children) and ignore other behaviours. Advantages — Researchers know exactly what behaviours they're looking for. Disadvantages — Potentially interesting behaviours could be ignored. **Time-interval sampling** — if the behaviours occur over a long time period you might choose to observe for only set time intervals e.g. the first 10 minutes of every hour. The time intervals could be chosen randomly. Advantages — Very convenient for the researchers to carry out. Disadvantages — If interesting behaviours occur outside the time sample they won't be recorded.
Inter-Observer Reliability	Even after you've **defined** the behaviours you're interested in, you have to make sure that the observers are actually putting each participant in the **right category** or giving the **right rating**. This might involve **comparing** the data from two or more observers to make sure they're giving the **same** scores (i.e. that they are 'reliable').

Observations, Questionnaires and Interviews

Questionnaires Need to be Designed *Carefully*

There are various things you need to consider when designing a questionnaire for a survey.

1) **Type of data** — whether you want **qualitative data** and/or **quantitative data** will affect whether you ask **open** and/or **closed questions**.
   a) **Open questions** are questions such as *What kinds of music do you like?* The participant can reply in **any way**, and in as much detail as they want. This gives detailed, qualitative information, although it may be **hard to analyse**, as the participants could give very different answers.
   b) **Closed questions** limit the answers that can be given, e.g. *Which do you like: Pop, Rock or neither?* They give **quantitative** data that is relatively **easy to analyse** — e.g. you can say exactly **how many** people liked each type of music. However, less detail is obtained about each participant.
2) **Ambiguity** — you have to avoid questions and answer options which are **not** clearly **defined**, e.g. *Do you listen to music frequently?* What is meant here by 'frequently'? — Once a day, once a week?
3) **Double-barrelled questions** — best not to use these, since a person may wish to answer **differently** to each part. For example, *Do you agree that modern music is not as good as the music of the 1960s and that there should be more guitar-based music in the charts?*
4) **Leading questions** — these are questions that **lead** the participant towards a particular answer. E.g. *How old was the boy in the distance?* They might have seen an older person, but by saying '*boy*' you're leading them to describe the person as young. You're also leading them to think that the person was male, but they might not have been sure. (It's really important to avoid leading questions in **eyewitness testimony** — see page 12.)
5) **Complexity** — whenever possible **clear English** should be used, avoiding **jargon**. However, if specialist terms are included, they should be clearly defined. (So the question *Do you prefer music written in unusual time signatures?* probably isn't ideal for most people.)

All of the Above Goes For *Interviews* As Well

But you also have to consider the following:

1) **How structured** the interview will be:
   Interviews can be very **informal** with **few set questions**, and new questions being asked **depending on** the participant's **previous answers**. This gives detailed qualitative data, which may be difficult to analyse. Alternatively, they may be more **structured**, with set questions and **closed answers**, giving **less detail** but being **easier to analyse**.
2) Using a **question checklist** — if the interview is structured, a checklist ensures that no questions are left out and questions aren't asked twice.
3) The behaviour or appearance of the **interviewer** — this could **influence** how the participants react.

Practice Questions

Q1 What is 'non-participant observation'?

Q2 Give two ways of rating behaviour in observational studies.

Q3 How can behaviour be sampled in observational studies?

Q4 Explain three of the issues involved in designing questionnaires and interviews.

Exam Questions

Q1 Outline three of the main issues that a researcher must consider when designing a questionnaire. [6 marks]

Q2 What are the advantages of choosing a participant observation design instead of a non-participant observation design? [6 marks]

Big Brother — naturalistic observation at its finest...?

This is all about observing behaviour that's as natural as possible. What you don't want is for people to put on an act just because they're aware that they're being watched — that defeats the object of doing the study in the first place. Makes you wonder about Big Brother — can they keep an act up for all those weeks, or do we actually get to see some natural stuff?

Selecting and Using Participants

It'd be great if you could study everyone in the world. It might take a while, but you're bound to find something interesting eventually. Most psychologists can't be bothered to do this though, so they just pick a selection of people to study instead...

Selecting a **Sample** of Participants Can Be Done in **Three Main Ways**

1) The part of a **population** that you're interested in studying is called the **target group** — e.g. all the people in a particular city, or all people of a certain age or background.
2) Usually you can't include everyone in the target group in a study, so you choose a certain **sample** of **participants**.
3) This sample should be **representative**, i.e. it should reflect the variety of characteristics that are found in the target group.
4) A sample that is unrepresentative is **biased**.

There are various methods of selecting a sample:

RANDOM SAMPLING

This is when **every** member of the target group has an **equal chance** of being selected for the sample. This could be done by giving everyone in the target group a number and then getting a computer to randomly pick numbers to select the participants. Sounds like being in a catalogue store. Order number 103 to the collection point...

Advantages: Random sampling is 'fair'. Everyone has an equal chance of being selected and the sample is **likely** to be representative.

Disadvantages: This method doesn't **guarantee** a representative sample — there's still a chance that some subgroups in the target group may not be selected (e.g. people from a minority cultural group). Also, if the target group is large it may not be practical (or possible) to give everyone a number that might be picked. So in practice, completely random samples are rarely used.

OPPORTUNITY SAMPLING

This is when the researcher samples whoever is **available and willing** to be studied. Since many researchers work in universities, they often use opportunity samples made up of students.

Advantages: This is a **quick** and **practical** way of getting a sample.

Disadvantages: The sample is **unlikely** to be **representative** of a target group or population as a whole. This means that we can't confidently **generalise** the findings of the research. However, because it's **quick** and **easy**, opportunity sampling is **often used**.

VOLUNTEER SAMPLING

This is when people actively **volunteer** to be in a study by responding to a request for participants advertised by the researcher, e.g. in a newspaper, or on a notice board.
The researcher may then select only those who are **suitable** for the study.
(This method was used by Milgram — see page 76.)

Advantages: If an advert is placed prominently (e.g. in a national newspaper) a **large number** of people may respond, giving more participants to study. This may allow more **in-depth analysis** and **more accurate** statistical results.

Disadvantages: Even though a large number of people may respond, these will only include people who actually saw the advertisement — no one else would have a chance of being selected. Also, people who volunteer may be more **cooperative** than others. For these reasons the sample is **unlikely** to be **representative** of the target population.

No method can guarantee a representative sample, but you should have confidence that your sample is (quite) representative if you want to generalise your results to the entire target group.

Selecting and Using Participants

Participants Sometimes **Act Differently** When They're Being **Observed**

Human participants will usually be aware that they are being **studied**. This may mean they don't show their **true response**, and so their data may not be **valid** or **reliable**. Some of these effects are explained below...

THE HAWTHORNE EFFECT: If people are **interested** in something and in the attention they are getting (e.g. from researchers), then they show a more **positive** response, try **harder** at tasks, and so on.

This means their results for tests are often **artificially high** (because they're trying harder than normal), which could make a researcher's conclusions **inaccurate**.

The opposite effect may occur if the participants are **uninterested** in the task.

DEMAND CHARACTERISTICS: This is when participants form an idea about the **purpose** of a study. If they think they know what kind of response the researcher is **expecting** from them, they may show that response to '**please**' the researcher (or they may **deliberately** do the **opposite**).

Either way, the conclusions drawn from the study would be **inaccurate**.

SOCIAL DESIRABILITY BIAS: People usually try to show themselves in the **best possible light**.

So in a survey, they may **not** be completely **truthful**, but give answers that are more **socially acceptable** instead (e.g. people may say they give more money to charity than they really do).

This would make the results **less accurate**.

The **Researchers** Can **Affect** the Outcomes in **Undesirable Ways**

The **reliability** and **validity** of results may also be influenced by the researcher, since he or she has **expectations** about what will happen. This can produce the following effects:

RESEARCHER (or EXPERIMENTER) BIAS: The researchers' **expectations** can influence how they **design** their study and how they **behave** towards the participants, which may then produce **demand characteristics**. Also, their expectations may influence **how** they take **measurements** and **analyse** their data, resulting in errors that can lead, for example, to accepting a hypothesis that was actually false.

INTERVIEWER EFFECTS: The interviewer's **expectations** may lead them to ask only questions about what **they** are **interested** in, or to ask **leading questions**.

Or, they may **focus** on the aspects of the participant's answers which **fit** their **expectations**.

Also, the participant may react to the **behaviour** or **appearance** of an interviewer and then not answer truthfully.

Practice Questions

Q1 What is random sampling?

Q2 Give a disadvantage of opportunity sampling.

Q3 Give an advantage of volunteer sampling.

Q4 What are demand characteristics?

Q5 How might a researcher's expectations affect a study?

Exam Questions

Q1 Describe three ways humans might alter their behaviour if they know they are being observed. [6 marks]

Q2 Outline three sampling strategies that researchers might use when recruiting people for a study. [6 marks]

Volunteers needed for study into pain and embarrassment... (and stupidity)

An interesting thing to bear in mind is that loads of the studies here were done in universities. Students are pretty easy to get your hands on in universities, so they make up a massive proportion of the samples. Trouble is, students are quite different to the rest of the population, so unless it's a study into sleep and beans on toast, the sample is probably unrepresentative.

Ethical Issues in Psychological Research

Ethics are standards about what's right and wrong, so an ethical issue is a dilemma about whether something is acceptable and justified. Try to imagine yourself as a participant in the studies you've read about so far — ask yourself if you would've been happy taking part, how you'd have felt, and if it would've had long-term effects on you.

The British Psychological Society (BPS) Produces **Ethical Guidelines**

The **British Psychological Society** (BPS) has developed ethical guidelines to help psychologists resolve ethical issues in research and protect participants. They include advice on **deception**, **consent** and **psychological harm**.

Deception Means Misleading or Withholding Information from Participants

Asch (see page 70) deceived participants about his study's purpose and about the confederates who pretended to be real participants. He argued that without deception the aim of this study could not be achieved. If deception has to be used, participants should be told of the true nature of the research as soon as possible, during the debriefing.

BPS Guidelines for Deception

Deception should be avoided wherever possible and only be used when it's scientifically justified — when the study would be meaningless otherwise.

Deception shouldn't be used if it's likely that the participant will be unhappy when they discover the study's true nature.

Informed Consent Should be Given Where Possible

Giving consent means **agreeing** to participate in a study. When a participant is told the research aim and procedure and then agrees to it, this is **informed consent**. They are fully informed before their decision to participate. If deception is used, participants **can't** give informed consent until they've been debriefed.

Asch's participants **did not** give informed consent when they agreed to take part. They were deceived about aspects of the study and didn't have enough information for an informed decision.

BPS Guidelines for Informed Consent

Participants should be given all the information they need to decide whether to participate in research and shouldn't be coerced or pressured.

Some people may not be able to give real informed consent — for example children. In these cases informed consent should be obtained from parents or guardians.

Psychological Harm Means Any **Negative Emotion** (e.g. Stress, Distress, Embarrassment)

Asch's participants may have experienced **stress** and were possibly **embarrassed** about being 'tricked' into conforming.

BPS Guidelines for Psychological Harm

Researchers have a responsibility to protect participants from physical and psychological harm during the study. Any risk of harm should be no greater than what the participant might experience in their normal life.

Researchers Have to Deal with **Ethical Issues in Their Studies**

Deception

Sometimes it's difficult to conduct meaningful research without a bit of **deception**. If participants know exactly what's being studied then their behaviour might change, and the data you get would be useless. Psychologists don't usually tell participants every last detail, but they do try to minimise deception. That way participants aren't likely to be upset when they find out the true nature of the study.
Milgram's experiment (page 76) is an example of a study that would probably not be considered ethical today. He deceived participants about the true purpose of the study and many of them showed signs of **stress** when taking part.

Consent

Gaining consent is central to conducting research ethically. But telling participants they're being observed could **change** the way they **behave**.
Milgram's participants couldn't give informed consent until after they were debriefed. If they'd known about the nature of the study, it wouldn't have worked.

Ethical Issues in Psychological Research

Confidentiality and ***Animal Rights*** are Also ***Ethical Issues***

Confidentiality means keeping information private.

1) Participants should feel safe that any **sensitive information**, **results** or **behaviour** revealed through research won't be discussed with others.
2) Information obtained during a study should remain confidential **unless** the participant agrees it can be shared with others.
3) The study's report shouldn't reveal information or data **identifiable** to an individual.
4) You shouldn't be able to tell who took part or what their individual data was — these should remain **anonymous**.

Research with non-human animals has caused heated debate.

1) In **support**, people argue that animal research has provided **valuable information** for psychological and medical research. Some **research designs** couldn't have been conducted on humans — e.g. Harlow's study on attachment, where young monkeys were separated from their mothers and reared alone (page 20).
2) Some **disagree** with the idea of conducting research with non-human animals. They may argue that it's **ethically wrong** to inflict harm and suffering on animals, and obviously animals can't give consent to take part.
3) Some argue that it's cruel to experiment on animals that have a **similar intelligence** to humans, because they might suffer the same problems we would. It'd be OK to experiment on animals that are far less developed than us, but there is no point because they'll be **too different** from us to give results that apply to humans.

Ethical Guidelines ***Don't Solve*** *All the Problems*

1) There may be researchers who **don't follow the guidelines** properly. Naughty.
2) If a psychologist conducts research in an unacceptable way, they **can't be banned** from research (unlike a doctor who can be 'struck off' for misconduct). But they'd probably be kicked out of their university and the BPS.
3) Even when guidelines are followed, it can be **difficult to assess** things like **psychological harm**, or to **fully justify the use of deception**.
4) Deciding whether the ends (benefits from the study) justify the means (how it was done and at what cost) is not straightforward either. This creates another dilemma for psychologists.

The lasting harm to Milgram's participants was beginning to show.

Practice Questions

Q1 If you have used deception, what should you do immediately after the study?

Q2 What does 'informed consent' mean?

Q3 For the issue of psychological harm, what level of risk is said to be acceptable in research?

Exam Questions

Q1 Identify one strength and one weakness of conducting research on non-human animals. [4 marks]

Q2 Outline the main ethical principles for conducting psychological research, as developed by the British Psychological Society. Indicate how psychologists deal with these issues in their studies. [12 marks]

Don't let someone debrief you unless you love them very much...

Psychological experiments create many ethical dilemmas. Take Milgram's study — there's no doubting that the results reveal interesting things about how people interact. But do these results justify the possible psychological damage done to the participants? There's no right or wrong answer, but the BPS guidelines are there to address exactly this sort of issue.

Data Analysis

Data analysis might sound vaguely maths-like — but don't run for the hills just yet. It isn't too tricky...

Data from **Observations** Should be Analysed **Carefully**

1) If you've got **quantitative** data (i.e. numbers), you can use **statistics** to show, for example, the most common behaviours. (Quantitative data can be obtained by **categorising** and **rating** behaviour — see page 38.)
2) **Qualitative** data might consist of a video or audio **recording**, or written **notes** on what the observers witnessed. Analysis of qualitative data is **less straightforward**, but it can still be done.
3) Whatever kind of data you've got, there are some important issues to bear in mind:

   a) There must be **adequate data sampling** to ensure that a **representative** sample of participants' behaviour has been seen.
   b) **Language** must be used **accurately** — the words used to describe behaviour should be **accurate** and **appropriate** (and must have valid **operationalised definitions** — see page 35). For example, it might not be appropriate to describe a child's behaviour as 'aggressive' if he or she is play-fighting.
   c) Researcher **bias** must be **avoided** — e.g. it's not okay to make notes **only** on events that **support** the researcher's theories, or to have a **biased interpretation** of what is observed.

The Same Goes for Data Obtained from **Interviews**

1) When **closed** questions are used as part of an interview's structure, **quantitative** data can be produced (e.g. the **number** of participants who replied 'Yes' to a particular question). **Statistics** can then be used (see pages 46-49) to further analyse the data.
2) When **open** questions are used, more **detailed**, **qualitative** data is obtained.
3) Again, whatever you've got, there are certain things you'll need to remember:

   a) **Context** — the **situation** in which a participant said something, and the way they were **behaving** at the time, may be important. It may help the researcher understand **why** something was said, and give clues about the **honesty** of a statement.
   b) The researcher should clearly distinguish **what** was said by the participant from **how** they interpreted it.
   c) **Selection** of data — a lot of **qualitative** data may be produced by an interview, which may be difficult for the researcher to **summarise** in a report. The researcher must **avoid bias** in selecting what to include (e.g. only including statements that support their ideas). The interviewees may be consulted when deciding **what** to include and **how** to present it.
   d) The interviewer should be aware of how *their* feelings about the interviewee could lead to **biased interpretations** of what they say, or how it is later reported.

And Likewise for Data from **Questionnaire Surveys**

1) Like observations and interviews, **surveys** can give you both **quantitative** and **qualitative** data, and so most of the points above are relevant to surveys as well.
2) Again, it's especially important to distinguish the **interpretations** of the **researcher** from the **statements** of the **participant**, and to be **unbiased** in selecting what to include in any report on the research.
3) However, the analysis of **written** answers may be especially difficult because the participant is not present to **clarify** any **ambiguities**, plus you don't know the **context** for their answers (e.g. what mood they were in, and so on).

Data Analysis

Qualitative Data Can Be **Tricky** to **Analyse**

Qualitative data is sometimes seen as 'of **limited use**' because it's difficult to **analyse**.
This is why it's often **converted** into **quantitative** data using **content analysis**.

CONTENT ANALYSIS

a) A **representative sample** of qualitative data is first **collected** — e.g. from an interview, printed material (newspapers, etc.) or other media (such as TV programmes).
b) **Coding units** are identified to analyse the data. A coding unit could be, for example, an **act of violence**, or the use of **gender stereotypes** (though both of these must be given valid **operationalised definitions** first — e.g. a definition of an 'act of violence').
c) The qualitative data is then **analysed** to see **how often** each coding unit occurs (or **how much** is said about it, etc.).
d) A **statistical analysis** can then be carried out (see pages 46-49).

ADVANTAGES OF QUANTIFYING DATA

1) It becomes **easier** to see **patterns** in the data, and easier to **summarise** and **present** it (see pages 50-51).
2) **Statistical analysis** can be carried out.

DISADVANTAGES OF QUANTIFYING DATA

1) Care is needed to avoid **bias** in defining **coding units**, or deciding which behaviours fit particular units.
2) Qualitative data has **more detail** (**context**, etc.), which is **lost** when it's converted into **numbers**.

1) Because of the **detail** (and hence the **insight**) that **qualitative** data can give, some researchers prefer to **avoid** 'reducing' it to **numbers**.
2) Instead they analyse the data into **categories** or '**typologies**' (e.g. sarcastic remarks, statements about feelings, etc.), **quotations**, **summaries**, and so on.
3) **Hypotheses** may be developed during this analysis, rather than being stated previously, so that they are 'grounded in the data'.

Audrey was disappointed to learn that she'd been reduced to a number.

Practice Questions

Q1 Distinguish between qualitative and quantitative data.
Q2 Why is data sampling an issue in observation studies?
Q3 Why might survey data be harder to analyse than interview data?
Q4 How is a content analysis done?

Exam Question

Q1 Outline the main differences between qualitative and quantitative data and give one strength and one weakness associated with each. [8 marks]

You must keep an open mind — but just don't let all the facts escape...

It's fairly obvious-ish, I guess, that qualitative data needs to be analysed with an open mind — it's not OK to fit the facts to your theory... you have to fit your theory to the facts. The same goes for analysing quantitative data — it's not just a case of 'doing some maths' — you have to be sure you're not being biased in your interpretations. Keep that mind open...

Descriptive Statistics

Run for your lives... panic. This really looks like maths... Well, actually, it's not too bad. So calm down.

Descriptive Statistics — Just Say What You See...

1) **Descriptive statistics** simply describe the **patterns** found in a set of data.
2) Descriptive statistics uses the fancy term '**central tendency**' to describe an **average**. For example, the central tendency (average) for the height of a group of 18-year-old boys might be about 1.70 metres.
3) Measures of **dispersion** describe **how spread out** the data is. For example, the difference in height between the shortest 18-year-old boy and the tallest might be 35 cm.

There are 3 Measures of Central Tendency (aka Average) You Need to Know

The Mean — This is the 'Normal Average'

You calculate the **mean** by **adding** all of the scores in a data set and then **dividing** by the number of scores.

Mean $= \bar{X} = \frac{\sum X}{N}$, where $\sum X$ is the sum of all the scores (and there are N of them).

Σ (pronounced 'sigma') just means you add things up.

Example: If you've got scores of 2, 5, 6, 7 and 10, then $\sum X = 30$ (since all the scores add up to 30), and N = 5 (since there are 5 of them)...

...so the **mean** is $\bar{X} = \frac{30}{5} = 6$.

For example, the scores 10, 40, 25, 20 and 650 have a mean of 149, which is not representative of the central tendency of the data set.

Advantages
a) It uses **all** the scores in a data set.
b) It's used in **further calculations** (e.g. standard deviation — see next page), and so it's handy to work it out.

Disadvantages
a) It can be **skewed** (distorted) by extremely **high** or **low** scores. This can make it **unrepresentative** of most of the scores, and so it may be **misleading**. In these cases, it's best to not use the mean.
b) It can sometimes give an **unrealistically precise** value (e.g. the average home has 2.4 children — but what does 0.4 of a child mean...?)

The Median — The Middle Score When the Data is Put in Order

Example: The **median** of the scores 4, 5, 10, 12 and 14 is **10**.

In this example there was one score in the middle. If there are two middle scores, add them together and then divide by 2 to get the median.

Advantages
a) It's relatively **quick** and **easy** to calculate.
b) It's **not** affected by extremely high or low scores, so it can be used on 'skewed' sets of data to give a '**representative**' average score.

Disadvantages
a) Not **all** the scores are used to work out the median.
b) It has **little further use** in data analysis.

The Mode — The Score that Occurs Most Often

Example: The **mode** (or the **modal score**) of 2, 5, 2, 9, 6, 11 and 2 is **2**.

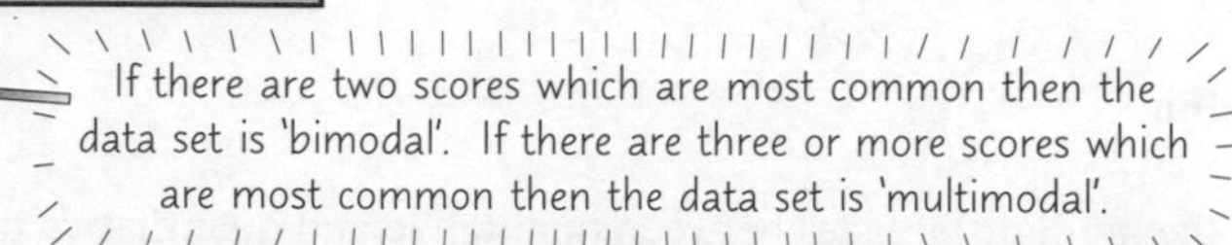

Advantages
a) It shows the **most common** or 'important' score.
b) It's always a result from the actual **data set**, so it can be a more **useful** or **realistic** statistic, e.g. the modal average family has 2 children, not 2.4.

Disadvantages
a) It's not very useful if there are **several** modal values, or if the modal value is only **slightly** more common than other scores.
b) It has **little further use** in data analysis.

Descriptive Statistics

Measures of Dispersion Tell You How Spread Out the Data Is

Range — Highest Score Minus the Lowest Score

Example: The **range** of the scores 6, 10, 35 and 50, is 50 – 6 = **44**

Note that (highest - lowest) +1 can also be used, so the range would then be 45.

Advantage — it's **quick** and **easy** to calculate.

Disadvantage — it completely ignores the **central** values of a data set, so it can be misleading if there are very **high** or **low** scores.

1) The **interquartile range** (**IQR**) can be calculated to help **avoid** this problem.
2) First the **median** is calculated (this is sometimes called **Q2**).
3) If there's an **odd** number of values then you take the middle number as the median. If there's an **even** number of values then you take the 2 middle numbers, add them together and divide them by 2 to find the median.
4) The **median** of the **lower half** of the data is called the **lower quartile** (or **Q1**). The **median** of the upper half of the data is called the **upper quartile** (or **Q3**)
5) The **IQR = Q3 – Q1**.

Example: 3, 3, **4**, 5, 6, **8**, 10, 13, **14**, 16, 19.
There are 11 values, so median (Q2) = 6th value = 8.
Then Q1 = 4, Q3 = 14, and so IQR = 14 – 4 = **10**.

Standard Deviation — Measures How Much Scores Deviate from the Mean

$$s = \sqrt{\frac{\sum (X-\bar{X})^2}{N}}$$, where s = standard deviation

Example: Scores = 5, 9, 10, 11 and 15. The mean = 10.
So the standard deviation is:

$$s = \sqrt{\frac{(5-10)^2 + (9-10)^2 + (10-10)^2 + (11-10)^2 + (15-10)^2}{5}} = 3.22 \text{ (3 s.f.)}$$

A high standard deviation shows more variability in a set of data.

Advantages — **all** scores in the set are taken into account, so it's **more accurate** than the range. It can also be used in further analysis.

Disadvantage — it's **not** as quick or easy to calculate as the range.

Practice Questions

Q1 Explain how to calculate the mean.

Q2 What is the difference between the mean and the mode?

Q3 How is the range calculated?

Q4 What is meant by 'standard deviation'?

Exam Questions

Q1 Work out the mean, median and mode for the following data set: 2, 2, 4, 6, 8, 9, 10. [4 marks]

Q2 Name two measures of dispersion and outline one advantage and one disadvantage of each. [4 marks]

Dame Edna Average — making stats fun, possums...

These statistics are used to describe a collection of scores in a data set (how big the scores are, how spread out they are, and so on), so they're called... wait for it... descriptive statistics. Don't be put off by the weirdy maths notation either — a bar on top of a letter (e.g. $\bar{X}$) means you work out the mean. And a sigma (Σ) means you add things up. There... not so bad.

Correlations

You know what they say — correlation is as correlation does.
Remember that as you read this page... then you won't go far wrong.

Correlation Measures How Closely Two Variables are Related

1) **Correlation** is a measure of the relationship between **two variables**, e.g. it can tell you how closely exam grades are related to the amount of revision that someone's done.
2) In a **correlational study** data is collected for some kind of **correlational analysis**.

The Correlation Coefficient is a Number Between –1 and +1

1) To find the correlation between two variables, you first have to collect some **data**.
   For example, you could ask every student in a class how many hours of study they did each week, and note their average test result.

Student	Hours of study	Average test score — %
A	4	58
B	1	23
C	7	67
D	15	89

2) You can then work out a **correlation coefficient** (e.g. Spearman's rho — see next page). This is a number between –1 and +1, and shows:

   a) **How closely** the variables are linked. This is shown by the **size** of the number — if it's **close to +1** or **–1**, then they are **very closely** related, while a smaller number means the relationship is **less strong** (or maybe not there at all if it's close to 0).
   b) The **type** of correlation — a **positive** correlation coefficient (i.e. between 0 and +1) means that the variables rise and fall together, while a negative correlation coefficient (i.e. between –1 and 0) means that as one variable rises, the other falls. (See below for more info.)

Correlation is Easy to See on Scatter Graphs

1) **Positive correlation** — this means that as one variable rises, so does the other (and likewise, if one falls, so does the other).
   Example: hours of study and average test score.
   The correlation coefficient is roughly **0.75** (close to +1).

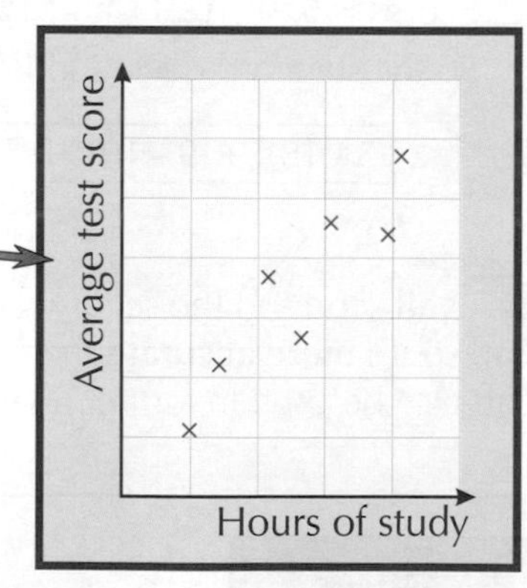

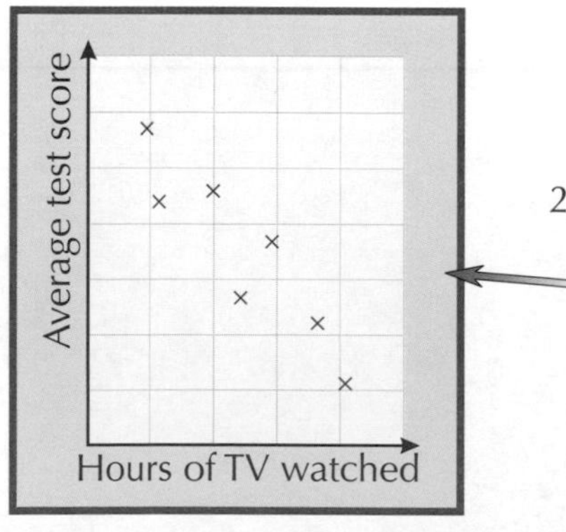

2) **Negative correlation** — this means that as one variable rises, the other one falls (and vice versa).
   Example: hours of TV watched each week and average test score.
   The correlation coefficient is roughly **–0.75** (close to -1).

3) **No correlation** — if the correlation coefficient is 0 (or close to 0), then the two variables aren't linked.
   Example: a student's height and their average test score.
   The correlation coefficient is roughly **0.01** (close to 0).

Average test score
Height

Correlations

Correlational Research has some Advantages...

1) Because correlational research doesn't involve **controlling** any variables, you can do it when (for **practical** or **ethical** reasons) you couldn't do a **controlled experiment**. Handy.
   For example, an experiment into the effects of smoking on humans probably wouldn't be done for ethical reasons, but a correlation between smoking and cancer could be established from hospital records.
2) Correlational analysis can give ideas for **future** research (e.g. biological research on the effects of smoking).
3) Correlation can even be used to test for **reliability** and **validity** (e.g. by testing the results of the same test taken twice by the same people — a good **reliable** test will show a **high correlation**).

...but some Limitations

1) Correlational analysis **can't** establish '**cause and effect**' relationships — it can only show that there's a **statistical link** between the variables.
   Variables can be closely correlated without changes in one causing changes in the other — a **third variable** could be involved. Only a **controlled experiment** can show cause and effect relationships.
2) Care must be taken when **interpreting** correlation coefficients — high correlation coefficients could be down to **chance**. To decide whether a coefficient is **significant**, you have to use a proper **significance test**.

For example, the number of births in a town was found to be positively correlated to the number of storks that nested in that town — but that didn't mean that more storks caused the increase. (It was because more people in the town led to more births, and also to more houses with chimneys to nest on.)

Spearman's Rho is a Correlation Coefficient

To work out (and then test the significance of) **Spearman's rho** correlation coefficient, you need values for two different variables (e.g. hours of revision and average test scores for 10 students).

a) The values for each variable are placed into **rank order** (each variable is ranked separately).
   The lowest value for each variable gets rank 1 (and in the above example, the biggest value will get rank 10).
b) The **difference** (**d**) in ranks for each student's variables is calculated. (So a particular student may have done the most revision, but got the 3rd best results, in which case the difference in ranks will be d = 3 – 1 = 2.)
c) The value of d for each student is **squared**, then the results are added together (to get $\sum d^2$).
d) Then the special **Spearman's correlation coefficient** calculation is done, which is $r_s = 1 - \frac{6 \times \sum d^2}{N \times (N^2 - 1)}$
   (where N is the number of students, or whatever).
e) To find out whether the result is **significant** (and so whether the variables are linked), you compare the outcome of that nightmarish calculation with a **critical value** that you look up in a **statistics table**.

Practice Questions

Q1 Explain what is meant by correlation.

Q2 What is a correlation coefficient?

Q3 What two things are shown by a correlation coefficient?

Q4 Explain the difference between a negative correlation and no correlation.

Exam Questions

Q1 A study has found a negative correlation between tiredness and reaction time. Explain what this means. [2 marks]

Q2 Outline the limitations of correlational research. [6 marks]

Stats sucks...

Look at the graphs showing the large positive and large negative correlations — all the points lie close-ish to a straight line, which slopes either upwards (positive correlation) or downwards (negative correlation). Just learn the steps involved in working out Spearman's rho — don't try to understand it too much. Well, that's my advice anyway...

Summarising the Data

It's not very scientific or anything, but the only bit about statistics I don't find mind-numbingly boring is the bit where you get to make all the lovely numbers look pretty... Ignore me — stats has turned my brain to mush.

Data** Can Be Presented in **Various Ways

1) **Qualitative** data from observations, interviews, surveys, etc. (see pages 32-33) can be presented in a **report** as a **'verbal summary'**.
2) The report would contain **summaries** of what was seen or said, possibly using **categories** to group data together. Also **quotations** from participants can be used, and any **research hypotheses** that developed during the study or data analysis may be discussed.
3) When **quantitative** data is **collected** (or **produced** from the data, e.g. by a **content analysis** — see page 45), it can be **summarised** and presented in various ways. Read on...

Tables** are a Good Way to Summarise **Quantitative Data

Tables can be used to clearly present the data and show any **patterns** in the scores.

Tables of **'raw data'** show the scores **before** any **analysis** has been done on them.

Other tables may show **descriptive statistics** such as the mean, range and standard deviation (see pages 46-47).

Edward's data was summarised nicely on his table.

Table To Show the Qualities of Different Types of Ice Cream

	Quality (score out of 10)		
Type of ice cream	Tastiness	Thickness	Throwability
Chocolate	9	7	6
Toffee	8	6	7
Strawberry	8	5	4
Earwax	2	9	8

Bar Charts** Can be Used for **Non-continuous Data

Bar chart showing the mean number of words recalled by two groups in a memory experiment.

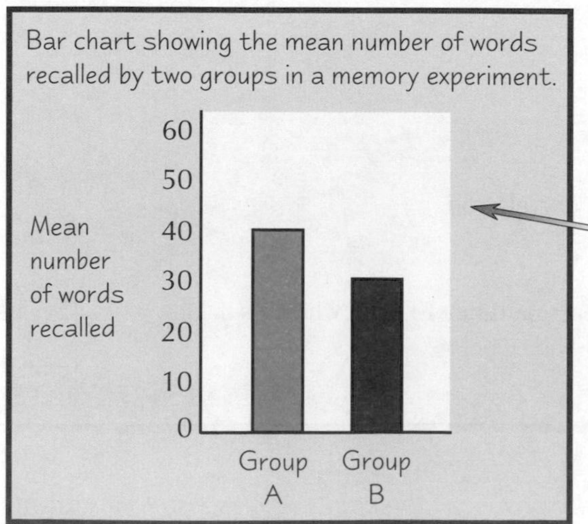

Bar charts (bar graphs) are usually used to present **'non-continuous data'** (like when a variable falls into **categories** rather than being measured on a numbered scale).

This bar chart shows the mean number of words recalled by different groups in a memory experiment.

Note that the columns in bar charts **don't touch** each other. Also, it's preferable to always show the **full vertical scale**, or **clearly indicate** when it isn't all shown (otherwise it can be **misleading**).

Summarising the Data

Nearly done — just a little bit more...

Histograms are for When You Have Continuous Data

Histograms show data measured on a '**continuous**' scale of measurement.

This histogram shows the time different participants took to complete a task.

Each column shows a **class interval** (here, each class interval is 10 seconds), and the columns **touch** each other.

It's the **height** of the column that shows the number of values in that interval. (**All** intervals are shown, even if there are **no scores** within them.)

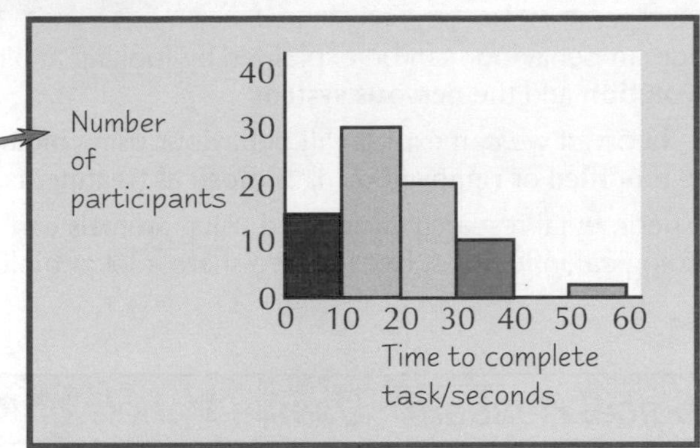

Frequency Polygons are Good for Showing More Than One Set of Data

Frequency polygons are similar to histograms, but use **lines** to show where the top of each column would reach.

It can be useful to combine **two or more** frequency polygons on the same set of axes — then it's easy to **make comparisons** between groups.

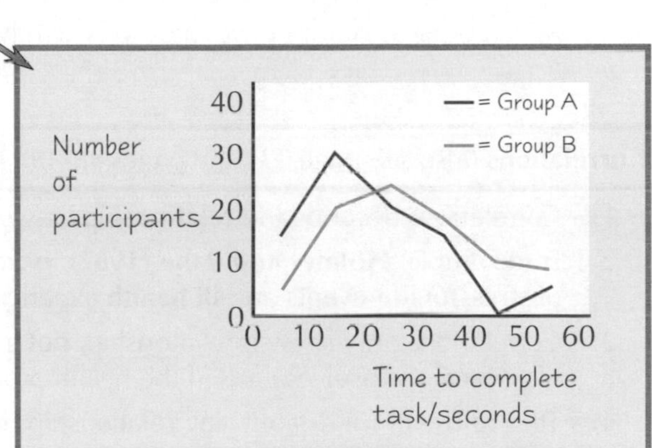

Practice Questions

Q1 What kind of information is typically shown in tables?

Q2 What kind of data is shown on bar charts?

Q3 What type of data do histograms represent?

Q4 What advantage do frequency polygons have over histograms?

Exam Questions

Q1 Describe three ways of summarising quantitative data. [6 marks]

Q2 Sketch a frequency polygon of the data in the table on p 50. [4 marks]

Is it too late to make a gag about Correlation Street...

Hmm I think I've missed the boat with that one. But if you like it, maybe turn back a page and imagine I put it there instead. How we laughed. Now wipe away the tears of joy and let's think about the fun of summarising data. Here's one — what did the histogram say to the bar chart... Oh who am I kidding, let's just be thankful it's the end of the section and move on...

The Biological Approach

The biological approach is all about looking at how physical, squidgy bits cause behaviour and determine experience. It's kind of a bit like Biology at school, except you won't have to dissect anything...

There Are Three Basic **Assumptions** of the Biological Approach

1) Human behaviour can be explained by looking at biological stuff such as **hormones**, **genetics**, **evolution** and the **nervous system**.
2) In theory, if we can explain all behaviour using **biological causes**, unwanted behaviour could be **modified** or **removed** using **biological treatments** such as medication for mental illness.
3) Experimental research conducted using **animals** can inform us about human behaviour and biological influences, because we share a lot of biological similarities.

Biological Research Uses a Variety of **Research Methods**

You also need to know about the ethical issues of these research methods — see pages 42-43.

Here are some that you should know about:

Experiments (also see page 32)

1) Experiments try to establish **cause and effect** by comparing groups and analysing any **differences** between them.
2) For example, **Krantz et al (1991)** conducted a laboratory experiment into the impact of stress on the heart (page 56).
3) Experiments are useful in this area because they can investigate possible **biological causes** of behaviour.
4) However, other **variables** have to be very tightly **controlled**, as they can affect the results of a study.

Correlations (also see page 33, and pages 48-49)

1) Correlations describe the **relationship** between two variables.
2) For example, **Holmes and Rahe (1967)** (page 58) found a positive correlation between the amount of **stressful life events** and **ill health** experienced. As one variable increases, so does the other.
3) Correlations only show a relationship, **not** a cause and effect — e.g. we can't say that the stressful life events themselves caused the health problems.
4) They're useful for establishing relationships between variables and often lead to **further research**.

Case Studies (also see page 33)

1) Case studies are used to investigate things that couldn't be investigated any other way.
2) For example, **Milner et al (1957)** reported a case study of a man who suffered memory loss after having part of his brain removed to reduce his epilepsy (see page 7).
3) Case studies are useful for investigating a situation in **great depth**.
4) However, they can't be **generalised** to other people as they're often unique situations.

Questionnaires and Interviews (also see page 33)

1) Questionnaires and interviews are used to collect information from people **directly**.
2) For example, **Holmes and Rahe (1967)** used these techniques to get people to rate how stressful individual events were to them (see page 58).
3) They rely on the **honesty** of the person but can provide **very detailed information**.

The Biological Approach

Brain Scanning *is Used to Investigate Possible* ***Abnormalities***

There are various types of brain scanning out there — some just look at the **structure** and others look at **function**.

1) **Magnetic Resonance Imaging (MRI)**

   MRI scans use **magnetic fields** to produce a **detailed image** of the brain that can show up abnormalities such as tumours and structural problems. It can also show **brain activity** by monitoring **blood flow** to different areas.

2) **Positron Emission Tomography (PET)**

   PET scans measure **brain activity** by using sensors placed on the head to track a radioactive substance that is injected into the person. PET scans can show which areas of the brain are more **active** when the person performs an activity such as counting. This helps us to understand about **function** and **communication** within the brain.

Both techniques are pretty **expensive** to use during research. However, it's useful to be able to see which parts of the brain are activated during certain activities, as different **functions** are performed in different parts of the brain. Certain functions, such as speech, problem solving and language processing, are generally localised more in one of the two **hemispheres** of the brain. This is known as **brain lateralisation**.

The Biological Approach Has ***Strengths*** *and* ***Weaknesses***

Strengths:

1) The approach can provide **evidence** to support or disprove a theory — it's a very **scientific** approach.
2) If a biological cause can be found for mental health problems or for unwanted behaviour such as aggression, then **biological treatments** can be developed to help individuals.

Weaknesses:

1) The approach doesn't take into account the influence of people's **environment**, their **family**, **childhood experiences** or their **social situation**. Other approaches see these as being important factors in explaining behaviour.
2) Using a biological explanation for negative behaviour can lead to individuals or groups avoiding taking **personal** or **social responsibility** for their behaviour.

Practice Questions

Q1 What are the basic assumptions of the biological approach?

Q2 What is a case study?

Q3 What does PET stand for?

Q4 Why is the biological approach described as being a very scientific approach?

Exam Questions

Q1 Outline one research method used in the biological approach. [6 marks]

Q2 Evaluate the biological approach in psychology. [6 marks]

MRI scans have shown that a student's brain patterns were identical when reading this page and when sleeping — coincidence...

Actually I think this is pretty interesting stuff. I mean the way your brain works must be one of the biggest remaining mysteries in medical science — sure, they can start to recognise areas of the brain and stuff — but there's a long way to go.

Stress as a Bodily Response

I'm sure you all know what stress is. It's having 3 hours left to revise before an exam, or having to visit your girlfriend or boyfriend's parents. We all feel it — but this is psychology, so it needs a proper scientific explanation.

*Stress is a Response to **Stimuli** in the **Environment***

Stress is one of those annoying words with two meanings... How helpful.

1) It can be the environmental **stimulus** that triggers a stress response, e.g. a giant cockroach dancing towards you. In other words, it's the thing that causes you to act stressed.
2) But it can also be the **response** to the stimulus — our reaction, e.g. running for the hills.

However, the white-coated ones have agreed to explain stress as '**the response that occurs when we think we can't cope with the pressures in our environment**'. This is shown in the diagram below:

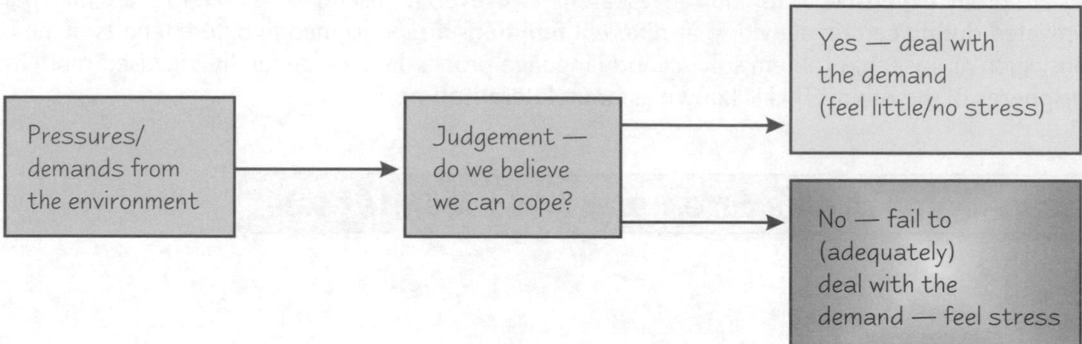

So, stress is the response that occurs when we think the demands being placed on us are greater than our ability to cope. These are our **own judgements** — so we could **over** or **underestimate** the demands, or our ability to cope. Whether the stress is justified or not doesn't matter — if we **think** we can't cope we get stressed. And when we get stressed something physically changes in us.

*The **Hypothalamus** is the Bit of the Brain that **Responds to Stress***

The evaluation of whether something is a **stressor** occurs in the **higher brain centres** — the **cerebral cortex**. When there's a stressor in the environment, these higher areas send a signal to the **hypothalamus**. This tiny part of the brain makes up for its size by having many functions — including controlling the **physiological activities** involved in stress. In response to the higher areas, the hypothalamus triggers **two processes** in the body:

*The activation of the **sympathomedullary pathway**...*

1) In the **initial shock response**, the **hypothalamus** triggers activity in the **sympathetic branch** of the **autonomic nervous system** — which is a branch of the **peripheral nervous system**.
2) The sympathetic branch becomes more active when the body is **stressed** and **using energy**.
3) It stimulates the **adrenal medulla** within the **adrenal glands**, which releases **adrenaline** and **noradrenaline** into the bloodstream.
4) These affect the body in several ways, including:
   - **Blood pressure** and **heart rate** increase to get blood quickly to areas of the body where it's needed for activity.
   - **Digestion decreases** so that blood can be directed to the brain and muscles.
   - **Muscles** become more **tense** so that the body is physically responsive.
   - **Perspiration increases** so that the body can cool down and burn more energy.
   - **Breathing rate increases** so that more oxygen can be sent to the muscles.

This happens pretty quickly, preparing us for 'fight or flight'.

5) The result of these changes is that the body is **ready to use energy** to deal with the stressful situation, e.g. running away from the rhino that's escaped from the zoo.

Stress as a Bodily Response

... Followed by the activation of the pituitary-adrenal system

If the stress is **long-term**, say several hours or more, then the sympathomedullary response will start to use up the body's **resources**. So, a second system produces a **countershock response** — which supplies the body with more fuel. It's like putting your body on red alert.

1) The hypothalamus also triggers the release of **CRH** (corticotropin-releasing hormone).
2) CRH stimulates the **anterior pituitary gland.**
3) This then releases a hormone called **ACTH** (adrenocorticotropic hormone).
4) ACTH travels through the body and then stimulates the **adrenal cortex**, which is near the kidneys.
5) The adrenal cortex then releases **corticosteroids** which give us energy by converting **fat** and **protein**.
6) This energy is needed to replace that used up by the body's initial reaction to the stress, e.g. running away.

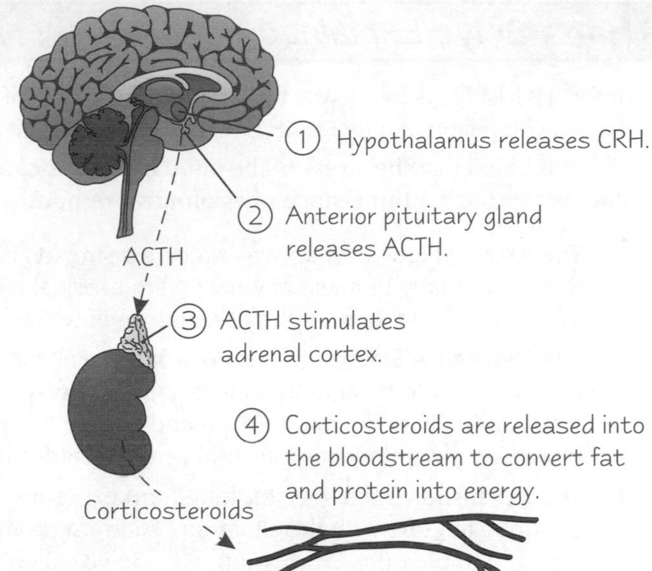

Changes in the Body Can Be Seen as Having Survival Value

1) During our evolution many threats to us would have been from **predators** or other **physical dangers**.
2) So, to successfully respond to them, we would have required **energy** to fight or run away — the **'fight or flight'** response.
3) However, in **modern society** stressors are more likely to be **psychological** than physical and are more **long-term**, e.g. the stresses of working at a desk, commuting, noisy neighbours, etc.
4) Therefore the physical stress response is not really needed, and in the long term it may actually be harmful to our bodies — the next two pages explain how.
5) Some stress can be positive and exhilarating — this is known as **eustress**, e.g. a parachute jump might lead to this kind of arousal.

Leo was finding the journey to work increasingly stressful.

Practice Questions

Q1 What is stress?

Q2 When does the sympathetic branch of the nervous system become more active?

Q3 Why does digestion decrease when the body is under stress?

Q4 What function do corticosteroids perform?

Exam Questions

Q1 A dog runs out into the road and Michael has to brake suddenly. He feels his heart start to pound. Explain why this happens. [6 marks]

Q2 Outline the response of the pituitary-adrenal system to long-term stress. [6 marks]

Well, as bodily responses go, I guess stress isn't so bad...

Stress is a natural reaction in response to anything which threatens you. In the past, it would have been a lion chasing you. Now it's more likely to be a deadline or late train. So next time you see someone getting stressed about something, try telling them, "relax, it could be worse — at least you're not being chased by a lion" — that'll soon calm them down.

Stress and Physical Illness

The last couple of pages made it blindingly obvious that stress isn't just something in your head — it's a physical response. These pages cover what stress can do to your physical state in the long run.

Hans Selye Explained Stress as a Three-Stage Response

In the 1930s, Hans Selye was researching the effects of hormones when he noticed that rats would become ill (e.g. develop stomach ulcers) even when they were given harmless injections (can't have been that harmless).

He concluded that the **stress** of the daily injections **caused the illness** and suggested that all animals and humans react to stressors through a **three-stage physiological response**. Selye called this the **General Adaptation Syndrome (GAS)** (1936).

1) **The Alarm Stage** — when we perceive a stressor, our body's first reaction is to increase arousal levels so that we're ready to make any necessary physical response (described on page 54). These mean we're able to run away (the 'fight or flight' response) if we're faced with a big-toothed hairy monster.
2) **The Resistance Stage** — if the stressor remains for a long time, our bodies can adapt to the situation and we seem to be able to cope in a normal way. For example, if we start a high-pressure job we would initially be unable to cope and go into the alarm stage, but after time we would seem to adapt. However, physiologically, arousal levels would still be higher than normal to cope with the situation.
3) **The Exhaustion Stage** — after long-term exposure to a stressor our bodies will eventually be unable to continue to cope with the situation. Alarm signs may return and we may develop illnesses, e.g. ulcers, high blood pressure, depression, etc. Selye called these 'diseases of adaptation'.

Comment — the stages Selye identified are supported by a lot of scientific research. However, the GAS theory describes a single type of response and so neglects the fact that the body's reaction to stress does vary, e.g. how much adrenaline is released depends on how the stressor is perceived by the person (how frightening it is, etc.). Also, a certain bacterium has been found to be involved in the formation of ulcers. It could still be the case, though, that stress weakens the immune system making ulcers more likely.

Long-Term Stress Can Affect the Cardiovascular System

The "cardiovascular system" is just a fancy name for the **heart** and **blood vessels**.
A **long-term stress response** may have a direct effect on this system:

	Krantz et al (1991) — stress and the heart
Method:	In a **laboratory experiment**, 39 participants did one of three stress-inducing tasks (a maths test, a Stroop test and public speaking). Their **blood pressure** and the extent to which the vessels around their heart **contracted** (low, medium or high myocardial ischaemia) was measured. Participants were instructed not to take any prescribed heart medication prior to the study.
Results:	Participants with the greatest myocardial ischaemia showed the highest increases in blood pressure. A small number of participants who showed mild or no myocardial ischaemia only had a very moderate increase in blood pressure.
Conclusion:	Stress may have a **direct influence** on aspects of body functioning, making cardiovascular disorders more likely.
Evaluation:	Although the effects were clearly **linked** to stress, it can't be said that one causes the other. Also, it wasn't shown whether the effects also occur at other times. They might sometimes happen even if the person feels relaxed — and therefore couldn't just be linked to feeling stressed. Not everybody showed the same reaction, which suggests that **individual differences** between the participants may also have played a role. The **ecological validity** of the study was reduced because it took place under **laboratory conditions** that weren't fully representative of real-life stress. However, the findings of the study are supported by **Williams (2000)** — it was seen that people who got angry easily or reacted more angrily to situations had a higher risk of cardiovascular problems.

Stress and Physical Illness

Stress Can Also Affect the *Immune System*

The immune system is made of cells (e.g. white blood cells) and chemicals that **seek and destroy bacteria** and **viruses**. When someone experiences stress over a long time (a **long-term stress response**) their immune system stops functioning properly. Loads of studies have tested whether long-term stress makes us more vulnerable to infection and illness.

Brady et al (1958) — stress and the development of ulcers

Method: Monkeys were put in pairs and given electric shocks every 20 seconds for 6 hour sessions. One monkey of each pair (the 'executive') could push a lever to postpone each shock. The other could not delay them.

Results: The 'executive' monkeys were more likely to develop illness (ulcers) and later die.

Conclusion: The illness and death was not due to the shocks but due to the stress that the executives felt in trying to avoid them. In the long term, this stress reduced the immune system's ability to fight illness.

Evaluation: The experiment has **ethical** issues — the experiment was very cruel and would not be allowed today. Also, we can't **generalise** results from monkeys to humans. Furthermore, we know that people with **little control** over their own lives (such as those with low-level jobs and the long-term unemployed), can experience **high levels** of stress, which this research cannot explain.

The same *Immune System Suppression* happens in *Humans*

Research on humans (fortunately not quite as unethical as the monkey study) has also supported the theory that stress can reduce the effectiveness of the immune system. Take the following study, for example:

Kiecolt-Glaser et al (1995) — stress and wound healing

Method: In a study with an **independent measures** design, a punch biopsy was used to create a small wound on the arms of 13 women who cared for relatives with Alzheimer's disease (a very stressful responsibility). A control group of 13 people also took part.

Results: Wound healing took an average of 9 days longer for the carers than those in the control group.

Conclusion: Long-term stress impairs the effectiveness of the immune system to heal wounds.

Evaluation: **Sweeney (1995)** also found that people caring for relatives with dementia took longer than a control group to heal their wounds. However, for both studies the two groups may have **varied in other ways** apart from the stress of being a carer. The effects on the carers could be due to poor diet, lack of sleep, etc, and not just the stress they experienced. The study only contained a small number of participants — for more reliable results it should be repeated with a larger number.

Practice Questions

Q1 What are the three stages of Selye's general adaptation syndrome?

Q2 What were the results of the Brady et al (1958) study?

Q3 Who were the experimental group in the Kiecolt-Glaser et al (1995) study?

Exam Questions

Q1 Sarah was promoted to team leader in a busy call centre and has noticed that she is experiencing more illness than she used to. Use psychological theories and studies to explain this. [10 marks]

Q2 Evaluate the strengths and weaknesses of studying stress under laboratory conditions. [12 marks]

No more exams thanks — can't be doing with ulcers...

If you think about it, it kind of stands to reason that being really stressed out all the time will have some effect on your body. You need to remember the actual physiological facts about how this happens, and as usual you need to know some criticisms of the studies too. Although, whilst you're at it, do take in the lessons for life on these pages — just chill out dude.

Sources of Stress — Life Changes

*There are loads of sources of stress — for some unfortunate individuals it's the thought of peanut butter sticking to their teeth, but for normal folk the two real biggies are **major life changes** and things at **work**.*

Life Changes are a Source of Stress

Throughout our lives, we all experience **major life events** — like the death of a close relative, getting married or moving house. These events and the adjustments they cause us to make can be a major source of stress. When psychologists want to find out what level of stress these events cause, they look at health because it's likely to be linked to stress.

Holmes and Rahe (1967) studied whether the stress of life changes was linked to illness

1) Holmes and Rahe assumed that both positive and negative life events involve change, and that change leads to experiencing stress.
2) To test this assumption, they studied approximately 5000 hospital patients' records and noted any major life events that had occurred before the person became ill.
3) It was found that patients were **likely** to have experienced life changes prior to becoming ill and that **more serious life changes** seemed to be more **linked to stress and illness**.

They ranked life events on the Social Readjustment Rating Scale (SRRS)

1) **Holmes and Rahe** made a list of 43 common life events and asked loads of people to give each one a score to say how stressful it was. They called the numbers that made up each score the **Life Change Units (LCU)**. The higher this number of LCUs, the more stressful it was.

2) Then they **ranked** the events from most stressful to least stressful and called it the **Social Readjustment Rating Scale (SRRS)**. Examples are shown in the table below.

Life Event	Rank	Score (LCU)
Death of a spouse	1	100
Divorce	2	73
Retirement	10	45
Change in school	17	37
Christmas	42	12

Retirement stressful — pah, I can't wait...

3) They found a **positive correlation** between the likelihood of illness and the score on the SRRS — as one variable increases, so does the other. So, the more stress a person experienced, the more likely they were to suffer illness.

Further Correlational Research Supported Their Findings

See above for a reminder of what LCU scores are.

Rahe et al (1970) — LCU score and illness

Method: In a **correlational study**, more than 2500 American Navy seamen were given a form of the SRRS to complete just before they set sail on military duty. They had to indicate all of the events that they had experienced over the previous six months.

Results: Higher LCU scores were found to be linked to a higher incidence of illness over the next seven months.

Conclusion: The stress involved in the changes that life events bring is linked to an increased risk of illness.

Evaluation: The results are **not representative** of the population and can only be **generalised** to American Navy seamen. Also, the results don't explain **individual differences** in response to stress. There are also limitations associated with using correlational research. You can't assume a **causal relationship** between the variables — the correlation might be caused by a third unknown variable. As well as this, there are problems with using the SRRS to rank stressful events (see the next page).

Sources of Stress — Life Changes

There are Some **Issues** with the SRRS

1) The SRRS doesn't separate **positive and negative life events**. Stress and illness might be more linked to negative life changes. For example, a wedding might be stressful, but positive overall, while the death of a spouse might have a very negative stressful effect.
2) Long-term, minor sources of stress, such as everyday **hassles** at work (see page 60), are not considered.

Despite criticisms the SRRS was useful for showing that changes in life may link to stress and illness.

The Research is **Correlational**, Not Experimental

1) **Correlational studies** aim to establish if two variables are **related** to each other.
2) They're useful because they allow us to investigate **relationships** between stress and lots of other variables.
3) For example, it's likely that our stress levels are the result of many **interrelated factors**, rather than one single factor.

Cynthia didn't need any experiments — she knew exactly what was causing her stress.

On the other hand...

1) **Experiments** aim to establish if a change in one variable **causes a change** in another.
2) They have an advantage if we want to find out exactly what is **causing** stress.

Several of the life changes within the SRRS could be **related** to each other. For example, a big change in **job conditions** or getting **fired** are likely to affect a person's **financial situation**. **Pregnancy** or a change in **personal habits** and **living conditions** may affect **personal health**. This means that life changes could be both the cause **and** effect of stress.

Practice Questions

Q1 What did Holmes and Rahe study?

Q2 What does SRRS stand for?

Q3 Which research method was used in the Rahe et al (1970) study?

Q4 What is the difference between correlational studies and experiments?

Q5 Suggest some life changes that could be related to each other.

Exam Questions

Q1 Explain how the SRRS was devised and evaluate the use of this technique. [10 marks]

Q2 Geoff lost his job, leading to financial difficulties. His doctor also recently diagnosed him as having high blood pressure. Explain how research into life events could explain his medical condition. [10 marks]

The sauces of stress — feels like you're always playing ketchup...

As a quick break, make your own SRRS by putting these stressful situations in order: 1) meeting your girl/boyfriend's parents, 2) walking into a job interview and realising your fly's undone, 3) feeling a spider run across your face in bed, 4) knowing that what you're writing will be read by thousands of cynical A-Level students and you can't think of anything funny to write.

Sources of Stress — In Everyday Life

Sometimes it's just the little things in life that get us down. If these start getting to us, and cause us to feel stressed, we can become ill. But I won't tell you too much here, or you won't bother reading the rest of the page...

Daily Hassles *are* ***Everyday Events*** *that are* ***Stressful***

Kanner et al (1981) suggested that stress is related to more **mundane events** than the major life events put forward by Holmes and Rahe. Examples of these daily hassles, which they named **irritants**, include having too many things to do, misplacing objects, and getting stuck in traffic.

Kanner et al (1981) — stress and daily hassles

Method: 100 adults completed a questionnaire each month which asked them to choose which hassles they had experienced that month from a list of 117. They then had to rate each hassle to show how severe it had been for them. This was repeated for 9 months.

Results: Certain hassles occurred more frequently than others, such as worrying about weight, family health and the rising cost of living. They found that those with high scores were more likely to have physical and psychological health problems. They also found that scores on an uplifts scale (containing events that make you feel good, e.g. finishing a task or getting on well with a partner) were negatively related to ill health — these events may reduce stress or protect us from it.

Conclusion: Daily hassles are linked to stress and health, with a stronger correlation than that found with the SRRS (see page 58).

Evaluation: The weaknesses of **correlational methods** are relevant here — it isn't possible to establish a cause and effect relationship between the variables. Using questionnaires resulted in **quantitative data**, which is useful for making comparisons, but they don't allow participants to explain why certain experiences are stressful to them, so potentially useful data is missed. They rely on **honesty** in order for the results to be valid — participants may not be completely truthful about admitting mundane daily events that they find stressful. They also rely on the participants' **recall** being accurate.

The ***Workplace*** *is a Massive Source of Stress*

Unfortunately, most people need to work. Some aspects of the **work they do**, **where they work**, or **who they have to work with**, become a source of stress. This is important because if a person is very stressed at work they may be more likely to get ill. This is not only bad for them, but also for their employer because they will take more days off sick.

Stress in the workplace comes from ***FIVE*** *key areas*

- **Relationships at work** — our relationships with our bosses, colleagues and customers may be stressful. For example, we might feel **undervalued** and that we **lack support**.
- **Work pressures** — having a large **workload**, maybe with **strict deadlines**.
- **The physical environment** — where we work may be very noisy, overcrowded, or too hot or cold (aren't we fussy...). Also, our work may involve health risks or unsociable working hours.
- **Stresses linked to our role** — worrying about **job security** or our **prospects for promotion**. Also, the range of our responsibilities may be unclear, and we may experience conflict, e.g. trying to please our bosses and the people who work for us.
- **Lack of control** — we may not have much **influence over the type and amount of work** we do, or where and when we do it. Check out the study by Marmot et al (1997) on the next page.

Sources of Stress — In Everyday Life

A ***Lack of Control*** *in the Workplace is Stressful*

Feeling that we don't have much influence over the type and amount of work we do can lead to stress.
This can be seen in Marmot et al's (1997) study:

Marmot et al (1997) — lack of control and illness in the workplace

Method: Over 7000 civil service employees working in London were surveyed. Information was obtained about their grade of employment, how much control they felt they had, how much support they felt they had, etc.

Results: When the medical histories of these employees were followed up 5 years later, those on lower employment grades who felt less control over their work (and less social support) were found to be more likely to have cardiovascular disorders. Participants on the lowest grade of employment were four times more likely to die of a heart attack than those on the highest grade.

Conclusion: Believing that you have little control over your work influences work stress and the development of illness.

Evaluation: The study only looked at '**white collar**' work (office-type jobs), so the results may not apply to other jobs. **Smoking** was found to be common in those who developed illnesses. So, perhaps those who felt less control at work were more likely to smoke — and the smoking caused the heart problems rather than stress. Other **factors** (e.g. diet and exercise) may be linked to job grade and could be causing illness rather than the perceived lack of control. The research is **correlational,** so it isn't possible to establish a cause and effect relationship between lack of control and illness. Data was obtained using **questionnaires**. This may have encouraged the participants to be more truthful than they would have been if interviewed. However, some people may have been concerned about admitting to experiencing stress at work in case it harmed their job prospects.

Frankenhaeuser (1975) also investigated the link between lack of control and stress in the workplace:

Frankenhaeuser (1975) — stress levels in sawmill workers

Method: Frankenhaeuser studied 2 groups of workers at a sawmill. One group had the repetitive task of feeding logs into a machine all day. The job was very noisy and the workers were socially isolated. They didn't have much control over their work as the machine dictated how quickly they should feed the logs in. The other group had a different task which gave them more control and more social contact. Stress levels were measured by testing urine samples and blood pressure.

Results: The workers who had minimal control and social contact had higher levels of stress hormones (adrenaline and noradrenaline) in their urine. They were more likely to suffer from high blood pressure and stomach ulcers.

Conclusion: A lack of control and social contact at work can lead to stress.

Evaluation: This was a field experiment, so it has high **ecological validity**. The findings are **supported** by Marmot's study. However, it doesn't take individual differences into account — some individuals may just be more prone to stress. The results could have been affected by extraneous variables, such as how much the workers were paid.

Practice Questions

Q1 Give one reason why the workplace might be a source of stress.

Q2 Who were the participants in Marmot's (1997) study?

Q3 Give an advantage of using questionnaires in this area of research.

Exam Questions

Q1 Describe a study investigating the relationship between daily hassles and stress. [6 marks]

Q2 Evaluate a piece of research into lack of control in the workplace and work-related stress. [6 marks]

Stress at work — I don't believe it — I live to work...

You might think that the bits about research methods are really boring and not worth learning. They are boring — I'll give you that. But they are worth learning. You'll pick up marks in the exam if you can identify what research method a study uses, and there's plenty more up for grabs if you can evaluate it. Don't go saying I never tell you anything useful.

Stress — Individual Differences

The last few pages have shown how stress affects the body, but that doesn't mean it affects everyone in the same way. If you stick two people in a pit and drop spiders on them, it's unlikely they're going to react in exactly the same way. Psychologists call different personal reactions 'individual differences'.

Different ***Personalities*** *Can Lead to Different Stress Levels*

Psychologists love sticking people into groups. One theory about personality is that you can split everyone into three groups called **'Type A'**, **'Type B'** or **'Type X'**. Type A people are competitive and ambitious. Type Bs are non-competitive, relaxed and easy-going. Type Xs have a balance of Type A and Type B behaviours. Friedman and Rosenman (1974) tested how these different types of personality affect the likelihood of CHD (coronary heart disease) — one of the most obvious effects of stress.

Friedman and Rosenman (1974) — Type A personality and illness

Method: Approximately 3000, 39-59 year old American males were assessed to class their personality characteristics into Type A, Type B or Type X using interviews and observation. At the start of the study none of them had CHD (coronary heart disease).

Results: Eight years later, 257 of them had developed CHD. 70% of these were classed as Type A personality. This includes being 'workaholic', extremely competitive, hostile to others, and always in a rush. Participants classed as Type B were less competitive and less impatient. They were found to have half the rate of heart disease of Type A. These results were found even when the extraneous variables of weight and smoking were taken into account.

Conclusion: Type A personalities seem to be at a **higher risk** of stress-related illnesses, such as CHD.

Evaluation: Having only three personality types seems a bit **simplistic**. The study doesn't prove that personality characteristics can **cause** stress and illness. It could be the other way round. For example, Type A personality may develop as a **response** to being under stress (from work etc.). Also, the **sample** used in the study was quite limited — middle-aged, male Americans. This means that it's not that easy to **generalise** the results to the rest of the population. In addition, participants may not have been completely **honest** in their interviews so that their characteristics appeared desirable to the researcher (**social desirability bias**).

Later research also identified **Type C** personalities — mild-mannered, easy-going people who may not react well to stressful situations and suppress their emotions. These people seem to have a higher risk of **cancer**. **Type D** personalities were identified as very negative/pessimistic people who worry too much about things and lack social skills. These people seem more at risk from **heart attacks**.

Kobasa (1979) Identified ***Hardiness*** *as an Important* ***Individual Difference***

Kobasa described people as being **hardy** or **non-hardy**. There are three main characteristics of hardy personalities:

1) Hardy personalities are very involved in what they do, and show a high level of **commitment**. This means that they work hard at relationships, jobs and other activities in life.
2) They view change in a positive rather than a negative way, seeing it as an opportunity for **challenge**. Hardy personalities enjoy a challenge and see it as an opportunity to develop themselves.
3) They have a strong feeling of **control** over their life and what happens to them. This is known as having an **internal locus of control**.

In comparison, **non-hardy** personalities view any life experiences in a much more **negative** way and feel that they're **unable to cope** with situations. They feel that **external agencies** have control over what happens to them and that it isn't worth trying to become more powerful. They **give up** easily and don't see any value in trying to change what's happening around them.

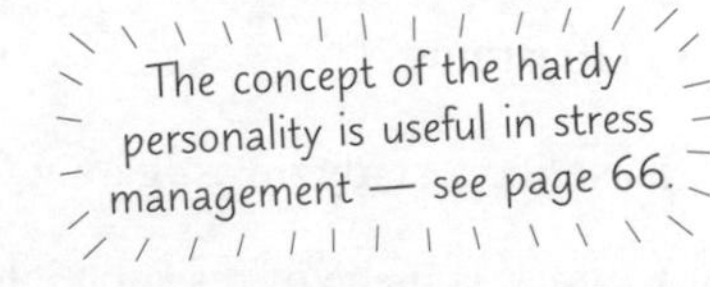

It's difficult to **quantify** what's meant by a hardy personality and therefore difficult to **measure** and test it. We also need to avoid making assumptions about **cause and effect** — it could be that some people have hardy personalities because of a lack of stress in their lives, rather than low stress being the result of personality. It could be that levels of hardiness **fluctuate** and may decrease when the person is experiencing lots of stress, such as after a bereavement.

Stress — Individual Differences

Stress can also be Related to **Gender**

Men and woman are pretty different in loads of ways, so psychologists (who don't miss a trick) thought that maybe these differences could affect what kinds of things men and women find stressful and how they cope. They looked at how **biological**, **social** and **cognitive** differences between males and females influence their response to stress.

Biological Explanation — through evolution, men in their role of 'hunter-gatherer' may have developed a stronger 'fight or flight' response than women, who had the role of caring for the kids. In this way, males and females may have developed different physiological responses to stress.

Taylor et al (2000) suggest that women produce a calmer response to stress due to a hormone. Oxytocin is released in response to stress and has been shown to lead to maternal behaviour and social affiliation. Taylor called this the 'tend and befriend' response (instead of the 'fight or flight' response) and thought it might make females more likely to seek social support to help them cope with stress.

Social Explanation — a Western stereotypical social role is that men are less open about their feelings than women. This means they're less likely to discuss stressful experiences with others and may use harmful coping methods instead, e.g. smoking and drinking.

Carroll (1992) found that women do generally make more use of social support to deal with stress. However, coronary heart disease has increased in women — but this could just be because a change in social roles means that it's now more acceptable for women to drink and smoke.

Cognitive Explanation — **Vogele et al (1997)** claim that women are better able to control anger and therefore respond more calmly to stressful situations. Men may feel that anger is an acceptable way to respond, and feel stress if they cannot show it. These cognitive differences could be the result of biology **or** the roles we are taught to follow, or a bit of both.

Stress Can be Related to **Culture**

1) **Culture** is a really vague term that is used to group people by **beliefs**, **behaviours**, **morals** or **customs** they share.
2) It influences how people live and how others react to them.
3) Variables such as **low socio-economic status** can lead to **poor living conditions** and experience of **prejudice** — which could lead to **negative thinking**.
4) Also, some people believe that **biological factors** could influence the link between culture, stress and illness.

Practice Questions

Q1 Explain the differences between the personality types A and B.

Q2 Give a criticism of Friedman and Rosenman's (1974) research.

Q3 What are the three characteristics associated with a hardy personality?

Exam Questions

Q1 Describe and discuss one explanation of how personality factors are associated with stress. [8 marks]

Q2 Sally has developed CHD. Use Friedman and Rosenman's (1974) study to explain how this could be a result of her personality. [8 marks]

We are all individuals, we are all individuals, we are all individuals...

This is an important thing to remember throughout psychology. People are divided into groups to show how different things affect people — but there are also individual differences, which means that when put in the same situation, people will often react differently. This seems pretty obvious but it's easy to forget if you get too wrapped up in all the theories.

Stress Management — Biological Approach

Biological methods of stress management help people cope with stress by changing the way the body responds to it. Drug treatments, biofeedback and exercise have been found to be effective. Best learn about them then.

Drug Treatments Work in Two Ways

1) They **slow down** the activity of the **central nervous system** (CNS).
   Anti-anxiety drugs called **benzodiazepines** (BZs) increase the body's reaction to its own natural anxiety-relieving chemical **GABA** (gamma-aminobutyric acid), which slows down the activity of neurones and makes us feel relaxed.

OR...

2) They **reduce** the activity of the **sympathetic nervous system** (SNS).
   The SNS increases heart rate, blood pressure and levels of the hormone **cortisol**. High levels of cortisol can make our immune system **weak** and also cause heart disease. The group of drugs called **beta blockers** reduce all these unpleasant symptoms.

Biofeedback Uses Information About What's Happening in the Body

Biofeedback gives people information about **internal physical processes** that they wouldn't otherwise be aware of, e.g. muscle tension. The idea is to give them more **control** over these internal processes and the ability to **alter** them. For example, if they can **modify** the physical aspects of stress then this may make them more **relaxed** in stressful situations. The process takes place as **training** in a **non-stressful** environment, which the person is then encouraged to use in real-life stressful situations.

There are 4 steps involved:

1) The person is attached to a machine that monitors and gives **feedback** on internal physical processes such as **heart rate**, **blood pressure** or **muscle tension**.
2) They are then taught how to **control** these symptoms of stress through a variety of techniques. These can include **muscle relaxation** — muscle groups are tensed and relaxed in turn until the whole body is relaxed. This teaches people to notice when their body is becoming tense. Other techniques include actively clearing the mind using **meditation**, or **breathing control** exercises.
3) This feeling of relaxation acts like a **reward** and encourages the person to repeat this as an involuntary activity.
4) The person learns to use these techniques in **real-life** situations.

Trisha didn't need biofeedback — she had stress totally sorted

Exercise is Another Biological Method of Managing Stress

1) **Exercise** and being physically active reduces the likelihood of stress-related illness.
2) **Morris (1953)** compared **bus conductors** and **bus drivers** and found that the conductors had lower rates of cardiovascular problems.
3) This could be the result of having a more **active job** or the stress of **driving**.
4) Or, it could be caused by any number of **other variables**...
5) However, it's difficult to get a clear idea of the relationship because active people may be less likely to engage in **harmful behaviours** like smoking and drinking. Active people are likely to **sleep better**, which will have both a **biological** and a **psychological** influence on levels of **stress**.

Stress Management — Biological Approach

The Biological Approach Has **Strengths** and **Weaknesses**

Both drugs and biofeedback are **effective**:

Drugs are **quick** and **effective** in reducing dangerous symptoms such as high blood pressure. **Kahn et al (1986)** found that benzodiazepines were superior to a placebo (sugar pill) when they tracked around 250 patients over an 8-week period.

Attanasio et al (1985) found that biofeedback helped teenagers and children with stress-related disorders to gain **control** over the symptoms of **migraine** headaches. They also showed an increase in **enthusiasm** and a more positive attitude.

Placebos are pills that do nothing at all. They're used to test if any effect happens just because people think they're being treated.

BUT both treat **symptoms** rather than the underlying causes of stress:

Drugs only help with the **symptoms** and only so long as the drugs are taken.

Biofeedback also aims to **reduce** symptoms, but using relaxation techniques can also give the person a sense of **control** and have more **long-lasting** benefits.

Drugs have **side effects**, biofeedback **doesn't**:

Drugs can have minor **side effects** such as dizziness and tiredness or more serious effects such as blurred vision and changes in sex drive. **Withdrawal symptoms** when people come off medication, such as increased anxiety, seizures, tremors and headaches, can be distressing. Benzodiazepines can be **addictive**, and are generally limited to a maximum of 4 weeks' use.

There are no side effects of biofeedback — just **relaxation**. This method's advantage is that it's **voluntary** and not invasive.

Drugs are **easier** to use than biofeedback:

Drugs are relatively **easy** to prescribe and use.

Biofeedback needs specialist **equipment** and expert **supervision**. Some argue that the benefits of biofeedback could be gained from other relaxation techniques and so this is an unnecessary expense.

Practice Questions

Q1 What is GABA?

Q2 What are the steps involved in biofeedback?

Q3 Give one problem of using drugs to deal with stress.

Q4 Why is biofeedback a more expensive form of treatment than drugs?

Exam Questions

Q1 Describe how drugs can help in the management of stress. [6 marks]

Q2 Explain and evaluate two different biological methods of managing stress. [12 marks]

Stress management — quite the opposite of traditional management...

This ridiculously stressed and hectic lifestyle we choose to live is turning us all into ill people. I can't understand it myself — personally I choose the more Caribbean attitude to time management. I'm quite confident I'll never need to take BZs or teach myself to think differently. But then again, I might get into trouble for not finishing this book on time. Hmmm...

Stress Management — Psychological Approach

Psychological Methods Involve Learning to *Think Differently*

The psychological approach helps you to cope better by **thinking differently** about the stressful situation. The techniques have been shown to be **effective** and deal with the **source** of the problem rather than just the symptoms. They provide **skills** that have more lasting value — like the **confidence** to cope with future problems and the belief of being in **control** and seeing life as a challenge rather than as a threat. (And other cheesy, upbeat things like that.)

Meichenbaum's Stress Inoculation Training (SIT):

This works like immunisation. Just like you might be inoculated against any attack from disease, you can protect yourself from the harmful effects of stress.

Training involves preparation so that you can deal with stress before it becomes a problem. 3 steps are involved:

1) **Conceptualisation**: Identify fears and concerns with the help of a therapist.
2) **Skill acquisition and rehearsal**: Train to develop skills like positive thinking and relaxation in order to improve self-confidence.
3) **Application and follow-through**: Practise the newly acquired skill in real-life situations with support and back-up from the therapist.

Meichenbaum (1977) found that SIT works both with short-term stressors such as preparing for public speaking, and longer-term stressors such as medical illness, divorce or work-related stress.

Hardiness Training:

Kobasa suggests that a strong and hardy person shows **3 Cs**:
Control over their lives, **commitment** (a sense of purpose in life) and **challenge** (life is seen as a challenge and opportunity rather than as a threat).
See page 62 for more about this.

Maddi introduced a training programme to increase hardiness, arguing that the more hardy the person, the better they cope with stress. This training has 3 steps:

1) **Focusing**: Learn to **recognise** physical symptoms of stress, e.g. increase in heart rate, muscle tension and sweating.
2) **Reliving stressful encounters**: Learn to **analyse** stressful situations to better understand possible coping strategies.
3) **Self-improvement**: Take on **challenges** that can be coped with and build **confidence**, thereby gaining a greater sense of **control**.

Threat? Nah — just another of life's great opportunities.

Maddi et al (1998) got 54 managers who went on a hardiness training programme to report back on their progress. They recorded an increase in hardiness and job satisfaction and a decrease in strain and illness.

Despite proven effectiveness, there are **weaknesses** with psychological methods:

1) Psychological methods only suit a narrow band of individuals who are **determined** to stick to the technique.
2) Research tends to be based on white, middle-class business folk and so can't necessarily be **generalised** to others.
3) The procedures are very lengthy and require considerable **commitment** of time and effort.
4) The **concepts** may be too complex. For example, a lack of hardiness might be just another label for negativity. It could be argued that it's just as effective to relax and think positively.

Stress Management — Psychological Approach

Cognitive Behavioural Therapy (CBT) Aims to Alter Thought Processes

1) CBT techniques were developed to treat abnormality using concepts from the **cognitive approach**.
2) The idea is that changing the way information is cognitively **processed** will result in a change in **behaviour**.
3) These techniques can be used in stress management — by changing the way we **think** in stressful situations we can **cope** better and **behave** in ways that help to minimise or remove the stressor.

See pages 94-95 for more on this.

Rational-Emotive Therapy (RET) was Developed by Ellis (1962)

Ellis (1962) suggested an **ABC model**:

1) It begins with an **activating event** (A) which leads to a **belief** (B) about why this happened.
2) This then leads to a **consequence** (C). If the beliefs are **irrational**, they will lead to maladaptive consequences — such as depression, anxiety or symptoms of stress.
3) For example, if somebody fails to get a promotion at work (A), they may believe that it happened because they're useless (B), and the emotional consequence (C) may be feeling depressed.
4) RET focuses on encouraging people to change irrational beliefs into rational beliefs, for a more **positive consequence**.
5) In this example, believing that they didn't get the promotion because it's not possible to always perform well in an interview may lead to a more positive cognitive mood and less stress.

Beck's Cognitive Restructuring Therapy Also Features Negative Beliefs

Beck (1963) identified a **cognitive triad** of types of negative thought which can be applied to stress management. These are thoughts about:

1) **Themselves** — "I'm useless at everything."
2) **The future** — "Nothing will change and I won't improve."
3) **The world** — "You need to be better than I am to succeed in life."

The therapist's goal is to **disprove** the negativity in a person's thinking. After a while they should be able to use **different cognitive processes**, leading to a more **positive belief system**. Beck initially developed the therapy for use with depression, but it's been adapted for use beyond this. For example, Proudfoot et al (1997) found that cognitive therapies were effective when used to deal with the psychological effects of unemployment.

Practice Questions

Q1 What does SIT stand for?

Q2 What are the three parts of Ellis's ABC model?

Q3 Who identified a cognitive triad of negative thoughts?

Exam Questions

Q1 Outline and evaluate the use of SIT for managing stress. [8 marks]

Q2 Explain how cognitive behavioural therapy can be used to help people cope with stressful experiences. [10 marks]

Aaaaaaaaaaaaaaaaaaaaarrrrrrrrrrrrrrrrrrrrrrrrgggggggggghhhhhh...

Makes sense, doesn't it? You get bossed around, told to write huge essays, told to write them again, told you can't go out until you've done your essay — of course you're going to feel stressed, it's only natural. But if you insist to yourself that it's all your own choice because it's the only path to a good job and lots of money, then you'll feel better. In theory anyway...

The Social Approach

Social psychology is about how we influence each other. Our behaviour is affected by the social situation we're in — so it might be normal to be naked in the bath, but it's not normal to be naked on the bus. To be fair, not all of the research is about being naked, but at least it's got your attention...

Social Psychology Looks at How **People Affect Each Other**

1) **Social behaviour** occurs when two or more people interact. People interact differently depending on the situation — so you may act differently with a parent, a friend, a stranger, or when you're in a group.
2) Social psychology also considers how we **think** about **other people**. This is **social cognition**, which can involve things like **stereotyping** and **prejudice**.
3) The influence of others can cause individuals to change their behaviour. Social psychologists have studied why people **conform** (change their behaviour to fit in with a group), and why they **obey** authority figures.

Social Psychologists Use Loads of Different **Research Methods**

Fortunately they're all methods that are used in some of the other approaches too. There's more general stuff on research methods on pages 32-33. And more on ethical issues on pages 42-43.

Laboratory experiments are conducted in **artificial settings** — e.g. Asch's study (page 70).

Advantages
- They're **highly controlled**, so the effect of the independent variable can be measured.
- This also means that it's possible to establish **cause and effect**, and to **replicate** the method.
- Participants in different conditions can act as comparisons.

Disadvantages
- They create an **artificial environment**, so studies have **low ecological validity** — most social interactions don't normally take place in labs. Unless you're a rat.
- This means there are problems with **generalising** the results.

Field experiments are conducted in **real-life settings** — e.g. hospitals.

Advantages
- The variables are still highly controlled, so it should be possible to establish **cause and effect**.
- Studies take place in the participants' natural environments, so they're more likely to capture natural social behaviour. This means they have **higher ecological validity** than lab experiments.
- **Demand characteristics** are reduced if the participants don't know they're being studied.

Disadvantages
- It's very difficult to control all the variables in a natural environment, so the results can still be affected by **confounding variables**.
- Lots of field experiments involve using **deception** (see page 42). This has **ethical implications** — you can't get **informed consent**, and it can be difficult to **debrief** participants.

Natural experiments look at **naturally occurring situations** — the independent variable isn't manipulated.

Advantages
- Studies take place in the participants' natural environments, and nothing is manipulated, so they're likely to capture natural social behaviour. This means they have **high ecological validity**.
- Researchers can investigate variables that it would be **unethical** to manipulate.

Disadvantages
- Because none of the variables are controlled, experiments tend to have **low internal validity**. It's really hard to tell what actually caused the results. This means it's difficult to establish **cause and effect**.
- Natural experiments often involve **deception**, which raises ethical issues.

The Social Approach

Naturalistic observation is when the experimenter just **observes** behaviour, without manipulating any variables.

Advantages

- Participants are in a natural environment, and are often unaware they're being observed. This means that studies should have **high ecological validity**.
- Results from observations can be used to **develop theories**, which can then be tested in experiments.

Disadvantages

- Not controlling the independent variable means it's very difficult to establish **cause and effect**.
- The results are **subjective** — observers can be biased about what they record.
- Observation can involve **deception**, which brings up problems of gaining **informed consent** and **debriefing** participants. Ethically it's OK to observe people in places where they might expect to be observed by strangers — so you can watch them in the street, but you can't train a telescopic lens on their bedroom.

Surveys are used a lot

Surveys can include **questionnaires** and **interviews**. They can be really useful, but the problem is that there's no way of knowing whether people are telling the truth. Unless you rig them up to a lie detector like on Jeremy Kyle.

Questionnaires can include **closed** or **open-ended questions**. Closed questions have a limited set of answers — e.g. yes or no. Open questions don't have a restricted set of answers — e.g. 'what do you think of Jeremy Kyle?'
Interviews can be **structured** or **unstructured**. Structured interviews use pre-decided questions that are the same for all of the participants. In unstructured interviews the interviewers give the participant more freedom, although they might still guide the conversation to cover certain topics.

Advantages

- With questionnaires you can gather lots of data quickly and cheaply. This means you can have a large sample, making the results more reliable.
- Closed questions and structured interviews produce **quantitative data**, which is really easy to analyse.
- Open questions and unstructured interviews produce **qualitative data**, which is really detailed.

Disadvantages

- Questionnaires and interviews rely on self-reporting. This means people can lie in order to show themselves in a good light — **social desirability bias**.
- Interviews can be very time-consuming.
- It's easy to write bad questions. Researchers have to avoid **leading questions** (ones that lead the participants towards certain answers), or questions that can mean different things to different people.

Practice Questions

Q1 What sorts of behaviour is social psychology concerned with?

Q2 Outline the experimental methods on these pages that involve manipulating the independent variable.

Q3 In terms of ethics, where can observational studies be conducted?

Q4 What's the difference between structured and unstructured interviews?

Exam Questions

Q1 Some social psychologists are investigating obedience. They design a questionnaire to ask students under what sort of conditions they would disobey their teachers.

a) Outline one disadvantage of using this method. [2 marks]

b) Explain one strength of quantitative data. [2 marks]

Q2 Outline one advantage and one disadvantage of field experiments. [4 marks]

Remember — social psychology is all about how people affect each other...

Phew, it's all gone a bit research methodsy round here. Not sure how that happened. Still, it's good really cos this stuff turns up all over the shop, so learn it now and you'll be laughing all the way to the exam hall. I can just picture you now, having a whale of a time. Just remember to cool it to a gentle giggle once you're in there though, else you might get hiccups.

Types of Conformity

__Conformity__ is when the behaviour of an individual or small group is __influenced__ by a larger or dominant group.

There's __More Than One Type__ of __Conformity__

__Compliance__ is __Going Along__ with Things Even if You __Disagree__ with Them

1) **Compliance** is where you go along with the majority, even if you don't share their views.
2) You do this just to appear **'normal'** — going against the majority might lead to exclusion or rejection from the group. This is called **normative social influence**.

__Internalisation__ Means Accepting the __Majority's__ Views as __Your Own__

1) **Internalisation** is following along with the majority and **believing** in their views — you've accepted and **internalised** them so they're now your own too.
2) This might happen if you're in an unfamiliar situation, where you don't know what the 'correct' way to behave is. In this situation, you'd look to others for **information** about how to behave. This is called **informational social influence**.

__Asch__ (1951) Looked at __Normative Social Influence__

Asch designed an experiment to see whether people would conform to a majority's incorrect answer in an **unambiguous task** (one where the answer is obvious).

Asch (1951) — conformity on an unambiguous task

Method: Asch carried out a **laboratory experiment** with an **independent groups** design. In groups of 8, participants judged line lengths (shown below) by saying out loud which comparison line (1, 2 or 3) matched the standard line. Each group contained only one real participant — the others were confederates (who acted like real participants but were really helping the experimenter). The real participant always went last or last but one, so that they heard the others' answers before giving theirs. Each participant did 18 trials.
On 12 of these (the **critical trials**) the confederates all gave the same wrong answer.
There was also a **control group**, where the participants judged the line lengths in isolation.

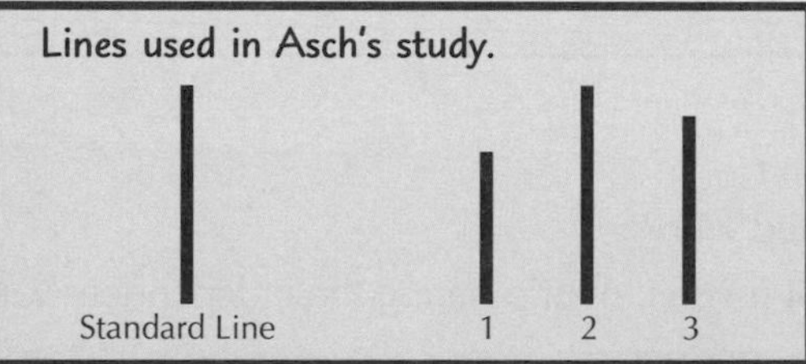

Lines used in Asch's study.

Seating plan for Asch's study. The real participant was always in position 7 or 8 and the others were confederates.

1 2 3 4 5 6 7 8

Stimulus Display

Results: In the control trials, participants gave the wrong answer **0.7%** of the time. In the critical trials, participants **conformed** to the majority (gave the same wrong answer) **37%** of the time. **75%** conformed at least once. Afterwards, some participants said they didn't really believe their answers, but didn't want to look different.

Conclusion: The control condition showed that the task was easy to get right. However, 37% were wrong on the critical trials. They conformed to the majority — this was **normative social influence**.

Evaluation: This was a **laboratory experiment**, so there was **good control** of the variables. This minimises the effects of **extraneous variables**. Strict control of the variables also means that you could easily **repeat** the study to see if you get the same results. However, because the participants weren't in a **natural situation**, the study lacks **ecological validity**. Whether they were right or wrong didn't really matter to the participants — they might have been less likely to conform if their answer had had real-life consequences. In terms of **ethics**, the participants were **deceived** and might have been embarrassed when they found out the true nature of the study.

Types of Conformity

Sherif *(1935) Tested the Effects of* ***Informational Influence***

Sherif researched whether people are influenced by others when they're doing an **ambiguous task** (one where the answer isn't clear).

Sherif (1935) — conformity and the autokinetic effect

Method: This was a **laboratory experiment** with a **repeated measures** design. Sherif used a visual illusion called the **autokinetic effect**, where a stationary spot of light, viewed in a dark room, appears to move. Participants were falsely told that the experimenter would move the light. They had to estimate how far it had moved. In the first phase, individual participants made repeated estimates. They were then put into groups of 3 people, where they each made their estimate with the others present. Finally, they were retested individually.

Results: When they were alone, participants developed their own stable estimates (**personal norms**), which varied widely between participants. Once the participants were in a group, the estimates tended to **converge** and become more alike. When the participants were then retested on their own, their estimates were more like the **group estimates** than their original guesses.

Conclusion: Participants were influenced by the estimates of other people, and a **group norm** developed. Estimates converged because participants used information from others to help them — they were affected by **informational social influence**.

Evaluation: This was a **laboratory experiment**, so there was strict control of the variables. This means that the results are unlikely to have been affected by a third variable, so it should be possible to establish **cause and effect**. It also means that the method could be **replicated**. The **repeated measures** design meant that **participant variables** that could have affected the results were kept constant. However, the method is flawed because the participants were being asked to judge the movement of a light that wasn't moving — this rarely happens in real life. This study is less successful than Asch's in demonstrating the effects of conformity — the answer was obvious, so the only reason Asch's participants conformed was to avoid standing out. This experiment created an **artificial situation**, so the study lacks **ecological validity**. As well as this, the **sample** used was quite limited — all of the participants were male, so the results can't be **generalised** to everyone. An **ethical problem** with this study was **deception** — the participants were told the light was moving when it wasn't.

Zimbardo *et al (1973) Studied* ***Conformity*** *to* ***Assigned Roles***

Zimbardo et al set up a mock prison to see if people would conform to the **assigned roles** of prisoner or guard.

Zimbardo et al (1973) — Stanford Prison Experiment

Method: Male students were recruited to act as either guards or prisoners in a mock prison. They were randomly given the roles of prisoner or guard, and their behaviour was observed. The prisoners were 'arrested' at home, taken to 'prison' and given uniforms and numbers. The guards also wore uniforms and mirrored sunglasses.

Results: Initially, the guards tried to assert their authority and the prisoners resisted by sticking together. The prisoners then became more passive and obedient, while the guards invented nastier punishments. The experiment was abandoned early because some prisoners became very distressed.

Conclusion: Guards and prisoners adopted their social roles quickly. Zimbardo claims this shows that our **social role can influence our behaviour** — seemingly well-balanced men became unpleasant and aggressive in the role of guard.

Evaluation: This was a **controlled observation**, so there was **good control** of variables. However, because it was an artificial environment, the results can't really be **generalised** to real-life situations. In terms of **ethics**, some participants found the experience very distressing. There's also a problem with **observer bias**, as Zimbardo ran the prison himself, and later admitted that he became too personally involved in the situation. This experiment doesn't take **individual differences** into account — not all of the participants behaved according to their new roles.

Types of Conformity

Reicher and Haslam (2006) Developed the Ideas in Zimbardo's Study

1) In the **Holocaust** during World War Two, approximately 6 million Jews were horrifically murdered by the Nazis.
2) Psychologists had different theories about the soldiers who'd carried out the killings. Some thought they must be 'evil' individuals, but others thought they were 'normal' people who'd committed atrocities because of the social role they were in.
3) **Zimbardo's** (1973) study showed that normal people will shape their behaviour in order to fit into a social role, even if it's only been randomly assigned.
4) It seemed that the participants' behaviour was **situational** (due to the social situation they were in), rather than **dispositional** (due to their internal characteristics).
5) **Reicher and Haslam** (2006) recreated a similar situation to Zimbardo's experiment, but they were particularly interested to see how the group dynamics changed over time.

Reicher and Haslam (2006) — the BBC Prison Study

Method: This was a **controlled observation** in a mock prison, which was filmed for television. The participants were 15 male volunteers who had responded to an advert. They were randomly assigned to 2 groups of 5 guards and 10 prisoners. They had daily tests to measure levels of depression, compliance with rules, and stress. The prisoners knew that one of them, chosen **at random**, would become a guard after 3 days. An independent **ethics committee** had the power to stop the experiment at any time in order to protect the participants.

Results: The guards failed to form a united group and identify with their role. They didn't always exercise their power and said they felt uncomfortable with the inequality of the situation. In the first 3 days, the prisoners tried to act in a way that would get them promoted to guard status. After one was promoted, they became a much **stronger group** because they knew there were no more chances of promotion. The unequal system collapsed due to the **unwillingness of the guards** and the **strength of the prisoner group**. On Day 6 the prisoners rebelled and the participants decided to live in a democracy, but this also collapsed due to tensions within the group. Some of the former prisoners then wanted to set up a stricter regime with them as leaders. The study was **abandoned** early on the advice of the ethics committee, as the participants showed signs of stress.

Conclusion: The participants didn't fit into their expected social roles, suggesting that these roles are **flexible**.

Evaluation: In contrast to Zimbardo's findings, Reicher and Haslam's prisoners were a strong group, and the guards were weak. However, it's possible that this was because Reicher and Haslam's guards were not as empowered as Zimbardo's, who were actively encouraged to maintain order. This study has been criticised for being made for TV — many people (including Zimbardo) argued that elements of it were staged and the participants played up to the cameras. Because this was an artificial situation, the results can't be **generalised** to real life. The **ethics** of this study were good — the participants were not **deceived**, so they were able to give **informed consent**. The participants were **protected** by the ethics committee and the study was abandoned as soon as they appeared to be becoming stressed. They were also **debriefed** and offered counselling afterwards.

Practice Questions

Q1 What is normative social influence?

Q2 Outline the strengths and weaknesses of the method in Asch's study.

Q3 What's the difference between situational and dispositional behaviour?

Exam Questions

Q1 Outline two types of conformity. [6 marks]

Q2 Outline and evaluate one study into conformity. [12 marks]

Oh doobee doo, I wanna be like you-oo-oo...

Conformity's handy because it means you don't have to make any decisions for yourself... It's all about wanting to fit in with a group, even if you think it's actually a bit rubbish. Personally I reckon joining a group that involves being arrested and put in a fake prison isn't really ideal. I'd probably just say thanks but I'm washing my hair that week.

Independent Behaviour and Social Change

Sometimes we're influenced by others and conform. But at other times we resist these influences and behave ***independently****. There are various factors that affect whether we resist the pressure to conform.*

Asch's Participants were Influenced by Situational Factors

1) **Group Size**

You might expect that the **bigger** the majority is, the more **influential** it will be. If that was the case, it would be easier to resist conforming when there were fewer people to influence you. To test this, **Asch (1956)** conducted his conformity experiment (page 70) with different numbers of confederates as the majority.

With only **two confederates**, the real participant **conformed on only 14%** of the critical trials. With **three confederates**, conformity rose to **32%**. There was **little change** to conformity rates after that — no matter how big the majority group got. So, very small majorities are easier to resist than larger ones. But influence doesn't keep increasing with the size of majority.

2) **Social Support**

Asch absolutely loved doing his conformity experiment, so he ran yet another version of it to test the effect of having a **supporter** in the group. When one of the confederates **agreed** with the **participant** rather than with the other confederates, the rate of conformity **fell to 5.5%**.

A fellow **dissenter** (someone who disagrees with the majority) made it easier for the participant to **resist** the pressure to conform.

Confidence and Expertise Might Affect Conformity

When Asch **debriefed** his participants, he found a common factor of **confidence** in the people who hadn't conformed. If someone felt confident in their judgements, they were more able to **resist** group pressure.

1) **Wiesenthal et al (1976)** found that if people felt **competent** in a task, they were **less likely** to conform.
2) **Perrin and Spencer (1980)** replicated Asch's study with participants who were engineering students. Conformity levels were much **lower**. This could have been due to the fact that engineers had **confidence** in their skills in making accurate observations.

Gender Might Also be a Factor

Until the mid-1970s the dominant view was that **females conform more than males**.
Then **Eagly and Carli** did a load of research that suggests it might not be as simple as all that...

Eagly (1987) argued that men and women's **different social roles** are responsible for the difference in conformity rates — women are more concerned with **group harmony** and **relationships**, so they're more likely to agree with the opinions of others. **Assertiveness** and **independence** are valued male attributes, so maintaining your own opinion under pressure fits with the perceived male social role.

This ties in with **Becker's (1986)** findings that women conform more than men in **public** settings, but not when their opinions are **private**.

Eagly and Carli (1981) did a **meta-analysis** of conformity research, where they re-analysed data from a number of studies. They did find some sex differences in conformity, but the differences were **inconsistent**. The clearest difference between men and women was in **Asch**-like studies where there was **group pressure** from an **audience**.

Eagly and Carli (1981) also pointed out that male researchers are more likely than female researchers to find female participants higher on conformity. This could be because **male researchers** use tasks that are more familiar to men (so they don't need to look to others as much for help). This is an example of **gender bias**.

Independent Behaviour and Social Change

How likely someone is to conform could all be down to something called their 'locus of control'. In a nutshell it comes down to the old question — do you believe you're in control of your destiny, or do you believe in fate?

*Aspects of **Personality** may Influence **Independent Behaviour***

Rotter (1966) developed a **questionnaire** to measure a personality characteristic called **locus of control**.
It indicates how much **personal control** people believe they have over events in their lives.
The questionnaire involved choosing between **paired statements** like these ones:

1) Misfortune is usually brought about by people's own actions.
2) Things that make us unhappy are largely due to bad luck.

If you agree with the first statement, you have an **internal locus of control**. This is categorised by a belief that what happens in your life results from **your own behaviour or actions**.

E.g. if you did well in a test you might put it down to how much work you did for it.

If you agree with the second statement, you have an **external locus of control**. This is a belief that events are caused by external factors, like **luck** or the **actions of others**.

E.g. if you did well in a test you might put it down to good questions coming up, or a lenient examiner.

People with an **internal locus of control** feel a stronger sense of control over their lives than people with an **external locus of control**. This means that they're more likely to exhibit **independent behaviour**.
People with an **external locus of control** may be more likely to conform.

Minority Influence** can be Quite **Powerful

1) Obviously people don't always go along with the majority — if they did, nothing would ever change.
2) Sometimes **small minorities** and even **individuals** gain influence and change the way the majority thinks.
3) In **minority influence**, it seems that a form of **internalisation** (see page 70) is taking place. Members of the majority actually take on the beliefs and views of a **consistent minority** — rather than just complying.

Moscovici et al (1969) did some research into **minority influence** that compared **inconsistent** minorities with **consistent** minorities.

Moscovici et al (1969) — Minority influence

Method: This was a laboratory experiment into **minority influence** using 192 women. In groups of 6 at a time, participants judged the colour of 36 slides. All of the slides were blue, but the brightness of the blue varied. Two of the six participants in each group were **confederates**. In one condition the confederates called all 36 slides 'green' (consistent) and in another condition they called 24 of the slides 'green' and 12 of the slides 'blue' (inconsistent). A control group was also used which contained no confederates.

Results: In the **control group** the participants called the slides 'green' **0.25%** of the time. In the **consistent** condition **8.4%** of the time participants adopted the minority position and called the slides 'green'. In fact, **32%** of the participants called the slides 'green' at least once. In the **inconsistent** condition the participants moved to the minority position of calling the slides 'green' only **1.25%** of the time.

Conclusion: The confederates were in the **minority** but their views appear to have influenced the real participants. The use of the two conditions illustrated that the minority **had more influence when they were consistent** in calling the slides 'green'.

Evaluation: This study was a laboratory experiment so it **lacked ecological validity** because the task was artificial. The participants may have felt that judging the colour of the slide was a **trivial** exercise. They might have acted differently if their principles were involved. Also, the study was only carried out on women so doesn't allow for **gender** differences and the results can't be generalised to men. However, owing to the use of a **control** group, we know that the participants were actually influenced by the minority rather than being independently unsure of the colour of the slides. In a similar experiment, participants were asked to **write down** the colour rather than saying it out loud. In this condition, even more people agreed with the minority, which provides **more support** for minority influence.

Independent Behaviour and Social Change

It's easy to see why you might go along with the majority. But minorities sometimes shake things right up...

Minorities** can Cause **Social Change

There are many examples in history of things changing because the ideas of a few have taken hold. Try these for starters:

The Suffragettes

1) In the early 1900s in Britain, a small minority began to campaign for women to be allowed to **vote**. This was called the **suffragette movement**.
2) Suffragettes **chained** themselves to railings outside Downing Street and Buckingham Palace.
3) The suffragettes' campaign involved **violent** methods such as assault and arson.
4) In 1913 a suffragette threw herself under the feet of the King's horse. She **died** from her injuries.
5) Eventually **the majority was influenced** by the suffragettes' point of view and in 1928 women were finally given the right to vote on the same terms as men.

Suzie was confident that it was only a matter of time before everyone started dressing like her.

Martin Luther King

1) In the 1950s in America, black people did not have the same **rights** as white people. For example, in parts of America, buses were **segregated** and black people had to give up their seats to white people.
2) **Reverend Martin Luther King** challenged the views of the majority to bring about **political and social rights** for black people. He and other activists used **peaceful** protests like marches and sit-ins. This was known as the **Civil Rights Movement**. His ideas were so unpopular that during this time his home was bombed by activists, he was subjected to personal abuse, and he was **arrested.**
3) In the end though, the actions of civil rights activists influenced the **majority**. Nowadays there are **laws** that ensure people are given equal rights regardless of racial origin, and in 1964 Martin Luther King was awarded the **Nobel Peace Prize.**

Gay Rights Movements

1) Homosexuality used to be **illegal** in the UK. It was **decriminalised** in England and Wales in 1967 — but the age of consent was 21 (higher than for heterosexual people) and homosexuals were still treated **negatively**.
2) Over the last decade, there have been moves towards equality as a result of **Gay Rights Movements**. These **minorities** have successfully **changed attitudes**. For example, the Equality Act (Sexual Orientation) 2007 made it **illegal to discriminate** against gay men and women in the provision of goods and services.

Practice Questions

Q1 What situational factors did Asch identify that affected conformity levels?

Q2 Why might social roles be responsible for gender differences in conformity?

Q3 What's the difference between an internal and an external locus of control?

Q4 According to Moscivici et al's (1969) study, how does consistency affect minority influence?

Exam Questions

Q1 Outline and evaluate one study into minority influence. [8 marks]

Q2 Outline two examples of social change caused by minority influence. [6 marks]

The times they are a-changing...

So minority influence can be a big deal. Here's an example: I think you should learn the stuff on this page — most people probably don't agree — but you will won't you? I've really got under your skin haven't I? Power to the minority. Woo!

Obedience to Authority

Atteeennnnnnnnnnshun! Obedience means acting in response to a direct order, usually from an authority figure. It's mostly not a bad thing, and in some situations it's really important. But it can also cause problems...

Milgram (1963) *did a* **Famous Study** *of* **Obedience**

Milgram (1963) — the original 'remote learner' experiment

Method: Milgram conducted **laboratory experiments** to test factors thought to affect obedience. This 'remote learner' condition tested whether people would obey orders to shock someone in a separate room. It took place at the prestigious Yale University. **40 men** took part, responding to newspaper adverts seeking **volunteers** for a study on 'learning and memory'. They received payment for attending, which didn't depend on them proceeding with the experiment. The experimenter wore a grey technician's coat. Each participant was introduced to a **confederate** (acting like a participant, but who was really part of the experimental set-up). They drew lots to see who would act as 'teacher' and 'learner', but this was fixed so the participant was always the teacher.
The participant witnessed the confederate being strapped into a chair and connected up to a shock generator in the next room. It didn't actually give electric shocks, but the participants thought it was real.
The switches ranged from 15 volts (labelled 'Slight Shock') to 450 volts (labelled 'XXX'). The participant taught the learner word-pairs over an intercom. When the learner answered incorrectly, the participant had to administer an **increasing level of shock**. As the shocks increased, the learner started to scream and ask to be let out. After the 330 V shock, he made no further noise. If participants hesitated, the experimenter told them to continue. **Debriefing** included an interview, questionnaires and being reunited with the 'learner'.

Results: **26 participants (65%)** administered **450 V** and **none stopped before 300 V** (when the learner started protesting). Most showed obvious signs of stress during the experiment, like sweating, groaning and trembling.

Conclusion: **Ordinary people** will **obey orders** to hurt someone else, even if it means acting against their consciences.

Milgram *did lots of* **Variations** *on his* **Experiment**

Ooh look, a table. That must say something good. Milgram carried out his experiment in loads of slightly different ways to investigate the effect that certain conditions would have on the results.

Some of Milgram's variations on this experiment	Percentage administering 450 volts
Male participants	65%
Female participants	65%
Learner's protests can be heard	62.5%
Experiment run in seedy offices	48%
Learner in same room as participant	40%
Authority (experimenter) in another room, communicating by phone	23%
Other teachers (confederates) refuse to give shock	10%
Other participant (a confederate) gives shock instead	92.5%

Milgram's Experiment *had* **Good** *and* **Bad** *Points*

1) **Internal validity**: It's possible that participants didn't really believe they were inflicting electric shocks — they were just going along with the **experimenter's expectations** (showing **demand characteristics**). But Milgram claimed participants' **stressed reactions** showed they believed the experiment was real.
2) **Ecological validity**: Milgram's participants did a task that they were unlikely to encounter in real life (shocking someone). So the study **lacks ecological validity**. However, because it was a **laboratory experiment** there was good control of the variables, so it's possible to establish **cause and effect**.
3) **Ethical issues**: The participants were **deceived** as to the true nature of the study. This means they couldn't give **informed consent**. They weren't informed of their **right to withdraw** from the experiment. In fact, they were prompted to continue when they wanted to stop. The participants showed signs of stress during the experiment, so they weren't **protected**. However, they were extensively **debriefed** and 84% of them said they were pleased to have taken part. As well as this, at the time of the experiment there weren't any formal ethical guidelines in place, so technically Milgram didn't breach any. There's more general stuff on ethics on pages 42-43.

Obedience to Authority

Milgram Identified **Factors** that **Affected Obedience**

1) **Presence of allies**: When there were 3 teachers (1 participant and 2 confederates), the real participant was less likely to obey if the other two refused to obey. Having allies can make it easier to resist orders than when you're on your own.
2) **Proximity of the victim**: Milgram's results suggest an important factor was the **proximity (closeness)** of the **learner**. In the 'remote learner' condition, 65% gave the maximum shock. This dropped to 40% with the learner in the same room, and 30% when the participant had to put the learner's hand onto the shock plate. Proximity made the learner's suffering harder to ignore.
3) **Proximity of the authority**: When the authority figure gave prompts by phone from another room, obedience rates dropped to 23%. When the authority figure wasn't close by, orders were easier to resist.

Milgram's **Agency Theory (1973)** Explains **Obedience**

1) When people behave on behalf of an **external authority** (do as they're told), they're said to be in an **agentic state**.
2) This means they act as someone's **agent**, rather than taking personal responsibility for their actions.
3) The opposite of this is behaving **autonomously** — not following orders.
4) Milgram claimed that there were some **binding factors** that might have kept his participants in the **agentic state**:

Reluctance to **disrupt the experiment** — participants had already been paid, so may have felt **obliged** to continue.

The **pressure** of the **surroundings** — the experiment took place in a prestigious university. This made the experimenter seem like a **legitimate authority**.

The **insistence** of the **authority figure** — if participants hesitated they were told that they **had** to continue the experiment.

Before his study, Milgram believed that people were **autonomous** and could **choose** to resist authority. His **agency theory** shows Milgram's findings changed his mind about how much impact legitimate authority figures have.

Evaluation of Agency Theory

1) There's lots of **experimental evidence** to support agency theory — Milgram's participants often claimed they wouldn't have gone as far by themselves, but they were just following orders.
2) Sometimes people **resist** the pressure to obey authority. This can be because of the situation, or because of individual differences (see page 79). Agency theory doesn't explain why some people are more likely to exhibit **independent behaviour** than others.

Practice Questions

Q1 Outline the method of Milgram's (1963) experiment.

Q2 In Milgram's original ('remote learner') experiment, what percentage of participants gave the maximum shock?

Q3 Why was the experimental validity of Milgram's study criticised?

Q4 What is meant by 'proximity' and why is it a factor in obedience?

Exam Questions

Q1 In social psychology, there are many ethical issues to be considered when involving human participants in research. Evaluate Milgram's (1963) study of obedience in terms of ethical issues. [6 marks]

Q2 Outline two factors that might affect obedience levels. [4 marks]

Pretty shocking results, don't you think?

Milgram crops up all the time, so you need to learn this stuff well. You've got to admit it's pretty incredible that people would give someone a 450 V shock just because they were told to. Everyone always thinks that they wouldn't have done it if they were one of the participants, but really it's impossible to know. I definitely would have done though. I love electricity.

Obedience to Authority

There are different factors that make people more or less likely to obey authority...

Milgram's Findings Tell Us About **Why** People **Obey**

An **Agentic State** is When You Act for Someone Else

1) Milgram's **Agency Theory** (page 77) stated that when we feel we're acting out the wishes of another person (being their agent), we feel **less responsible** for our actions.
2) This effect is seen in Milgram's studies. Some participants were concerned for the **welfare** of the learner and asked who would take **responsibility** if he were harmed. When the experimenter (authority) took responsibility, often the participant would continue.
3) This **agentic state** was also in the experiment's set-up. The participants voluntarily entered a **social contract** (an obligation) with the experimenter to take part and follow the procedure of the study.
4) People can start off acting in an **autonomous** way (thinking for themselves), but then become obedient. This is known as an **agentic shift**. When Milgram's participants arrived for the experiment they were in an **autonomous state**, but as soon as they started following orders they underwent an **agentic shift**, and entered an **agentic state**.

Gradual Commitment Can Make Us More Obedient

1) Gradual commitment means agreeing to something gradually — in **small steps**. It makes it **harder to refuse** the next request. In Milgram's study, participants were asked to deliver only a 15 volt shock at the start. This was gradually built up to very large shocks.
2) Participants might have been more **reluctant** to obey if they'd been asked to deliver the 450 volt shock at the start. They obeyed at the lower levels, so it was harder for them to justify disobeying the later requests.
3) Gradual commitment is also known as the '**foot-in-the-door**' effect. Once you've gone along with a minor request, the request could be gradually increased until you're doing something you might never have agreed to in the first place.

We See Some People as **Justified Authorities**

1) We're socialised to recognise the authority of people like **parents**, **police officers**, **doctors**, **teachers** etc.
2) These kinds of people are **justified authorities** — they're given the **right** to **tell us what to do**. This means we're more likely to obey them.
3) When Milgram re-ran his study in some **run-down offices**, obedience rates were lower than when the study was run in the university.
4) He argued that the experimenter's authority was higher in the university situation because of the **status** of the university.
5) **Bickman (1974)** conducted a field experiment where researchers ordered passers-by to do something like pick up a bit of litter. They were dressed either in a guard's uniform, as a milkman, or just in smart clothes. People were much more likely to obey the person in a guard's uniform. This was because he seemed to be the most **legitimate authority figure**.

Boris's authority may not have been justified, but he was the best damn cop in Düsseldorf.

Some Things Can Act as **Buffers**

1) **Buffers** are things that **protect us** — in this case **from the consequences of our actions**.
2) Milgram's participants were **more obedient** in conditions where they **could not see or hear** the victim receiving the shocks. When they were in the same room as the learner, there wasn't any buffer.
3) So... losing the buffer made it harder for Milgram's participants to act against their conscience and go along with someone's unjust orders to hurt the learner.

Obedience to Authority

Sometimes People **Resist** the **Pressure** to **Obey Authority**

The **Situation** Can Make People **More** Resistant

1) More of Milgram's participants resisted orders if there were **other participants present** who refused to obey (see page 77). This suggests that people find it easier to stand up to authority if they have support from others, because they no longer have to take full responsibility for rebelling.

Gamson et al (1982) found that support can help people resist authority, particularly if the request is unreasonable or unjust. They studied a **group** of participants **who felt they were being manipulated**. Participants rebelled against the unjust authority figure. This happened through a process of **minority influence** — with one or two people resisting the authority's requests at first. This rebellion then spread to the whole group.

Conclusion: The presence of **allies** and **collective action** seemed to help the participants in their resistance.

2) This ties in with Asch's research on conformity. He found that participants were more likely to resist the pressure to conform if one of the confederates agreed with them (page 73). It seems that people are more likely to display independent behaviour if they've got support from others.
3) It doesn't really make sense to call this behaviour **independent**, seeing as it depends on having someone else there to agree with you... But just go with it...

Resistance to **Authority** can be Explained by **Individual Differences**

1) If an individual has a high level of **moral reasoning** (thinking about right and wrong) they may be more able to resist an order that goes against their conscience.
2) One of Milgram's participants had experienced a Second World War concentration camp. She **refused** to administer any level of shock, because she didn't want to inflict pain on another person.
3) Those who resisted may have still felt personally responsible — they **weren't** in an **agentic state**.

Rotter (1966) claimed that people could be categorised as having an **internal** or **external locus of control** (page 74). People with an **internal locus of control** take responsibility for their actions more than people with an **external locus of control**. This means that they're more likely to exhibit **independent behaviour** — they're less likely to conform, or be obedient, than people with an **external locus of control**.

Sometimes people feel that they're being pushed too far or a rule restricts them too much. In this situation they might react by doing the **opposite** of what they're told. This is known as the '**boomerang effect**'.

Practice Questions

Q1 Why might obedience rates have dropped when Milgram's study took place in run-down offices?

Q2 Give an example of a buffer that reduced obedience rates in one of Milgram's studies.

Q3 What did Gamson et al (1982) conclude from their research on independent behaviour?

Q4 How do individual differences influence independent behaviour?

Exam Questions

Q1 Rosie was approached by a man at the bus stop, who told her to go and stand somewhere else.
Outline two factors that might make Rosie more likely to obey his authority. [4 marks]

Q2 Outline two factors that may help people resist authority. [4 marks]

I can never resist a man in uniform...

The good thing about this obedience stuff is that it's mostly quite obvious. Everyone knows some people are more likely to obey authority than others. And the only explanation anyone can come up with for why this happens is that they just are, and that's that. So it shouldn't be too difficult to learn. And buffers is a pretty funny word too, which always helps...

Research into Conformity and Obedience

I don't want to blow my own trumpet, but these pages are brilliant — look at all those lovely words just waiting to be read. They're all about the implications of research into conformity and obedience for social change — basically, what we can learn from people like Milgram.

Milgram's (1963) Findings Were Revolutionary

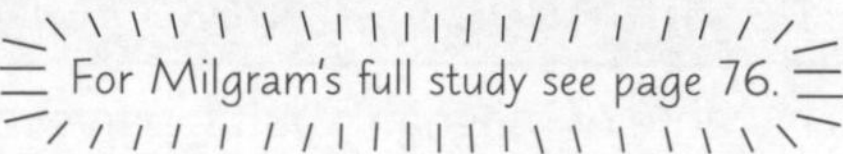

1) Before the study Milgram asked different experts on human behaviour (e.g. psychiatrists) to predict the results. They thought the maximum average shock that participants would go up to was 130 V, and that only someone with a **psychopathic personality disorder** would administer a 450 V shock.
2) He actually found that 65% of participants went up to 450 V, even when they clearly didn't want to.

Milgram's study completely changed what people thought about obedience, and it's had a huge impact ever since.

It showed that his participants **deferred responsibility** for their actions onto the authority figure. Milgram found the highest rate of obedience when the experiment took place in a university and he wore a lab coat. This exposed the huge amount of trust that people have in **justified authorities**. **Hofling et al (1966)** also showed this when they got nurses to break hospital rules because they thought they were following a doctor's orders.

Application to real life

We often have no choice but to place our trust in experts, but with this comes the potential for abuse of power. A contemporary example of this is the case of **Harold Shipman** — a doctor who murdered patients by injecting them with huge overdoses. He was able to do this because his patients **trusted** him, and he's thought to have got away with killing over 200 of them before anybody became suspicious. Scary...

Zimbardo Looked at the Effect of Deindividuation

Deindividuation is when people lose their personal identity (stop feeling like **individuals**), and identify with a group.

1) **Zimbardo (1970)** replicated Milgram's experiment and examined the effect of different conditions.
2) He compared participants who wore their own clothes and were treated as individuals, to ones who wore **hoods** covering their faces and were spoken to as a group.
3) He found that the average level of electric shock **doubled** when the participants were wearing a hood.

When the participants were **deindividuated**, they became more **obedient** and more **antisocial**. Zimbardo later demonstrated this in the **Stanford Prison Experiment (1973)** (page 71). The prison guards wore **uniforms** and **sunglasses**, and they quickly became aggressive towards the prisoners. It seems that they stopped taking **personal responsibility** for their actions, and changed their behaviour to fit into their social role.

Deindividuation Also Happens in Large Crowds

Mann's (1981) study looked at newspaper coverage of suicide attempts. It focused on the crowds that gathered below when someone was threatening to jump off a tall building or a bridge. The newspaper reports showed that people in large crowds were likely to start jeering and telling the person to jump. This was even more common when it was dark. Mann concluded that the **anonymity** you get in a big group can lead to more extreme behaviour, because the sense of personal responsibility is **shifted onto the group**.

Application to real life

These studies help explain problems like police brutality and rioting behaviour. Zimbardo's research suggests there are ways of combating the negative effects of deindividuation — he found that when participants wore name tags instead of hoods, they gave less severe electric shocks. This has implications for social change — e.g. hoodies are banned in some public places. It could be that wearing hoodies makes people more likely to behave in an antisocial way. Or it could be that people find hoodies threatening because the people wearing them can't be identified. Or it could just be a load of rubbish.

Research into Conformity and Obedience

People in Groups Feel Pressure to Conform

1) **Sherif (1935)** and **Asch (1956)** (pages 70-71) showed that participants' responses to tasks changed when they were in a group.
2) In Sherif's study this was because they were in an **unfamiliar situation**, so they looked to other people for information on how to behave. Asch's participants felt pressure from the group to give the wrong answer, just so they would **fit in**.
3) These findings have wider implications for society, as we rely on groups to make important decisions — e.g. governments and juries.

Chris wasn't sure why the players had to be naked, but he wanted to fit in.

Janis (1972) found that groups having to make important decisions can be guilty of **Groupthink**. This happens especially in very **cohesive** groups, which are isolated from other influences, and have very **powerful leaders** — e.g. governments. Janis saw that members of the group converge their thinking so that it falls in line with what they imagine the general view of the group is. This leads to a unanimous decision that doesn't actually reflect what everyone in the group wants. It happens because individuals want to preserve the unity of the group. **Groupthink** is most common in situations where there's lots of **pressure** to make a quick, important decision.

Janis proposed ways of combating Groupthink:

1) Initially, group leaders shouldn't express their opinions, so other members won't feel **pressured** to agree with them.
2) One member should be given the role of **devil's advocate** (always expressing the opposite argument) to make sure that all possibilities are explored.
3) **Objective people** outside of the group should be consulted.

Research into Conformity and Obedience has Ethical Implications

There are loads of ethical issues surrounding studies like Milgram's. The participants were deceived and put under stress. However, it's important with every study to do a **cost / benefit analysis** — consider whether the cost to the participants was worth the benefit of the findings to society.

1) Despite feeling pressured during the studies, a high proportion of Milgram's participants said they were **pleased to have taken part**. This was because they felt they'd learned valuable lessons about themselves.
2) Research into conformity and obedience can lead to **social change**. Studies like Milgram's **raised awareness** of the possible negative outcomes of blind obedience. Janis's ideas on **Groupthink** showed that some conflict within a group is necessary, not destructive. His ideas have been taken on board by group leaders to help ensure they make the best decisions.

Practice Questions

Q1 What is deindividuation?

Q2 When is Groupthink most likely to occur?

Exam Question

Q1 Apply findings from the social approach to explain a real-life instance of conformity or obedience. [6 marks]

Now all repeat after me — conformity is bad...

The trouble with a lot of this research is that it forgets about all the good things that come from obedience and conformity. If you weren't so obedient and conformist then you wouldn't be sitting here revising right now, and that would be a crying shame. And anyway, a bit of good old-fashioned discipline never hurt anyone. Although a 450 volt shock might have done...

The Individual Differences Approach

This section's all about individual differences — basically the fact that everyone is different. And an individual. Mind-blowing stuff. What psychologists want to know is how, and why... They're never satisfied.

Individuals **Differ** in Their Psychological Characteristics

The **individual differences approach** studies how psychological characteristics, like aggression and memory span, differ from person to person.

Psychologists argued for ages about whether an individual's personality is influenced by **nature** (inherited factors) or **nurture** (environmental factors). This is known as the **nature-nurture debate**. It's now thought most likely that **both** have an effect and interact with one another, so there shouldn't be much more debate over which one is solely to blame.

There are Lots of Different **Perspectives** Within the Approach

These will be covered in more detail further on in the section, but for now, here's a brief overview...

The Biological Approach (see pages 88-89)

This approach explains behaviour in terms of **physiological** or **genetic** factors. It focuses on physical treatments for psychological disorders, e.g. using **drugs** or **electroconvulsive therapy**.

The Psychodynamic Approach (see pages 90-91)

The psychodynamic approach puts abnormal behaviour down to underlying **psychological problems**, often caused by past events and experiences. Treatment comes in the form of **psychoanalysis**, where the therapist tries to find and sort out these underlying problems.

The Behavioural Approach (see pages 92-93)

The behavioural approach claims that all behaviour, including abnormal behaviour, is **learned**. It's believed that old behaviours can be '**unlearned**' — treatment of abnormal behaviour is based on this.

The Cognitive Approach (see pages 94-95)

This approach puts abnormality down to **irrational and negative thoughts**. So, as you can probably guess, treatment focuses on changing the way a person thinks about things.

Several Different **Methods** are Used in the Individual Differences Approach

1) Case Studies (see page 33)

In a **case study** you use **interviews** and **observation** to collect **information** about an individual or group. You can study behaviour over a **long period of time** — this means you could observe some behaviours that might not be seen in another type of study. Also, it's often possible to observe behaviour in a **natural setting**. However, in a natural setting it's harder to control all **variables**, and it's mighty tricky to **replicate** the study.

2) Meta-analysis

This is where you analyse the results from loads of different studies and come up with some **general conclusions**. They're a good way of **bringing together data** (which is a general aim of the scientific process), and by doing this they reduce the problem of **sample size**. However, one problem is that there are loads of **conflicting results** out there, which obviously makes doing a meta-analysis a bit tricky...

3) Correlational Studies (see page 33)

These use **statistics** to compare two **variables**. For instance, you might give a questionnaire to all participants to measure their stress levels on a scale. They'd then do another task, e.g. a memory test, for which they'd also get a score. A correlation would **compare** the scores to see if there is a **relationship** between stress and memory. But you couldn't use this to show that one **causes** the other.

4) Physiological Studies

These include methods such as **brain scanning**, which can produce a detailed picture showing up any **structural abnormalities**. This means psychologists can make links between **structures** in the brain and **behavioural abnormalities**. However, scanning is a pretty **expensive process**, so it's not always possible.

The Individual Differences Approach

Psychologists Try to **Classify** People

The **DSM-IV** is the fourth edition of the American Psychiatric Association's Diagnostic and Statistical Manual of Mental Disorders. It contains all known mental health disorders, and offers a new **method of classification** — a **multiaxial classification**:

1) Individuals can be rated on **multiple axes/dimensions**. Diagnostic categories are used, for example organic mental disorders, personality disorders etc.
2) DSM-IV made diagnosis more **concrete and descriptive** than it had been.
3) Classifications are useful to acquire new information about a disorder. This can help in the development of new **treatments** and medication.
4) This type of classification has been criticised for **stigmatising** people and ignoring their 'uniqueness' by putting them in **artificial groups**.

Rosenhan (1973) — psychiatric classification can be inaccurate.

Method 1: In a field study, eight 'normal' people tried to be admitted to 12 different psychiatric hospitals around the USA, with only one symptom — claiming they heard voices, saying 'empty', 'hollow' and 'thud'.

Results 1: Seven were diagnosed with **schizophrenia** and all eight were **admitted** to psychiatric hospital. On admission, they said they were sane and had faked symptoms to get admitted, but this was seen as a symptom itself. It took, on average, 19 days before they were released, usually with a diagnosis of 'schizophrenia in remission'. Other, real patients could tell that these people were not mentally ill.

Method 2: Rosenhan later told staff at a psychiatric hospital that one or more **pseudopatients** (normal people pretending to have schizophrenia) were trying to be admitted to the hospital.

Results 2: No pseudopatients appeared, but 41 genuine patients were judged to be pseudopatients by staff.

Conclusion: Medical staff could not distinguish the sane from the insane (although many of the real patients could).

Evaluation: Being a field study, it wouldn't have been possible to control all variables, and so the results lose some of their **reliability**. Staff would probably not **expect** 'normal' people to try to gain admission to a psychiatric hospital, and so this might explain why the participants were initially admitted. 'Schizophrenia in remission' is a diagnosis that is **rarely** used, which suggests the psychiatrists concerned may not have believed they were really suffering from schizophrenia. There are **ethical** considerations in this study — people had their freedom taken away, mentally healthy people may have received treatments, professionals were deceived, and the study risked genuine patients not being treated.

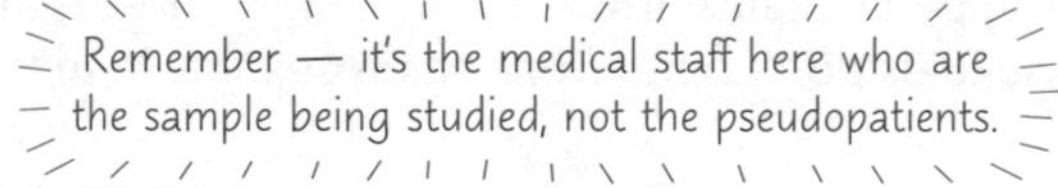

Practice Questions

Q1 What does the individual differences approach study?

Q2 List the four different perspectives within the individual differences approach.

Q3 What is meant by multiaxial classification?

Q4 Who were the sample in Rosenhan's (1973) study?

Exam Questions

Q1 Explain one strength and one weakness of using case studies in individual differences research. [4 marks]

Q2 Outline and evaluate Rosenhan's (1973) study of psychiatric hospital admission. [12 marks]

Get me out of here, I'm not crazy — I'm as sane as any other rabbit...

The first pages of a new section. Isn't it thrilling... It's like all your birthdays have come at once. Anyway, before you get over-excited just make sure you've got to grips with the basics here first. Think of these pages as the sausage rolls before you get stuck into the jelly and ice cream, and start pouring hundreds and thousands straight into your mouth from the tub...

Defining Abnormality

Defining what's abnormal is easy — it's just what's not normal. But what's normal...?

Abnormality Can be Described as **Deviation from Social Norms**

1) All societies have their **standards** of behaviour and attitudes. Deviating from these can be seen as abnormal.
2) But **cultures vary**, so there isn't one universal set of social 'rules'.
3) One problem with defining abnormality as deviation from social norms is that it can be used to **justify** the removal of 'unwanted' people from a society. For example, people opposing a particular political regime could be said to be abnormal.

The concept of deviation from the majority can be expressed statistically in terms of the **normal distribution**:

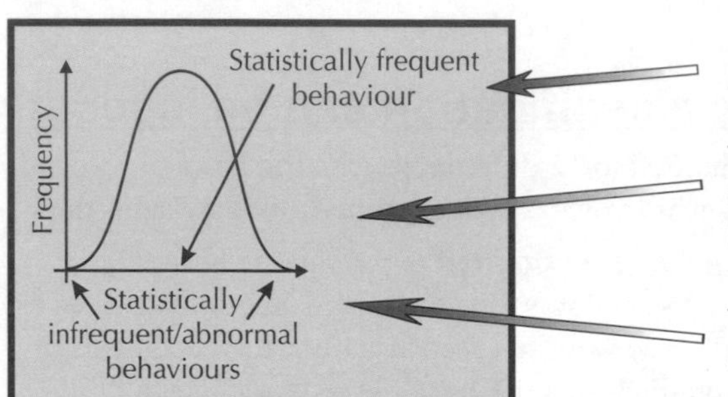

People who behave in the average way make up the middle of the bell-shaped curve.

Those people who behave 'abnormally' make up the tail ends of the bell curve — this behaviour is rare (statistically infrequent).

This axis shows a numerical measure of the behaviour, e.g. the number of hand washes per week.

Not all traits show a normal distribution.

However, there are **problems** with defining abnormality simply in terms of statistical infrequency:

1) It doesn't take account of the **desirability of behaviour**, just its frequency. For example, a very high IQ is abnormal, as is a very low one, but having a high IQ is desirable whereas having a low IQ is undesirable.
2) There's **no distinction** between **rare, slightly odd** behaviour and **rare, psychologically abnormal** behaviour.
3) There's **no definite cut-off point** where normal behaviour becomes abnormal behaviour.
4) Some behaviours that are considered psychologically abnormal are quite common, e.g. mild depression. **Hassett and White (1989)** argue that you cannot use statistical infrequency to define abnormality because of this. Using the statistical infrequency idea, some disorders would not be classed as anything unusual.

Interestingly, as recently as 1974, homosexuality was classified in the DSM as a **disorder**. However, the diagnosis was dropped because it was found that homosexuality **wasn't as infrequent** as previously thought, and that homosexuals don't differ from heterosexuals in terms of **psychological well-being**.

Failure to Function Adequately *is Another Definition of* ***Abnormality***

You can't function adequately if you can't cope with the demands of day-to-day life.
Various **criteria** are used for diagnosis, including:

1) **Dysfunctional behaviour** — behaviour which goes against the accepted standards of behaviour.
2) **Observer discomfort** — behaviour that causes other individuals to become uncomfortable.
3) **Unpredictable behaviour** — impulsive behaviour that seems to be uncontrollable.
4) **Irrational behaviour** — behaviour that's unreasonable and illogical.
5) **Personal distress** — being affected by emotion to an excessive degree.

If you can tick the box for **more than one** of the criteria above, the person's behaviour is considered to be **abnormal**. It does seem a bit unfair though — we've probably all done stuff that could fit under these categories at some point. People are always uncomfortable around me, but that could be because I've got fleas.

Defining Abnormality

Jahoda (1958) Identified Six Conditions Associated with Good Mental Health

Jahoda's six conditions were:

1) Positive self-attitude
2) Self-actualisation (realising your potential, being fulfilled)
3) Resistance to stress
4) Personal autonomy (making your own decisions, being in control)
5) Accurate perception of reality
6) Adaptation to the environment

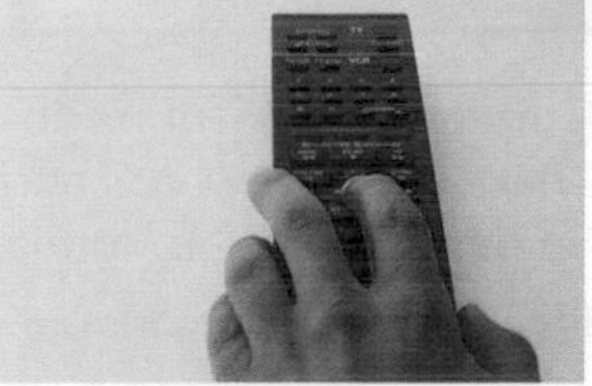

As far as Doug was concerned, he was in control of everything he needed in life.

However, it can be **hard to meet** all the standards set in this list, and they're **subjective** (ideas of what is required for each will differ from person to person).

Also, a violent offender, for example, may have a positive self attitude and be resistant to stress etc. — yet society wouldn't consider them to be in good mental health.

The Idea of Ideal Mental Health Varies Across Time and Between Cultures

What's considered mentally 'healthy' at one time, wouldn't necessarily be at another.
For example, in some cultures today, it's considered **abnormal** for women to **enjoy sex** — they may be forced to have their clitoris surgically removed to prevent their enjoyment. In Victorian times here, women who enjoyed sex were deemed abnormal and hence Freud coined the term '**nymphomania**'. There's still influence from this today — there are still **double standards** about male and female sexual activity.

But the idea of 'ideal' mental health can be a useful one because it moves away from focusing on mental 'illness'.

Some Symptoms are Associated with Mental Illness

The Department of Health provides a guide to assess symptoms associated with mental illness.
To be classified as a mental illness, there should be **one or more** of the following (**not temporary**) symptoms:

1) Impairment of **intellectual functions**, such as memory and comprehension.
2) Alterations to **mood** that lead to **delusional appraisals** of the past or future, or lack of any appraisal.
3) Delusional **beliefs**, such as of persecution or jealousy.
4) Disordered **thinking** — the person may be unable to appraise their situation or communicate with others.

Practice Questions

Q1 Define abnormality using the deviation from social norms explanation.

Q2 What does Jahoda (1958) say are the six conditions associated with mental health?

Q3 Give three of the symptoms that the Department of Health uses to classify mental illness.

Q4 If someone's forgotten their trousers, should they be allowed on the bus?

Exam Questions

Q1 Outline the problems with defining abnormality in terms of deviation from social norms. [6 marks]

Q2 Outline the key features of the idea of abnormality as the failure to function adequately. [6 marks]

I'm not abnormal — I'm just a little socially deviant...

Ah, wouldn't it be easier to just be a fish... Nobody minds if you're abnormal when you're under the sea — you can swim around any way you like. You could befriend a manatee and have an adventure. The kindly sea cow — he'd never judge you for your dysfunctional and unpredictable behaviour. Yes, life is much better down where it's wetter, take it from me...

Defining Abnormality

Maybe trying to define abnormality is just wrong altogether. I mean, calling someone 'abnormal' isn't exactly very nice. I got called abnormal the other day and it cut me pretty deep. Mothers can be so cruel...

*The Concept of Abnormality **Varies** from One **Culture** and **Time** to Another*

1) **Cultural relativism** means that judgements made about abnormality are relative to individual cultures. That's because what's normal in one culture is sometimes considered to be abnormal in another. So definitions of abnormality are **limited** because they're **culturally specific**.
2) It's important to work out whether an abnormality is **absolute**, **universal**, or **culturally relative**.

> a) **Absolute** — occurring in the same way and frequency across cultures.
> b) **Universal** — present in all cultures, but not necessarily with the same frequency.
> c) **Culturally relative** — unique to a particular culture.

3) Many **physical** conditions are **absolute**. The same goes for some mental conditions. However, **social norms** vary from one culture to another. This can affect how these conditions are **perceived**. For example, in some **cultures** it's considered normal to experience **hallucinations**, but in other cultures it can be seen as a **symptom** of **schizophrenia.**
4) Some abnormal behaviours are **universal**, e.g. **depression** occurs in all cultures, but is more common in women and in industrial societies.
5) Some abnormal behaviours are **culturally relative** — these are known as **culture-bound syndromes**.

> '**Witiko**' is an example of culturally relative behaviour. It is a culture-bound syndrome, suffered by native Canadians, who **lose their appetite** for ordinary food, feel **depressed** and believe they are **possessed by the Witiko**, who is a **giant man-eating monster**. This can result in cannibalism, murder or pleas for death from the sufferer. It is thought to be an extreme form of **starvation anxiety**.

*Attempts to **Define** Abnormality May Be **Biased***

There are often problems when it comes to defining abnormality — these often relate to **stereotypes**.

Gender...

Factors such as **biological** or **hormonal** differences, and the different ways that men and women are **brought up**, could lead to gender differences in the frequencies of disorders.

However, the **gender stereotype** can lead people to believe that women are generally moodier, and men generally more violent and antisocial. This could be a factor in clinicians tending to diagnose more **mood** disorders in women and more **antisocial** disorders in men — the clinicians **expect** to find them.

Race...

Several studies have found that very large numbers of **black people** in Britain are being diagnosed with **schizophrenia**. Surveys of inpatients by **Bagley (1971)** and **Cochrane (1977)** found that **immigrant groups** in Britain are more likely to be diagnosed as schizophrenic than native-born people. This is particularly so for people originating in Africa, the Caribbean and Asia. It was first thought that this could be explained in terms of **genetic** or **biological** factors, except that the same rates of occurrence were **not found** in the **countries of origin**.

Therefore, possible reasons include **racial stereotypes** in diagnosis and **greater stress**. Stress could be due to poorer living conditions, prejudice, or the general stress of living in a new culture.

Even if stereotypes alone are to blame for a diagnosis, the person could 'develop' the disorder. Once a person is **labelled** with a mental disorder, they may begin to behave in the expected way due to the label. The diagnosis then becomes a **self-fulfilling prophecy**.

Defining Abnormality

Classification Systems **Pigeon-Hole** People

A major **problem** with systems for classifying abnormality is that they can lead to pigeon-holing people into **certain categories**. This leads to **practical**, **theoretical** and **ethical considerations**, which **you need to know** about.

1) **Diagnosis** — when people report how they feel 'psychologically', these are **subjective** feelings. One person's "I'm extremely depressed" may mean the same as someone else's, "I'm fed up". A more **idiographic approach** would be useful — that is, focusing on each unique case and viewing patients on their merits.
2) There are many **different theories** of abnormality — psychodynamic, learning, cognitive, etc. They all have their own definitions and ideas of what causes abnormality.
3) There's little evidence of **validity** — how much any of the classification systems measure what they're supposed to. It's hard to find a central cause **(aetiology)** for most disorders. And, if patients have more than one disorder it can be difficult to spot symptoms of one disorder.
4) Psychiatrists may not always agree from category to category, so classification systems may not always be **reliable**.
5) **Treatment** — grouping patients can be useful for prescribing treatments, but treatment often depends on diagnosis. Therefore, if the diagnosis is subjective initially, the treatment may not be correct.
6) **Labelling theory (Scheff, 1966)** argues that if people are treated as mentally ill, their behaviour will change and become more like that expected from their diagnosis.
7) **Szasz (1974)** said that psychiatric labels were **meaningless**. He said illness was a bodily problem, so 'mental' illness could not exist. He believed the term was used to exclude non-conformists from society.
8) Finally, it's hard to say where normality ends and abnormality starts anyway.

Just so you know, there's a difference between psychologists and psychiatrists. Psychiatry is a part of medicine that deals with the prevention, diagnosis and treatment of mental disorders. So, a psychiatrist is trained in medicine as well as psychology.

In some cultures marrying your horse is perfectly normal.

Practice Questions

Q1 What is cultural relativism?

Q2 What is meant by a universal abnormality?

Q3 What are culture-bound syndromes?

Q4 What is meant by an idiographic approach to abnormality?

Q5 What did Scheff (1966) propose in his labelling theory?

Exam Questions

Q1 Outline how stereotypes can cause problems in defining abnormality. [8 marks]

Q2 Evaluate the use of classification systems for defining abnormality. [10 marks]

In the seventies people thought men with huge perms were normal...

You've got to know all the stuff on these pages if you're going to answer a 'defining abnormality' question in the exam. I reckon the best way is to read the pages and make a list of all the main points in note form. Then cover the pages up, and try to write them out again from the notes you've just made. This process is known as 'learning' or 'revision'...

The Biological Model of Abnormality

There are many different models of abnormality that describe symptoms and treatments differently. Firstly, you need to know about the biological model, including its strengths and weaknesses.

The Biological Model Assumes Psychological Disorders are ***Physical Illnesses***

The **biological (or medical or somatic) model** assumes that psychological disorders are **physical illnesses** with physical causes. In principle they're no different from physical illnesses like flu, except they have major psychological symptoms. When the same symptoms frequently occur together, they represent a reliable **syndrome** or **disorder**. The cause or '**aetiology**' may be one or more of the following:

1) **Genetics** — Faulty genes are known to cause some diseases that have psychological effects, e.g. Huntington's disease that leads to a deterioration of mental abilities.
2) **Neurotransmitters** — Too much or too little of a particular neurotransmitter may produce psychological disorders, e.g. an increased level of **dopamine** is linked to schizophrenia — **drugs** like cocaine, which increase dopamine levels, can lead to schizophrenia-like symptoms.
3) **Infection** — Disorders may be caused by infection. **General paresis** is a condition involving delusions and mood swings, leading to paralysis and death. It is caused by **syphilis**, and can now be treated.
4) **Brain injury** — Accidental brain damage may produce psychological disorders. E.g. in 1848 an explosion sent an iron rod through **Phineas Gage's** head, destroying parts of his frontal lobes. He survived, but he became more impulsive and disorganised, couldn't plan for the future and had a strangely different personality.

Research Has Been Done into the ***Genetic Basis*** *of* ***Schizophrenia***

Twin Studies

Identical twins share **100%** of their genes. So in theory, if schizophrenia has a purely **genetic basis**, if one twin suffers from schizophrenia then the other twin will too. **Non-identical twins** share **50%** of their genes, so the risk of both suffering should be lower.

	Gottesman (1991) conducted a meta-analysis of twin studies
Method:	Gottesman carried out a meta-analysis of approximately 40 twin studies.
Results:	It was found that having an **identical twin** with schizophrenia gave you a **48%** chance of developing the condition. This reduced to **17%** in **non-identical twins**.
Conclusion:	Schizophrenia has a strong **genetic basis**.
Evaluation:	The meta-analysis was carried out on field studies, giving the research **high ecological validity**. Because identical twins share 100% of their genes, it might be expected that both twins would always suffer from the same conditions. The fact that both twins had developed schizophrenia in only about half of the cases means that **another factor** must also be involved. Identical twins tend to be treated more similarly than non-identical twins, and so the **family environment** might play a large role.

Adoption Studies

Adoption studies have also provided evidence for a **genetic basis** of schizophrenia.

	Heston (1966) conducted an adoption study
Method:	47 adopted children whose biological mothers had schizophrenia were studied. The control group consisted of 50 adopted children whose biological mothers didn't suffer from schizophrenia. The children were followed up as adults and were interviewed and given intelligence and personality tests.
Results:	Of the experimental group, 5 of the 47 became schizophrenic, compared to 0 in the control group. Another 4 of the experimental group were classified as borderline schizophrenic by the raters.
Conclusion:	The study supports the view that schizophrenia has a **genetic basis**.
Evaluation:	Interview data can be unreliable and affected by **social desirability bias**. However, interviews are a good way of getting data in a **naturalistic way**. The adopted children whose mothers didn't suffer from any conditions might have not shown any symptoms of schizophrenia **yet** — it can't be completely ruled out.

The Biological Model of Abnormality

Biological Disorders Can Be **Treated** with Biological Therapies

The biological model says that once the physical cause of a psychological disorder has been identified, a physical (biological) therapy is needed to treat the physical problem. One or more of the following may be used:

1) **Drugs** — Drugs can be used to change **neurotransmitter levels** in the brain. For example, **phenothiazines** reduce levels of dopamine and can therefore relieve symptoms of schizophrenia.
2) **Psychosurgery** — Psychosurgery is brain surgery involving destruction or separation of parts of the brain. **Moniz** developed the '**frontal lobotomy**' in the 1930s to separate parts of the frontal lobes from the rest of the brain. This reduced aggression and generally made people more placid. However, it's **not a cure**, but a change — the **irreversible** changes to personality may have just made patients easier to manage. Psychosurgery is now only a last resort treatment for some disorders, e.g. very serious depression.
3) **Electroconvulsive therapy (ECT)** — During ECT, an electric shock of around 225 volts is given to a person's brain. This can help to relieve depression, but can also produce memory loss. Although quite commonly used in the past, it's now only used as a last resort therapy.

The **Biological Model** Has **Strengths** and **Weaknesses**

Strengths:

1) It has a **scientific** basis in biology and a lot of evidence shows that biological causes **can** produce psychological symptoms.
2) It can be seen as **ethical** because people are **not blamed** for their disorders. They just have an illness.
3) Biological **therapies** have helped relieve conditions (e.g. schizophrenia) that could not be treated very well previously.

Weaknesses:

1) Biological therapies raise **ethical** concerns. Drugs can produce addiction and may only suppress symptoms rather than cure the disorder. The effects of psychosurgery are irreversible.
2) Psychological disorders may not be linked to any physical problem. **Psychological therapies** can be just as effective as biological treatments, without any interference to biological structures.

Practice Questions

Q1 Give two possible causes of psychological disorders according to the biological model.

Q2 What type of studies have been used to investigate the genetic basis of schizophrenia?

Q3 What is psychosurgery?

Q4 What is electroconvulsive therapy?

Q5 Give one strength and one weakness of the biological model.

Exam Questions

Q1 Outline the key features of the biological model relating to the causes of abnormality. [6 marks]

Q2 Outline and evaluate a piece of research conducted into the genetic basis of schizophrenia. [8 marks]

Biological, medical, somatic — it just needs to make up its mind...

That's the first of many models of abnormality. Make sure you know this one thoroughly before you look at the next one. And that means the key features, the studies, the treatments and the strengths and weaknesses. Phew. You don't want to start getting all the details mixed up with the other models. So, when you're ready, on to the psychodynamic model...

The Psychodynamic Model of Abnormality

You've probably forgotten what you read about the psychodynamic approach back on page 82. So, luckily for you, here it is again. And even better, it's in more detail. What more could you possibly want...

The Psychodynamic Model is Based on **Conflict in Development**

1) The model is based on **Freud's** division of personality into the **id**, **ego** and **superego**.
2) It also uses his **stages of development** — the oral, anal, phallic, latency and genital stages.
3) The model suggests that **conflict** and **anxiety** may occur during childhood because the **ego** is not yet **developed** enough to deal with the id's desires, understand real-world issues or cope with the superego's moral demands (e.g. knowing right from wrong).
4) Psychological disorders may also come from **conflict** or **anxiety** which happens in a certain **stage** of development. For example, during the anal stage, conflict may occur during potty training.
5) Anxiety from the conflicts is repressed into the **unconscious mind**. **Stress** or **trauma** in adulthood may 'trigger' the repressed conflicts, leading to **psychological disorders**.

Psychoanalysis is Used as a **Treatment** in the Psychodynamic Model

1) Freud introduced **psychoanalysis** as a treatment in the early twentieth century.
2) Its aim was to allow the patient to **access** repressed thoughts and unconscious conflicts — Freud called this **'insight'**.
3) Patients were then encouraged to **deal** with the conflicts.
4) Freud recognised that this process would be painful and cause anxiety, and that people would be **resistant** at first. However, patients were encouraged to focus on the **feelings** that the repressed thoughts brought about.

Freud used three psychoanalytic techniques to uncover his patients' repressed thoughts:

Hypnosis

Hypnosis is an **altered mental state**, involving deep relaxation. Freud believed that people could access repressed thoughts whilst in this state. He gradually lost interest in the technique for two main reasons — he found it **difficult** to hypnotise people, and also found that people become very **suggestible** when hypnotised.

Free Association

In free association, the patient is given a **cue word** and is asked to say any **ideas** or **memories** that come into their mind. Freud believed that by doing this repressed thoughts would eventually **emerge**, giving an **insight** into the unconscious problems causing abnormal behaviour.

Dream Analysis

Dream analysis was also used by Freud. It was thought that a certain part of the mind keeps repressed thoughts in the **unconscious** and that this part is **less active** during **sleep**. Therefore, Freud believed that repressed thoughts are likely to appear in **dreams**.

So, your dream of a cow eating corn. Had any corned beef lately...?

The Psychodynamic Model of Abnormality

The *Psychodynamic Model* Also Has *Strengths* and *Weaknesses*

Strengths:

1) It's quite a unique approach to abnormality, suggesting that disorders may be linked to **unresolved conflicts** related to **biological needs**.
2) It offers methods of **therapy** which may also uncover unconscious conflicts. The client can then **understand** the causes of their problems and so **resolve** them and release their anxieties.
3) It was the first theory to focus on **psychological causes** of disorders. Before this, the focus had been on **physical causes** or things like possession by **evil spirits**.

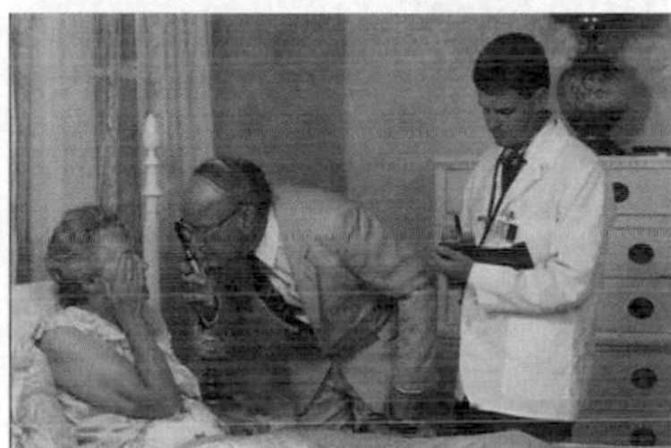

So... hearing voices. Ever get pushed out of the sand pit at school...?

Weaknesses:

1) Freud's claims are based on his subjective interpretations of his patients' dreams, etc. Therefore they're hard to **scientifically test** and so can't be proved right or wrong.
2) **Psychoanalysis** may take a long time and so be very expensive. The childhood conflicts that are 'uncovered' may be emotionally distressing and possibly inaccurate, depending on the reliability of the patient's memory, the techniques used to uncover them and the analyst's interpretations.
3) The focus is on the patient's **past**, rather than on the problems that they are **currently suffering.**

Practice Questions

Q1 Who introduced psychoanalysis as a treatment?

Q2 According to the psychodynamic model, what might lead to psychological disorders?

Q3 What did Freud mean by 'insight'?

Q4 Why might people be resistant to psychoanalysis at first?

Q5 What is 'free association'?

Q6 Tell me about your mother...

Exam Questions

Q1 Outline the assumptions of the psychodynamic model relating to the treatment of abnormality. [6 marks]

Q2 Evaluate the strengths and weaknesses of the psychodynamic model. [8 marks]

We all experience conflict during childhood — that's what siblings are for...

My sister once pinned me down and spat on my face. I wouldn't mind, but I was 21 at the time and it seemed a little undignified. Still, at least it didn't happen before my ego was properly developed, else it might have messed me up good and proper. Isn't that right, Freud? Freud? Sigmund? He's not answering — how rude. His silence speaks volumes...

The Behavioural Model of Abnormality

Nearly there on all the different models of abnormality now — just this one and the cognitive one to go. The behavioural one's my favourite, although I'm not too keen on the picture at the bottom of the next page...

The Behavioural Model of Abnormality says **Behaviours** are all **Learnt**

Behaviourists argue that abnormal behaviours are learnt in the same way that all behaviours are learnt — through **classical** and **operant conditioning**. This page is all about their take on the matter.

1. Behaviourists reckon that classical conditioning can be used to explain the development of many abnormal behaviours, including **phobias** and **taste aversions**.

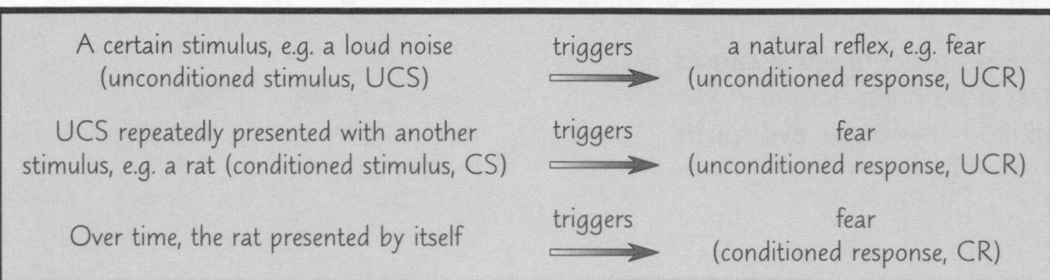

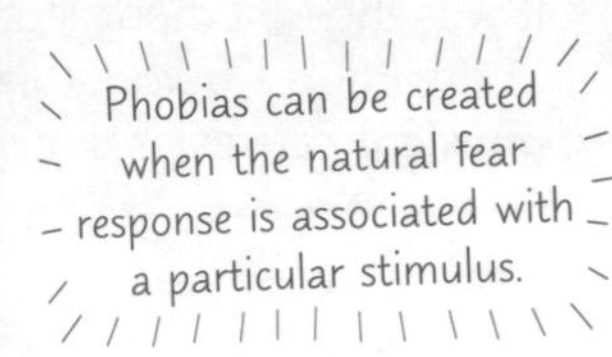

1) **Watson and Rayner (1920)** experimented with an 11-month-old boy, **'Little Albert'**, producing fear of a white rat by associating it with a loud, scary noise. This is a classic, old-school crazy study.
2) **Taste aversions** are often created if you're ill after a certain food or drink. Its taste will become a CS, producing a CR of nausea. So, if you were ill after eating a curry with bad meat, the taste of curry might always make you feel ill.

2. **Operant conditioning** is learning from the **consequences** of actions. Actions which have a good outcome through **positive reinforcement** (reward) or **negative reinforcement** (removal of something bad) will be repeated. Actions which have a bad outcome (**punishment**) will not be repeated. Some examples include:

a) Maintaining **phobias** — we get anxious around phobic stimuli (heights, spiders etc.) and avoid them. This prevents the anxiety, which acts as negative reinforcement.
b) **Bulimics** feel guilt and disgust, so make themselves sick. The removal of these feelings is negative reinforcement.
c) **Anorexics** desire to lose weight, or to have more control of their life, so not eating is positive reinforcement.

Behavioural Therapies are Based on **Changes** Through **Conditioning**

Behaviourists try to identify what **reinforces** unwanted behaviours and try to change them through conditioning.

1) **Operant conditioning therapies** are often used in psychiatric hospitals. They control abnormal behaviour by removing the reinforcements which maintain the behaviour, and giving new reinforcements for better behaviour. For example, psychiatric patients might receive **tokens** for behaving 'normally'. These can be exchanged for **reinforcements**, such as sweets or being able to watch TV. This is called a **token economy**.
2) Behavioural therapies can also use **classical conditioning** to change behaviour, for example...

1) Aversion Therapy

This removes an undesired behaviour by associating it with **unpleasant feelings**. For example, alcoholics are given alcohol at the same time as a drug that naturally produces nausea. Nausea becomes a conditioned response to alcohol, so they should then feel no urge to drink, but instead feel sick at the idea of it.

The Behavioural Model of Abnormality

2) Systematic Desensitisation

This is a treatment for **phobias**.

1) First, the phobic person makes a '**fear hierarchy**'. This is a list of feared events, showing what they fear least (e.g. seeing a picture of a spider) through to their most feared event (e.g. holding a spider).
2) When put in the situation of their least feared event, they're **anxious**.
3) Then they're encouraged to use a **relaxation** technique.
4) Relaxation and anxiety can't happen at the same time, so when they become relaxed and calm, they're no longer scared.
5) This is repeated until the feared event is only linked with relaxation.
6) This whole process is repeated for each stage of the fear hierarchy until they are **calm** through their **most feared** event.

Margaret was still anxious around beards, but she'd learnt to grin and bear it.

The Behavioural Model Has **Strengths** and **Weaknesses**

Strengths:

1) It's a **scientific** approach — it has clear **testable** concepts, which have been supported in many experiments.
2) Behavioural **therapies** can be very **effective** for treating phobias, eating disorders, obsessions and compulsions.

Weaknesses:

1) It cannot explain all behaviours because it neglects:
   a) The influence of **genetics** and **biology** — for example, how brain functioning affects behaviour.
   b) The influence of **cognitions** — how thought processes contribute to disorders (see pages 94-95).
2) Behavioural therapies are **not effective** for **all** disorders, e.g. conditioning doesn't cure schizophrenia.
3) The procedures sometimes raise **ethical** issues, e.g. aversion therapy may be quite distressing.
4) It only treats the behaviour, so it doesn't address any underlying causes for it.

Practice Questions

Q1 How might classical conditioning explain abnormal behaviour?

Q2 Give an example of how operant conditioning could explain behaviour.

Q3 What are taste aversions?

Q4 What is a token economy?

Q5 Outline one strength of the behavioural model of abnormality.

Exam Questions

Q1 Explain an assumption of the behavioural approach to abnormality and give a criticism of this approach. [6 marks]

Q2 Outline the process of systematic desensitisation. [4 marks]

So, you're scared of spiders — oooh, look what I have here...

Hmmm... you wouldn't be able to use the excuse of 'phobia of revision' if your teacher was a behaviourist. So I guess you'd better just get on with it just in case. Doing well in your exam will be a positive reinforcement — or something... Anyway, it's just the usual stuff — features of the approach, treatments, and the good old strengths and weaknesses.

The Cognitive Model of Abnormality

Guess what... Another model you've got to learn. And if all the models are a bit right, I guess that means they're all a bit wrong, which is rather annoying really... Still, at least it's the last one you've got to learn.

The Cognitive Model of Abnormality Concentrates on **Thoughts** and **Beliefs**

The cognitive model assumes that behaviours are controlled by thoughts and beliefs. So, irrational thoughts and beliefs cause abnormal behaviours. A few different versions of the model have been suggested:

Ellis (1962) — The '**ABC model**' claims that disorders begin with an **activating event (A)** (e.g. a failed exam), leading to a **belief (B)** about why this happened. This may be rational (e.g. 'I didn't prepare well enough'), or irrational (e.g. 'I'm too stupid to pass exams'). The belief leads to a **consequence (C)**. Rational beliefs produce adaptive (appropriate) consequences (e.g. more revision). Irrational beliefs produce maladaptive (bad and inappropriate) consequences (e.g. getting depressed).

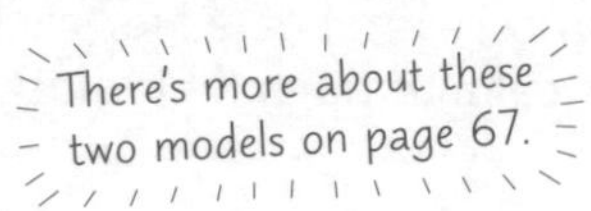
There's more about these two models on page 67.

Young Arthur grasped the ABC model at a very young age.

Beck (1963) — Beck identified a '**cognitive triad**' of negative, automatic thoughts linked to **depression**: negative views about **themselves** (e.g. that they can't succeed at anything), about the **world** (e.g. that they must be successful to be a good person) and about the **future** (e.g. that nothing will change).

Cognitive Therapies Try to Change **Faulty Cognitions**

Cognitive therapies assume that we can treat psychological disorders by **eliminating** or **changing** the original faulty thoughts and beliefs. They're used to treat a wide range of conditions, and can be particularly helpful with problems such as **depression** and **anxiety**. They've also been shown to be as effective as **medication** for some conditions.
This is generally what happens during cognitive behavioural therapy:

1) The therapist and client **identify** the client's faulty **cognitions** (thoughts and beliefs).
2) The therapist then tries to show that the cognitions aren't true, e.g. that the client doesn't always fail at what they do.
3) Together, they then set **goals** to think in more positive or adaptive ways, e.g. focusing on things the client has succeeded at and trying to build on them.
4) Although the client may occasionally need to look back to past experiences, the treatment mainly focuses on the **present situation**.
5) Therapists sometimes encourage their clients to keep a **diary** — they can record their thought patterns, feelings and actions.

Examples of cognitive therapies are **Hardiness Training** and Meichenbaum's **Stress Inoculation Training (SIT)**, which, as you can probably guess, was developed to reduce stress (see page 66).

The Cognitive Model of Abnormality

The Cognitive Model, Surprise Surprise, Has **Strengths** and **Weaknesses**

Strengths:

1) The cognitive model offers a **useful** approach to disorders like depression and anorexia. This is because it considers the role of **thoughts** and **beliefs**, which are greatly involved in problems like depression.
2) Cognitive therapies have often **successfully treated** depression, anxiety, stress and eating disorders.
3) It allows a person to **take control** and make a positive change to their behaviour.

Strengths — looks good in pink. Weaknesses — only has half a pair of trousers.

Weaknesses:

1) Faulty cognitions may simply be the **consequence** of a disorder rather than its cause. For example, depression may be caused by a chemical imbalance in the brain, which causes people to think very negatively.
2) Cognitive therapies may take a long **time** and be **costly**. They may be more effective when **combined** with other approaches, e.g. cognitive-behavioural methods.
3) The treatments work **better** with some conditions than others.
4) The person could begin to feel like he or she is to **blame** for their problems.

So, you're probably getting the point by now. All these different models and approaches are great in some ways, but are actually kinda dodgy in other ways. It makes it tricky to see which model best explains abnormality, or whether they're all partially right.

Practice Questions

Q1 Outline the ABC model of abnormality.

Q2 What three factors make up Beck's 'cognitive triad'?

Q3 What are the main features of cognitive therapy?

Q4 For which conditions are cognitive therapies particularly effective?

Q5 Give two examples of cognitive therapies.

Exam Questions

Q1 Outline the assumptions of the cognitive approach to the causes and treatment of abnormality. [6 marks]

Q2 Evaluate the strengths and weaknesses of the cognitive model of abnormality. [8 marks]

I think I'm mentally ill, therefore I am...

What's a bit confusing is that all these theories seem to make sense — you read them and think, 'So that's what it's all about. Get in. I must be well brainy.' The tricky thing is, they probably can't all be right... If I had to back one, I'd go with the cognitive people — I wouldn't want to mess with anyone who'd had 'hardiness training'. Those guys are built...

The Wonderful World of Psychology

I bet you'll find yourself applying psychological theories to everything. You can impress your friends by explaining what's happening in the news whilst they're just trying to watch. I'm sure they'll really appreciate it...

Social Psychology Could Explain the Abuse at Abu Ghraib

1) In 2004 reports came out that American soldiers had been **abusing** Iraqi detainees in **Abu Ghraib** prison.
2) The guards took **photos** of each other **posing** and **smiling** while they **tortured** prisoners.
3) The American government **condemned** the guards' behaviour, and some of them were given prison sentences.
4) However, it was revealed that soldiers had been **told** to **'take the gloves off'** when they interrogated prisoners. It seemed that they'd interpreted this as giving them **absolute power** to treat the prisoners however they wanted.

In **Zimbardo et al's (1973)** study (page 71) people were randomly assigned the role of prisoner or guard. After only a couple of days the guards started to act aggressively and cruelly, and the prisoners displayed 'learned helplessness'. These findings are mirrored in the real-life situation at Abu Ghraib. Like the American soldiers, Zimbardo's guards were given **absolute power** over the prisoners. They seem to have adapted their behaviour to fit into their social role. This was heightened by the fact that they wore uniforms, which **deindividuate** people, meaning that they feel less personal responsibility for their actions.

Reicher and Haslam (2006) (page 72) also did a prison experiment, but didn't explicitly tell the guards how much power they had over the prisoners. In their study the guards were much more reluctant to display their authority over the prisoners than in Zimbardo's. This suggests that the behaviour of the guards at Abu Ghraib can be explained by the fact that they felt they were **given authority** to treat the prisoners **however they wanted**.

1) **Sherif's (1935)** study of **informational influence** (page 71) showed that people will look to **each other** for **information** on how to behave in an **unfamiliar situation**. One of the **criticisms** of the American army was that some of the soldiers were **inexperienced**. It could be that the guards at Abu Ghraib were **following** each other because they were **unsure** about how to behave.
2) **Asch's (1956)** study of **normative influence** (page 70) showed that people will **conform** towards a **group norm** so they don't **stand out**, even when they think what the group's doing is **wrong**. They could have been going along with everyone else because they didn't want to seem **different**.

- These two types of **conformity** then lead to a situation where people feel even less **individual responsibility**, because they're just doing what everyone else is doing. This could be why the guards took **photos** of the abuse — in the environment they'd **created**, they began to think of it as **normal** and **acceptable**.
- On the other hand, all Sherif and Asch's participants had to do was give an opinion about a **spot of light** or the **length of a line**. It's difficult to see how that's the same as **torture**. This shows that there are still always **problems** with **generalising** the results of these experiments to **real life**.

Then There's the Whole Art Thing

Art hasn't escaped from the influence of psychology either — there's tons of **Freudian** stuff hiding in paintings.

Surrealists loved Freud's ideas. I reckon **Salvador Dali** is one of the biggies. Take any one of his paintings — they're packed full of ideas of the **unconsious mind** and **dreaming**. Every single object or idea in his paintings is a **symbol** for something else. For example, ants and grasshoppers stand for death and decay (nice...) whereas sex can equal cannibalism (also nice). This is just like Freud's ideas that the things in our **dreams** symbolise things going on in our **unconscious mind**.

Stuart's painting symbolised his tortured life during what felt like years of psychology revision.

So there you have it. Freud's ideas may have been wacky, but they've certainly **influenced** people.

Summary of the Exam

*Here's what you can expect to see in your **two AS Psychology** exams...*

*The Exam Papers Are **Broken Down** into Sections*

Unit 1 is broken down into just **two** sections, like this:

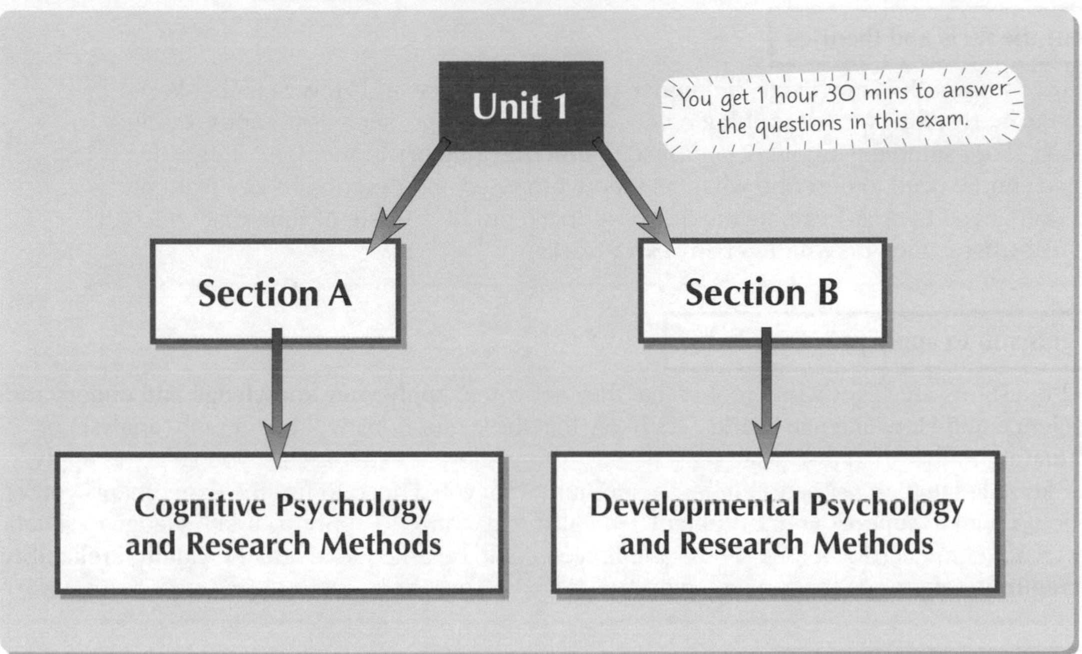

You get **mainly shortish answer questions**, but **one whopping 12 mark question**.
There are **72 marks** up for grabs in Unit 1.

Unit 2 has **three** wonderful sections:

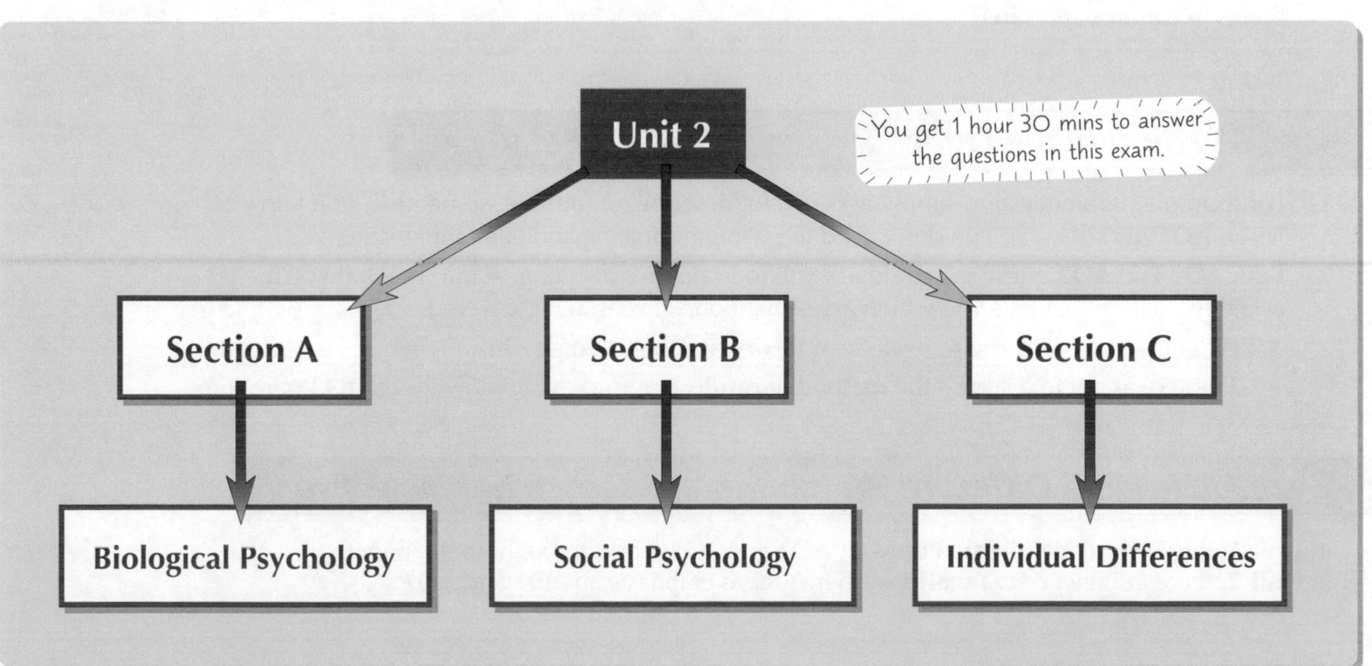

This unit also has **mainly shortish answer questions** — but there could be a **couple of 8 mark questions**.
There'll also be **one or more big 12 mark question**.

There are **72 marks** up for grabs in Unit 2.

Assessment Objectives

You can get loads of clues about your answers from the exam paper.

You Need to Meet Certain **Assessment Objectives**

There are three **assessment objectives** — **AO1**, **AO2** and **AO3**.

AO1 is about the facts and theories

These questions cover the **knowledge and understanding of science** and **How Science Works**. You get marks by **recalling** and **describing** psychological knowledge, such as theories, studies and methods. For example, you might get asked to **describe a theory** of memory. To get the marks, you'd simply need to describe what the theory proposed and describe its key features. What you don't need to do is evaluate the theory — that'd just be a **waste of time** that you could use elsewhere, and you **won't get any extra marks**.

AO2 gets you to apply your knowledge

AO2 questions are slightly different in that they get you to **apply your knowledge and understanding of science** and **How Science Works**. It's likely that these questions will begin with '**analyse**' or '**evaluate**'. Rather than just recalling stuff, e.g. listing relevant experiments, you've got to **apply your knowledge** to the situation in these questions. So, you'd need to use the experiments you've come up with to **support your argument**. You also might have to apply your knowledge to situations you've not come across before. For example, you could be asked to assess the **validity**, **reliability** or **credibility** of a study that's new to you.

AO3 is about 'How Science Works'

'**How Science Works**' focuses on how scientific experiments are carried out. You need to be able to suggest a suitable **experimental design** and know how to make sure measurements and observations are **accurate** and **precise**. You could also be asked to **analyse** and **evaluate** the **methodology** and **results** of a study described in the exam. When you're doing this, don't forget about things like **ethics** and **safety**.

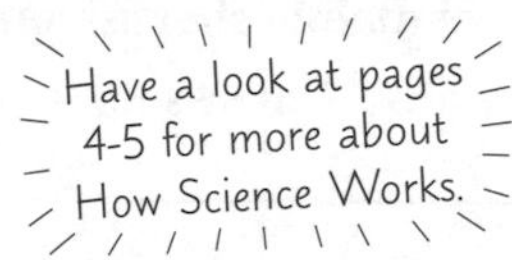

The **Wording** of the Question Can Tell You What to Do

1) For example, if the question simply asks you to '**describe**' or '**outline**' something, you know it's an **AO1** question. So you don't need to go into evaluating and explaining stuff.
2) Both **AO2** and **AO3** questions could ask you to **evaluate** something — but it's **what** you're asked to analyse that tells you which assessment objective is being covered:
   - If the question asks you to evaluate a **theory**, it's an **AO2** question.
   - If you're asked to evaluate the **method** or **results** of a study, you know it's an **AO3** question.

Each Unit Has a **Different Weighting** of Assessment Objectives

In **Unit 1**, there's an **equal division** of AO1, AO2 and AO3 marks throughout the paper.
In **Unit 2**, there are **fewer AO3 marks** — there's more emphasis on AO1 and AO2.

		Assessment Objective		
		AO1	AO2	AO3
Weighting (%)	Unit 1	16.7	16.7	16.7
	Unit 2	20.8	20.8	8.3

What You Need to Write

The Number of Marks Tells You How Much to Write...

1) The number of marks that a question is worth gives you a pretty good clue of **how much to write**.
2) You get **one mark per correct point** made, so if a question is worth four marks, make sure you write four decent points.
3) There's no point writing a massive answer for a question that's only worth a few marks — it's just a **waste of your time**.
4) For the longer essay-style questions, make sure that you've written **enough** to cover the 12 marks, but don't just waffle.

Martha suddenly realised that the question was worth 8 marks, not 88.

...But You Can't Just Write About Anything

1) It's important to remember that it's not just a case of blindly scribbling down **everything** you can think of that's related to the subject. Doing this just **wastes time**, and it doesn't exactly impress the examiner.
2) You only get marks for stuff that's **relevant** and **answers the question**.
3) So, make sure you read over the question a couple of times before you start writing so that you really understand what it's asking.

An Example Answer to Show You What to Aim for...

This is the sort of answer that would get you full marks.

The model has three features, and the question's worth 6 marks. So, you'd just need to write enough about each feature to get you two marks. The answer might look short, but it's all you'd need to write.

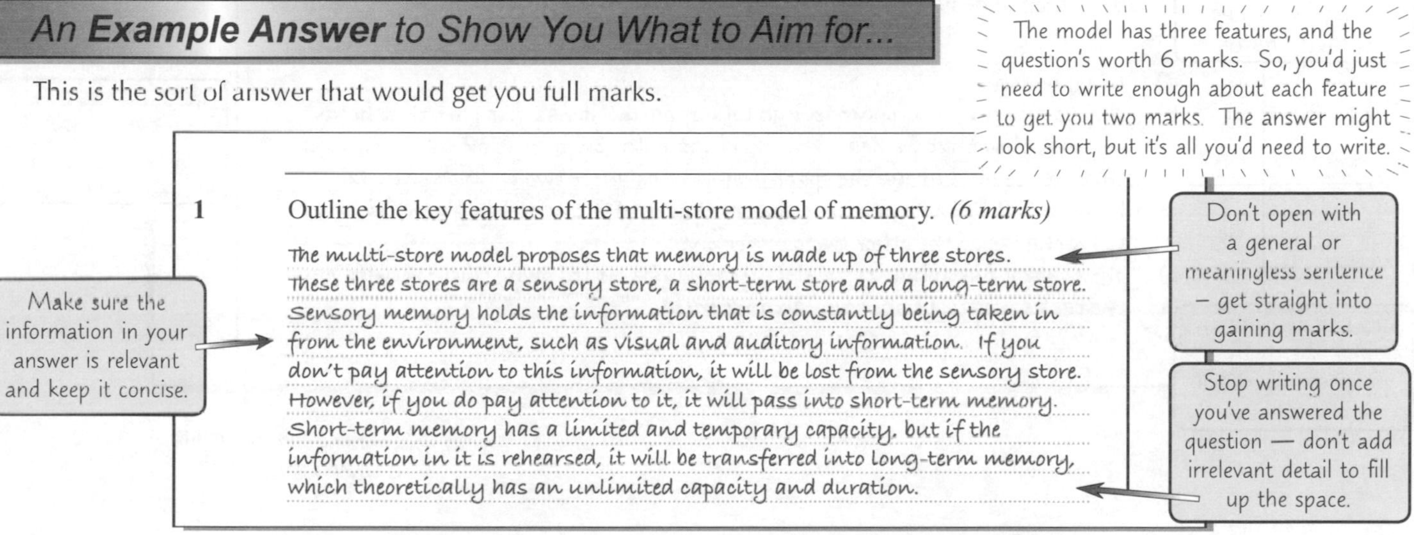

1 Outline the key features of the multi-store model of memory. *(6 marks)*

The multi-store model proposes that memory is made up of three stores. These three stores are a sensory store, a short-term store and a long-term store. Sensory memory holds the information that is constantly being taken in from the environment, such as visual and auditory information. If you don't pay attention to this information, it will be lost from the sensory store. However, if you do pay attention to it, it will pass into short-term memory. Short-term memory has a limited and temporary capacity, but if the information in it is rehearsed, it will be transferred into long-term memory, which theoretically has an unlimited capacity and duration.

Make sure the information in your answer is relevant and keep it concise.

Don't open with a general or meaningless sentence — get straight into gaining marks.

Stop writing once you've answered the question — don't add irrelevant detail to fill up the space.

...And an Alternate Answer to Show You What Not to Write...

I repeat... What **NOT** to write...

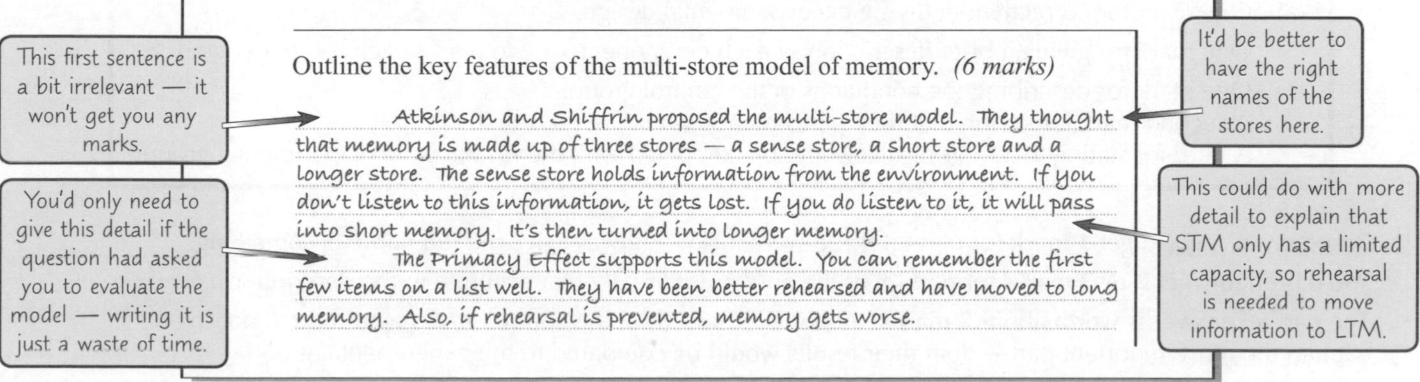

Outline the key features of the multi-store model of memory. *(6 marks)*

Atkinson and Shiffrin proposed the multi-store model. They thought that memory is made up of three stores — a sense store, a short store and a longer store. The sense store holds information from the environment. If you don't listen to this information, it gets lost. If you do listen to it, it will pass into short memory. It's then turned into longer memory.

The Primacy Effect supports this model. You can remember the first few items on a list well. They have been better rehearsed and have moved to long memory. Also, if rehearsal is prevented, memory gets worse.

This first sentence is a bit irrelevant — it won't get you any marks.

You'd only need to give this detail if the question had asked you to evaluate the model — writing it is just a waste of time.

It'd be better to have the right names of the stores here.

This could do with more detail to explain that STM only has a limited capacity, so rehearsal is needed to move information to LTM.

The second answer lacks the **detail** of the first — it only sketches over the features of the model. It wouldn't earn all the possible marks. Also, there's quite a bit of **irrelevant information** that wouldn't get you any marks.

Worked Exam

Over the next 8 pages we've given you examples of exam questions and answers. For each question, there's a C grade and an A grade answer — look carefully to see what makes the difference between the two grades.

*This is a Typical **C Grade** Answer*

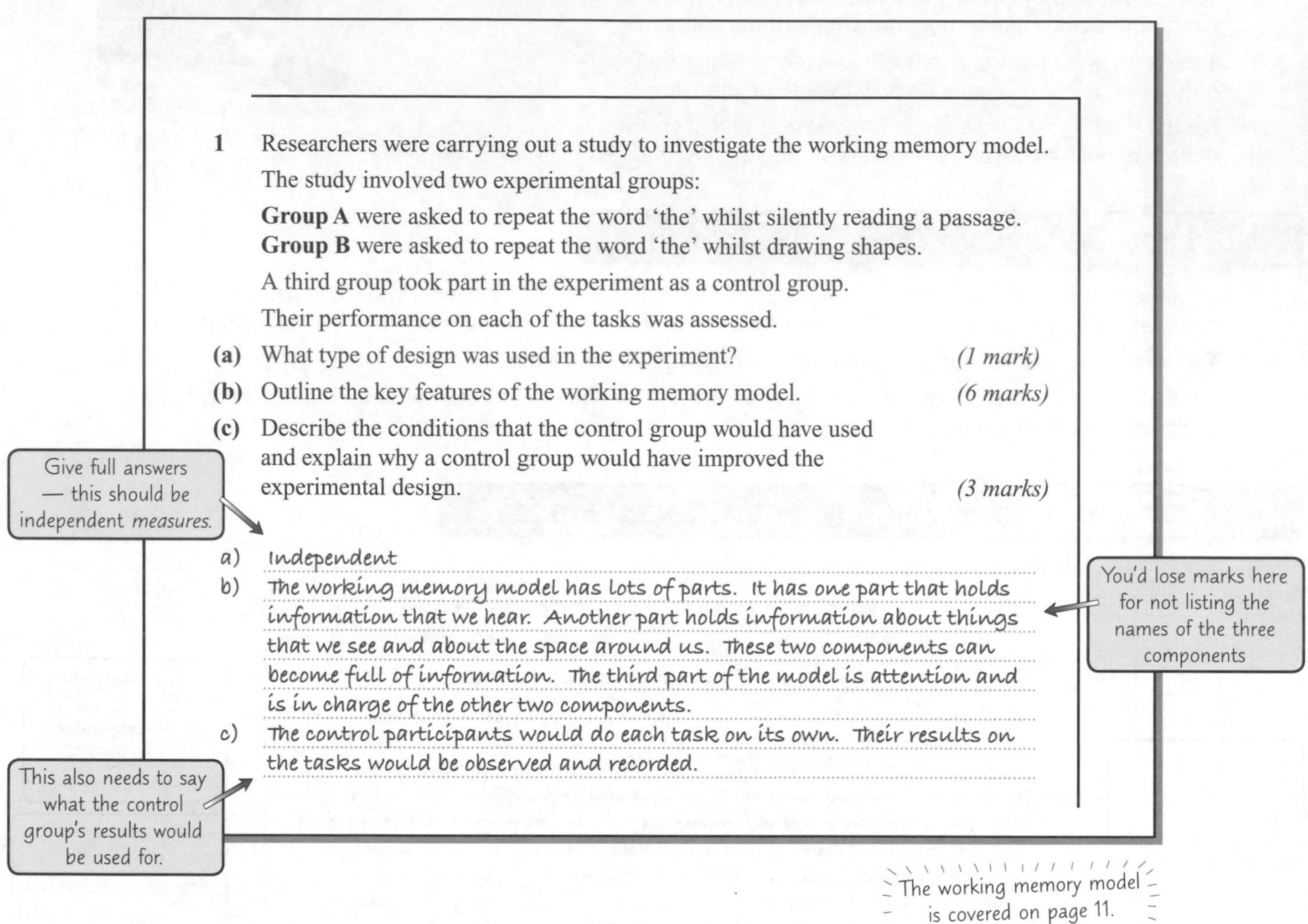

1 Researchers were carrying out a study to investigate the working memory model.

The study involved two experimental groups:

Group A were asked to repeat the word 'the' whilst silently reading a passage.
Group B were asked to repeat the word 'the' whilst drawing shapes.

A third group took part in the experiment as a control group.

Their performance on each of the tasks was assessed.

(a) What type of design was used in the experiment? *(1 mark)*

(b) Outline the key features of the working memory model. *(6 marks)*

(c) Describe the conditions that the control group would have used and explain why a control group would have improved the experimental design. *(3 marks)*

a) Independent

b) The working memory model has lots of parts. It has one part that holds information that we hear. Another part holds information about things that we see and about the space around us. These two components can become full of information. The third part of the model is attention and is in charge of the other two components.

c) The control participants would do each task on its own. Their results on the tasks would be observed and recorded.

Give full answers — this should be independent *measures*.

You'd lose marks here for not listing the names of the three components

This also needs to say what the control group's results would be used for.

The working memory model is covered on page 11.

*The **Mark Scheme** Would Be Something Like This:*

Your answers to the questions above would be marked with these points in mind:

(a) One mark for correctly identifying the experimental design.
(b) One mark for giving a brief description of each component, or two marks each for more detail.
(c) One mark for describing the conditions of the control group.
A second mark for saying that their performance would be recorded.
A third for stating that their results would be compared with the results of the experimental group.

Based on this, you'd get **1 mark** for part (a) if you were lucky — always give the full name of something.

You'd probably get **2 or 3 marks** for part (b) as the answer isn't really that accurate in the descriptions.

The part (c) answer is worth about **2 marks**. Although it says what the control group would do, it doesn't explain the most important part — that their results would be compared to the experimental group.

Worked Exam

This is a Typical **A Grade** Answer

1 Researchers were carrying out a study to investigate the working memory model.
The study involved two experimental groups:
Group A were asked to repeat the word 'the' whilst silently reading a passage.
Group B were asked to repeat the word 'the' whilst drawing shapes.
A third group took part in the experiment as a control group.
Their performance on each of the tasks was assessed.

(a) What type of design was used in the experiment? *(1 mark)*

(b) Outline the key features of the working memory model. *(6 marks)*

(c) Describe the conditions that the control group would have used and explain why a control group would have improved the experimental design. *(3 marks)*

a) The experiment used an independent measures design.

b) The working memory model was developed by Baddeley and Hitch and consists of three stores — the articulatory-phonological loop, the central executive and the visuo-spatial sketchpad. The articulatory-phonological loop holds speech-based information, and contains a phonological store (the inner ear) and an articulatory process (the inner voice). The visuo-spatial sketchpad temporarily holds visual and spatial information. These two components are slave systems and have limited capacity. They are controlled by the central executive. The central executive is the key component of the model and can be described as 'attention'.

c) Participants in the control group would perform each task without verbal interference. Their performance on each of the tasks would be recorded and used as a baseline. The performances of the experimental groups could then be compared to this.

A good, full response that answers the question.

You don't need to say who developed the model — this is just showing off.

Make sure you've answered both parts of the question.

Make a **Plan** Before You Start Your Answer

1) Examiners will stick to their mark scheme pretty strictly. So they won't give you extra marks for writing loads if it doesn't answer the question — to them it's just pointless and **irrelevent information**.

2) Also, when you're writing your answers, try to **structure** them in an **organised** way. If there's one thing that examiners find worse than a load of pointless information, it's being unable to make head nor tail of an answer — it just makes it really difficult for them to mark.

3) Before you start, it's worth jotting down a quick **plan** of what you want to write so that you don't just end up with a really jumbled answer.

For example, if a question asks you to outline and evaluate a study, your plan might look something like this:

1. Brief description of the method, results, conclusion
2. Strengths of the study design
3. Weaknesses of the study design

Worked Exam

Here's a second example. Notice how the research methods are mixed in with a developmental question. Quite sneaky. But I guess it's better than being faced with one massive research methods question.

*This is a Typical **C Grade** Answer*

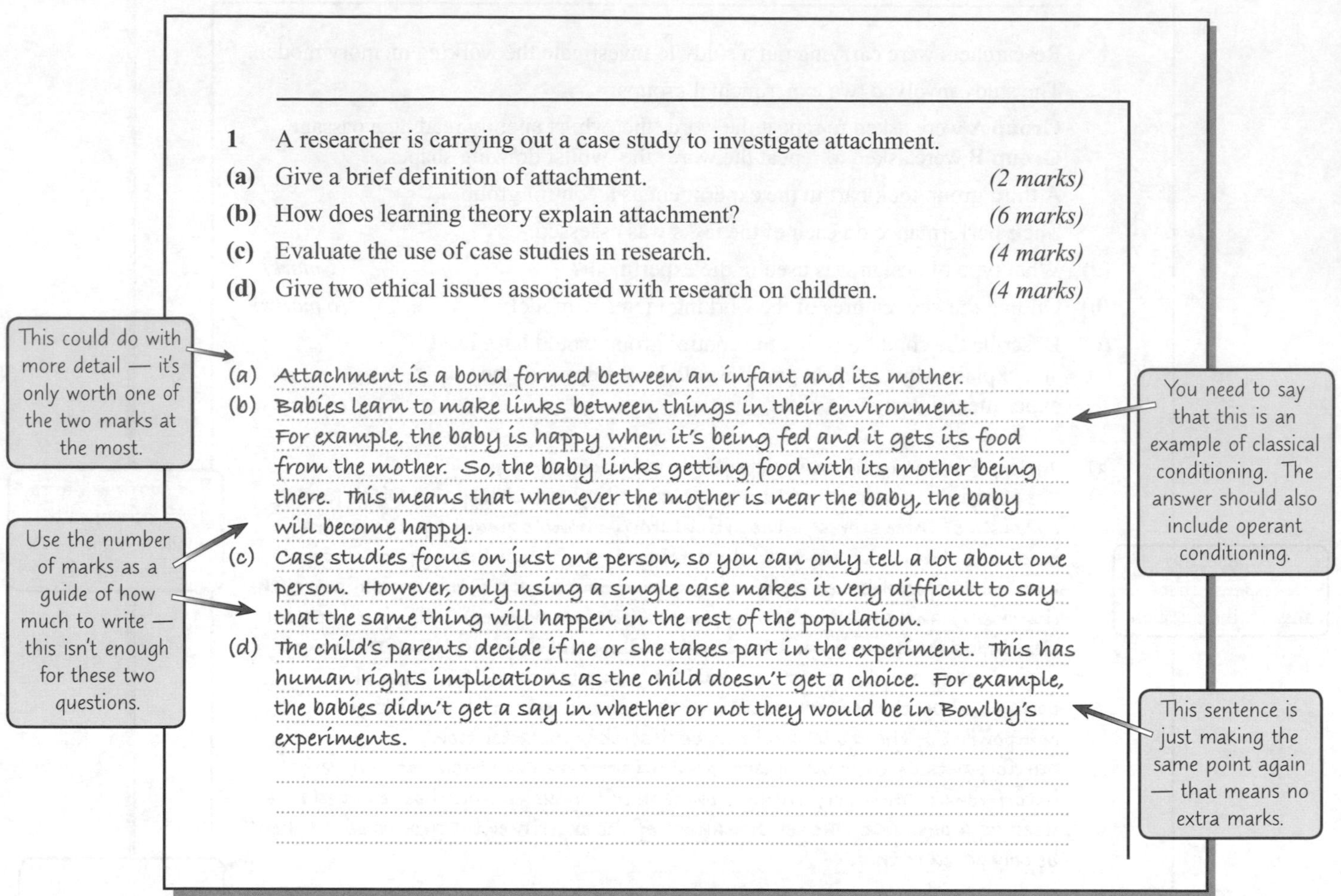
1 A researcher is carrying out a case study to investigate attachment.

(a) Give a brief definition of attachment. *(2 marks)*

(b) How does learning theory explain attachment? *(6 marks)*

(c) Evaluate the use of case studies in research. *(4 marks)*

(d) Give two ethical issues associated with research on children. *(4 marks)*

(a) Attachment is a bond formed between an infant and its mother.

(b) Babies learn to make links between things in their environment. For example, the baby is happy when it's being fed and it gets its food from the mother. So, the baby links getting food with its mother being there. This means that whenever the mother is near the baby, the baby will become happy.

(c) Case studies focus on just one person, so you can only tell a lot about one person. However, only using a single case makes it very difficult to say that the same thing will happen in the rest of the population.

(d) The child's parents decide if he or she takes part in the experiment. This has human rights implications as the child doesn't get a choice. For example, the babies didn't get a say in whether or not they would be in Bowlby's experiments.

*The **Mark Scheme** Would be Something Like This:*

Your answers to the questions above would be marked with these points in mind:

(a) One mark for a basic description of attachment.
Or, two marks for giving a detailed description of attachment.

(b) Three marks for a description of classical conditioning.
Another three marks would come from a description of operant conditioning.

(c) Up to two marks for a strength of the use of case studies.
Up to two more marks for a weakness of the use of case studies.

(d) Two ethical issues are needed here.
Up to two marks for each, depending on the detail and accuracy of the description.

Based on this, you'd probably get **1 mark** for part (a) as it's only a really basic description.

Part (b) would only be worth **2 marks**. You need to describe classical and operant conditioning in terms of attachment. However, this answer doesn't mention either of these, and only roughly describes classical conditioning.

You'd also get **2 marks** for part (c). The answer gives a strength and a weakness, but they're not very detailed.

Part (d) is worth **2 marks**. It only gives one ethical issue to do with research on children.

Worked Exam

This is a Typical *A Grade* Answer

1 A researcher is carrying out a case study to investigate attachment.

(a) Give a brief definition of attachment. *(2 marks)*

(b) How does learning theory explain attachment? *(6 marks)*

(c) Evaluate the use of case studies in research. *(4 marks)*

(d) Give two ethical issues associated with research on children. *(4 marks)*

(a) Attachment is a close emotional bond formed between infants and their caregivers. Attached infants show a desire to be close to their primary caregiver and will show distress when separated.

(b) Learning theory uses conditioning to explain attachment. In classical conditioning, the baby learns associations between things in its environment. For example, being fed gives the baby pleasure and the baby's desire for food is fulfilled when its mother is there. In this way, an association is formed between the mother and food. Whenever the mother is close, the baby will feel pleasure.

In operant conditioning, the baby's behaviour is reinforced. The baby will feel discomfort when it is hungry. It discovers that if it cries, its mother will come and provide food, removing the discomfort. This is negative reinforcement. The mother becomes associated with food and the baby will desire to be close to her.

(c) As case studies focus on just one person, researchers have the opportunity to study phenomena in great detail and collect a large amount of data. However, only using a single case makes it very difficult to generalise the results to the population. The results of the study might only apply to that one individual.

(d) Firstly, until they are 18 years old, someone's participation in a study is up to their parents. Even if the child doesn't understand the implications of participating in the study, their parents can give informed consent for them. This has human rights implications.

Secondly, children generally view adults as being more powerful than themselves. This may mean that the child is less inclined to use their right to withdraw from an experiment.

This is a good, full answer that would get both of the marks.

Use clear explanations of the two types of conditioning.

Use psychology terms, e.g. conditioning and reinforcement, where possible.

For 4 marks, fully describe one strength and one weakness.

These are well structured ethical arguments.

Take a look at pages 18 and 19 for the research methods and ethics bits. Page 20 covers attachment and the learning approach.

You Need to be Able to *Apply* Your Knowledge

1) For example, part (b) asks how learning theory can explain attachment.
2) It's no good just explaining what **learning theory** is — you won't get very many marks.
3) You need to talk about learning, associations and reinforcers in relation to a **child** and its **caregiver**.

Tasha really wanted to answer her exam but it hadn't started ringing yet.

Worked Exam

Not all of the exam questions will be made up of three or four parts. Some of them will just be single essay-type questions worth 12 marks. Because we're so nice to you, here are some examples of answers to these.

*An Example of a **C Grade Answer** to a 12 Mark Essay Question*

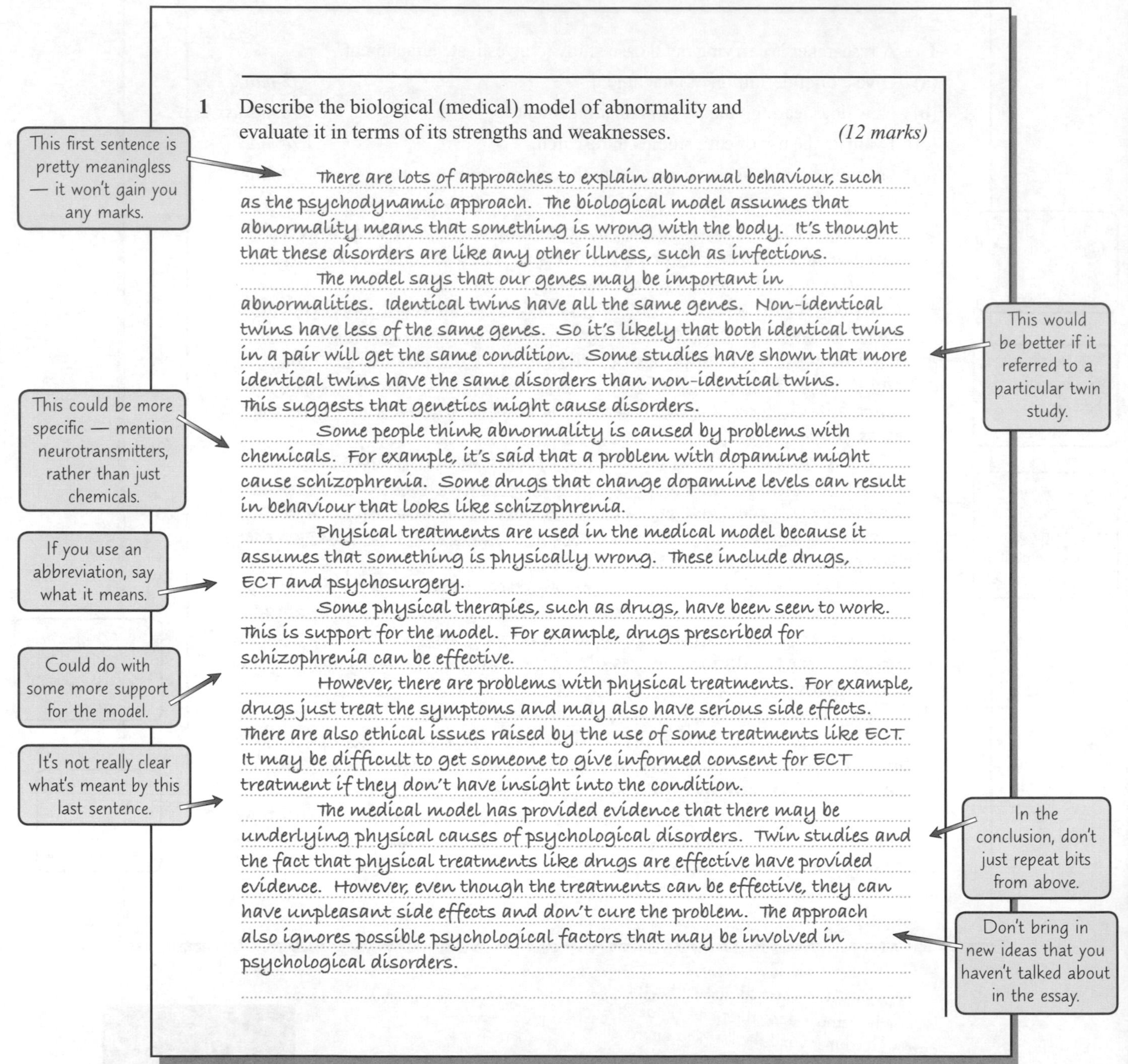

*This Type of Question Has Both **AO1** and **AO2** Marks*

1) You'll get **AO1** marks for giving a **description** of the theory (or study, if that's what the question is about).
2) **AO2** marks come from your **evaluation** of the theory. Don't forget that an evaluation needs both strengths and weaknesses — you need to show in your answer that you can weigh them up.
3) Examiners are looking for **detailed** and **accurate** answers, that are written in a **coherent** and **concise** way.

Worked Exam

An Example of an **A Grade Answer** to a 12 Mark Essay Question

1 Describe the biological (medical) model of abnormality and evaluate it in terms of its strengths and weaknesses. *(12 marks)*

Don't open with a general or meaningless sentence – get straight into gaining marks.

The biological model of abnormality assumes that there is an underlying physiological cause of psychological disorders. Such disorders are considered as illnesses in the same way as the body can be affected by illnesses.

The model includes the idea that genetic factors may be important in psychological disorders. As identical twins are 100% genetically identical and fraternal twins don't share all of their genes, identical twins might be more similar if a condition is inherited. Gottesman (1991) conducted a meta-analysis of twin studies, and found that people had a 48% chance of developing schizophrenia if their identical twin had the condition. This reduced to 17% with non-identical twins. This suggests that schizophrenia could have a genetic basis.

Interpret findings using sentences beginning with 'This suggests that...' etc.

Another explanation of abnormality is that it is caused by biochemical imbalance. For example, the dopamine hypothesis suggests that excess dopamine may cause schizophrenia. Evidence for this includes the effects of drugs such as amphetamines, which increase dopamine levels and can result in behaviour similar to schizophrenia. However, an alternative explanation is that people with schizophrenia are more sensitive to dopamine, rather than they have more of the chemical.

Most AO2 marks will be awarded for your evaluation of strengths and weaknesses – so don't spend too long describing the model.

AO2 marks for discussing alternative explanations of findings.

Because the medical model assumes there is a physical cause of abnormality, it uses physical treatments. These include drug therapy, electro-convulsive therapy (which is sometimes used in very severe depression) and psychosurgery such as prefrontal lobotomies.

One strength is that there is evidence supporting the view that there are physical causes underlying some psychological disorders. Physical therapies, such as drugs, have proved effective in treating psychological conditions. Antipsychotic drugs prescribed for schizophrenia are often effective in reducing positive symptoms such as hallucinations and delusions. In some cases, these treatments have enabled people to lead more independent lives. The effectiveness of drugs supports the idea that there are physical causes of psychological conditions.

Provide relevant evidence to support the statement.

Write a balanced essay by discussing both strengths and weaknesses.

However, there are problems associated with physical treatments. For example, drugs treat symptoms rather than the cause and so do not cure psychological disorders. They may also have serious side effects. Another weakness of the medical model is that there are ethical issues raised by the use of treatments like ECT. It may be difficult to gain informed consent for treatment from someone with a psychological problem, especially if they don't have insight into the condition.

In conclusion, the medical model has provided evidence that there may be underlying physical causes of psychological disorders. The treatments derived from the approach are often effective, but can have unpleasant side effects and don't provide a cure. However, despite its weaknesess, the strengths of the model have maintained its popularity.

Don't repeat stuff in the essay, but do put in a conclusion for full marks.

The biological model is on pages 88 and 89.

Worked Exam

And one more for luck...

An Example of a **C Grade Answer** to a 12 Mark Essay Question

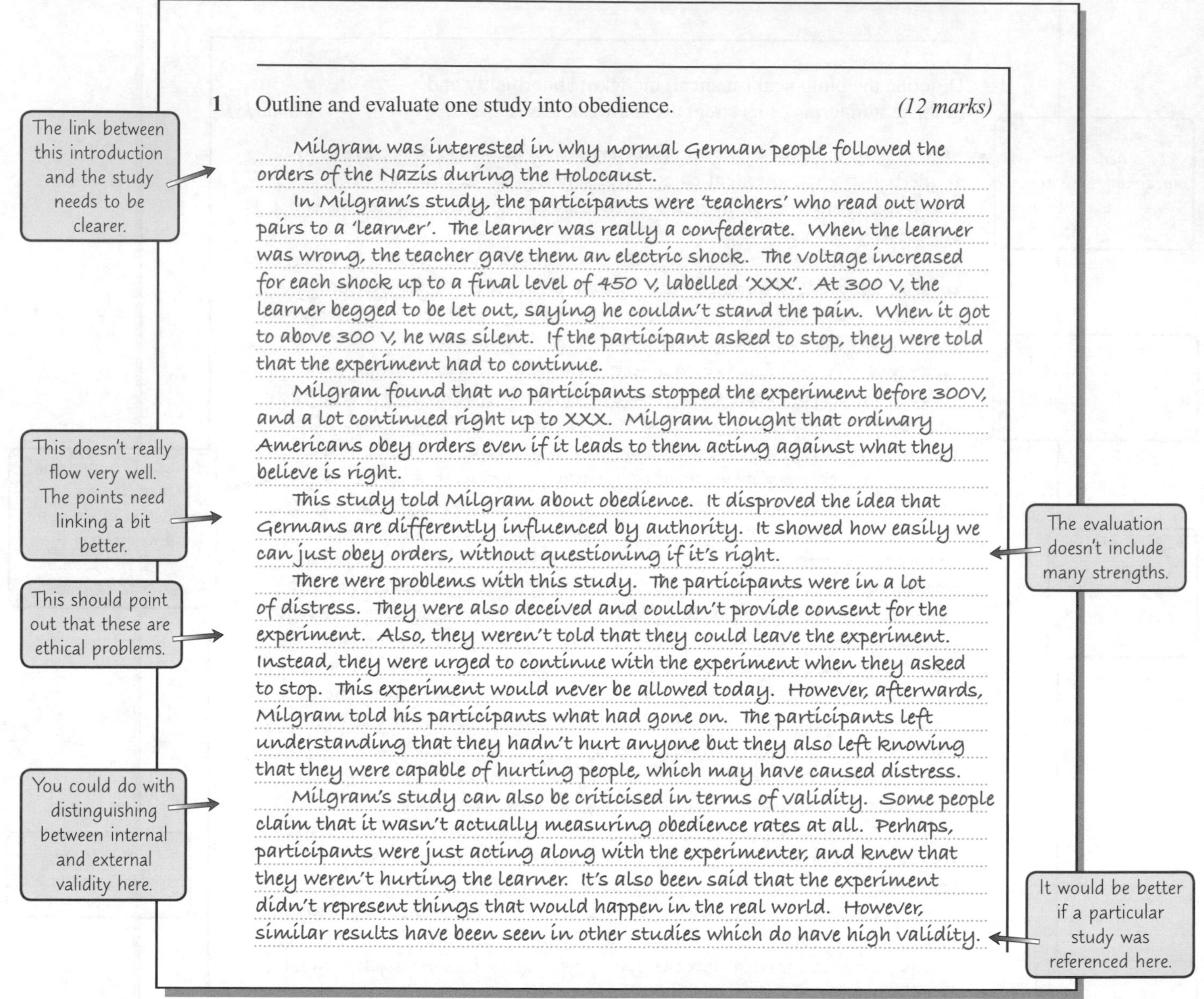

You Get Marks for **Quality of Written Communication** (QWC)

In some of these questions, you get marks for QWC. It assesses things like:

1) whether your scribble, sorry, writing is **legible.**
2) whether your **spelling**, **punctuation** and **grammar** are accurate.
3) whether your **writing style** is appropriate.
4) whether you **organise** your answer clearly and coherently.
5) whether you use **specialist psychology vocabulary** where it's appropriate.

On the front of the paper, you'll be told which of the questions this is being assessed in.
However, **stop** right there. This doesn't mean that you don't need to think about it in all the other questions though.
If your writing is easy to read and your answers make sense it makes the examiner's job much easier.

Worked Exam

An Example of an **A Grade Answer** to a 12 Mark Essay Question

All this Milgram stuff is on pages 76-79.

1 Outline and evaluate one study into obedience. *(12 marks)*

Milgram was interested in why normal German people followed the orders of the Nazis, leading to their treatment of the Jews. He was interested in whether normal Americans would also blindly follow instructions from authority, even if it led to them hurting other people.

Milgram set up a study where participants believed they were taking part in a learning experiment. Each participant was a 'teacher' who read out word pairs to a 'learner' (who was actually a confederate). Every time the learner gave an incorrect response, the participant had to give them an electric shock. With each shock, the voltage was increased up to a final level of 450 V, labelled 'XXX'. At 300 V, the learner pleaded to be let out, saying he couldn't stand the pain. Above 300 V, he was silent. If the participant asked to stop, they were told that the experiment had to continue.

Milgram found that no participants stopped the experiment before 300 V, and 65% actually continued as far as 450 V. Milgram concluded that ordinary Americans obey orders even if it leads to them acting against their conscience and hurting others.

This was a very influential study, which provided great insights into human behaviour. It disproved the 'Germans are different' hypothesis, and led to increased awareness of how easily we can just blindly obey orders, without questioning whether we morally should. However, there are a number of criticisms, including ethical issues and issues of validity.

The participants in Milgram's study suffered a lot of psychological distress. They were also deceived as to the nature of the experiment, which meant they couldn't provide informed consent. Additionally, they were not informed of their right to withdraw, which is now common practice in psychology experiments. Instead, they were urged to continue with the experiment when they asked to stop. This experiment was therefore very ethically questionable, and would never be allowed today. However, Milgram extensively debriefed his participants, including reuniting them with the learner. The participants therefore left understanding that they hadn't hurt anyone. They did, however, leave in the knowledge that they were capable of hurting people, which may have caused them distress.

Milgram's study can also be criticised in terms of external and internal validity. Some people claim that it lacks internal validity — that it wasn't actually measuring obedience rates at all. Perhaps instead, participants were just acting along with the experimenter, not actually believing they were hurting the learner (showing demand characteristics). The experiment has also been criticised in terms of external validity — that it doesn't represent traits that would happen in the real world, with different people, and different situations. However, similar obedience rates have since been shown in other studies (e.g. Hofling et al), which do have high external validity.

Don't get carried away describing all the details — you just need the aim, method and conclusion.

Make sure the study you choose is the one you can describe and evaluate best — not just your favourite.

Don't worry if you can't remember exact figures — just make sure you know the general findings and what they mean.

Evaluations need to include positive points too — not only problems.

Explain what you mean when you use terms like 'external validity' etc.

Make sure you know the different types of validity — you'll probably need to mention them in any evaluation.

Referencing other studies shows that you have a broad knowledge of the subject.

1) You'll have gathered that to get the higher grades, your answer needs to show **detailed** and **accurate** knowledge.
2) Basically, you need to show the examiner that you **understand** stuff really well.
3) Picking out studies and theories to **support** your answers is great — but keep it all **relevant** to the question.

A2-Level
Psychology

Exam Board: AQA A

Introduction to A2 Psychology

These pages are here to give you a quick intro to A2 Psychology — recapping some stuff that you did at AS and giving you a brief overview of what exciting topics A2 has got in store for you. Are you sitting comfortably? Then let's begin...

A2 Psychology is Made Up of Two Units

A2 Psychology is made up of two units — imaginatively named **Unit 3** and **Unit 4**.

Unit 3

Unit 3 contains eight topics — **Biological Rhythms and Sleep**, **Perception**, **Gender**, **Relationships**, **Aggression**, **Eating Behaviour**, **Intelligence and Learning**, and **Cognition and Development**. The good news is you only have to answer questions on **three** of these topics and you get to choose which ones you do.

Unit 4

Unit 4 covers **Psychopathology** (where you'll have to choose **one** disorder to study out of **three**) and **Psychology in Action** (where you'll study one application of psychology from a choice of three). There's also a visit to the old favourite, **Research Methods**.

You learnt about the different **approaches** that are used to study psychology during AS level. You'll need these again for A2, so here's a quick recap:

The Cognitive Approach Focuses on Internal Processes

1) Cognitive psychologists focus on **internal processes** to understand behaviour — for example, how we perceive or remember things.
2) They compare the human mind to an advanced **computer** system, so they use **computer models** to try to understand human cognition (thinking).
3) Using concepts from information processing, cognitive psychologists describe the brain as a **processor** — it receives **input**, **processes** it, and produces an **output**. Obviously it's a bit more complicated than that, but the general idea is the same.
4) Cognitive psychology studies are often laboratory-based and **artificial**, so they can lack **validity** in the **real world** (**ecological validity**).

If brains are like computers, Sarah's crashed the day she packed for her holiday.

Developmental Psychology is About How Humans Develop... Obviously...

You covered **developmental psychology** at AS level and it's back again for A2. Bet you're pleased about that.

Developmental psychology is a bit of a jumble of ideas from different approaches. It deals with how people **develop** and **change** over their lifetime. It also involves looking at how children are **qualitatively different** to adults in their understanding, abilities and feelings.

Chloe had just seen that solid food was next on her timetable and she couldn't wait.

Researchers like **Piaget** and **Samuel and Bryant** looked at children's **cognitive** development. They studied the way children approach problems depending on their age and the stage of development they've reached.

They found that the brain appears to have a **timetable** of **what** we can do and **when** we can do it — e.g. children don't start speaking or progress with potty training until they reach a certain stage of development.

Introduction to A2 Psychology

The Biological Approach Explains Behaviour as a Product of Nature

The biological approach involves three **key assumptions**:

Human behaviour can be explained by looking at internal, biological stuff, like hormones and the nervous system.

Experimental research that uses **animals** can be generalised to **human behaviour**.

Abnormal behaviour can be removed using **biological treatments** — e.g. medication for mental illnesses such as schizophrenia.

So, as far as this approach is concerned, it's what's inside that counts...

1) Researchers look at **genetics**, **hormones**, the **brain**, and the **nervous system** to explain behaviour.
2) It's very scientific — research is mostly carried out in **laboratory experiments**.
3) Common research techniques include **animal studies**, **brain scans** and **correlational studies**.

Individual Differences is About Differences Between... erm... Individuals

You've met **individual differences** before as well. It's another one that's made up of bits from loads of approaches. The main thing that researchers want to find out is **how** and **why** we're all **different** from each other. You might think it's pretty obvious that we're all different, but psychologists have got to find something to fill the day.

1) Other areas of psychology tend to assume that people are broadly the **same** — e.g. developmental psychologists assume that we all go through the same basic stages of development.
2) However, this usually isn't the case. Not everyone hits the stages of development at the same **age**, and we all differ to some extent in our **psychological characteristics** — for example, our levels of motivation, aggression and intelligence, etc.
3) So, the individual differences approach looks at what **causes** these differences.

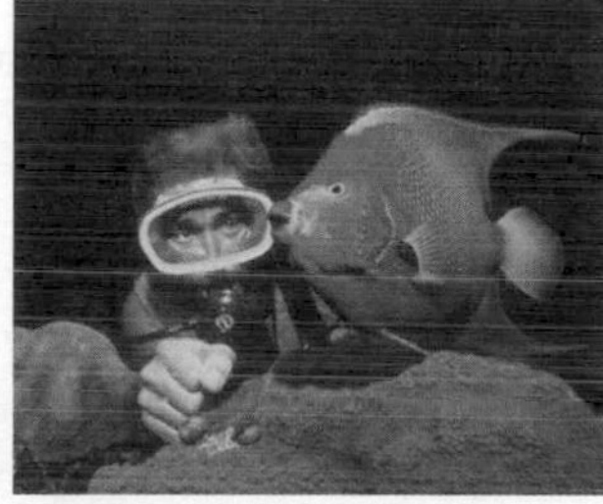

For example, Brian and his friend Flippy differ from each other in a few ways.

Social Psychologists Look at How We Interact with Each Other

Last one, hurrah. Social psychology isn't new to you either — you covered it for AS.

1) This approach is all about how we **influence** each other's thoughts, feelings and behaviour — either as **individuals** or as **groups**.
2) Major areas of research include **conformity** and **obedience**.

Probably the most famous experiment in social psychology is **Milgram's Behavioural Study of Obedience** (1963). In the experiment he tested people's obedience by asking participants to give someone electric shocks if they made mistakes in a learning task. Most of his participants carried on giving the shocks, even when they thought they were causing harm. He concluded that most people will follow orders even if it means doing something they don't think is right. Pretty scary stuff.

3) Other areas of research include **persuasion**, **attitudes** and **relationships**.
4) Common research methods include **correlational studies**, **observational studies** and **experimental methods**. If you don't remember what these are don't stress — there's a whole section on research methods starting on page 218.

And that's all there is to A2 Psychology...

OK, that's a lie. Clearly there's a lot more to A2 psychology than just these two pages. There's the whole rest of this book. And there's nothing for it than to make your way through it one page at a time. But don't fret — if you look after the pages then the sections will look after themselves (as the saying almost never goes) and very soon you'll be ready for the exam.

The Scientific Process

You've already met the stuff on this page at AS. It's the nuts and bolts of science though — and that's pretty important stuff. So, if you're not sure how we develop and test scientific theories then read on...

Science Answers Real-life Questions

Science tries to explain **how** and **why** things happen — it **answers questions**. It's all about seeking and gaining **knowledge** about the world around us. Scientists do this by **asking** questions and **suggesting** answers and then **testing** them, to see if they're correct — this is the **scientific process.**

1) **Ask** a question — make an **observation** and ask **why or how** it happens.
2) **Suggest** an answer, or part of an answer, by forming a **theory** (a possible explanation of the observations).
3) Make a **prediction** or **hypothesis** — a **specific testable statement**, based on the theory, about what will happen in a test situation.
4) Carry out a **test** — to provide **evidence** that will support the prediction (or help to disprove it).

What happens if you spend too long on your own? Send your hypotheses on a postcard please.

Suggesting explanations is all very well and good, but if there's **no way to test** them then it just ain't science. A theory is **only scientific** if it can be tested.

Science is All About Testing Theories

It starts off with one experiment backing up a prediction and theory. It ends up with all the scientists in the world **agreeing** with it and you **learning** it. Stirring stuff. This is how the magical process takes place:

1) The results are **published** — scientists need to let others know about their work, so they try to get their results published in **scientific journals**. These are just like normal magazines, only they contain **scientific reports** (called papers) instead of celebrity gossip. All work must undergo **peer review** before it's published.

- **Peer review** is a process used to **ensure the integrity** of published scientific work. Before publication, scientific work is sent to **experts** in that field (**peers**) so they can assess the **quality** of the work.
- This process helps to keep scientists **honest** — e.g. you can't '**sex-up**' your conclusions if the data doesn't support it, because it **won't pass** peer review.
- Peer review helps to **validate conclusions** — it means published theories, data and conclusions are more trustworthy. But it **can't guarantee** that the conclusions are 100% right. More **rounds** of predicting and testing are needed before they can be taken as '**fact**'.
- Sometimes **mistakes** are made and bad science is published. Peer review **isn't perfect** but it's probably the best way for scientists to **self-regulate** their work and to ensure **reliable** scientific work is **published**.

2) Other scientists read the published theories and results, and try to **repeat them** — this involves repeating the **exact experiments**, and using the theory to make **new predictions** that are tested by **new experiments**.
3) If all the experiments in all the world provide evidence to back it up, the theory is thought of as scientific 'fact' (**for now**).
4) If **new evidence** comes to light that **conflicts** with the current evidence the theory is questioned all over again. More rounds of **testing** will be carried out to see which evidence, and so which theory, **prevails**.

If the Evidence Supports a Theory, It's Accepted — For Now

Our currently accepted theories have survived this '**trial by evidence**'. They've been tested **over and over and over** and each time the results have backed them up. **BUT**, and this is a big but (teehee), they never become totally undisputable fact. Scientific **breakthroughs or advances** could provide new ways to question and test a theory, which could lead to **changes and challenges** to it. Then the testing starts all over again...

And this, my friend, is the **tentative nature of scientific knowledge** — it's always **changing** and **evolving**.

The Role of Science

So what's it all about then — why do scientists get to flounce around in long white swishy lab coats, with their goggles pushing back their flamboyant hairstyles and the smell of ammonia wafting after them?

Science Helps Us Make **Better Decisions**

Lots of scientific work eventually leads to **important discoveries** that could **benefit humankind**. Oh yes. These results are **used by society** (that's you, me and everyone else) to **make decisions** about the way we live. All sections of society use scientific evidence to make decisions:

1) **Politicians** use science to devise policy. E.g. **cognitive behavioural therapy** is available on the NHS because there's evidence to show it can help people with **depression**.
2) **Private organisations** use science to determine what to make or develop — e.g. evidence has shown that the number of people being diagnosed with **depression** is increasing, so drugs companies might put **more money** into this area of research.
3) **Individuals** also use science to make decisions about their **own lives** — e.g. evidence suggests that we should exercise and eat healthily, but it's up to individuals to **decide** whether they take that advice or not.

Other **Factors** Can **Influence** Decision Making

Other factors can influence decisions about science or the way science is used:

Economic factors

- Society has to consider the **cost** of implementing changes based on scientific conclusions — e.g. the **NHS** can't afford the most expensive drugs without **sacrificing** something else.
- Scientific research is **expensive** so companies won't always develop new ideas — e.g. developing new drugs is costly, so pharmaceutical companies often only invest in drugs that are likely to make **money**.

Social factors

- **Decisions** affect **people's lives.** How psychologists decide what's **normal** and what's **abnormal** affects how people are treated — e.g. homosexuality was defined as an **abnormal behaviour** until 1987.

Environmental factors

- Scientists believe **unexplored regions**, like parts of rainforests, might contain **untapped drug** resources. But some people think we shouldn't **exploit** these regions because any interesting finds might lead to **deforestation**, **reduced biodiversity** and **more CO_2** in the atmosphere.

Science Has **Responsibilities**

Yes, you've guessed it — **ethics**. Science has to be **responsible** in many ways. Scientists aren't allowed to test something just because they can. They have to think about the **ethical considerations** surrounding the experiment design and how the results could affect society.

1) **Design** — e.g. experiments involving **animals** are tightly controlled and monitored. **Studies** are checked to ensure they aren't placing individuals in **unnecessary danger**. If a study shows a drug has a highly **beneficial effect**, it's stopped and those in the **placebo** (negative) group are given the drug too.
2) **Results** — e.g. scientists' understanding of some **genetic disorders** could lead to tests to detect members of the population that carry the genes for them. But would people want to know?

Society does have a say in what experiments take place. **Controversial experiments** involving ethical issues have to be approved by scientific and **ethics councils** before they are allowed to be carried out.

So there you have it — how science works...

Hopefully these pages have given you a nice intro to how science works — what scientists do to provide you with 'facts'. You need to understand this, as you're expected to use it to evaluate evidence for yourselves — in the exam and in life.

Biological Rhythms

George Gershwin. Gloria Estefan. 90s dance maestros Snap. They all had rhythm, and so do you. You don't have to write a song on it (unless you really want to) but you do need to know about it. And these lovely pages are here to help.

Biological Rhythm Cycles **Vary in Length**

Biological rhythms can be classified according to how long their cycle lasts.

1) **Circadian rhythms** — have cycles that generally occur **once every 24 hours**. For example, we will usually go through the **sleep-waking cycle** once every day.

2) **Infradian rhythms** — have cycles that occur **less than once every day**. For example, the menstrual cycle. **Sabbagh and Barnard (1984)** found that when women live together their menstrual cycles may **synchronise**. It isn't clear why, but it may be linked to **pheromones** (chemicals that can affect the behaviour or physiology of others).

Stan and Paul had more than enough rhythm for everyone.

3) **Ultradian rhythms** — have cycles that occur **more than once every 24 hours**. For example, the sleep cycle has several repeating stages of light and deep sleep (see p.116). Research using **EEGs** (electroencephalograms) to monitor brain activity during sleep has shown that a **regular** sleep pattern is really important. Disrupting these cycles can have very **serious consequences** — see the next page.

Biological Rhythms are **Regulated** by **Internal and External Influences**

The timing of biological rhythms is determined by factors both **inside** and **outside** our bodies.

Endogenous pacemakers

1) Some aspects of our biological rhythms are set by **genetically determined** biological structures and mechanisms **within the body**.
2) The **suprachiasmatic nucleus** (SCN), part of the **hypothalamus**, seems to act as an **internal clock** to keep the body on an approximate 24-hour sleep-waking cycle.
3) It is sensitive to light and regulates the **pineal gland**, which secretes **melatonin** — a hormone which seems to induce sleep. When there is **less** light, more melatonin is produced. When there is **more** light, secretion is reduced and waking occurs.
4) **Menaker et al (1978)** lesioned this structure in hamsters — their sleep-waking cycle was **disrupted**.

Exogenous zeitgebers

1) These are influences outside of the body that act like a **prompt**, which may trigger a **biological rhythm**.
2) **Light** is the most important zeitgeber. **Siffre (1975)** spent six months in a cave. He had **no clocks** and **no natural light** as zeitgebers. His sleep-waking cycle **extended** from a 24-hour to a 25-30 hour cycle. It therefore seems that natural light is needed to fine-tune our normal 24-hour cycle.

Endogenous and Exogenous Factors **Interact**

Endogenous and exogenous factors **interact** to regulate the timing of our biological rhythms.

1) In some cases, endogenous factors may **completely determine** a cycle. **Pengelly and Fisher (1957)** found that squirrels will hibernate even when kept in laboratory conditions very different from their natural environment.
2) However, many animals can **react more flexibly**, especially humans who are able to adapt to their surroundings. We can make ourselves stay awake and **change the environment** to suit our needs, e.g. by using artificial light.
3) **Cultural factors** are also important. For example, Eskimos often live in permanent daylight or permanent night-time but can maintain **regular daily sleep cycles** — so the cycle can't just be determined by levels of light acting on the pineal gland.
4) **Individual differences** can also affect the rhythms. **Aschoff and Wever (1976)** found that in a group of people isolated from daylight, some maintained their **regular** sleep-waking cycles. Other members of the group displayed their own very **extreme** idiosyncrasies, e.g. 29 hours awake followed by 21 hours asleep. This also shows that factors must interact to control or influence biological rhythms.

Biological Rhythms

Disrupting *Biological Rhythms can have* ***Negative Consequences***

1) In the natural environment, zeitgebers normally **change slowly**, e.g. light levels during the year change gradually.
2) However, in modern society, zeitgebers can change quickly. This can have **negative effects** on our ability to function — slowing **reaction times**, impairing **problem-solving skills**, and limiting our **ability to concentrate**.

Jet lag

1) Jet planes allow fast travel to **different time zones**. Leaving the UK at 9am means that you'd get to New York at about 4pm UK time. New York is 5 hours behind the UK, so the local time would be about 11am.
2) Consequently you'll feel sleepy at an **earlier (local) time**. If you then went to sleep you would wake-up earlier and be **out of sync** with local timing. It appears easiest to **adapt** by forcing yourself to stay awake.
3) It can take **about a week** to fully synchronise to a new time zone. **Wegman et al (1986)** found that travelling east to west (**phase delay**) seems easier to adapt to than travelling west to east (**phase advance**).
4) **Schwartz et al (1995)** found that baseball teams from the east coast of the USA got **better results** travelling to play in the west than teams based in the west did when travelling to play in the east.

Shift work

Modern work patterns mean some people work shifts throughout the 24-hour period, disrupting their sleep cycle.

Czeisler et al (1982) studied workers at a factory whose shift patterns appeared to cause sleep and health problems. The researchers recommended **21-day shifts** (allowing more time for workers to adapt), and changing shifts **forward in time** (phase delay). After implementing the changes **productivity** and **job satisfaction** increased.

Research on Biological Rhythms has ***Limitations***

1) Findings from animal studies can't accurately be **generalised** to humans — humans have greater **adaptability**.
2) Studies that have deprived humans of natural light have still allowed **artificial light**, which may give many of the **benefits** of natural light — this reduces the **validity** of these studies.
3) Things like **individual differences** need further study. Some people are more alert early in the day, and others later on, and the speed with which we **adapt to disruptions** can vary. It's difficult to determine whether a person's lifestyle is a **cause or effect** of their biological rhythms.
4) If we fully understand what causes the problems linked to jet lag and shift work, we can **minimise** or **avoid them**, reducing accidents in work environments. However, there are different ways to deal with these problems, e.g. taking time to **naturally adjust**, or using **drugs** to reduce the effects of sleep deprivation.

Practice Questions

Q1 What is the difference between circadian, infradian and ultradian rhythms?

Q2 Explain what is meant by 'endogenous pacemakers' and 'exogenous zeitgebers'.

Q3 Why does jet lag occur?

Q4 Why is shift work disruptive to biological rhythms?

Q5 Give two criticisms of research on biological rhythms.

Exam Question

Q1 a) Outline the roles of endogenous pacemakers and exogenous zeitgebers in biological rhythms. [8 marks]

b) Discuss research studies that have examined the role of endogenous and exogenous factors in human biological cycles. [16 marks]

"I didn't mean to fall asleep Miss — the melatonin made me do it..."

It's scientific fact that if you're a rock star, your biological rhythm immediately changes to 'Here I Go Again' by Whitesnake. Actually, that's not scientific at all. Nor is it fact. When you can answer the practice questions, and you've had a crack at the essays, think about what your rock rhythm would be... Are you ready? It's 'Here I Go Again', by Whitesnake. Fact.

Sleep States

Sleep — a topic that's surely close to all our hearts. We spend about a third of our lives asleep, so it must be pretty important. Amazingly, no one's quite sure why. I reckon I know though — it's because staying in bed all day is brilliant.

Sleep Can Be Split into Stages of Different Brain Activity

Electroencephalograms (EEGs) measure electrical activity in the brain, and are used to record the stages of sleep.

1) Adults pass through the stages about **five times a night**, with each cycle lasting about **90 minutes**. Who'd have thought we were so busy...
2) As you fall into deeper sleep, brain activity becomes **higher voltage** and **lower frequency**. These are the stages of slow wave sleep (SWS):

    Stage 1 is a bit like deep relaxation, with lowered heart rate, muscle tension and temperature. It's quite easy to wake people up.

    Stage 2 has slower and larger EEG waves, with some quick bursts of high frequency waves called **sleep spindles**.

    Stage 3 has even larger, slower waves.

    Stage 4 has the largest, slowest waves of all, because it's the deepest stage of sleep. Metabolic activity is pretty low in general, and the sleeper is very hard to wake.

Stage	EEG
Stage 1	
Stage 2	
Stage 3	
Stage 4	
REM Sleep (active sleep)	

3) After stage 4 the cycle reverses back through stages 3 and 2. A period of **active sleep** occurs instead of stage 1.
4) During the active stage, metabolic activity increases, and the body appears almost paralysed except for **rapid eye movement (REM)**. The EEG pattern is almost like when you're awake. The cycle is repeated about five times during the night, but we only enter stages 3 and 4 in the first two. Periods of REM increase with each cycle.

There are Lots of Different Theories of Sleep

Evolutionary approaches relate to the **environment**, **evolution** and **survival of the fittest**.

1) **Webb (1968)** suggested that everyday sleep is similar to **hibernation** — sleep conserves energy at times when it's harder to get resources (i.e. at night time). Using energy would be **inefficient**.
2) **Meddis (1977)** suggested that sleep helps keep animals **safe**. By being quiet and still, they are less likely to attract predators (especially at night). However, sleep also makes animals **vulnerable** to predators if discovered.
3) Not sleeping at all would be very advantageous, but as it seems to occur in all animals, it must have an **important function** — although how much sleep animals have **varies**. Animals that **graze** often and must avoid predators **sleep less**, while **predators**, that don't eat as frequently and aren't hunted, **sleep more**.

- The evolutionary approach, focusing on survival and environmental adaptation, is useful for understanding **how and why** behaviours occur. Behaviours have evolved to help survival and adapt us to our environment.
- Evolution occurs over **long periods** so it's hard to test theories about why some behaviours have been **naturally selected**. So, it's difficult to **prove them wrong**, making them **less useful** from a scientific perspective.

Restoration approaches suggest that sleep restores the body's ability to **function**, after being busy during the day.

1) **Oswald (1980)** suggested that SWS/non-REM sleep is for restoring bodily functions linked to **physical activity**, and REM sleep is for restoring **brain functions**.
2) **Horne (1988)** distinguished between two types of sleep: **core sleep**, which is made up of stage 4 SWS (for body restoration) and REM sleep (for brain restoration), and **optional sleep**, which is made up of the other sleep stages. Although optional sleep is not necessary, having it can help to conserve energy.

- It seems that important **brain and body restoration** occurs during sleep. Babies, whose brains are developing, spend more time in REM sleep and release more **growth hormone** during SWS.
- **Shapiro et al (1981**) found that long-distance runners had more SWS after a race, implying that the exercise **increased** the need for bodily restoration.
- However, **Horne and Minard's (1985)** study found that when participants did physical and cognitive activity they fell asleep **more quickly**, but did not sleep for longer. It may be that there was a **reduction** in the amount of **optional sleep** that they had.

Sleep States

Several **Techniques** are Used in Sleep Research

The following equipment and techniques are often used in **sleep laboratories**:

1) Equipment such as **EEGs** measure electrical activity in the brain and provide **quantitative reports** which can easily be compared to others. They have high **reliability** and changes in sleep stages can be easily identified.
2) Other equipment used includes **EOGs** (electrooculograms) which measure the electrical activity of the **eyes**, and **EMGs** (electromyograms) which measure the electrical activity in **muscles**.
3) **Self reports** involve participants keeping a record of their dreams or estimating their length. They're useful for gaining information which couldn't be collected in any other way, but they're limited by the **accuracy of recall**.
4) **Observations** of patterns and directions of **eye movements** can be recorded and related to sleep stages.
5) Variables, such as noise and distraction, are **controlled** to increase the **reliability** of the research. However, research in sleep laboratories creates an **artificial environment**, which may affect the participants' sleep patterns and so reduce **validity**.

Our **Sleeping Patterns Change** During Our **Lifespan**

The **amount** we sleep and our **patterns** of sleep **change** as we get older.

1) The **older** we get the **less** we tend to sleep — babies sleep up to 20 hours a day, whilst most adults average 7-8 hours and people over 50 average only 6 hours.
2) Also, as we get older we tend to have **less REM sleep** — Kleitman (1963) found that newborn babies may spend 8-9 hours every day in REM sleep. Children have less REM sleep than infants, and adults have less than children.
3) Kales and Kales (1974) found that elderly people are more likely to **wake up** several times during their night's sleep than younger people.

Comments

1) Most evidence for changes in sleep patterns comes from laboratory research using **EEG recordings**. These recordings are obtained by attaching **electrodes** to participants. This creates an **unfamiliar sleeping environment** for the participants, which may **disrupt** their usual **sleep patterns**.
2) However, Empson (1989) suggests that after the first night participants **adjust** to the conditions and their sleep is representative of their usual patterns.
3) More research is needed to find out the **reasons** for lifespan changes in sleep. For example, REM sleep in childhood may be linked to brain development.

Practice Questions

Q1 Summarise the four stages of slow wave sleep.

Q2 What is active sleep?

Q3 How does the average amount of sleep that we have every day change over our lifespan?

Q4 Give a limitation of sleep research using EEG recordings.

Exam Question

Q1 a) Outline the stages of human sleep. [4 marks]

b) Outline the lifespan changes in human sleep. [4 marks]

c) Evaluate research on the functions of sleep. [16 marks]

REM sleep — not the same as dozing off with your headphones on...

Don't know about you but I'm not looking forward to getting down to six hours sleep a night — talk about falling standards. Bring back the good old days of 20 hours snoozing out of 24. Anyway, seeing as you've got so much more time awake than ever before, I suggest that you put it to good use and learn about the nature, functions and lifespan changes of sleep. Enjoy.

Disorders of Sleep

There are lots of different sleep disorders — some are common, like insomnia, others are more unusual, like narcolepsy. And then there's sleepwalking — which can lead to some very bizarre situations. You need to know about all three.

Insomnia is a Sleep Disorder

1) People with **insomnia** have **difficulty falling asleep**, **difficulty staying asleep**, or **both**.
2) They may feel **sleepy** and **irritable** during the day, with **impaired concentration** — this can affect their daily life and their relationships.
3) Insomnia may be **acute**, lasting a few nights, or **chronic**, lasting for weeks, months or years.
4) Research has suggested that about **10%** of adults may suffer from **chronic** insomnia.
5) There are different types of insomnia:

Primary Insomnia

Primary insomnia is insomnia that **isn't linked** to any existing **physical** or **psychological** conditions. Instead, it may be caused by:

1) **Stimulants**. Stimulants such as caffeine or nicotine increase arousal and can lead to insomnia. This can also lead to a vicious circle of frustration and anxiety.
2) **Disruptions to circadian rhythm**. Jet-lag, shift work and sleeping at irregular times (e.g. staying-up late at weekends) may all disrupt sleep patterns and lead to insomnia.

Secondary Insomnia

Secondary insomnia is the result of existing **physical** or **psychological** conditions. For example:

1) **Physical complaints**. A number of physical complaints such as arthritis, diabetes and asthma can cause insomnia.
2) **Psychological conditions**. A number of psychological conditions, e.g. depression, can cause insomnia.
3) **Stress or anxiety**. Worrying about something causes anxiety (higher bodily arousal), which may in turn cause insomnia. Failure to get to sleep can cause frustration, which creates more anxiety, making it even harder to get to sleep and producing a vicious circle.
4) **Medication**. Some medications may have side effects which disrupt sleep. Also, medications taken to improve sleep may cause problems if their effects are too long-lasting (leaving the person sleepy the next day), or if their effects wear off too early. Some people may become dependent on sleeping pills and suffer even worse insomnia if they stop taking them.

Insomnia is Influenced by Many Factors

An episode of insomnia can be influenced by many factors. For example:

1) **Sleep apnoea**. This is a condition where a person's airways become temporarily **blocked** whilst they are sleeping, causing their **breathing** to be **interrupted**. This **disrupts** their **sleep pattern** — either causing a person to wake up or to move into a lighter stage of sleep. Sleep apnoea is linked to snoring and may be caused by various abnormalities in brain or respiratory functioning. It's also linked to obesity — especially in males.
2) **Personality traits**. Characteristics like being **overly sensitive**, **worrying**, having a very **serious attitude** to life issues and being **overly dependent** on other people can lead to insomnia.
3) **Depression and anxiety**. These increase **emotional arousal** — which may then increase **physiological arousal**, causing insomnia.

Claire broke the news gently — Jake's nap time snoring was the cause of the insomnia epidemic in Class 1.

Research into insomnia is **difficult** as there are **many variables** that can cause or influence the condition. This problem is compounded by the fact that some of the variables are **hard to control**. Much of the research that's been done has produced **correlational evidence** rather than showing cause and effect.

Disorders of Sleep

Sleepwalking is a Sleep Disorder...

Sleepwalking is a disorder associated with **stage 3** and **stage 4** sleep. It affects approximately **15% of children** and **2% of adults**. The causes of sleepwalking are not fully known but it's thought it can be triggered by...

- **Sleep deprivation**, especially in people with a history of sleepwalking
- An **irregular sleep schedule**
- **Stress** or **anxiety**
- Some **drugs**, e.g. anti-psychotics or stimulants

Dauvilliers et al's (2005) study suggests there may be a **genetic component** to sleepwalking as well — they found higher concordance rates for the disorder in identical twins than in non-identical twins.

...and so is Narcolepsy

Narcolepsy is a disorder causing sudden episodes of **day-time sleepiness**, leading to a person falling asleep for a short period of time (seconds or minutes). They may also experience **features** of sleep such as **weak muscles** (**cataplexy**) and **dream-like imagery**. Narcolepsy affects **0.02-0.06%** of the population, most of whom develop the condition in early adulthood. The causes of narcolepsy may include:

- **Reduced levels of hypocretin**. Hypocretin is a chemical that's involved in regulating arousal levels. It's thought narcolepsy may be caused by the body's immune system attacking the cells that produce hypocretin, reducing the body's ability to regulate sleep.
- **Genetics**. Studies have shown a 25-31% concordance rate for the condition between identical twins — this suggests a genetic link. This concordance rate is fairly low, so environmental influences must also be important. It could be that a virus, e.g. that causes measles, may trigger a genetic predisposition to narcolepsy. So a person would need the genetic predisposition for narcolepsy as well as contact with the virus before developing the condition — meaning the cause would be both genetic and environmental.

Alfie might claim it was narcolepsy but he was fooling no-one. They knew a lazy seal when they saw one.

Practice Questions

Q1 What is insomnia?

Q2 What is the difference between primary insomnia and secondary insomnia?

Q3 How can depression influence insomnia?

Q4 List three possible causes of sleepwalking.

Q5 List some possible causes of narcolepsy.

Exam Question

Q1 a) Outline explanations for insomnia. [6 marks]

b) Describe and explain how sleep apnoea and personality traits can influence insomnia. [12 marks]

c) Evaluate the evidence for one explanation for narcolepsy. [6 marks]

Revision — it cures insomnia and induces narcolepsy in one go...

Now stay with it — you need to remember this stuff. It's not too bad really, three sleeping disorders — insomnia, narcolepsy and sleepwalking, with explanations for all of them. Once you've learnt that, you can give yourself a pat on the back, make yourself some cocoa and have a little nap if you like — because you've reached the end of this very short section. Huzzah.

Theories of Perception

Perception is how we make sense of things around us. Without it the world would be a mish mash of meaninglessness — so it's pretty important. With that in mind, you'd better have a look at some theories of perception. Here they come...

Perception is the Process of **Giving Meaning to Stimuli**

1) Our senses are constantly detecting **stimuli** in the environment around us.
2) The information the stimuli provide has to be **processed** in order to **make sense of it**.
3) This processing is known as **perception**.
4) Theories of how the information is understood are known as **theories of perception**. You need to know about two of them — Gibson's **direct theory** and Gregory's **indirect theory**.

Gibson's Direct Theory of Perception is a **Bottom Up** Theory

'Bottom up' means information is pieced together to make sense of it.

1) **Gibson's** (**1979**) **direct theory** of perception suggests that stimuli provide **visual information** which the cognitive system then **processes**, allowing the person to make sense of the stimuli.
2) Previously stored knowledge **isn't needed** — the information provided by the stimuli is enough.
3) Gibson argues that this is possible because of the large amount of information provided by the **optic array**:

The Optic Array

The optic array is the **pattern of light** that enters the eye, allowing things to be seen. It's a really **complicated** pattern — it's made up of all the light rays reflecting off all the objects and surfaces in view, so it holds **lots of information.** To make things even more complex, it **changes** each time you **move**. The optic array gives rise to **texture gradients, horizon ratios** and **optic flow patterns**. These are all involved in perception.

Texture gradients

Objects that are **far away** take up less of the optic array and are **closer together** than objects that are near. This is known as the **texture gradient**. It provides information on the **depth** and **distance** of objects.

Horizon ratios

Objects that are the **same height** are cut in the **same place** by the horizon, regardless of how far away they are. This is known as a **horizon ratio** and provides us with information on the **size** and **distance** of objects.

Optic flow patterns

As we move, the place we're moving towards appears to be stationary whilst other objects appear to **move past us**. Objects that are **close** to us seem to be moving **quickly**, whilst those **far away** seem to move much more **slowly**. For example, when you travel in a car, signposts and nearby buildings zoom by in comparison to mountain ranges in the distance. This is due to **changes in the optic array** as we move. These are known as **optic flow patterns**. They give us information on the **position** and **depth** of objects.

Although the optic array **changes** when a person **moves**, the information provided by texture gradients, horizon ratios and optic flow remains **constant**. This enables us to perceive the world around us.

4) The optic array explains our perception of the **position** of objects relative to each other. However, it doesn't address how we're able to perceive what objects **are** or how they should be **used**.
5) Gibson proposed that we perceive how an object should be used from the object itself. An object **affords** (offers) **itself** to certain **behaviours**, e.g. a bed affords itself to lying down.
6) The **affordances** of objects can **change** depending on the **circumstances**, e.g. a box might afford itself to storing something or afford itself to being stood on to reach a high object.

Comments on Gibson's Theory

1) Gibson studied perception in real-world situations, so his theory has **ecological validity**. His theory also has **practical applications** — the concept of optic flow has been used to help train pilots.
2) However, the idea of **affordances** has been **criticised**. Many psychologists believe that the uses of some objects can't be perceived without drawing on **stored knowledge** or **experience**.

Theories of Perception

Gregory's Indirect Theory of Perception is a Top Down Theory

'Top down' means perception is steered by context and prior knowledge.

1) **Gregory's (1966) indirect theory** of perception suggests that stimuli often **don't** provide the cognitive system with **enough information** for it to make sense of a situation.
2) This could be because the stimuli are **ambiguous** or because the information they provide is **limited**.
3) Instead, stimuli are treated as **hypotheses** which are tested within different **contexts** using **stored knowledge**.
4) **Visual illusions** provide support for Gregory's theory:

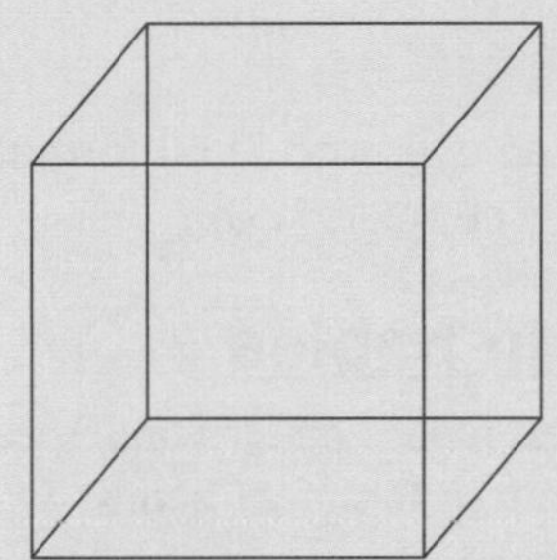

The diagram on the left shows a **Necker cube**. As you look at it your perception of which face is the **front face** changes. Gregory suggests that this is your brain **testing different hypotheses**. As there's **no context** to help you decide which the front face is, your brain continues to switch between them. This **supports** Gregory's theory that stimuli alone don't always provide enough information for the cognitive system to work out what's going on.

Comments on Gregory's Theory

1) There's plenty of evidence to support Gregory's theory — however, it's based on **laboratory experiments** so **lacks ecological validity**.
2) The theory can explain **errors** in perception — for example, those caused by **optical illusions**.
3) However, many psychologists reckon that if perception is based entirely on hypothesis testing we would make **more errors** in perception than we do.

Perception is Probably a Combination of Top Down and Bottom Up Processes

1) Many psychologists believe that perception stems from a **combination** of **top down** and **bottom up** processes.
2) **Bottom up** processes are most likely when the information provided by stimuli is **unambiguous** and **plentiful**.
3) **Top down** processes become more dominant when the amount or the quality of information provided by stimuli is **reduced**. We become more dependent on **stored knowledge** and **past experiences**.
4) When this happens, unconscious 'educated guesses' play a greater part in perception.

Practice Questions

Q1 What is perception?

Q2 Give an example of a bottom up theory of perception.

Q3 What is the optic array?

Q4 What do texture gradients provide information on?

Q5 Which features of the optic array provide information on the size of objects?

Q6 Why does Gregory's (1966) theory lack ecological validity?

Exam Question

Q1 Outline and evaluate Gregory's indirect theory of perception. [24 marks]

Bottom up theory — not the same as bottoms up. That's for after the exam.

Before you get to the celebratory times after finishing exams you need to get through the not-so-great times of learning for the exam. And as part of that, you definitely need to take the time to learn about Gibson's and Gregory's perception theories. So stuff your brain with info on affordances, visual illusions, hypotheses and the like — not forgetting that mysterious optic array.

Development of Perception

The odd visual illusion aside, we're pretty good at perception and can make sense of most things most of the time. Hmmm, I wonder if we're born with this skill or if we learn it. Oh yes — it's nature vs nurture time again.

There Have Been Lots of **Studies** on The **Development of Perception**

There's been much debate over whether our perceptual abilities are **innate** (inbuilt) or are **learned** through experience. In other words, whether they're down to **nature** or **nurture**. Studies have been carried out to investigate the development of perceptual abilities such as **depth perception** and **visual constancies**.

Some Studies Suggest **Depth Perception is Innate**

Depth perception allows us to change a 2D image on the retina (the inner lining of the eye) into 3D information. We do this using cues such as relative size, texture gradients and optic flow patterns (see page 120).

Gibson and Walk (1960) — depth perception in babies

Method: A '**visual cliff**' was created using a layer of glass with **two levels** of a checkerboard pattern underneath. The shallow level had the pattern just below the glass, the deep level had the pattern **four feet below**. 36 six-month old babies were placed on the shallow side and encouraged by their mothers to crawl on to the deep side.

Results: Most babies **wouldn't** crawl on to the **deep side** of the visual cliff.

Conclusion: Babies can perceive depth so **depth perception** is the result of **nature**, not nurture.

Evaluation: The **validity** of this study is questionable as the babies were six months old and could have **learnt** depth perception by this age. **Campos (1970)** tested **babies** by measuring their heart rate when they were on different sides of the cliff. He found that the heart rate of two-month old babies (who **couldn't crawl**) was the **same** on both sides, suggesting they didn't perceive any change in depth. Nine-month old babies (who **could crawl**) had a **increased** heart rate on the deep side, suggesting they had learned depth perception, i.e. through **nurture**.

Studies Have Suggested That **Visual Constancies** are **Innate**

1) As you look at an object, an image of it forms on the **retina**, allowing it to be seen.
2) The **closer** an object is, the **larger** the image it creates on the retina. However, when the brain interprets the image it's able to identify the object as being closer rather than larger. This is known as **size constancy**.
3) Similarly, when an object is rotated, e.g. a door opening, the **shape** of the image on the retina **changes** but the brain doesn't interpret this as the object changing shape. This is known as **shape constancy**.
4) Size and shape constancy are both **visual constancies** and important perceptual abilities.
5) Several studies have been carried out to determine whether visual constancy is a result of **nature** or **nurture**:

Slater and Morrison (1985) — shape constancy in babies

Method: **Newborn** babies were shown a square held at **different angles**. At some angles the image on the retina would be a **trapezium**. Once the baby was familiar with the square they were shown a trapezium **alongside it**.

Results: The babies were more likely to look at the new **trapezium** than the square.

Conclusion: Babies can distinguish between the trapezium and the square held at an orientation where it looks like a trapezium. So, babies have an **innate** ability to apply **shape constancy** to objects.

Bower (1964, 1966) — size constancy in babies

Method: **Two-month-old** babies were conditioned to look at a **30 cm cube** held **1 m away** from them, by being given a reward each time they looked at it. Once they could do this they were presented with new stimuli. Firstly they were shown a **90 cm cube** held **1 m away**. This would create a **larger** retinal image than the original cube. Then they were shown a **90 cm cube** held **3 m** away, producing the **same size** retinal image as the original. Lastly, the **original 30 cm cube** was held at a distance of **3 m**, producing a **smaller** retinal image than before.

Results: The babies preferred to look at the **original 30 cm cube** held at a distance of **3 m** than the 90 cm cubes.

Conclusion: Babies can distinguish between objects of different sizes regardless of the size of the image they create on the retina. So, babies have an **innate** ability to apply **size constancy** to objects.

Development of Perception

Cross Cultural Studies *Have Been Carried Out On* ***Perceptual Abilities***

1) If perceptual abilities are the result of **nature** they're likely to be present in **everyone** regardless of culture.
2) However, if they're the result of **nurture** they're likely to **vary** between people of different cultures.
3) So, **cross-cultural studies** can help to determine whether perceptual abilities are the result of **nature** or **nurture**:

1) The **Müller-Lyer illusion** shows two lines of the **same length** that can appear to be different lengths due to inward or outward facing arrow heads (see diagram on right).
2) **Segall et al (1966)** showed the illusion to a sample of **urban** South Africans and a sample of **rural** Zulus.
3) Most of the urban South Africans identified the line with the **inwardly pointing arrows** (**a**) as being **longer** than the line with the **outwardly pointing arrows** (**b**). The Zulus were **less susceptible** to the illusion, with a high proportion identifying the lines as being the same length.
4) Segall suggested that the urban South Africans, who were used to an environment dominated by **straight lines** (e.g. in buildings, furniture, roads, etc.), interpreted the diagram in **3D**.
5) In 3D, **line a** resembles an object receding **away** from the observer (e.g. the inner corner of a room). **Line b** resembles an object projecting **towards** the observer (e.g. the outer corner of a building).
6) As **line a** appears to recede away from the observer the brain interprets it as being **further away** than **line b**.
7) So, the brain interprets **line a** as being **larger** than the image it forms on the retina (**size constancy**) and **perceives** it to be **longer** than **line b**.
8) The **Zulu** people were **less familiar** with buildings made from **straight lines** — their huts were circular. Segall suggested that they saw the lines in **2D**, so didn't apply size constancy and didn't perceive any difference in the length of the lines.
9) He saw this difference in perception across cultures as evidence that perceptual abilities are **developed** in response to the **environment**, i.e. perception is the result of **nurture**.

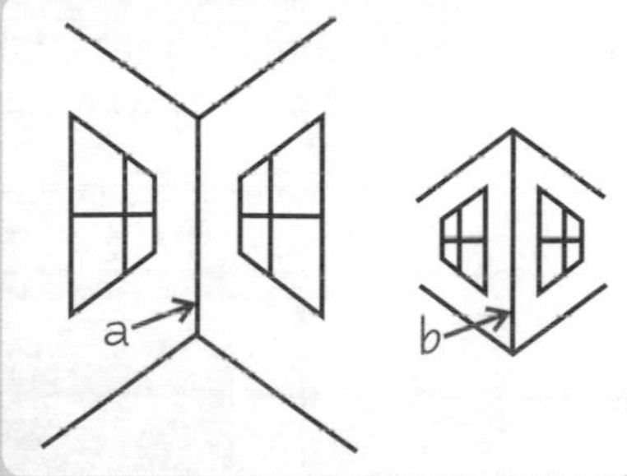

Practice Questions

Q1 What did Gibson and Walk's (1960) 'visual cliff' study test?

Q2 What is size constancy?

Q3 What is shape constancy?

Exam Question

Q1 a) Outline one cross-cultural study into the development of perceptual abilities. [8 marks]

b) Discuss the nature-nurture debate in relation to explanations of perceptual development. [16 marks]

I perceive you might not care whether it's down to nature or nurture...

...however, I also perceive that the examiners don't care that you don't care. I'm perceptive like that. And I perceive that, regardless of your cultural background, your perceptual abilities will lead you to concur. So, in short, learn these pages.

Face Recognition and Visual Agnosia

Of all the very clever things we can do, being able to recognise thousands of different faces is surely one of the most useful. So you'd think someone would have come up with a theory of how we do it. And you'd be right. Read on...

Bruce and Young's (1986) Theory Suggests How We Recognise Faces

1) **Face recognition** is an important perceptual ability — allowing us to **form relationships** and **function socially**.
2) It lets us tell the **difference** between thousands of faces, even though they have the **same basic features**, e.g. eyes.
3) We're also able to **identify familiar faces** — those of friends, family or famous people.
4) **Bruce and Young** (**1986**) suggest that the process of face recognition is **different** from recognition of other objects. Their model outlines a number of different **components** involved in face recognition:
   - **Structural encoding** — physical features are interpreted to determine **basic information** (e.g. age, gender). This allows a **structural model** of the face to be built up.
   - **Expression analysis** — facial features are analysed to work out the person's **emotional state**.
   - **Facial speech analysis** — facial movements (e.g. lip movements) are used to help **interpret speech**.
   - **Directed visual processing** — processing of **specific features** (e.g. whether the person has a beard).
   - **Face recognition units** — these contain information about the structure of **familiar faces**.
   - **Person identity nodes** — these contain information known about the **person** (e.g. their job, interests).
   - **Name generation** — this helps us to retrieve the **name** of a familiar person and relate it to their face.
   - **Cognitive system** — this contains **extra information** (e.g. the context in which a face is likely to be seen). It also helps determine which of the **other components** involved in face recognition are activated.
5) Bruce and Young suggested that some of these components are activated in a **specific sequence**, whilst others can work in **parallel** with each other. The diagram below shows how they suggest the components are linked.

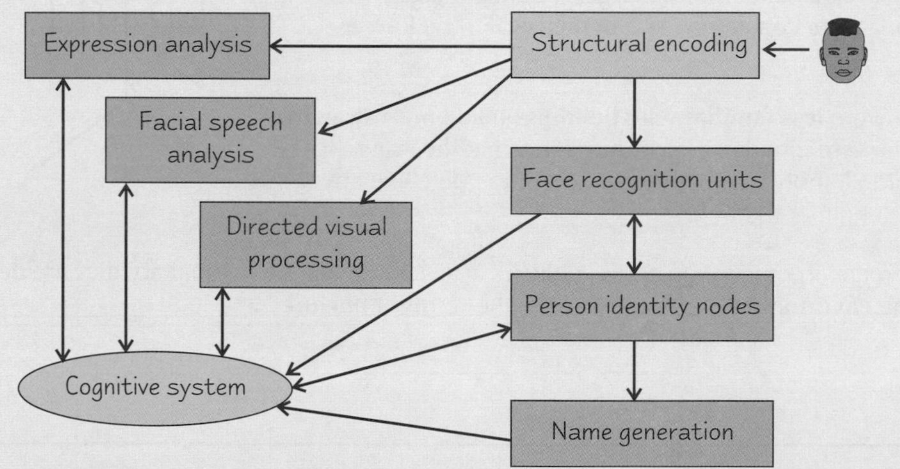

It might well be familiar, but no-one ever seemed to look at Troy's face.

- For example, **structural encoding** is always the **first** component to be activated. After this either **face recognition units**, **facial speech analysis**, **expression analysis** or **direct visual processing** may be activated. These components work in **parallel**.
- However, **person identity nodes** can only be activated **after** the **face recognition units**, and only **after this** can **name generation** be activated. These components work in **sequence**. Makes sense — you can't come up with information about someone until you've realised they're familiar.

The Components Used Depend on Whether the Face is Familiar or Not

Bruce and Young's model proposes that we use **different components** to process **new** and **familiar** faces.

1) They suggest that processing of a **new face** involves **structural encoding**, **expression analysis**, **facial speech analysis** and **directed visual processing**.
2) Recognition of **familiar faces** uses **structural encoding**, **face recognition units**, **person identity nodes** and **name generation**.

Face Recognition and Visual Agnosia

People with **Prosopagnosia** Have Trouble **Recognising Faces**

1) **Prosopagnosia** is a condition where people have difficulty **recognising familiar faces**.
2) It's usually caused by **brain damage**, but some evidence suggests that it could also be **congenital** (present at birth).
3) There are **different types** of prosopagnosia, with the most serious forms leaving people unable to recognise their spouse, close family and friends. Some patients can't even recognise their own face.
4) Some studies of prosopagnosia have provided support for Bruce and Young's model of face recognition:

- **Farah (1994)** studied a patient (LH) who developed prosopagnosia as a result of **brain damage** caused by a **car crash**.
- Along with a control group of participants who didn't have prosopagnosia, he was shown pictures of **faces** and pairs of **spectacles** and then given a **recognition memory test**.
- LH performed **as well** as the control group in recognising **spectacles** but much **worse** than the control group in recognising the **faces**.
- This suggests that prosopagnosia is caused by damage to the area of the brain involved in **face recognition** but not **object recognition**.
- This supports Bruce and Young's proposal that face recognition and object recognition are **separate processes**.

- **Kurucz and Feldmar (1979)** saw a patient with prosopagnosia who was **unable** to **identify familiar faces** but could interpret the **emotional state** of the person.
- This suggests that recognition of familiar faces and interpretation of emotional states are processes that work **independently** of each other.
- This supports Bruce and Young's concept of expression analysis and face recognition units as **separate components** that work in **parallel** with each other — one can be functional even if the other isn't.

5) These case studies suggest that the various types of prosopagnosia are caused by problems with one or more of the components of Bruce and Young's model. For example, the patient in Kurucz and Feldmar's study would have suffered damage to **face recognition units** or **person identity nodes** but **not** to the **expression analysis component**.

There's Some **Evidence** That Bruce and Young's Model **Isn't Correct**

Some studies suggest that Bruce and Young's model **isn't accurate**. For example:

1) **de Haan et al (1991)** found that when given the names and faces of famous people, a patient with amnesia was able to correctly match **88%** of the **faces** to the **names** even though they couldn't give any other information about the person.
2) This doesn't support Bruce and Young's model — the study suggests that activation of **face recognition units** was followed by **name generation**, bypassing **person identity nodes** entirely.

Practice Questions

Q1 What is the role of expression analysis in Bruce and Young's (1986) theory of face recognition?

Q2 Which components of Bruce and Young's (1986) model contain information about familiar faces?

Q3 What is prosopagnosia?

Exam Question

Q1 a) Outline Bruce and Young's (1986) theory of face recognition. [8 marks]

b) Using case studies, discuss the evidence for and against Bruce and Young's theory. [16 marks]

Prosopagnosia's not so bad — there are some faces you want to forget...

So, final two pages for this section. Best to go out with a flourish and learn them really well I think. Especially as there's only ONE theory here. I'm unbelievably kind to you when you think about it. Anyway, enough about me. You need to learn Bruce and Young's theory and the info on prosopagnosia, including the case studies. And then you're done with perception.

Formation, Maintenance and Breakdown

Relationships are a bit of a song and dance at the best of times. But learn these lovely pages and you'll be able to explain — WITH evidence — why you went off on one when Kevin nicked one of your chips without asking.

We Might Form Relationships for **Selfish Reasons**

1) **Reward/need satisfaction theory** states that we form friendships and relationships to receive **rewards** or **reinforcement** from others.
2) Relationships provide **rewards** (approval, sex, status, love, money, respect, agreement with our opinions, smiling, information, etc.) that satisfy our **social needs** (for self-esteem, affiliation, dependency, influence, etc.)
3) So, in terms of operant conditioning, being in a relationship is **positively reinforced** because it is rewarding.
4) **Byrne and Clore's (1970)** Reinforcement-Affect theory suggests that both **operant** and **classical conditioning** play a part in relationships. The theory states that we **learn** to associate people with **positive or enjoyable situations**, even if they are not **directly rewarding** us in these instances.

Economic Theories Consider Relationships to be a **Trading Process**

1) **Social Exchange Theory** (Thibaut & Kelley, 1959) suggests that people try to **maximise rewards** (e.g. attention, self-esteem, happiness) from a relationship and **minimise costs** (e.g. time, effort, emotional support).
2) If the relationship is to continue, then the rewards must not be **outweighed** by the costs — we should end up in **profit**. So, relationships are formed using a sort of 'cost-benefit' analysis.
3) But if we are striving to **get more** and **give less**, this may result in an **unequal relationship**.

1) **Equity theory** suggests that people expect relationships to be **fair and equal**.
2) They want to receive rewards from relationships that are **in balance** with the rewards they provide for the other person.
3) If a relationship is unequal or unfair then it produces **discomfort and distress** in both partners, even if you are the one getting more and giving less.
4) The disadvantaged person may try to **make things fairer** if it seems possible.

"This doesn't seem very fair."
"Well... it is, so keep pushing."

Relationships can be **Perceived Very Differently**

People within a relationship may have different feelings about the relationship and have different levels of satisfaction.

Hatfield et al (1979) asked newlyweds to assess what they and their partner **contributed** to the relationship and their level of **contentment** with the marriage:

- The least satisfied were those who were **under-benefited** (unhappy about giving the most).
- The next least satisfied were those who were **over-benefited** (perhaps they felt a bit guilty about giving the least). Equal relationships were the **most satisfactory**.

But there may be sex differences in how we feel about unequal relationships. **Argyle (1988)** found that:

- Over-benefited **men** were almost as satisfied as those in equitable marriages.
- Over-benefited **women**, however, were much **less satisfied** than women in equal relationships.

Theories of relationship formation can also give an insight into **relationship maintenance**.

- A relationship in which your needs are satisfied would be important for you to **protect and maintain**.
- In the same sense, equity theory says that people in an unbalanced, unfair relationship may **attempt to change things** in order for the balance to be restored.

Formation, Maintenance and Breakdown

A Range of Factors can Influence the *Breakdown of a Relationship*

These are some common reasons for the breakdown of a relationship:

- **dissatisfaction** or **boredom** with the relationship
- **breaking agreed rules** (e.g. being faithful, confidentiality)
- **interference** from other relationships (e.g. family or friends)
- **abuse** (e.g. violence, drugs, alcohol)
- an attractive **alternative relationship** exists
- costs **outweigh** benefits
- **conflict** or **dispute** (e.g. over finances)
- **jealousy** over a real or imagined rival

Theories Suggest Relationships *End in Stages*

Lee (1984) conducted interviews with over 100 couples who had broken up.
He identified **five stages** in the process of the breakdown of a relationship:

1) **Dissatisfaction** in one or both partners
2) **Exposing** the dissatisfaction and identifying problems
3) **Negotiating** the exposed problems
4) **Resolution** — attempting to solve problems
5) **Termination** of the relationship if no resolution

Not all couples went through **all the stages**. It seems that less intimate relationships may progress to the termination stage **more quickly**. Stronger relationships took **longer** to go through the stages and took longer to get over.

Duck (1988) developed a **four-phase model** of the ending of an intimate relationship.

1) **Intra-psychic** phase — inside the head of **one person**. One partner becomes **dissatisfied** with the relationship.
2) **Dyadic phase** — between **two people**. The other partner is told about the dissatisfaction.
3) **Social phase** — beyond the couple. The break-up is **made public** to friends and family. **Implications** are discussed (e.g. care of children). The relationship **can still be saved** here (e.g. intervention of family, external marital support).
4) **Grave-dressing phase** — finishing the relationship completely. The ex-partners organise their lives post-relationship. They tell their own version of the break-up and of their current relationship with their ex.

However, the theories don't take **individual differences** into account and **research evidence** suggests these models don't show how **complex** relationship dissolution can be.

- **Rusbult and Zembrodt (1983)** said some people in relationship breakdowns **actively lead** the process (to resolve the problems or speed up the ending). Others are **passive** (believing things will resolve themselves).
- **Akert (1992)** said people who do the breaking up are **less likely** to be upset and show physical symptoms (e.g. loss of appetite and sleep) — not surprising really.
- Finally, these theories don't take **cultural differences** in relationships into account (see page 131).

Practice Questions

Q1 List some needs and rewards provided by relationships.

Q2 Give three examples of reasons for the breakdown of a relationship.

Q3 What are Lee's five stages of relationship breakdown?

Q4 Describe the dyadic phase of Duck's model.

Exam Questions

Q1 Outline and evaluate two or more theories of relationship formation. [24 marks]

Q2 Discuss research (theories and/or studies) relating to the dissolution of relationships. [24 marks]

People might try and tell you that a relationship is the best kind of ship...

... but that's clearly a lie. The best kind of ship is probably like that one out of Pirates of the Caribbean. It had cannons. And pirates. But I doubt psychologists are cut out for the high seas. Duck might cope, I suppose. Now, make sure you can describe the main theories concerning the formation and dissolution of relationships, and then we can quack on...

Reproductive Behaviour

If you've ever wondered why we find certain characteristics attractive in people, or why parents put so much time and effort into bringing kids up, you've come to the right pages. If you've never wondered this, these are still the right pages.

Sexual Selection Explains Certain *Reproductive Behaviours*

1) Within a species there are certain **characteristics** that make individuals **attractive** to potential mates.
2) For example, female peacocks find the **long**, **brightly coloured tails** of male peacocks attractive.
3) Males with very brightly coloured tails are more noticeable to **predators**. Those with very long tails find it **difficult to escape** from predators. So, long, brightly coloured tails **reduce** male peacocks' **chances of surviving**.
4) However, as female peacocks are **attracted** to this feature, males with long, brightly coloured tails have a **higher chance of reproducing** and passing their genes on to the next generation than other males.
5) This means that the characteristic **evolves** in the species even though it reduces the survival chances.
6) This evolution of characteristics which are attractive to potential mates is known as **sexual selection**.
7) In **humans**, characteristics affecting attractiveness include **physical** and **mental health** and some **physical features**.
8) These influence potential mates as they indicate ability to **reproduce** and **provide for offspring**.

There Are *Different Types* of *Sexual Selection*

Intrasexual selection

Intrasexual selection takes place when males compete (often aggressively) and the winner is rewarded with the female. The female is **passive** in this process — she doesn't choose her own mate.

Intersexual selection

Intersexual selection takes place when males compete for the **attention** of a female. The female plays an **active role**, choosing her mate.

Sperm Competition is a Form of *Intrasexual Selection*

1) Short's (1979) **Sperm Competition Theory** suggests that males are motivated to ensure that their sperm is **successful in fertilisation** and compete against other males to make this happen.
2) In **humans** this has resulted in men evolving to release **large amounts** of sperm during ejaculation.
3) This is a form of **intrasexual selection** and increases the likelihood of **successful fertilisation**.

Buss (1989) Carried Out *Cross Cultural Research* Into *Intersexual Selection*

Buss (1989) — gender differences in mate selection

Method: **Questionnaires** were used to collect data from over 10 000 men and women from 37 different cultural groups. The questionnaires covered **demographic information** such as age, gender and marital status. They also asked about preferences for variables such as marriage, age differences and characteristics in a mate (e.g. intelligence, sociability and financial prospects).

Results: **Women** valued variables associated with **gaining resources** (e.g. money, safe environment) more highly than men. **Men** valued variables associated with **reproductive capacity** (e.g. youth) more highly than women.

Conclusion: Historically, women have had limited access to the **resources** needed to provide for themselves and their offspring. So, they've evolved to select mates who can **provide** these resources. Men have been limited by access to **fertile women**, and so have evolved to be attracted to women with a high likelihood of **reproducing**.

Evaluation: The study supports an **evolutionary explanation** of gender differences in sexual selection. **Similar findings** were found across a range of **different cultures**. However, it **wasn't** a truly **representative** study as it was hard to include rural and less educated populations. The study also didn't take **social influences** on mate selection into account. For example, changes in society mean that women in many cultures are now able to provide for themselves and their offspring, and aren't as dependent on men for resources.
Also, **homosexual relationships** aren't explained, as reproduction isn't a goal in same-sex relationships.

Reproductive Behaviour

Parental Investment Can be Explained in Terms of *Evolution*

1) **Parental investment** refers to any **time**, **effort** and **energy** that a parent puts towards the **conception**, **gestation** and **rearing** of a child that **reduces** their ability to invest in **other offspring**.
2) In species where gestation is **short** and offspring become independent **quickly**, **less** parental investment is needed.
3) However, in **humans**, parental investment is **more demanding** — gestation takes nine months and children don't become independent for many years.
4) **Sex differences** are an **evolutionary factor** that affects parental investment. For example:

Sex differences

1) Parental investment in humans shows **sex differences**.
2) Men only need to be involved at **conception** whilst women also have to invest during **pregnancy**.
3) There are differences when the offspring is born too, e.g. women have to invest in **breast-feeding**. Historically, men provided **protection**, **shelter** and other **resources** (e.g. food) whilst women invested more time and energy in the **day-to-day care** of children.
4) The **number of children** women can have is **limited** so they're likely to invest **heavily** in the survival of each one. Men can have many more children so investment in each individual is **less important**.
5) **Trivers (1972)** suggests the sex that invests **most** in the offspring (usually females) will **discriminate** when choosing a mate. The sex that invests **least** (usually males) will **compete** more for the higher investing mates.
6) Trivers' parental investment theory explains why men are usually **bigger** than women. Men who were **strong** and **aggressive** were more likely to win the **competition** for a higher investing female. This meant that their **genes** were more likely to stay in the gene pool.
7) Trivers' theory also offers an explanation for differences in **sexual promiscuity** between men and women. Men are more willing to engage in **one-night stands** and to have sex with lots of **different partners**, whereas women are more **choosy**. Trivers argued that this was because the parental investment per child is usually much **lower for men** than for women. Men need to make as **many** offspring as possible whereas women need to find a mate who will **protect** their offspring.

- Not all psychologists agree that parental investment theories explain the differences in reproductive behaviour between men and women. Some women are willing to have one-night stands, and get involved with short-term relationships. Also, **Sternglanz and Nash (1988)** argued that one-night stands aren't likely to result in pregnancy.
- It's possible that **culture** has also played a big role in shaping human reproductive behaviour. For example, it's often seen as **socially acceptable** for men to be promiscuous, but promiscuous women are **shunned**.
- **Buss (2000)** accepts **evolutionary explanations** for reproductive behaviour, but points out that sexual discrimination in women and sexual competition in men could be **problematic** for modern relationships.

Practice Questions

Q1 List some characteristics that influence attractiveness in humans.

Q2 What is meant by parental investment?

Q3 Male chimpanzees can be around 1.3 times bigger than female chimpanzees. Suggest why this might be.

Exam Question

Q1 a) Outline the relationship between sexual selection and human reproductive behaviours. [8 marks]

b) Discuss and evaluate the influence of sex differences on parental investment. [16 marks]

Research into sexual selection — sounds like a very dodgy excuse to me...

Sexual selection may sound made up, but it's actually a proper psychological term — along with sex differences and parental investment. Once you've got those straight you'll be able to wow those examiners with your reproductive knowledge.

Adult Relationships

We form relationships with lots of people throughout our lives. The relationships we form when we're young and the ones we see around us can affect our own ability to form successful adult relationships. A scary thought indeed...

Hazen and Shaver (1987) Linked Attachment Theory to Adult Relationships

1) **Childhood** experiences can influence **adult relationships** as they provide **examples** of how to behave.
2) **Hazen and Shaver** (**1987**) noticed similarities between the attachments infants form with their caregivers and the behaviour shown by adults in romantic relationships.
3) They investigated the link between the **attachment type** individuals showed as children and the way they felt about **adult relationships**:

Hazen and Shaver (1987) — attachment and adult relationships

Method: Descriptions of three attitudes towards adult relationships were published in a newspaper. These attitudes were based on **Ainsworth et al's attachment types**. Readers were asked to choose the attitude that best suited them. They were also asked to describe their relationships with their own caregivers.

Results: The **attachment type** that an individual had shown as a child was **significantly related** to how they felt about **adult relationships**. Those who showed a **secure** attachment type in childhood were more likely to enjoy **secure** relationships as an adult. Those with an **anxious-avoidant** attachment type in childhood were more likely to find it **difficult to trust people** in adult relationships. Those with an **anxious-resistant** attachment type in childhood were more likely to feel **anxious** in adult relationships and find it hard to get others as close to them as they wanted.

Conclusion: Relationships formed with parents during childhood affect relationships in adulthood.

Evaluation: The study was based on **self-report data** which is **subjective** and therefore may be **unreliable**. The data was also **retrospective**, further reducing the reliability of the study. Also, because the study relied on people replying to a newspaper article, the sample might not be **representative** of the whole population.

Look back to AS (p.22) if you can't remember about Ainsworth.

Parental Divorce Can Also Affect Adult Relationships

1) Many studies show that people who experienced **parental divorce** during childhood have **more negative attitudes** towards relationships than those who didn't experience parental divorce.
2) These negative attitudes include being **less optimistic** about having a successful relationship, feeling **less trustful** of partners, having a **more favourable attitude** towards **divorce** and a **more negative attitude** towards **marriage**.
3) Silvestri (1991) found that having **divorced parents** significantly increased an individual's **own chances** of getting divorced. Johnston and Thomas (1996) suggest that this could be because individuals model their adult behaviour on their parents' behaviour.
4) Alternatively, it could be a result of **learnt negative behaviour**, **disruption** caused by family tension, or **separation** from a parent or siblings during normal child developmental stages.
5) If one parent is absent the child doesn't have a **template** on which to model their own adult relationships. Franklin et al (1990) found that this can create problems with children's future adult relationships.
6) Not all children of divorced parents go on to have unsuccessful adult relationships. There are many factors which can influence the long-term effects, e.g. **quality of relationship** with parents and **support after divorce**.
7) This research can be used to **minimise** the **effect of divorce** on children.

Peer Interaction in Adolescence Develops Skills For Adult Relationships

1) Arnett (2007) suggests that friendships with **peers** during childhood and adolescence give opportunities to develop the **skills** needed to form **successful adult relationships**. These include how to **resolve conflict** and how to take on different **roles** needed in relationships.
2) Collins and van Dulmen (2006) support this theory and also suggest that relationships with peers give individuals the opportunity to learn **behaviours** and **expectations** involved in relationships.
3) So, experiences during childhood and adolescence influence the **quality** of adult relationships.

Adult Relationships

Different Cultures have Different Attitudes to Relationships

Western societies tend to be **individualist** and **Eastern** societies tend to be **collectivist**.

1) A **collectivist** society sees the individual as part of an **interdependent social group**. Obligations to others and the good of the group are very important.
2) Relationships are more likely to be **non-voluntary** (e.g. arranged marriages), where marriage joins **families** as well as individuals. Extended families are more likely to **live together**, providing support for each other.
3) In Western societies, the emphasis is on the **individual's** freedom, achievements and rights. So relationships are formed for individual happiness and are mostly **voluntary**, where a person chooses their partner for themselves.

The Attitudes and Values of Cultures Affect Relationships

Hsu (1981) stated that Western cultures value **change** and **new things**, but that Eastern cultures value **ancestry**, **history** and **continuity**. **Values** affect relationships in different parts of the world.

Duration

- Relationships are more likely to be **permanent** in non-Western cultures.
- In Western societies, we are more likely to split up and have **new relationships**.

Marriage

- Arranged marriages are often associated with collectivist cultures, and involve **whole families**. Arranged marriages also seem to have more **stability** than those based on 'romantic love'.
- However, **De Munck (1996)** found that in a Sri Lankan community with an emphasis on arranged marriages, **romantic love** was still considered when choosing a partner.
- **Ghuman (1994)** stated that arranged marriages were **common** among Hindus, Muslims and Sikhs in Britain, but **Goodwin (1997)** found that only **9%** of Hindu marriages he studied were arranged.
- **Levine et al (1995)** found a higher percentage of people from **collectivist** societies would marry a person with the **right qualities** whom they didn't love, compared to members of **individualistic** societies.

Divorce

- **Goodwin (1999)** calculated the US divorce rate to be **40-50%**.
- However, the Chinese regard divorce as shameful to the **families involved** as much as the divorcing couple — **fewer** marriages end in divorce. This is beginning to change though, as a result of **westernisation**.

Barry got his family's seal of approval before agreeing to anything.

Practice Questions

Q1 Describe the effect of parental divorce on a person's attitude towards adult relationships.

Q2 Give an example of a skill used in peer relationships that can also be used in adult relationships.

Q3 List some differences between trends in relationships in individualistic and collectivist cultures.

Exam Question

Q1 a) Discuss the influence that childhood experiences may have on adult relationships. [8 marks]

b) Discuss research relating to cultural differences in relationships. [16 marks]

I'm the anxious-resistant-avoidant type when it comes to exams...

Just like 40-50% of US marriages, you've reached the end of the road — or at least the end of the section. The key things to learn here are how childhood experiences affect adult relationships, and how relationships vary between cultures. Which is basically everything on these pages. Apart from Barry and the seals — you don't have to learn about him. He's very strange.

Social Theories of Aggression

This section is about aggression — GRRRR! Eeek, I scared myself a bit there. Maybe some theories will calm me down...

Deindividuation Theory Says Being Anonymous Encourages Aggression

One **social psychological** theory of aggression suggests we're **disinhibited** when we're an **anonymous** part of a **crowd**. People may feel less **personal responsibility** and less fear of **public disapproval** when they're part of the group. **Festinger et al (1952)** coined the term **deindividuation** to describe this state.

Aggression is behaviour intended to harm — including physical and psychological harm.

There's some **real-world evidence** for this effect:

1) **Mullen (1986)** analysed newspaper reports of **lynch mob violence** in the US. The **more people** there were in the mob, the **greater** the level of violence.
2) **Mann (1981)** analysed 21 reports of **suicides** and identified ten cases where a crowd had **baited** the person threatening suicide (e.g. shouting 'jump'). Baiting was more likely to happen **at night**, when the crowd was **at a distance** and when the crowd was **large** (more than 300 people).

Research studies have also supported deindividuation:

1) **Zimbardo (1969)** showed that **anonymity** affects behaviour. Participants in his study believed they were administering **shocks** to another participant in a learning experiment. **Individuated** participants wore normal clothes, large name badges and were introduced to each other. **Deindividuated** participants wore coats with hoods, were instructed in groups and weren't referred to by name. The **more anonymous** participants administered more and longer shocks.
2) **Diener et al (1976)** observed 1300 trick-or-treating children in the US. If they were **anonymous** (in costumes, masks or large groups) they were **more likely** to steal money and sweets.

This evidence supports the idea that deindividuation **increases** aggression. But there are also examples of it having **no effect** or even **reducing** aggression. For example, individuals in crowds at religious festivals often express goodwill to others. It could be that being in a group means that you **conform to group norms**. If group norms are **prosocial**, the individual may behave that way too.

Social Learning Theory Says Experience Explains Aggressive Behaviour

Social learning theory says behaviours are learnt in two ways:

1) **directly** through **reinforcement** (i.e. reward and punishment).
2) **indirectly** by seeing others being rewarded or punished for behaviours (**vicarious learning**).

Bandura (1965) conducted the **Bobo Doll Experiment** to investigate whether **aggressive behaviour** can be learnt through reinforcement and punishment.

A Bobo doll is an inflatable figure with a weight in the bottom.

Bandura (1965) — Bobo Doll Experiment

Method:	In a **controlled observation** with an **independent measures** design, children watched a video of a male or female model behaving aggressively towards a Bobo doll. Their behaviour was distinctive — e.g. they used a hammer or shouted certain things. The children either saw the model being told off (**punished**) or being rewarded with sweets (**reinforced**). In a **control condition**, the model was neither rewarded nor punished. The children were then allowed to play in a room of toys, including the Bobo doll.
Results:	Children who'd seen the model being rewarded and those in the control condition imitated **more** aggressive behaviours than those who saw the model being punished.
Conclusion:	Children learn aggressive behaviour through **observation** and **imitation**, particularly if it's rewarded.
Evaluation:	The models used distinctive actions that the children were unlikely to produce spontaneously, meaning that Bandura could be sure that **imitation** was taking place. However, the conditions were pretty **artificial** — it's unlikely that children would see adults behaving aggressively towards toys in real life, so the study lacks **ecological validity**. The study also didn't consider the differences between **playfighting** and aggression towards other people. The **previous** behaviour of the children wasn't considered, and no **follow-up** was done to see if the aggressive behaviour was long-term.

Institutional Aggression

Institutional Aggression is Often Seen as *Acceptable*

Aggression doesn't always involve red faces, bulging eyes and throbbing veins. It can be calm, organised, and even respectable. Certain groups in society are actually relied on to show aggression, so the rest of us don't have to...

Aggression in the police force

To uphold the **rules** and **norms** of society the police are allowed to use aggression against people breaking the law. In this situation, aggression can be seen as a **prosocial behaviour** and many people think the threat of police aggression is critical in maintaining order in society. To make sure their aggressive behaviours are **controlled** and **appropriate** to the situation police officers have to go through training — uncontrolled police aggression or abuse of police power isn't tolerated by society. The **Independent Police Complaints Commission** helps make sure that police aggression is controlled and appropriate by holding police officers accountable for their actions.

Aggression in the military

Wars are usually started and coordinated by **politicians**. Their motivations may be very different to those of the soldiers who join up to fight. For example, a soldier may join the military in order to become part of a **group** and feel a **sense of belonging**, leading to increased **self-esteem**.

Aggression, or the threat of aggression, is an important feature of a soldier's job. However, like in the police force, the aggression needs to be **controlled** and used for **specific purposes** only. For this reason soldiers receive training on **when** to behave aggressively and what **types** of aggression are appropriate. For example, the use of guns to return enemy fire is deemed acceptable, but violence towards prisoners and innocent civilians is not.

However, organised aggression isn't always respectable or accepted by society.
Terrorist groups are an example of aggressive organisations that **aren't** tolerated by society.

Aggression in terrorist groups

People who join **terrorist organisations** may be motivated by a wide range of reasons, including the sense of belonging that comes with joining a group. Many join believing it will bring them certain **benefits**, e.g. young Palestinians living in poverty are often recruited as suicide bombers with the promise of glory in the afterlife. The difference between military organisations and terrorist groups is **relative**, depending on who the target of aggression is — enemy soldiers or civilians.

Practice Questions

Q1 What does deindividuation mean?

Q2 Outline a laboratory experiment that linked deindividuation and aggression.

Q3 Give two criticisms of Bandura's (1965) Bobo Doll experiment.

Q4 Give two examples of institutional aggression.

Q5 Give three reasons why an individual might decide to join the army and fight for their country.

Exam Question

Q1 a) Outline two social psychological theories of aggression. [8 marks]

b) Evaluate the theories of aggression outlined in part (a). [16 marks]

That wasn't aggression — my fist slipped... And then so did my foot...

It doesn't seem at all surprising that a small child will mimic behaviour that they've recently seen, especially if there's been no harmful outcome of the behaviour they witnessed. But is hitting a doll the same as hitting another child because you've seen someone on TV doing it... Hmm, not too sure about that one — it's a really big jump, and not something you can easily test.

Biological Explanations of Aggression

Aggression is a tendency that humans share with almost all species of animal, as anyone who's tried to give a cat a bath will know. It's a response that can be partially explained by biology. Not sure that'd go down well as an excuse though...

There Are **Genetic Influences** Underlying Aggression

1) Species of various animals have been **selectively bred** to produce highly **aggressive** individuals — e.g. Doberman dogs were originally bred by humans to behave aggressively towards intruders so they can be used as guard dogs.
2) This ability to select the most aggressive dogs and breed them together to give **new generations** with the **same** aggressive tendencies suggests that there are specific **genes** that determine levels of aggression.
3) In humans, evidence for a genetic component to aggression comes from **twin studies** and **adoption studies**, where **criminality** is used as a measure of aggression.

Christiansen (1977) — Twin study into aggression

Method: A **concordance analysis** of all 3586 pairs of **twins** born between 1881 and 1910 in a region of Denmark was conducted. From this sample, **926** individuals were registered by the police for **criminal activity**. **Identical** (**MZ**) and **non-identical** (**DZ**) twins were compared for the rate at which **both** twins of the pair were registered.

Results: **Male MZ twins** showed **35% concordance** for criminality, compared to the **12% concordance** shown between **DZ twins**. **Female MZ** twins showed **21% concordance** compared to **8%** for **DZ** twins.

Conclusion: There's a **genetic component** to aggressive behaviour.

Evaluation: Genetics can't be the only factor, as the concordance rate for MZ twins (who share all of their genetic material) wasn't 100%. In previous twin studies, **samples** have been used where at least one twin had committed a crime. This gave **inflated** concordance rates. However, by studying **all** the twins born in a specified time frame, this study gives a more **representative** rate of concordance. As with all twin studies, **shared environment** for MZ twins is a **confounding variable**.

Mednick et al (1984) — Adoption study into aggression

Method: A **concordance analysis** of 14 427 Danish **adoptees** was conducted. Rates of concordance for **criminality** between the adoptees and their **adopted** and **biological parents** were compared.

Results: **13.5%** of adoptees with parents (adoptive or biological) **without** a criminal conviction had a criminal conviction themselves, compared to **14.7%** of adoptees with at least one criminally convicted **adoptive** parent, **20%** of adoptees with at least one criminally convicted **biological** parent, and **24.5%** of adoptees with at least one convicted adoptive **and** one convicted biological parent.

Conclusion: A **genetic link** is supported. However, the **concordance rates** are quite **low**, suggesting that there are **other** factors that lead to criminality.

Evaluation: Adoption studies allow **separation** of the genetic and environmental influences. However, criminal convictions may not be a **valid indicator** of aggression — the convictions could have been for non-violent crimes. Also, just because a person has not been **convicted** of a crime does not necessarily mean that they have never committed one.

Areas of the **Brain** Have Been Linked to Aggression

Different areas of the **brain**, including the **temporal lobe** and the **limbic system**, have been linked to different forms of aggressive behaviour. One part of the limbic system, the **amygdala**, has been found to have a particularly strong connection to aggression. Animal studies have shown that **electrical stimulation** of different parts of the amygdala can either **cause** or **reduce** aggression. **Lesions** to the amygdala have been found to cause cats to **attack**, but caused dogs to become **more submissive** and **less aggressive** — they needed **more stimulation** to provoke a response.

There is some evidence for the role of the amygdala in **human** aggression too. **Charles Whitman**, a sniper who killed 14 innocent people and wounded 31 others, left a note that pleaded for his brain to be examined after death for possible dysfunction. An autopsy showed that he had a **temporal lobe tumour**, pressing on his amygdala.

Biological Explanations of Aggression

Hormones May Also Be Involved in Aggression

High levels of **testosterone** (an androgen) are linked to aggression.

1) Levels of testosterone have been **compared** in **males** and **females**, and in **violent** and **non-violent** criminals.
2) **Males** in general, and **violent criminals** in particular, have **higher** levels of testosterone. This may explain their higher levels of **aggression**.
3) However, there's a problem with establishing **cause and effect** — this data is only **correlational**. Another factor could be causing aggressive behaviour, or it could be that being aggressive raises levels of testosterone.

Cindy wasn't the aggressive type, but if she ever saw that hairdresser again...

Van Goozen et al (1994) studied the effects of testosterone **directly**. This avoided having to depend on correlational data, which made it easier to establish cause and effect.

Van Goozen et al (1994) — Aggression in sex-change participants

Method:	In a **repeated measures** design, 35 female-to-male and 15 male-to-female transsexuals completed **questionnaires** to assess **proneness to aggression**. They completed the questionnaires before and after receiving hormone treatment to 'change' their sex. Female-to-male transsexuals were given testosterone (an androgen) and male-to-female transsexuals were given anti-androgens. Treatment lasted 3 months.
Results:	**Female-to-male** transsexuals reported an **increase** in aggression proneness, whereas **male-to-female** transsexuals reported a **decrease**.
Conclusion:	Levels of **testosterone** determine the likelihood of displaying **aggressive behaviours**.
Evaluation:	By controlling levels of testosterone **experimentally**, the **direction** of cause and effect between testosterone and aggression can be established. However, **self-report** measures of aggression were used, which are subjective and so may not be valid. The participants may have been conforming to **stereotypes** of their new gender roles by expressing an increase or decrease in aggression.

Practice Questions

Q1 Give two possible biological causes of aggression.

Q2 Outline the conclusion of the study by Christiansen (1977).

Q3 Describe the method used in the study by Mednick et al (1984).

Q4 Which parts of the brain have been linked to aggression?

Q5 Which hormone has been linked to aggression?

Q6 Give one advantage and one disadvantage of the method used in the study by Van Goozen et al (1994).

Exam Question

Q1 a) Outline the role of hormones in aggression. [8 marks]

b) Discuss the genetic explanation for aggression. [16 marks]

Pardon me for being aggressive — it was not me, it was my amygdala...

Not quite as snappy as the original, but I still have high hopes that it'll catch on. It's quite surprising that biological parents have more influence on criminal behaviour than the adoptive parents you've grown up with. But, as the study pointed out, the concordance rates are still quite low, so there must be other factors involved — e.g. your friends and where you live.

Evolutionary Explanations of Aggression

Aggression often (though not always) serves a purpose. That doesn't give you licence to go stomping around throwing things about though — it's not big and it's not clever. Speaking of clever, you'd best get on and learn this stuff...

*There's an **Evolutionary Explanation** For Aggression*

Lorenz proposed a theory of aggression based on **animal behaviour**. He used the idea of **natural selection** (that only the best adapted will survive and pass on their genes) to explain how the behaviour of animals is shaped. Lorenz suggested his theory could also be applied to **humans**.

1) Aggression is an **innate tendency** that's triggered by **environmental stimuli**.
2) Aggression is an **adaptive response**. An individual will be more likely to pass on their **genes** if they're able to gain the **upper hand** in competition for food, mates or territory.
3) Aggression is **ritualised**. A behaviour won't be passed on in the genes if it gets an animal **killed** before it produces offspring. So, there are ritual behaviours in place to stop confrontations being fatal, e.g. wolves end a fight by the loser exposing his jugular vein as a sign of **submission**. This puts the winner in prime position to kill their rival, but in fact the winner takes no further action. If animals were **routinely killed** during everyday power struggles or mating contests, it's likely the species would become **extinct**.

Lorenz's theory has been **criticised** on the fact that aggression **isn't always** adaptive and ritualised — there are many species that **do** fight to the death. Also, the relevance of the theory to **humans** is limited, as **cultural** influences are highly influential in the expression of aggression, e.g. a person's religious beliefs may shape their actions, as may the availability of weapons or the occurrence of war. However, an **evolutionary** approach may be relevant in explaining **some** aggressive human responses.

Jealousy** is Aggression to **Deter a Partner's Infidelity

Tony didn't see it as infidelity, more a service to mankind — genes as good as his should be passed on.

1) In a survey by **Kinsey (1948)**, **50%** of married **men** and **26%** of married **women** reported having had sex with somebody else while married.
2) Infidelity can be seen as an **evolutionary adaptive strategy** for a man to increase the **quantity** of offspring carrying his genes, and for a woman to improve the **quality** of her offspring.
3) However, it's obviously **not** in the **genetic interests** of their **partners** to be cheated on — it won't be their genes being passed on to the next generation.
4) Indicators that a partner is being unfaithful often lead to **jealous rage**. Jealousy has been explained as a product of **evolution**, although this response is triggered **differently** in each sex.

Buss et al (1992) — Sex differences in jealousy

Method: This was a **cross-cultural questionnaire study**. Participants were presented with the **hypothetical scenario** that someone they were in a serious, committed romantic relationship with had become interested in someone else. They were asked what would distress them more — imagining their partner forming a deep **emotional attachment** to that other person, or enjoying passionate **sexual intercourse** with the person.

Results: Across all studies, **more men** than women reported **sexual infidelity** to be most upsetting. On average, **51%** of the men versus **22%** of the women chose this to be more distressing than **emotional infidelity**.

Conclusion: Men's jealousy is innately triggered by the threat of uncertainty over the **paternity** of children produced within the relationship. However, women are more threatened by **emotional involvement** as it could mean being left for another woman, and so reducing the resources available to her children.

Evaluation: The fact that the evidence was **consistent** across **different cultures** suggests that these different responses are **innate** rather than learned. However, the fact that the questionnaires were based around a **hypothetical** situation, and the responses available to the participants were **multiple choice**, means that the **validity** of the results is questionable — they may not accurately reflect what participants would actually do if they found themselves in that situation.

Evolutionary Explanations of Aggression

Group Aggression Also Has an Evolutionary Explanation

Aggression can be used by groups to establish dominance in **status** or to gain better **resources**. Warfare and sport are two examples of **group displays** of aggression in humans. There's an **evolutionary explanation** for them both:

Warfare

1) **Buss and Shackelford (1997)** suggest that aggression is an **adaptive response** as it encourages the **reproductive success** of the species. **Sexual selection** means that we choose between prospective mates who we will breed with. Aggression through warfare is one way to **eliminate rivals** and increase the likelihood of our genes being passed on.
2) According to **Waller (2002)**, **terrorist attacks** and **genocides** can be explained by evolutionary theory. Because humans have evolved living in **groups**, a sense of 'them' and 'us' has become important to us. Warfare and other violence against 'outsiders' are ways of defining the **boundaries** of our groups.

- **Tinbergen (1968)** pointed out that aggression in humans **doesn't always** have an **adaptive survival function**. Humans are **one of the few species** that use aggression purely to cause harm.
- Tinbergen said that advances in **technology** mean we're now able to fight each other from **long distances**. In face-to-face aggression we use **signals of appeasement** and **submission** (e.g. emotional tears blur vision and so reduce the efficiency of attack and defence — this acts as a signal of submission to the opponent). In **modern warfare**, these signals no longer apply as we can't clearly see our opponent. In other words, changes in technology have **outstripped** the evolution of adaptive behaviour.

Sport

1) **Podaliri and Balestri (1998)** studied Italian **football supporters**. They found that **aggressive chants** and **aggressive behaviour** strengthened the **cultural identity** of the different supporters, so that the differences between the groups were emphasised.
2) They argued that being **associated** with the **winning team** at a football match gives us **increased status** and makes us more **attractive** to potential partners. This has **adaptive value** because we increase the likelihood of genes from our group being passed on — aggressive behaviour has **survival value**.
3) A weakness of this approach is that similar levels of aggression are **rare** in supporters of **other types of sports**. Also the role of **testosterone** (see page 135) and **social learning theory** (see page 132) aren't considered.

Anthony had listened carefully in psychology class — drowning the opposition at the water polo game had worked very nicely indeed.

Practice Questions

Q1 Describe the findings of the study by Buss et al (1992).

Q2 Why have we evolved the adaptive response of aggression?

Q3 What were the findings of the Podaliri and Balestri (1998) study?

Exam Questions

Q1 "Aggression is an adaptive response." Discuss this statement. [20 marks]

Q2 Rob is at a football match where the crowd becomes aggressive.
How could an evolutionary approach to aggression explain this behaviour? [4 marks]

Forget infidelity — it's people with no exams that make me jealous...

The point to remember about evolutionary arguments is that a modern man or woman probably wouldn't have an affair in order to spread their genes about or improve the quality of any offspring. But these may be deeply buried motives that have been passed down from their early ancestors and still affect their behaviour today, even if they're not aware of it. Spooky.

Factors Influencing Eating Behaviour

This section is all about food and eating, so if you're feeling peckish I suggest you go and grab some biscuits before you start reading. Or a nice bar of chocolate. Maybe even some toast. Actually, forget that, where's the takeaway menu...

Cultural Influence** Affects Attitudes Towards **Food** and **Size

In the UK today we tend to assume that you have to be **skinny** to be **beautiful**. But that's actually quite a **recent** idea.

1) Throughout human history, being **voluptuous** (curvy) was considered an attractive trait in a potential partner — it signalled **health** and access to **plentiful resources** in times of scarcity. People were proud to gorge themselves on food and drink because it signalled their **wealth** and **status**.
2) However, in the last 40 years the '**supermodel**' and '**size zero**' figure has become popular in Western culture. Highly profitable diet, exercise and surgery industries have sprung up as a result of this popularity.
3) In many other places big is **still** seen as best though — for example, in many **African** cultures plump females are regarded as wiser and more fertile, in **Asian** cultures weight is often still linked to affluence and success, and **Pacific Islanders** (Hawaiians/Samoans) equate large physical size in both genders with beauty and status.

Food is also an important part of many **religions**:

1) Some **fast** to show devotion (e.g. **Muslim** Ramadan).
2) Some **feast** to celebrate important events (e.g. **Christian** Christmas).
3) Some **forbid** certain foods (e.g. **Judaism** — pork isn't eaten).
4) Some incorporate food in **rituals** (e.g. **Catholicism** — communion wafers).

Different cultures attach different **meanings** to foods and eating forms a major part of many **celebrations** and **ceremonies** worldwide. Imagine birthdays without cake, or Christmas without sprouts...

*Attitudes to Food Can Be Affected By **Mood***

Anyone who has been unable to eat when **stressed** or who has 'pigged out' on junk food when they're feeling **down** will know that mood and food are **linked**.

1) A reduced appetite or bad diet, caused by a lack of motivation, is a common symptom of **depression**.
2) If you don't have the **energy** to prepare healthy meals you might be more likely to resort to unhealthy pre-packaged ready meals and quick snacks.
3) Some people may impulsively '**comfort eat**' or **binge eat** in the hope that a quick indulgence will make them feel better — usually choosing foods high in carbohydrates, fat, sugar and salt to provide that quick 'hit'.
4) This can lead to a **vicious cycle** of mood swings caused by unnatural highs and lows in blood sugar levels, which trigger further cravings.

Psychologists are currently investigating the role **emotional intelligence (EI)** plays in the relationship between mood and eating behaviour. They believe that people with a **high level** of personal EI make better food choices and are less likely to use food to regulate their mood. These people are also less likely to find that their appetite is affected (reduced or increased) by **stress**.

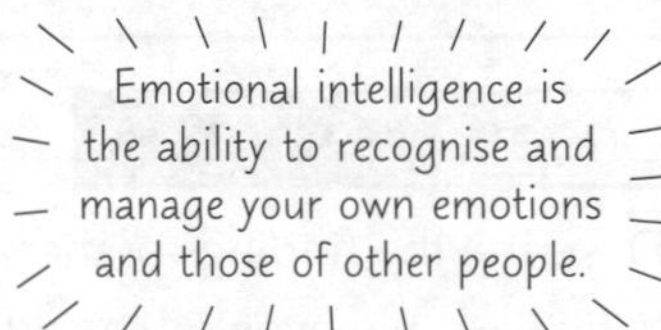

Health Concerns** Can Affect **Eating Behaviour

Health concerns (e.g. high blood pressure) can affect what and how much we eat. However, eating healthily can become an **obsession** for some people:

Orthorexia is an **eating disorder** where people survive on a **highly restricted diet** to try and avoid anything they think might be 'unhealthy'. This can range from pesticides, herbicides, artificial additives or genetically modified ingredients to fats, animal products, or anything except raw fruit and vegetables. In extreme cases this can lead to **malnutrition** or even **death**.

More familiar examples of eating disorders include **anorexia** and **bulimia** (see p.142–145). Sometimes these can begin with a desire to lose weight and be more **healthy**, which then gets out of hand and becomes a dangerous **obsession**.

Factors Influencing Eating Behaviour

Dieting Doesn't Always Lead to *Weight Loss*

It's not as easy as just going on a diet and watching the weight drop off. Whether a person **succeeds** in losing weight depends on things like motivation, willpower, genetics, lifestyle and medical conditions (e.g. diabetes or thyroid problems). Other factors include:

Support and Encouragement

1) Eating is often a part of **social interaction**, so many experts think dieting should be too.
2) Informing friends and family of weight loss goals should help reduce the **temptations** of food and encourage **positive reinforcement** (and punishment) from others. Lots of dieters also join a weight loss group or diet with a friend or partner to maintain **motivation**.
3) But this approach doesn't work for everyone — some people find constant monitoring by others stressful and use **secretive binge eating** as a defence mechanism.

They were meant to be on a diet, but Mike sensed that his wife's resolve had slipped.

Physiological Changes Due to Dieting

1) Your body has evolved to cope with **chronic food shortages** by lowering your metabolic rate and protecting fat stores in times of **starvation**. Extreme dieting triggers this response.
2) If you then return to normal eating you end up with **more excess calories** than before which are then converted to fat. To overcome the feeling of deprivation during the diet people often also **overeat** afterwards, which gives an even bigger weight gain.
3) You may then start **another**, even more restrictive diet to undo the weight gain. But this will just reduce the metabolic rate **further** and so the pattern of **'yo-yo' dieting** continues.

Polivy and Herman (1975) — Psychological effects of dieting

Method:	In a study with an independent measures design, samples of **dieting** and **non-dieting** students were placed in three **'pre-load'** conditions — drinking either one or two glasses of milkshake or nothing at all. They were then given unlimited supplies of ice cream.
Results:	The non-dieters ate **less** ice cream the more milkshakes they had drunk. The dieters ate **more** ice cream the more milkshakes they had drunk.
Conclusion:	Drinking the milkshake had damaged the dieters' determination — they gave in to total indulgence after failure. This is known as **'the counter-regulation effect'**.
Evaluation:	These findings **support** what we already know about dieting (the 'diet starts tomorrow' mentality). **Follow-up studies** have found that many people have an 'all-or-nothing' mentality to dieting — if they break the diet they tend to see it as immediate failure and so eat as much as they like.

Practice Questions

Q1 Explain why a fuller figure has traditionally been considered attractive in many cultures.

Q2 Suggest a reason why dieting might fail.

Q3 Describe a physiological effect of dieting.

Exam Question

Q1 Discuss the factors that affect eating behaviour and attitudes to food. [24 marks]

Eating behaviour — now that's the kind of study I'd volunteer for...

There's now such pressure on people, especially women, to look slim in order to feel attractive that it's hard to believe it's all just down to fashion. But from an evolutionary point of view the old-fashioned preference for a curvier figure makes more sense. This showed you had the physical resources to grow and provide for a baby successfully.

Biological Explanations of Eating Behaviour

As the title suggests, there are biological reasons for why you feel hungry or full at different times. And here they are...

Neural Mechanisms** Control Eating and **Satiation

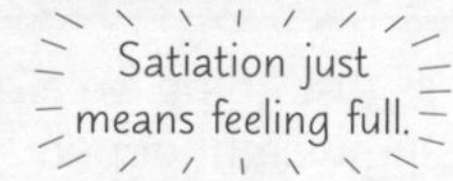

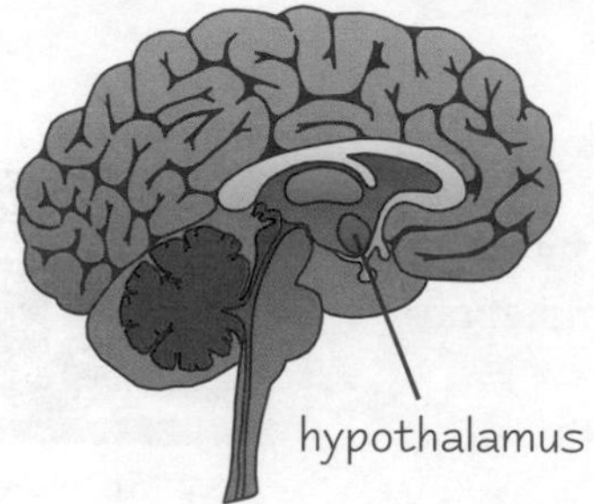

1) The **hypothalamus** is a gland in the brain responsible for **homeostasis** (keeping conditions in the body constant).
2) It helps to **regulate** things like temperature, circadian rhythms and intake of food and drink.
3) The **ventromedial nucleus (VMN)** and the **lateral nucleus (LN)** are the parts of the hypothalamus that are thought to be involved in **food regulation**.

*The **Ventromedial Nucleus** is the **Satiety Centre***

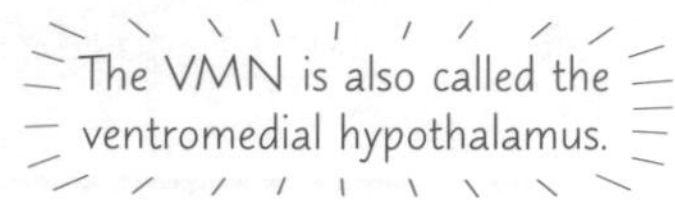

1) Satiety is the **unconscious physiological process** that **stops** you eating.
2) The **VMN** provides the signal to stop eating when it picks up **hormonal messages**. For example, when food is being digested the level of the hormone CCK in the bloodstream is high. This stimulates receptors in the VMN.
3) Experimental **electrical stimulation** of the VMN has been shown to **reduce food intake**.
4) Malfunctions in the VMN may cause **obesity**. This was demonstrated by Baylis et al (1996).

	Baylis et al (1996) — VMN lesioning in rats
Method:	Two **symmetrical lesions** (injuries) were made in the VMN of eight male and five female rats. Their body weight was later compared with **age-matched controls**.
Results:	The rats with lesions in their VMN had become **obese**, while the control rats had not.
Conclusion:	Lesions in the VMN cause **hyperphagia** (overeating) and obesity, so the VMN must play a role in satiation.
Evaluation:	This was a very **small sample** using only one breed of rat, so the findings can't be generalised. Also, **other tissues** surrounding the VMN might have been damaged when the lesions were created, so it might not necessarily just be the VMN that is involved.

*The **Lateral Nucleus** is the **Hunger Centre***

1) When the body's blood sugar level drops, homeostatic responses kick in to help restore the **equilibrium**.
2) **Receptors** in the LN detect the drop in blood sugar. This then causes neurons to fire that create the sensation of hunger.
3) The person is driven to eat and blood glucose levels increase. Receptors then send a hormonal message to the **VMN** to give the sensation of fullness (see above).

The LN is also called the lateral hypothalamus.

Damage to the LN can reduce food intake. For example, chemical lesions are known to produce **aphagia** (failure to eat). However, as with VMN studies, there may be **methodological problems** muddying the water.

	Winn et al (1990) — LN lesioning in rats
Method:	The toxin **NMDA** was used to make **lesions** in the LN of rats. A small dose (lesions in **LN only**) and a large dose (lesions spread to **adjacent areas**) condition was used, and there was also a **control group**.
Results:	Rats that had the small dose of NMDA showed **no changes** in their eating behaviour after a brief recovery period. However, rats that had the large dose showed **long-term deficits** in their eating behaviour.
Conclusion:	Damage to the **hypothalamus** impairs feeding responses, but the LN may **not** have as much of an effect as previously thought.
Evaluation:	This research is useful as it shows that the localisation of brain function is **more complex** than originally thought. However, this was an **exploratory study** to test whether NMDA was an effective toxin for use on the hypothalamus and wasn't originally intended to investigate hunger. Therefore, all the relevant variables may not have been controlled, reducing the **reliability** of the results.

Biological Explanations of Eating Behaviour

There Are *Evolutionary* Reasons For *Food Preferences*

People need food to **survive** and throughout history it's been a driving force for **evolution**. This can help explain why so many people would rather have a chocolate eclair than a slice of grapefruit.

Why we like sweet stuff...

- **Harris (1987)** found that **newborn babies** have a preference for sweet things and dislike bitter things.
- These preferences and dislikes are **universal**, suggesting a **genetic** (therefore evolutionary) explanation.
- Early mammals were **frugivores** (ate mainly fruit). Sweet food now triggers the release of the pleasure-inducing brain chemical **dopamine** which acts as a reinforcer.
- Most **poisons** have a strong bitter taste — so our dislike of this type of taste could be a **survival reflex**.

Why we prefer food that's bad for us...

- **Burnham and Phelan (2000)** suggest that a preference for **fatty foods** would have helped our ancestors survive in times of **food scarcity** — these foods are full of energy-giving **calories**.
- Even though food is no longer scarce, we're still programmed to stuff ourselves with burgers and cakes when they're available in order to **build up fat reserves** in case there's ever a shortage. Again, **dopamine** may act as a reinforcing reward.

Why we like our meat spicy...

- **Sherman and Hash (2001)** analysed almost 7000 recipes from 36 countries and found that **meat** dishes contained far more **spices** than **vegetable** dishes. They hypothesised that this was because spices have **antimicrobial** properties — meat is more vulnerable to being infested with bacteria and fungi than vegetables are.
- This may also explain why people in **hot climates** tend to eat **more** spicy food — microbes grow faster in warmer conditions.

For the ultimate dopamine hit Jessie liked to take her sugar neat.

Why we won't eat green bananas or mouldy bread...

We've learned to avoid food that seems **unripe** or **mouldy**. Knowledge passed on from other people as well as our own experiences tell us that good food means life and bad food means death (or at least a dodgy tummy and wasted energy).

Practice Questions

Q1 Describe the function of the hypothalamus in eating behaviour.

Q2 How do Burnham and Phelan (2000) explain our preference for fatty foods?

Q3 Explain how Darwin's theory of natural selection can be applied to food preferences.

Exam Question

Q1 Describe and evaluate research studies into hunger and satiation and explain what they tell us about the neural mechanisms involved. [24 marks]

I can't help it — I've evolved to eat cheesecake...

This explains the mystery of why people seem to love chips, kebabs and anything bad, and shudder at the thought of broccoli and spinach. Our ancestors would be surviving on plants and thinking themselves lucky, and now and again having a big blow-out on a dead mammoth to keep them going through the lean times. Mmmm, barbecued mammoth. My favourite.

Anorexia Nervosa

Lots of people are worried about their weight, but for some this preoccupation leads to really serious health problems. Eating disorders like anorexia nervosa have become increasingly common over the past couple of decades.

Anorexia Nervosa Leads to Significant *Weight Loss*

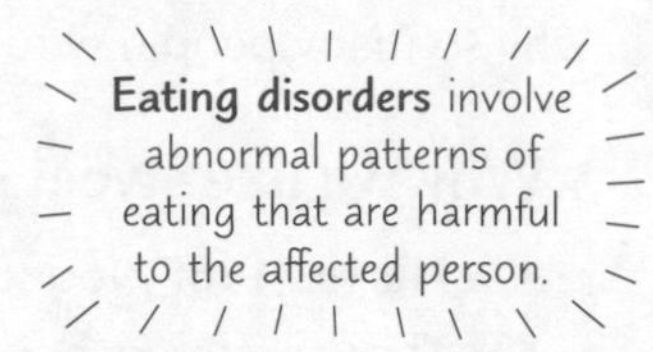

Anorexia nervosa is one of the most common eating disorders in the UK. About **90%** of cases are **females** aged **13–18** years old. About **1 in 250 females** and **1** in **2000 males** in the UK between **15 and 30** suffer from anorexia. It involves a dramatic reduction in the amount of food eaten, leading to significant **weight loss**.

The **DSM-IV** (the main diagnostic manual for mental disorders) describes four main characteristics of anorexia:

Low weight — anorexia is characterised by a refusal to maintain a normal body weight. This is usually classified as consistently weighing **less than 85%** of the expected weight for their build, age and height.

Body-image distortion — people with anorexia have **distorted self-perception**. They believe they're overweight even when very thin, judge themselves based largely on their weight and refuse to accept the seriousness of their condition.

Anxiety — anorexics are very **fearful** of gaining weight or getting fat even when they're seriously underweight.

Amenorrhoea — females usually **stop menstruating** due to their low body weight. Missing **three consecutive periods** is a clinical characteristic of the disorder.

There Are *Biological Explanations* For Anorexia Nervosa

Genetic Explanations Have Been Suggested

	Holland et al (1988) — concordance rates in twins
Method:	**Concordance rates** (extent to which twins share the same traits) were studied in 45 pairs of twins. At least one twin of each pair had been diagnosed as having anorexia nervosa — the study examined how often the other twin also suffered from the disorder.
Results:	The concordance rate was **56%** for **identical** (MZ) twins and only **5%** for **non-identical** (DZ) twins.
Conclusion:	Anorexia has a **genetic basis**.
Evaluation:	Identical twins share 100% of their genetic material, so **other factors** must also be involved in causing anorexia nervosa as the concordance rate was only **56%**. The higher concordance in MZ twins could be due to **environmental** rather than genetic factors, as looking the same may lead to more shared experiences.

Neural Causes Have Also Been Investigated

1) Researchers have suggested that anorexia nervosa may be due to **damage to the hypothalamus**, specifically the **lateral nucleus** (the area of the brain responsible for controlling hunger, see page 140). Lesion studies show that damage to this area can produce **aphagia** (a failure to eat) in animals, and recent research suggests that anorexics have **reduced blood flow** to this area. But it hasn't yet been proven whether this is a **cause** or an **effect** of the disorder.
2) Anorexics often also have **abnormally high levels** of the neurotransmitter **serotonin** and this causes abnormally high levels of **anxiety**. Serotonin production is stimulated by biological components (amino acids) in **food**, so starvation may actually make anorexics feel better. But again, it's not clear whether these serotonin levels are a **cause** or an **effect** of the disorder.

Anorexia Nervosa

The *Psychodynamic Approach* Suggests *Unconscious* Motivations

1) **Anorexia nervosa may be a reaction to sexual abuse.**

   If a person is sexually abused they may then **loathe their body** for appearing attractive to an abuser — anorexia nervosa is a way to help **destroy the body** and so make it less attractive to others.

2) **Anorexia nervosa may reflect a reluctance to take on adult responsibilities.**

   Anorexia nervosa prevents females developing **breasts or hips** — instead of gaining a womanly shape they **remain physically childlike** and so are able to remain **dependent** on their parents for longer.

3) **Anorexia nervosa may reflect low self-esteem.**

   Very low self-esteem may cause a person to believe their needs (in this case food) to be **wrong** in some way, or that they're **not worthy** of having food. They then **deny themselves** food.

4) **Anorexia nervosa may be a battle against controlling parents.**

   Bruch (1978) found that parents of anorexics tend to be **domineering**. Anorexia might be an attempt to regain some **control** by manipulating the one thing they have control of — their body.

Remember though — it's hard to find **empirical evidence** for theories like these, and there are many **counter arguments**, e.g. not everyone with anorexia nervosa has experienced sexual abuse or has controlling parents.

The *Behavioural Approach* Suggests *Conditioning* May Be the Cause

Classical conditioning

Leitenberg et al (1968) claimed that anorexia nervosa could be a result of someone learning to associate **eating** with **anxiety** — often to **phobic proportions**. Losing weight helps to **reduce** that anxiety.

Operant conditioning

Praise and admiration for initial weight loss acts as **positive reinforcement** for more extreme food avoidance. A constant feeling of **hunger** then acts as a **reward** in itself. **Gilbert (1986)** reported that anorexics experience pleasure and pride as a result of not eating. The **guilt** associated with eating is lessened (**negative reinforcement**), as well as the fear that their weight will attract negative attention (**punishment**).

Practice Questions

Q1 Outline the clinical characteristics of anorexia nervosa.

Q2 Explain how Holland et al's (1988) study provides evidence for a genetic explanation of anorexia nervosa.

Q3 Describe two psychodynamic explanations of the possible causes of anorexia nervosa.

Q4 Explain how operant conditioning may play a role in the development of anorexia nervosa.

Exam Question

Q1 a) Describe one biological explanation for anorexia nervosa. [4 marks]

b) Outline and evaluate psychological explanations for anorexia nervosa. [20 marks]

Anorexia nervosa isn't as recent a problem as you might think...

...in fact, it was first diagnosed in 1868 by William Gull. And although it's most common in teenage girls, it can affect all kinds of different people from all walks of life. It's probably caused by a mixture of the factors listed on these pages and each individual case will be different. Sufferers are often just as confused by their motivation as everyone else.

Bulimia Nervosa

Bulimia nervosa is another type of eating disorder that's common in the UK. It's a different condition from anorexia — sufferers don't starve themselves — but they can still have really serious health problems due to the condition.

Bulimia Nervosa Follows a Pattern of Binge Eating and Purging

Bulimia nervosa involves a pattern of binge eating followed by some kind of purge so that weight isn't gained — for example by inducing vomiting, doing excessive exercise or using laxatives. So, the person's weight fluctuates but stays within a normal range.

The **DSM-IV** (the main diagnostic manual for mental disorders, see p.175) describes five main characteristics of bulimia:

Bingeing — eating a large quantity of food in a short time frame. During a binge the person feels **out of control**, i.e. they can't stop themselves from eating.

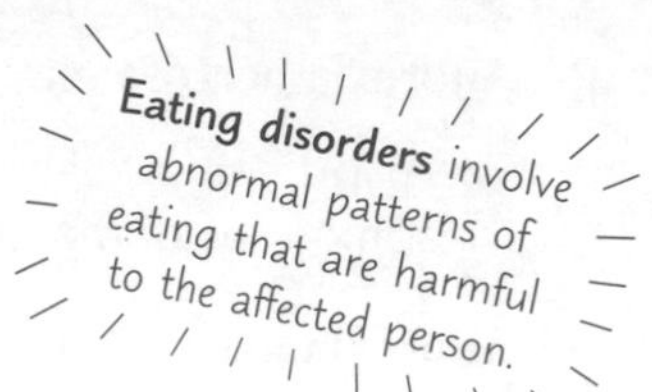

Purging — after **bingeing** the person tries to **prevent weight gain**. This may involve vomiting, using laxatives, not eating for a long period of time or excessive exercise.

Frequent bingeing and purging — the binge-purge cycle needs to have been repeated about **twice a week** for at least **3 months** before a diagnosis of bulimia is given.

Distorted self-evaluation — people suffering from bulimia judge themselves based largely on their **body shape** and **weight**.

Separate condition to anorexia — bulimia isn't just a feature of anorexia, it can exist as a condition **on its own**.

There Are Biological Explanations For Bulimia Nervosa

Concordance rates are the extent to which twins share the same trait.

Genetic Explanations Have Been Suggested

Kendler et al (1991) studied over 1000 pairs of twins where at least one twin had bulimia nervosa and found **concordance rates** of **23%** in **identical** twins and **9%** in **non-identical** twins. Although this suggests **genetics** may play a part in bulimia nervosa, it can't be the full story. As identical twins share all of their genetic material, a concordance rate of 100% would be expected if genetics were the only factor.

Neural Causes Have Also Been Investigated

	Kissileff et al (1996) — The role of cholecystokinin (CCK)
Method:	25 people with bulimia nervosa and 18 **controls** were asked to binge eat (i.e. eat as much as they could in one sitting).
Results:	The participants with bulimia nervosa consumed an average of **3500 calories** whereas the controls only managed **1500 calories** on average. The participants with bulimia nervosa were also found to have **depressed levels of CCK** (a hormone related to satiety, see page 140).
Conclusion:	Depleted levels of CCK allowed bulimic patients to carry on eating without feeling full.
Evaluation:	This would seem to fit with the **enhanced appetite** that many bulimics report and their pattern of overeating. However, a lot of the research into the effects of CCK on satiety is based on **animal models**, so there's no guarantee that the same findings apply to humans. The study also used a fairly **small sample size**, so it might not be valid to generalise the results to the whole population.

It's also been found that bulimics often have **abnormally low levels** of the neurotransmitter **serotonin** leading to bouts of abnormally **low mood**. Serotonin production is stimulated by biological components (amino acids) in **food**, and so overeating may actually make bulimics feel temporarily better — although it later leads to guilt and purging.

Bulimia Nervosa

The *Psychodynamic Approach* Says Bulimia is a *Defence Mechanism*

1) **Bulimia nervosa may be a reaction to sexual abuse.**

The binge-purge cycle helps to express **self-disgust** for attracting an abuser by punishing the body. **Wonderlich et al (1996)** interviewed 1099 American women and found a **correlation** between childhood sexual abuse, dissatisfaction with appearance and bulimia. 16-33% of cases of significant bulimia could be attributed to sexual abuse in childhood.

2) **Bulimia nervosa may be a result of emotional damage caused by poor relationships with parents.**

According to **Halmi (1995)**, bulimics often **mistake** their emotions for **hunger**, as poor parental relationships stunted their ability to **distinguish** between internal **needs** and **feelings**.

3) **Bulimia nervosa may be a defence mechanism to help guard against trauma.**

Bulimia is often **triggered** by a specific **traumatic event**, e.g. a divorce or long-term illness. Bulimics may try to **block out** unhappy feelings by indulging in overeating.

Theories from the psychodynamic approach are difficult to find **empirical evidence** for, and there are many **counter arguments**. For example, not everyone with bulimia has experienced sexual abuse or suffered a trauma that could be pinpointed as a trigger.

The *Behavioural Approach* Suggests Bulimia is *Learned*

Operant conditioning

Bulimics often have **poor eating habits** before they develop the disorder fully, e.g. they often reduce their food intake as part of a diet, then overeat to compensate for their deprivation. Both of these behaviours would bring about **positive reinforcement** — praise for weight loss and satisfaction from indulgence. However, overeating may lead to **anxiety** (a **punishment**) which is then reduced by purging (**negative reinforcement**). This makes the purging behaviour more likely to happen again.

Social learning theory

Hamilton and Waller (1993) found that bulimics **overestimated** their own size and shape after seeing **fashion magazine photos**. **Rodin (1991)** found that they often had **mothers** who also had the disorder, or who constantly dieted. This would suggest that exposure to **models** who are positively reinforced for their weight loss may lead to **imitation**.

Practice Questions

Q1 Outline the clinical characteristics of bulimia nervosa.

Q2 Explain why Kendler et al's (1991) study does not offer a complete explanation of bulimia nervosa.

Q3 How does social learning theory explain why some people suffer from bulimia nervosa?

Exam Question

Q1 Outline and evaluate one biological and one psychological explanation of bulimia nervosa. [24 marks]

Bulimia nervosa was only recognised as a condition in 1979...

...but it can have really serious health effects — for example, those who purge by vomiting (which accounts for 75% of people with the condition) can get peptic ulcers, become dehydrated and suffer from electrolyte imbalances. Electrolyte imbalances are especially worrying as they can lead to an irregular heartbeat that can prove fatal. Not good at all.

Obesity

It might seem odd to include obesity in a section on eating disorders — but overeating to the point of being clinically obese certainly counts as an abnormal eating pattern that's harmful to the person affected. And that's why it's in here.

Obesity is When Someone Has an *Abnormally High Body Mass Index*

1) A person is classed as obese if they have a **BMI** (body mass index) of **30 kg/m² or higher**. This is about 20% above normal for their height and body frame, i.e. they're carrying too much adipose (fatty) tissue.
2) Obesity is generally caused by a person **taking in more calories** (food) than they **burn off** (by exercise), but there are some genetic conditions and medications that can increase the risk of obesity.
3) It's estimated that by 2050 over half of the people in the UK will be obese. This is pretty worrying when you consider that it's already one of the leading **preventable** causes of death worldwide — it increases the risk of **illnesses** like heart disease, diabetes and cancer.
4) The most effective way to treat obesity is with a **sensible diet and plenty of exercise**. However, increasingly people are turning to quick fixes — 'miracle' pills or surgery such as stomach stapling, gastric band fitting or gastric bypass surgery.

Body mass index is a measurement of height relative to weight. A normal BMI is between 18.5 and 25.

Exercise is the best way to combat obesity, but that still didn't excuse Kristy's outfit.

Obesity Can Have *Biological Explanations*

Some studies have shown that there is a **genetic** element to obesity.

Stunkard et al (1986) — Adoption studies and obesity

Method: The weight of 540 **adult adoptees** from Denmark was compared with that of both their **biological and adoptive parents**. The adoptees were split into 4 weight classes — thin, median, overweight and obese.

Results: There was a **strong relationship** between the weight of the adoptees and that of their biological parents. There was **no relationship** between the weight of the adoptees and their adoptive parents in any of the weight classes.

Conclusion: Genetic influences have an important role in determining adult weight, whereas **environment** seems to have **little effect**.

Evaluation: This finding is **supported** by other biological versus adoptive relative research and even by some **twin studies**. However, it's probably too **reductionist** to say that genetics alone are responsible for obesity. Also, the participants were all from Denmark, so the results **can't be generalised** to the whole population.

In some cases obesity is caused by a **chemical** problem.

Montague et al (1997) — Leptin's role in obesity

Method: Two severely obese children (male and female cousins) were studied — a large proportion of their total body weight was made up of **adipose (fatty) tissue**.

Results: A **mutation** on the part of their DNA responsible for controlling their supply of **leptin** was found — they didn't produce enough leptin. Leptin is a protein produced by adipose tissue to signal that **fat reserves** in the body are **full**.

Conclusion: Their leptin deficiency had caused the children's obesity. They did not have enough of this chemical to **suppress appetite** in the normal way.

Evaluation: A number of trials in which obese patients were given doses of leptin have had **very little success**. Research now suggests that most people with obesity in fact have **high levels** of leptin — they're just **resistant** to its effects. This was a **case study** of only two children, so although it revealed a lot about their particular situation, the findings **weren't relevant** to the majority of obese people.

Obesity

The *Psychodynamic Approach* Links Obesity With *Emotional Conflict*

1) **Obesity may be the result of an oral fixation.**

   It's been suggested that obese people experienced trauma at the **oral stage** of psychosexual development, and so developed a fixation there. This means that they derive **pleasure from food** and are **unable to delay gratification**, as they're ruled primarily by the **id** (the pleasure principle).

2) **Obesity may reflect a lack of coping skills.**

   Lots of people binge eat as a result of **stress** — it's a form of **denial** used to escape negative feelings that the person **can't cope** with.

3) **Obesity may be due to our thanatos instinct (death drive).**

   Psychodynamic psychologists believe that attempting to eat ourselves to death reflects the unconscious human **desire for self-destruction.**

4) **Parental overfeeding may be a reaction to trauma.**

   Parents who have experienced the **death of a child** are sometimes prone to **overfeeding** remaining or subsequent children to the point of morbid obesity. They feel **unable to deprive** the child of anything.

Psychodynamic theories are difficult to find **empirical evidence** for. Also, there are many **counter arguments**. For example, not everyone who is obese has parents who experienced a trauma.

The *Behavioural Approach* Suggests Obesity is *Conditioned*

Children learn from an early age to **associate** eating with happiness (i.e. classical conditioning) for several reasons:

1) Parents or teachers may use food to **reinforce good behaviour**, e.g. sweets as **rewards**.
2) Parents may **praise** children for clearing their plate or **punish** them for wasting food at mealtimes.
3) Advertisers use **brightly coloured** packaging, friendly **characters** and **free gift** giveaways.
4) **Celebrations** are always accompanied by food, e.g. birthday parties.

As adults they may then overeat to try to recapture these happy emotions (**positive reinforcement**) or to remove a negative state such as sadness, anger or boredom (**negative reinforcement**). So, operant conditioning is also in effect.

Practice Questions

Q1 Outline the clinical characteristics of obesity.
Q2 Why did Stunkard et al (1986) reject environmental factors as causes of obesity?
Q3 What did Montague et al's (1997) study suggest as a possible cause of obesity?
Q4 Explain why parents may overfeed children.
Q5 Describe how operant conditioning can cause obesity.

Exam Question

Q1 a) Outline one or more biological explanation(s) for obesity. [8 marks]

b) Evaluate one or more psychological theories of obesity. [16 marks]

So it could be your genes stopping you fitting into your jeans...

Hmmm, this chapter has given me some food for thought and no mistake. In fact, my thoughts have been full of nothing but food. Too little, too much, too much rapidly followed by too little — eating can be a complicated business and trying to explain it isn't straightforward either. As usual, a single, simple explanation just won't cut it. Terribly sorry about that.

Psychological Influences on Gender

You'd think gender would be straightforward — you're either masculine or feminine. But that would make for some insultingly easy exam questions. And no-one likes to be insulted. So there's a bit more to it. I knew you'd be pleased.

Cognitive Developmental Theory *Suggests Ideas on Gender* ***Change With Age***

1) **Gender** is the way someone acts and identifies themselves — the behavioural characteristics that make a person **masculine** or **feminine**.
2) **Cognitive developmental theory** was first proposed by Piaget. It suggests that children's thoughts and views on the world **change** as they develop.
3) Many theories use Piaget's ideas to explain how ideas about **gender** change with age.

For more on Piaget's cognitive developmental theory see p.160.

Kohlberg (1966) *Developed a* ***Theory of Gender Consistency***

1) **Kohlberg's** (**1966**) theory of **gender consistency** is part of his wider cognitive developmental theory. It identifies **three stages** of gender development:
   - **Gender identity** — the child is aware that they're **male** or **female**, but think their gender might **change** (e.g. by wearing opposite sex clothes). This stage usually occurs between the ages of 2 and 3½ years old.
   - **Gender stability** — the child realises that their gender will remain **fixed** over **time** (e.g. boys will become men). However, they may think that gender can **change** in **different situations** (e.g. when doing an 'opposite-sex activity'). This stage usually occurs between the ages of 3½ and 4½.
   - **Gender consistency** — the child is aware that gender remains fixed in **different situations** (e.g. cross dressing doesn't change gender). This usually occurs between the ages of 4½ and 7.
2) There is some evidence for Kohlberg's theory. For example, **McConaghy's** (**1979**) study showed that children in Kohlberg's **gender stability** stage determined the gender of dolls by their **clothing** rather than their genitals. This suggests they believe that when the situation (e.g. clothing) changes, gender does too.
3) Munroe et al's (1984) study found the same stages in children from **different cultures**.
4) However, Kohlberg's theory has been criticised for ignoring the effects of **social influences** and **conditioning**. Also, it describes what happens, but doesn't explain **why**.

Martin *and* ***Halverson (1981)*** *Developed the* ***Gender Schema Theory***

1) Martin and Halverson's gender schema theory **combines** cognitive developmental theory and social learning theory to suggest how **gender stereotyping** helps children learn what is and what isn't appropriate for their gender.
2) It proposes that, by the age of **three**, children have developed a **basic gender identity**. They also have a **gender schema** which contains the child's ideas about **gender appropriate behaviour**.
3) Through **observation**, children continue to learn gender appropriate behaviours and **add** them to their schema.
4) A child's gender schema is based on the concept of an **in-group** and an **out-group**:
   - Activities, objects and behaviours associated with their **own sex** are seen as **in-group**. Those associated with the **opposite sex** are **out-group**.
   - So, for example, a boy might **label objects** such as cars and trousers as in-group and objects like dolls and skirts as out-group.
   - Through reference to their **in-group/out-group schema**, children will show a **bias** towards **in-group** behaviours.
5) Having a gender schema can help children to manage all the information that they're exposed to. They can focus on **processing** information related to their **in-group** and **filter out** information related to their **out-group**.
6) However, there are also **disadvantages** — reinforcing stereotypical gender roles can discourage children from showing interest in things related to their out-group. This can limit their opportunities and lead to **discrimination**.
7) There is some evidence to support gender schema theory. For example, **Bradbard et al** (**1986**) gave children unfamiliar toys and found they were more likely to play with them (and remember them) if they were described as being for their **own gender** rather than the other.
8) As children get older they are capable of **more complex cognition** and understand that their gender doesn't limit them rigidly to in-group objects and behaviours.

Psychological Influences on Gender

*People Who **Don't Fit** Gender Stereotypes Show **Psychological Androgyny***

1) **Bem (1974)** developed a self report questionnaire known as the **Sex Role Inventory**. It aimed to measure the mix of stereotypically masculine and feminine traits present in an individual.
2) Individuals rate how likely they are to display certain **character traits**, e.g. shyness. Those who score highly for both masculine and feminine traits are said to be **psychologically androgynous**.
3) Bem suggests that androgyny is **advantageous** in society as it means people have the traits needed to cope with a **range of situations**. Those who score highly on only one scale have a more limited range of skills.
4) Several studies suggest that **environmental factors** are the cause of psychological androgyny. For example:

- Weisner and Wilson-Mitchell (1990) compared children raised in families that put an **emphasis** on traditional gender roles with children raised in families that actively **downplayed** traditional gender roles.
- They found that androgyny was **higher** in children who had been encouraged to **ignore** traditional gender roles.

__Gender Dysphoria__ is Also Known as __Gender Identity Disorder__

1) **Gender dysphoria** is a mental disorder which causes a person to feel that they're **biologically** one gender but **psychologically** the other — they feel that they're trapped in the wrong body.
2) For example, a boy may behave **effeminately**, want to wear **female clothes** and have a **baby**.
3) Some studies have indicated that gender dysphoria could be caused by **parental psychiatric problems** or **absent fathers**. For example, Rekers and Kilgus (1997) studied families where offspring had gender dysphoria and found that:

- **80%** of the gender dysphoria sufferers had **mothers** with **mental health problems**.
- **45%** had **fathers** with **mental health problems**.
- **37%** of sufferers had **absent fathers** (or no male role model).

4) However **not all** children who experience these problems during childhood go on to develop gender dysphoria — so there must be **other explanations**.

Practice Questions

Q1 Give the three stages of gender development outlined in Kohlberg's (1966) theory of gender consistency.

Q2 According to Martin and Halverson's (1981) gender schema theory, what is an in-group?

Q3 Why did Bem consider psychological androgyny to be advantageous?

Exam Question

Q1 a) Outline Kohlberg's cognitive developmental theory of gender development. [8 marks]

b) Discuss Martin and Halverson's (1981) gender schema theory. [16 marks]

In-group, out-group, shake-it-all-about group...

Told you there was more to it — but it shouldn't be too bad to learn. It's just Kohlberg's theory (which is pretty simple) and gender schema theory (which there's a bit more to, but nothing to make your head spin). Then psychological androgyny (which could be good for you) and gender dysphoria (a.k.a. gender identity disorder). And then you're done (yay).

Biological Influences on Gender

Biological factors influence gender. No surprises there — the title gives that one away. You need to know what these factors are and how they influence gender. Luckily, these two pages are here to help you out. I'm too kind to you.

Gender Development *is Affected by* ***Genes*** *and* ***Hormones***

Males *and* ***Females*** *Have Different* ***Sex Chromosomes***

1) **Females** have a **pair of X** chromosomes — XX. So all ova contain an X chromosome.
2) **Males** have **one X** chromosome and **one Y** chromosome — XY. This means sperm may contain either an X chromosome or a Y chromosome. It's the **Y chromosome** that leads to **male development**.
3) If an ovum is fertilised by a Y carrying sperm, the offspring will be **XY** (**male**). If an ovum is fertilised by an X carrying sperm the offspring will be **XX** (**female**). Which sperm fertilises the ova is determined by chance.
4) Some humans are born with **variations** in the standard sex chromosome pattern. Studies of people with such variations indicate that **gender differences** can be caused by **different sex chromosomes** in males and females.

Sperm and ova only contain one sex chromosome.

For example, in **Klinefelter's syndrome** males are born with **XXY sex chromosomes** — they have an **extra X chromosome**. Males with this syndrome are **sterile** and tend to be **less muscular** and have **less facial and body hair**. They can have problems using **language** to express themselves and may have trouble with **social interaction**.

Males *and* ***Females*** *Have Different* ***Hormone Levels***

1) The major male and female hormones are **androgens** and **oestrogens**.
2) Both types of hormone are present in males and females, but in very **different amounts**.
3) **Men** produce more **testosterone** (an androgen) each day than females, and **females** produce more **oestrogens** than males.
4) However, some humans produce **smaller** or **larger** quantities of these hormones than normal.

For example, sometimes people are born with much more **testosterone** than normal — a particular form of a syndrome called **CAH**.

1) This form of CAH can cause **early sexual development** in males, but doesn't have much of an effect otherwise.
2) The **behaviour** of **girls** with this type of CAH tends to be **masculinised** — they have a preference for playing with boys' toys and enjoy 'tomboyish' activities.
3) **Physically**, girls tend to look more **masculine**. Their **growth** is fast and **puberty** can happen early.
4) CAH can also cause **physical abnormalities** such as **ambiguous genitalia**. This can make it difficult to tell whether someone is **male** or **female** at birth.

5) Case studies of conditions like this suggest that the effect of **testosterone** on the **developing brain** is responsible for the **differences in gender behaviour**.

There are ***Evolutionary Explanations*** *For Differences in* ***Gender Roles***

Gender roles are the behaviours seen as **appropriate** for one sex and not the other. For example, traditional gender roles would include men being the breadwinner and women staying at home to bring up the children. Many psychologists believe that gender roles originally developed through **evolution**. For example:

1) **Shields** (**1975**) suggests that men and women evolved to have roles that **complemented** each other — dividing the behaviours necessary for survival.
2) **Buss** (**1995**) suggested that the different behaviours shown by men and women are the result of different **reproduction strategies**. For example, Trivers (1972) suggests that women invest more in offspring than men do and so discriminate more when choosing a mate. This could lead to some stereotypically female behaviours, e.g. coyness. In contrast, men have to compete for mates so demonstrate more aggressive behaviours.

Timmy hoped his dad would give up on traditional gender roles soon — he was taking a pounding.

Biological Influences on Gender

The **Biosocial Approach** Can Explain **Gender Development**

The **biosocial approach** explains gender development as a result of both **biological** and **social factors**. **Money and Ehrhardt's (1972)** biosocial theory of gender has two main aspects:

1) During **foetal development**, **genetics** and **physiological changes** (such as the inheritance of an X or Y chromosome and the presence of hormones like testosterone) lead to the development of male or female **physical characteristics**.
2) Once the baby is **born** people **react differently** to it depending on its **gender** — it's given a **social label**. This labelling means that males and females are treated differently from birth and learn different attitudes and behaviours as a result — they are **socialised** in different ways.

Money and Ehrhardt suggest that the **social labelling** of infants and children has a **greater influence** on their behaviour than physiological differences do.

Smith and Lloyd (1978) investigated differences in behaviour towards male and female babies:

Smith and Lloyd (1978) — Behaviour towards male and female babies

Method: A sample of women were asked to play with an **unfamiliar baby**. A variety of toys were available for them to use. A number of babies were used in the experiment — some were **male** and some were **female**.

Results: Participants were likely to offer **gender stereotyped toys** to the baby they played with. They also used **different verbal communication styles** depending on the given gender of the child. Boys were given encouragement for **motor activity**, girls were more likely to be spoken to **calmly** and in a **soothing manner**.

Conclusion: People's behaviour towards babies alters depending on the babies' **gender**.

Evaluation: This study supports the **biosocial theory**, showing that people react differently to boys and girls. This imposes different ideas of what it is to be a boy or a girl on the baby, i.e. they are **socialised differently** and so learn to behave according to a particular gender role. However, the participants might have shown **demand characteristics** — they could have worked out the purpose of the experiment and acted to fit in with it.

Gender Dysphoria Could have a **Biological Influence**

1) Although **gender dysphoria** (see p.149) is currently classed as a **psychiatric condition**, recent studies have suggested a **biological cause**. For example, one study showed a link between male-female gender dysphoria and low **testosterone levels** in the **developing brain**. This could cause the development of a **female gender identity**.
2) The **biosocial approach** to gender development can be used to explain **gender dysphoria**. For example, a child might **biologically** be female, but be treated **socially** as a male. This could happen if parents were desperate to have a son but gave birth to a daughter. This could lead to the child feeling **confused** about their **gender identity**.

Practice Questions

Q1 Which chromosome leads to development of male features? And which are the major male hormones?

Q2 Explain what is meant by gender roles.

Exam Question

Q1 a) Outline the roles of hormones and genes in gender development. [8 marks]

b) Discuss the biosocial approach to gender development. [16 marks]

So, your gender is influenced by biology — never saw that one coming...

Ah, hormones. They're always popping up as reasons for this, that or the other. Maybe they're why you're feeling so restless and depressed now. No... wait... that would be the revision. Anyway, biological influences on gender — get learning.

Social Influences on Gender

Like most things in psychology, gender is influenced by social factors. These factors include the way that family and friends behave, the media you're exposed to, the school you go to and the culture you grow up in. Read on...

Parents and Peers Can Influence Gender Roles

1) **Social learning theory** suggests that we learn by **observing** and **copying** the behaviour of people around us.
2) This learning can be **passive** (when the behaviour is simply watched and copied) or it can be **active** (when the behaviour is reinforced by rewards or discouraged by punishments).
3) **Gender typical behaviours** can be learnt this way, with males copying the behaviour of other males and females copying behaviour of other females. For example, girls may imitate the behaviour of their mothers — the behaviour becomes part of their idea of the female gender role.
4) There's also evidence that parents and peers **react differently** to children depending on their gender:

Parents

- Rubin et al (1974) found that fathers used words like '**soft**' and '**beautiful**' to describe newborn **daughters** and '**strong**' and '**firm**' to describe **sons**.
- Culp et al (1983) found that women treated babies differently according to how they were dressed — **talking** more to those dressed as **girls** and **smiling** more at those dressed as **boys**.
- Hron-Stewart's (1988) study found that adults were **quicker** to comfort a crying baby **girl** than a crying baby boy, expecting boys to be hardier and braver. Also, mothers were more likely to help a **daughter** complete a task than a son.

Peers

- Maccoby and Jacklin (1987) found that children as young as three prefer **same-sex playmates**. Maccoby (1990) found that when children organise their own activities they tend to segregate themselves according to their **gender**.
- Serbin et al (1984) suggest that girls try and influence situations by **polite suggestion** whilst boys use **direct commands**.
- Lamb and Roopnarine's (1979) study of nursery behaviours found that children **encouraged** gender appropriate behaviour and **criticised** gender inappropriate behaviour.

5) The different behaviours that girls and boys observe and experience can lead to development of gender roles.

*The **Media** Can Also Influence **Gender Roles**...*

TV, **films**, **magazines** and **computer games** usually show **gender stereotypical behaviour**. Several studies have shown that the behaviour displayed in these media can influence gender roles. For example:

1) Some studies have shown that the **more TV** a child watches the **more stereotypical** their views on gender are.
2) Williams (1986) carried out a two year **natural experiment** in Canada. He looked at the effect of introducing TV to a town (Notel), by comparing it to a nearby town that already had TV (Multitel). At the start of the experiment, gender stereotyping was much greater in Multitel than Notel. Williams found that gender stereotypes of Notel children **increased** and became more like those of Multitel children after the introduction of TV.

*...and So Can **Schools***

1) The attitude of **schools** and **teachers** can influence gender roles.
2) For example, if teachers hold gender stereotypes this may influence their beliefs about the **abilities** and **preferences** of girls and boys.
3) Bigler (1995) compared students in classes that were **divided by gender** with students in classes where gender **wasn't emphasised**. Students divided by gender were more likely to have **stronger gender stereotypes** and a stronger belief that all males are similar and all females are similar.

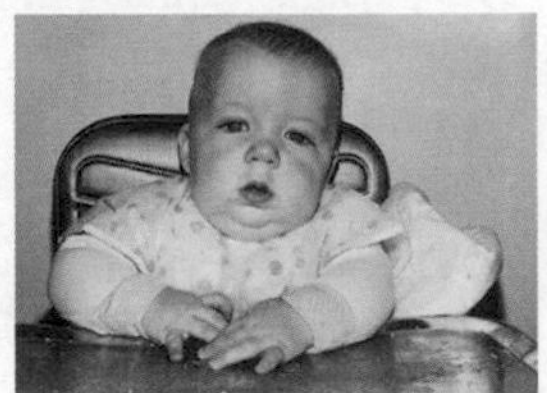

Boris tried not to conform to the stereotype of the 'cute baby'. Everyone agreed it was a great effort.

Social Influences on Gender

There's Been **Cross-Cultural Research** Into **Gender Roles**

1) **Cross-cultural research** has been carried out to identify how gender roles differ between cultures.
2) Cross-cultural research can also help us to understand the **causes** of gender roles — if roles are **similar** in different cultures it suggests a **biological** explanation. However, if they **vary** between cultures a **social** explanation of gender roles is more likely.

- Whiting and Edwards (1988) observed the behaviour of children in the USA, Mexico, Japan, India, the Philippines and Kenya.
- They found that gender behaviour was very **similar to Western stereotypes** and that there were clear differences between **male** and **female** behaviour.
- For example, girls were more **caring** than boys, and boys were more **aggressive** than girls.
- In societies where children were expected to work to contribute towards the family, there were further gender differences. Girls were more likely to look after **younger siblings** and do **domestic work**, whilst boys were more likely to look after **animals** and were less likely to work within the home.

Responsibility for **Childcare** May Determine **Gender Roles**

1) Katz and Konner (1981) looked at **80 different cultures** — they found that in **90%** of them **women** had the main responsibility for child rearing.
2) This **gender division** has implications for men and women in terms of **occupation**, **finance** and **mobility**.
3) D'Andrade (1966) looked at information from **224 societies** to investigate what **types of tasks** and jobs were performed by males and females. He found that:

- **Men** were more likely to **travel further** from the home, and be involved in **weapon making**, **metal work** and **hunting**.
- **Women** were more likely to **make** and **repair clothes**, **prepare** and **cook food**, and **make objects** for use in the **home**.

4) Segal (1983) suggested that the differences in **activities** associated with gender roles are related to the differences in **involvement in childcare**.

Max was slightly hurt by his sisters' reaction to his offer of looking after the baby.

Practice Questions

Q1 What did Rubin et al (1974) discover about the way fathers describe their newborn children?
Q2 What did Maccoby and Jacklin (1987) find from their study on the type of playmates children prefer?
Q3 Which students in Bigler's (1995) study had the strongest gender role stereotypes?
Q4 How can cross-cultural research help us to understand the causes of gender roles?
Q5 Outline the activities associated with males and females in the D'Andrade (1996) study.

Exam Question

Q1 a) Discuss how parents and peers may influence gender roles. [8 marks]

b) Describe and discuss cross-cultural research into gender roles. [16 marks]

A whole town with no TV. Not a single one. In Canada. In 1986. Scary.

It seems everyone's plotting to force us into gender roles and turn us into stereotypes — parents, friends, teachers and the media. There's no getting away from it. I say we fight back. We could start off by getting rid of TVs. We'll just chuck 'em out — it's proven to work and then we'll be free. Life with no TV, it'll be great. Hmmm... maybe gender roles aren't so bad...

Theories of Intelligence

You might have thought intelligence was pretty straightforward — if you do well in your exams you're smart, if you don't you're not. Turns out it's not that simple — there are several theories of intelligence and you need to know them all...

The **Learning Approach** Suggests Intelligence is Developed by **Reinforcement**

1) The **learning approach** to intelligence suggests intelligent behaviours are developed through **conditioning**.
2) For this to happen there needs to be an initial **change in behaviour** that's then **rewarded**. This is known as **reinforcement** and encourages the person to **repeat** the behaviour.
3) For example, Skinner taught pigeons to play ping-pong by providing **positive reinforcement** in stages — for standing on the court, then for touching the ball, then for hitting it correctly, etc.
4) Intelligent human behaviours, e.g. **driving a car** or **writing**, can be learnt in the same way.

Comments

- This approach has been criticised for being **reductionist** — it ignores other aspects of intelligence, e.g. the biological approach.
- More understanding is needed of what **cognitive abilities** are involved in intelligence and what **biological** and **environmental factors** influence individual differences in intelligence.

The **Psychometric Approach** Focuses on **Intelligence Testing**

1) The **psychometric approach** involves measuring intelligence to produce an **intelligence quotient** (**IQ**) **score**.
2) This is done through **intelligence tests** that are focused on mathematical ability and abstract, logical reasoning.
3) Spearman (1904) found that people who did well on **one** kind of test, e.g. arithmetic, usually did well in **other** kinds of tests, e.g. spatial reasoning. In other words, their test scores showed a **positive correlation**.
4) So, he proposed that everyone has a **general intelligence** that's **genetically determined** and **unchangeable**. He termed this '**g**'. He also suggested that people develop **specific abilities**, '**s**', which are influenced by **learning**. This can explain why, for example, some people are better at maths than at English.

Comments

- Thurstone (1938) argued **against** the concept of g, claiming that there are **7 independent groups** of primary mental abilities (e.g. numerical, verbal, spatial) rather than one general intelligence.
- There are many issues with the use of IQ tests. Many things, e.g. musical ability, are **difficult to measure**. Also, tests may be biased towards one culture.
- **Developmental factors** are not considered by the psychometric approach — g may be influenced by **education** and **nutrition**, which could promote or impair the development of intelligence.

The **Information Processing Approach** Focuses on **Cognitive Processes**

1) The **information processing approach** to intelligence focuses on the use of a **set** of **cognitive processes**.
2) **Sternberg** (**1985**) suggested that these underlie intelligence and can be split into **three components**:
   - **Metacomponents** — planning and control processes used in problem solving and decision making.
   - **Performance components** — processes that allow us to carry out actions, e.g. memorising, calculating, etc.
   - **Knowledge acquisition components** — processes used to learn new information.
3) Sternberg proposed that these three components are **universal** and apply to **three aspects of intelligence**:
   - **Analytical intelligence** — the ability to solve problems, see solutions, monitor and plan.
   - **Creative intelligence** — the ability to react to stimuli and develop ideas, either new or familiar.
   - **Practical intelligence** — the ability to adjust to different environments and contexts.

   These three kinds of intelligence make up **Sternberg's triarchic model of intelligence**.

Comments

- Sternberg's model allows for the influence of both **internal** and **external factors** on intelligence.
- It also addresses intelligence in relation to **practical**, **real-life scenarios** rather than just academic contexts.
- However, Gottfredson (2003) argues that Sternberg's concept of practical intelligence is **faulty** — it simply represents a set of skills developed to cope with a particular environment, rather than a kind of intelligence.

Theories of Intelligence

*Gardner's (1985) Theory Identifies **Seven Kinds** of Intelligence*

1) Traditionally, intelligence has been seen as a **single concept**, emphasising verbal, logical and mathematical skills.
2) Gardner's theory of **multiple intelligences** suggests that we have **several different kinds** of intelligence. These each involve different cognitive structures so are **independent** of each other, although they do interact.
3) So, a person could have a **high level** of ability in **some areas** of intelligence, but a **low level** in **other areas**.
4) Gardner identified **seven** kinds of intelligence:

- **Logical-mathematical** — ability in mathematics and logical and abstract reasoning.
- **Verbal-linguistic** — speaking, reading, writing and the ability to learn languages.
- **Visual-spatial** — ability in mental visualisation and art.
- **Musical** — abilities relating to sound, rhythm and tone.
- **Bodily kinaesthetic** — use of body, e.g. athletic and dance ability.
- **Intrapersonal** — associated with self-understanding, feelings, motivations and objectives.
- **Interpersonal** — social skills, empathy and ability to cooperate with others.

5) In 1997, Gardner added an **eighth** kind of intelligence to his model — **naturalistic intelligence**. People with high naturalistic intelligence are able to relate well to **nature** and **animals**.

Comments on Gardner's Theory

- Gardner's theory is based on a **range** of **research methods**, including psychometric tests and case studies of people who have low IQ scores but high ability in particular kinds of intelligence. For example, Horwitz et al (1965) found that some people who were considered to have low intelligence could rapidly calculate the day of the week that a particular date fell on.
- The concept of multiple intelligences can be **applied to education**. This would give a **broader approach** than the traditional emphasis on verbal and mathematical skills. It can also help teachers to understand the best ways for different students to **learn** things.
- The theory has been criticised because some aspects are **vague**, e.g. intrapersonal and musical intelligence are **difficult to define**. They're also **difficult to measure precisely**.
- Also, some people believe that some of the types of intelligence identified by Gardner are really just names for **talents** or **personality traits**, rather than a kind of intelligence.

Practice Questions

Q1 Give a problem associated with IQ tests.

Q2 In the psychometric approach to intelligence what does 'g' represent?

Q3 Give the three aspects of intelligence identified in Sternberg's (1985) theory.

Q4 Which of Gardner's multiple intelligences is associated with the ability to learn languages?

Q5 Give one criticism of Gardner's (1985) theory of multiple intelligences.

Exam Question

Q1 a) Outline the information processing approach to intelligence. [8 marks]

b) Describe and evaluate Gardner's (1985) theory of multiple intelligences. [16 marks]

Idle-slacker intelligence — the ability to do nothing, common in students...

Who'd have thought there were so many different kinds of intelligence. I wonder what they'll come up with next — maybe the ability to put together great outfits, or a high potential for buying exceedingly good birthday presents, or intelligence in the area of competitive eating perhaps. Tell you what is impressive though, those ping-pong playing pigeons. Marvellous.

Animal Learning and Intelligence

So, humans have varying levels of intelligence and are able to learn — even though it might not feel like much is going in sometimes. These pages look at whether the same applies to other animals or if us humans are a special case.

Classical Conditioning Involves Reflexive Responses

Classical conditioning occurs when a stimulus produces a response in an organism because it's become **associated** with **another** stimulus which normally produces that response. Animals can be classically conditioned.

> **Example**
>
> When dogs see food, they salivate. This is an automatic, unlearned response — a **reflex**. The food is an **unconditioned stimulus** (**UCS**) and salivation is an **unconditioned response** (**UCR**). **Pavlov** (**1927**) studied laboratory dogs that **always** received their food after a **bell** was rung. After a while the dogs would salivate when the bell was rung (before getting the food) as they **associated** the bell with food. The bell had become a **conditioned stimulus** (**CS**), and salivation had become a **conditioned response** (**CR**).

The principles of classical conditioning are:

1) **Generalisation** — when stimuli similar to the original CS (e.g. a bell with a different pitch) produce the CR (e.g. salivating).
2) **Discrimination** — when stimuli similar to the original CS don't produce the CR. This can be achieved by withholding the UCS (e.g. food) when the similar stimulus is used. The animal will begin to discriminate between the CS and the similar stimulus and will only respond to the CS.
3) **Extinction** — when the CR (e.g. salivating) isn't produced as a result of the CS (e.g. bell). This happens when the CS is repeatedly presented without the UCS (e.g. food) following it.
4) **Spontaneous recovery** — when a previously extinct CR is produced in response to the CS. This happens when the CS is presented again after a period of time during which it's not been used.
5) **Higher order conditioning** — when a new CS (e.g. a light) produces the CR because the animal associates it with the original CS. This can be achieved by consistently presenting the new CS before the original CS.

Operant Conditioning Involves Voluntary Behaviours

Operant conditioning occurs when organisms learn to associate **particular behaviours** with **particular consequences**. **Positive** consequences encourage them to **repeat** the behaviour, **negative** consequences discourage them from repeating the behaviour. Operant conditioning can involve **positive reinforcement**, **negative reinforcement** or **punishment**:

- **Positive reinforcement** — the behaviour produces a positive outcome, e.g. food, so the behaviour is reinforced.
- **Negative reinforcement** — the behaviour removes a negative stimulus, e.g. pain, so the behaviour is reinforced.
- **Punishment** — the behaviour is punished, e.g. electric shock, deterring the animal from repeating the behaviour.

Operant conditioning can be used to teach animals certain behaviours:

> **Example**
>
> Skinner (1938) studied laboratory rats to see if they could learn behaviour through operant conditioning. He placed the rats in boxes containing a lever. Pushing the lever provided the rat with food pellets — a **positive consequence**. Over time, the rats pushed the lever more frequently as they **associated** the behaviour with the reward of food.

Comments

1) Most research into conditioning has involved **laboratory experiments**. This **reduces ecological validity** so the results can't be **generalised** to real-life. More **field research** would be useful.
2) Different **species** have different **capacities** for learning by conditioning. Some may also learn by simple observation, with no reinforcement involved.
3) **Genetics** seem to **influence** and **limit** what different species can learn by conditioning. For example, Breland and Breland (1951) gave food to pigs when they carried wooden coins (in their mouths) to a 'piggy bank'. However, they started to drop them on the floor and push them towards the bank with their snout (showing an **instinctive** foraging behaviour), so taking longer to get the food.

Animal Learning and Intelligence

Non-human Animals *May Show Some Kinds of* ***Intelligence***

Self-recognition, **social learning** and **Machiavellian intelligence** are all seen as evidence of intelligence.

Self-recognition

Self-recognition may be assessed by the **mark test** — an animal is anaesthetised and red dye is put on its forehead. Later, the animal is placed in front of a mirror. If it touches the mark on its head it provides evidence that it **identifies** the image in the mirror as **itself**. A few animals, e.g. chimpanzees, have shown self-recognition. However, Heyes (1994) claims that this doesn't prove that they're self-aware in the same way that humans are.

Machiavellian Intelligence

Machiavellian intelligence is the ability to **manipulate social situations** to reach a goal. For an animal to do this it needs to have **theory of mind** — an ability to imagine the world from the perspective of **others**. Theory of mind allows animals to attribute behaviour to intentions, beliefs and feelings, and enables them to **deceive** others.

Woodruff and Premack's (1979) laboratory experiment

Method: Chimpanzees watched as a trainer placed food under one of two containers, both of which were out of their reach. One of two trainers then entered. One trainer wore a green coat, the other a white coat. If the chimps were able to guide the **green-coated** trainer to where the food was, they were **given the food**. If they guided the **white-coated** trainer to the food, the trainer **kept the food**. However, if the white-coated trainer **did not** find the food, it would be given to the chimp.

Results: After repeating the test several times, all of the chimps learned to guide the green-coated trainer to the food. Some of the chimps **intentionally deceived** the white-coated trainer, pointing to the opposite container to where the food was, whilst the rest **withheld information** about the location of the food.

Conclusion: Chimps have **theory of mind** and are able to **deceive**.

Evaluation: The chimps may have learnt to guide the green-coated trainer to the food through **conditioning** (with food acting as a **positive reinforcer**) rather than actively attempting to deceive the white-coated trainer. This doesn't require a theory of mind so wouldn't be an example of Machiavellian intelligence.

Social Learning

Social learning occurs when an animal **copies** behaviour that it sees another animal receive a **benefit** from. This is known as **vicarious reinforcement**. Kawai's (1965) **naturalistic observations** of macaque monkeys showed that one of them started to wash potatoes in the sea before eating them. Other monkeys soon seemed to **imitate** this. However, Nagell et al (1993) suggest that animals may just notice environmental features that others are **interacting** with, so also **explore** them and learn by **trial and error**.

Practice Questions

Q1 Outline Pavlov's (1927) experiment on classical conditioning in dogs.

Q2 What is spontaneous recovery?

Q3 What is Machiavellian intelligence?

Exam Question

Q1 a) Outline theories of simple learning in non-human animals. [8 marks]

b) Discuss evidence for intelligence in non-human animals. [16 marks]

I can't come out — I'm conditioning my hair...

So animals are able to learn things — nothing new there. After all, you can train parrots to talk and horses to jump, not to mention all the stuff that guide dogs learn. Don't know why everyone gets so excited about Pavlov's slobbery dogs.

Human Intelligence

Many animals are bigger, stronger or faster than humans but appear to be less intelligent. Many factors may explain why humans are more intelligent than other species, and why intelligence varies between individuals...

Evolutionary Factors** May Have Affected the **Development of Intelligence

1) **Darwin's** (1859) theory of **natural selection** suggests that characteristics that increase an animal's chances of **surviving** and **reproducing** are likely to be passed from one generation to the next.
2) If **intelligence** is **beneficial** to survival, the **most intelligent** members of a population are the **most likely** to **survive** and **reproduce**. This gives rise to **intelligent offspring**, who are also likely to survive and reproduce.
3) In this way the species **evolves** over time to become **more intelligent**.
4) Humans are a **highly intelligent species**. This suggests that intelligence is a characteristic that's been **beneficial** to the survival of humans and has **evolved** through **natural selection**.
5) **Several factors** may have contributed to the evolution of human intelligence. For example:

1 Ecological Demands

1) The **ecological demands** of the environment may have stimulated the development of intelligence.
2) For example, a hunter-gatherer or foraging lifestyle requires **memory** and **navigational skills**, so higher intelligence levels would be beneficial for survival.

2 Social Complexity

1) Humans are **social animals**. Living in **groups** could have contributed to the development of intelligence.
2) The **social complexity** of group living may help survival, e.g. by giving **protection** from predators and **cooperation** when hunting. However, social living also creates **competition** and **conflict**, e.g. for a mate.
3) Successful social living is more likely if animals are **intelligent** and have **theory of mind**, allowing them to understand others' intentions and feelings. This also allows for **Machiavellian intelligence** — where individuals and groups can deceive others for their own advantage.
4) There is some evidence that **social complexity** and **intelligence** are **linked**:
   - Other animals considered to be intelligent, e.g. **primates** and **dolphins**, also live in social groups.
   - Cosmides and Tooby (1992) found that people are better at solving logical problems if they are put in terms of **everyday social situations**, rather than presented in an abstract form. This suggests that intelligence may have evolved to deal with **social situations**. However, it's not clear which evolved first — intelligence or group living.

3 Brain Size

1) Jerison (1973), found a **positive correlation** between **body size** and **brain size** in animals. However, humans have brains **seven times larger** than expected for a mammal of our size.
2) Early hominids had a brain size of about 600 cubic centimetres. This remained relatively constant for 1.5 million years before **doubling** in size over the last 0.5 million years.
3) This is despite the fact that larger brains require **more energy** and make **childbirth** more **difficult** and **dangerous**.
4) However, these evolutionary costs are **balanced** by **increased intelligence**. Higher intelligence requires **more brain cells** and possibly **more specialised brain areas** — and so **bigger brains** evolved.
5) Research on brain size as a proportion of body size **supports** this theory. Willerman et al (1991) used MRI scanning to measure the brain size of college students. Those with **higher IQ scores** had **larger brains** (proportionate to body size). However, a limited, unrepresentative sample was used, meaning that it's hard to generalise the results. Also the type of IQ test may have had an effect on the results.

Human Intelligence

Intelligence Test Performance is Influenced by *Genetics* and the *Environment*

1) There's a lot of debate about the role **genetic** and **environmental factors** play in intelligence test scores.
2) Closely related people, e.g. siblings, tend to have more highly correlated IQ scores than less closely related people, e.g. cousins.
3) Bouchard and McGue (1981) did a meta analysis of 111 studies and found that the people with the **highest** IQ correlations were **identical** twins reared **together**. They showed a correlation of **0.86** compared to **0.6** for **non-identical** twins reared together. This suggests that intelligence is influenced by **genetics**.
4) However, **environmental factors** must influence intelligence to some extent otherwise the identical twins would show a correlation of **1**.
5) Another way of testing for genetic influences is to **compare** the correlations **adopted children** show with their **biological** and **adoptive relatives**. A **higher correlation** with their **biological relatives** than with their adoptive relatives (whose environment they share) suggests a strong **genetic** link.
6) But Schiff et al (1978) found that children from lower socio-economic backgrounds who were adopted into families with higher socio-economic status showed **higher IQs** than their **biological relatives**. This suggests that intelligence is affected by **environmental factors**.
7) Also, Bouchard and McGue (1981) found that identical twins reared **apart** showed a **lower correlation** in IQ scores (0.72) than identical twins reared together. This supports the theory that environmental factors affect IQ.
8) So, genetics and environmental factors are **both important** in IQ test performance, and probably **interact**. For example, variations in intelligence caused by genetics could be **compounded** or **reduced** depending on the **environment** (e.g. quality of nutrition or education).

Comments

1) Different studies have used **different kinds of IQ test**, making **comparisons** difficult.
2) Closer relatives often share **more similar environments** (e.g. the same home) than more distantly related people. This makes it difficult to separate genetic influences from environmental influences.

Intelligence is Linked to *Culture*

1) Sternberg's (1985) **triarchic model** of intelligence suggests that intelligence is shown by successfully adapting to the **physical** and **social demands** of the surrounding environment.
2) Sternberg et al (2001) found that some Kenyan children knew a huge amount about **herbal medicines** but didn't perform very well on normal **IQ tests**.
3) So intelligence must be understood in relation to the **culture** that a person lives in.
4) In some cultures the ability to **pass exams** could be seen as evidence of intelligent behaviour, whilst in others the ability to **hunt** has greater value.
5) Any **intelligence testing** that's carried out must take these differences into account.

Some behaviour isn't considered intelligent in any culture.

Practice Questions

Q1 List three evolutionary factors that may have contributed to the development of human intelligence.

Q2 How can group living help survival?

Q3 Give one piece of evidence that suggests that genetics influences intelligence.

Exam Question

Q1 a) Discuss the role of at least two evolutionary factors in the development of human intelligence. [16 marks]

b) Evaluate the roles of genetic and environmental factors associated with intelligence test performance. [8 marks]

Evolution of intelligence — feels like mine is going the other way...

That's the last pages on intelligence done — learn this stuff and you'll have this very clever topic wrapped up. The key things here are the development of human intelligence and the whole genetic vs environmental factors issue. Learn and enjoy...

Development of Thinking

This bright and shiny new section is all about thinking, and how your thinking develops as you get older. As you might be learning to expect by now, there are a lot of different theories about this. And I bet you want to know all about them. Well, as luck would have it, these pages are all about these theories. It's almost like they were designed just for you...

Piaget *Proposed That* ***Cognition*** *Progresses in* ***Stages***

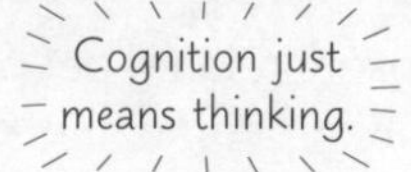

Piaget said that we're all born with the **basics** to allow **cognitive progression** — reflexes and senses. He reckoned that more **complex** abilities become possible as children move through **stages of development** as they get older:

Sensorimotor stage (0–2 years)	The child's knowledge is limited to what their senses tell them when they're exploring their surroundings. This exploration brings about an understanding of the concept of object permanence (if you put a towel over a toy, the toy is still there).
Preoperational stage (2–7 years)	The child has some language now, but makes logic mistakes — e.g. cats have four legs, so everything with four legs must be a cat. They typically can't do the three mountains task (see below) or conservation tasks (see next page). Children at this stage show egocentrism, irreversibility and centration (see below).
Concrete operational stage (7–11 years)	The child's use of logic improves and they can do conservation tasks. They no longer show egocentrism, irreversibility and centration but can't yet use abstract reasoning (reasoning in their head).
Formal operational stage (11+ years)	The child is much more advanced now, and can use abstract reasoning in problem solving. They can also use hypotheses and theoretical principles, and deal with hypothetical situations.

1) Piaget used the idea of **schemas** a lot in his work. A schema contains all the information you **know** about an object, action or concept — e.g. the schema of a human face has two eyes, a mouth and a nose, and the schema of riding a bike contains all the movements you'd need to make.
2) Schemas help you to **organise** and **interpret** information — new experiences are taken into our schemas (**assimilated**) and are **accommodated** by them. Accommodation just involves altering existing schemas.
3) Piaget reckoned that children try to find a **balance** between assimilation and accommodation during cognitive development.

Piaget *Used the* ***Three Mountains Task (1956)*** *as Evidence for His Theory*

1) Piaget built a **3-D model** of **three mountains** (well, he was from Switzerland).
2) The mountains had different **landmarks** on them — e.g. one had a cross on it, and another had a house.
3) Piaget put a small doll on one of the mountains and then showed children photos of the mountains taken from **various angles**. The children were asked to pick the photo that matched what the **doll** could see.
4) He found that children at his **preoperational stage** (2–7 years old) picked the photo taken from their **own perspective**, rather than the one taken from the **doll's perspective**.
5) He concluded that children at this stage were unable to put themselves in the doll's shoes.

Piaget used this and other experiments as evidence that children at his preoperational stage have the following qualities:

1) **Egocentrism** — they can only view the world from their **own viewpoint**. They're not sensitive to the fact that others may have **different** views or thoughts (as demonstrated by the three mountains task).
2) **Irreversibility** — they don't understand that you can undo an action (e.g. that you can reform a sausage-shaped piece of clay into its original ball shape).
3) **Centration** — they focus on small aspects of a task, not the task as a whole.

Development of Thinking

Piaget Showed How **Other Skills** Develop in **Later Stages**

Understanding of conservation

1) **Conservation** is the understanding that a **set quantity** stays the **same**, even if it **looks** different. For example, if liquid is poured from a short, fat glass into a tall, thin glass, the amount of liquid is still the same. Another example is counters in a row — two rows of five counters both have the same number of counters, even if the counters in one row are spaced out so that it looks longer.
2) Children at the **concrete operational stage** can **correctly identify** that the amount of liquid or the number of counters stays the same even after they've been rearranged. But children at the **preoperational stage** will say that the spaced out row contains **more** counters or the tall glass **more** liquid.
3) However, **McGarrigle and Donaldson (1974)** found that if a puppet (Naughty Teddy) **'accidentally'** knocked the counters so that the row looked longer, even younger children at the **preoperational stage** said that the number of counters was the **same**. This suggests that they **did** understand conservation.

The four beaker problem

1) **Piaget and Inhelder (1956)** gave children four beakers, each containing a colourless liquid. When two of the liquids were mixed the liquid turned yellow. Children had to work out the **right combination**.
2) Children at the **formal operational stage** used **systematic testing** of different mixtures to find the answer, whereas children at the **concrete operational stage** used a **random** approach.
3) However, some researchers have argued that **not everybody** gets to this stage of systematic hypothesis testing, so it might not be a **universal** stage of development.

There's Evidence **For** and **Against** Piaget's Stages of Cognitive Development

1) There's **cross-cultural similarity** in the stages — studies have suggested that children of all backgrounds progress through the stages in the same way, which provides **support** for Piaget's theory.
2) Piaget **underestimated abilities** at each age — for example, the experiment with Naughty Teddy showed that preoperational children **can** in fact understand the concept of conservation.
3) He said that **practice** and **teaching wouldn't** speed up progression through the stages but this isn't true — it's been found that teaching **can** help to move children on through the stages.
4) Piaget didn't think that **language** was important in cognitive development. He thought you needed **cognitive development first** in order to allow language to develop. But other theorists, such as **Vygotsky**, take a different view on this, as you'll find out on the next page...

Practice Questions

Q1 Name Piaget's four main stages of cognitive development.

Q2 How is the preoperational stage different from the concrete operational stage?

Q3 Did McGarrigle and Donaldson's (1974) experiment provide evidence for or against Piaget's theory?

Q4 Give two criticisms of Piaget's theory.

Exam Question

Q1 Describe and evaluate Piaget's theory of cognitive development. [24 marks]

Naughty Teddy! You've wrecked my theory...

Piaget's stages were an attempt to explain how children's understanding of the world changes as they develop, and the stages do help to show this. The trouble with any stage theory is that they tend to overestimate any differences between stages, and underestimate differences between individuals within the same stage. Oh well, nothing's perfect I suppose...

Development of Thinking

Some more highly interesting theories on cognitive development coming up — over to you, Vygotsky and Bruner.

Vygotsky Reckoned Culture Plays a Big Part in Cognitive Development

1) **Vygotsky** said there were two types of mental function — **elementary** and **higher**. Elementary functions can be thought of as **innate reflexes**, **sensory abilities** and certain types of **memory**. Higher functions include more complex tasks like **language comprehension** and **decision-making**.
2) **Social** and **cultural factors** play a necessary part in moving from one type of functioning to the other — it's the influence of **others** around you that drives cognitive development.
3) One of Vygotsky's ideas was the **zone of proximal development**. This is the difference between the problem solving a child can do on their **own** and the problem solving they can do with a **more able peer** or **adult**.
4) If your teacher has an idea of what your **potential** is, they can help you reach it by pushing and guiding. So it's **interaction** with the teacher that's important (unlike Piaget's idea that progression happens on its own).
5) Instruction is **social** and driven by the teacher using **language** and **cultural** influences. The intention is to help the child to be **self-regulated** and responsible for their own learning.

Language is Also Important in Cognitive Development

Vygotsky suggests that **language** is a **driving influence** on cognitive development:

1) Children first learn language as a means to **communicate** with caregivers. It's also a tool that allows adults to communicate **social** and **cultural information** to children.
2) As the child grows older they use language not only to communicate but also to **guide** their **behaviour** — they use **self-talk** (talking out loud) to **regulate** and **direct** themselves.
3) This self-talk eventually becomes **internalised** and becomes silent **inner speech**. At this point the child has developed two very different forms of language — **inner speech** and **external oral speech**.
4) **Oral speech** is used socially for **communication**, whilst **inner speech** is a **cognitive tool** that allows individuals to **direct** and **monitor** their **thoughts** and **behaviour**.
5) If someone finds a task difficult they may re-employ **self-talk** to exert greater **control** over their thoughts.

Vygotsky Also Came Up With Stages of Development

Vygotsky's stages **aren't as rigidly defined** as Piaget's — they're broader areas of development (without specified ages) giving an idea of the stages children go through as their thinking matures (**concept formation**).
He came up with these 4 stages after studying how children of various ages went about solving a problem:

1) **Vague syncretic** — **trial and error** methods are used, with **no understanding** of the underlying concepts.
2) **Complex** — use of **strategies** begins but they're **not** used successfully.
3) **Potential concept** — successful strategies are used but only **one at a time**.
4) **Mature concept** — **lots** of strategies used at the same time. Thinking becomes **mature** and **developed**.

Vygotsky's Theory Has Strengths and Weaknesses

Vygotsky carried out **very few studies** whilst coming up with his theory. However, other people have carried out studies that have provided evidence that **supports** Vygotsky's theory:

1) **Gardner and Gardner (1969)** found that with **instruction** animals can reach **higher levels** of functioning. This is evidence for the role of **culture** in learning.
2) **Chi et al (1989)** showed that pretending to **talk to the author** as you read (self-explanation) can help increase understanding. This is evidence for the use of **speech in thought**.
3) **Berk (1994)** found that children who used **more self-talk** when solving maths problems did better over the following year. This is evidence for the use of **self-talk** in problem-solving.

Another strength is that the theory can be **successfully applied to education** (see page 164). However, a **major criticism** is that the theory over-emphasises social and cultural factors in intelligence and **ignores biological factors**.

Development of Thinking

Bruner's *Theory Focuses on* ***Representations of Knowledge***

Bruner (1966) claimed that our brains use three **modes of representation** for knowledge:

1) **The Enactive Mode** — at first, knowledge is only in the form of **physical actions**, i.e. learning by doing. For example, a baby's knowledge of a rattle would involve how to hold and shake it. Later, this mode is used to represent knowledge such as how to swim. So, knowledge just involves '**muscle memory**'.

2) **The Iconic Mode** — at 2–6 years we begin to also store knowledge in the form of **mental images** involving different senses like vision, smell and touch. For example, our knowledge of what an apple is includes what it looks like and tastes like.

3) **The Symbolic Mode** — from about 7 years old we develop the ability to think in **symbolic ways** — we can store things as words and numbers. Language and thinking become strongly linked, e.g. we use language to talk about experiences. This allows us to **mentally manipulate** concepts and ideas, and to think in **abstract** ways.

Like Vygotsky, Bruner thought that **language** was very important for cognitive development. So, **language instruction** might help achieve understanding. However, **Sinclair-de-Zwart (1969)** found that although language appropriate for **conservation tasks** could be taught to children who couldn't conserve, most were still **unsuccessful** at the conservation tasks. Further development seems to be necessary before the next stage can be reached.

There is Some ***Evidence*** *to* ***Support*** *Bruner's Theory*

	Bruner and Kenney (1996) — Iconic and symbolic thinking
Method:	Children aged 5–7 were shown a grid with an arrangement of different sized glasses on it. These were removed and the children had to **replace** them as they had been (requiring **iconic thinking**), or **rearrange** them, e.g. in a mirror image (requiring **symbolic thinking**).
Results:	**All** the children **replaced** the glasses correctly, but only the **older** children could **rearrange** them. Children without the appropriate language to talk through the problem were only able to do the **replacement task**.
Conclusion:	Mental manipulation of ideas requires **symbolic representation**, and children must have progressed to the **symbolic mode** of cognitive development in order to think in this way. Language is important for more complex thinking.
Evaluation:	This was a **laboratory experiment** so there was **good control over variables**. However, all the study really showed was that **older** children can manage more **complex tasks** — so, this could also be used as support for Piaget or Vygotsky's theory.

Practice Questions

Q1 According to Vygotsky, what is inner speech used for?

Q2 Give two pieces of evidence that support Vygotsky's theory of cognitive development.

Q3 What is the difference between iconic and symbolic representation?

Q4 What did Bruner and Kenney conclude from their 1996 experiment?

Exam Question

Q1 a) Outline one theory of cognitive development. [8 marks]

b) Evaluate the theory of cognitive development outlined in (a). [16 marks]

I like Bruner's theory best — he's the easiest to spell...

I wonder how many different spellings of Vygotsky's name crop up on exam papers. Quite a few, I imagine. If you're like me and struggle to remember how to spell your own name, it's worth taking the time to learn it now. Vygotsky, that is — not your name. If you really can't spell that by now I doubt you'll ever be able to. Sorry to be the one to break it to you.

Applying the Theories to Education

Psychologists don't spend their time carrying out experiments and coming up with theories just for fun, you know. Well, maybe some of them do, but even then the theories they develop can have practical applications, such as using ideas about cognitive development to improve education — which, funnily enough, is the next thing you need to learn...

Piaget's Theory Has Implications for *Education*

Piaget's theory suggests a **child-centred approach** to education, in which children can learn for themselves through their own experience. It can be applied to find ways to help children **learn** more effectively:

1) **Learning by discovery** — according to Piaget, when children encounter new experiences that their current **schemas** can't deal with adequately, they develop new schemas through the process of **accommodation** (see page 160). This implies that providing opportunities to **actively** experience new things in a stimulating classroom with lots of **different** resources will help promote cognitive development.
2) **Readiness** — Piaget claimed that development is limited by the process of **maturation**. So, children **can't** learn particular kinds of knowledge until they're **ready** to develop the necessary schemas. For example, a child at the **preoperational** stage isn't ready to understand conservation of volume.
3) **Appropriate materials** — teachers must provide **appropriate challenges**, e.g. **preoperational** children should be given **concrete examples** of new ideas to help their understanding. Teachers must also be sensitive to **developmental differences** between students, because some children mature and learn more quickly than others.

The Plowden Report (1967)

The Plowden Report reviewed **primary level** education and made **recommendations** for UK schools. The report included research and surveys. Some of the recommendations it made were based on **Piaget's theory**. For example, Piaget's ideas about **discovery learning**, **readiness** and a **set sequence** of developmental stages were used in the report. However, Piaget's theory **isn't** now as widely accepted as it once was. It's now known that children generally have **more abilities** than Piaget claimed, e.g. **operational** thinking may develop **earlier** than Piaget suggested.

Vygotsky's Theory Emphasises *Social Interaction*

Vygotsky's theory is a **teacher-guided approach** and suggests that **interactions** with others are important in learning. In other words, **other people** are needed to stimulate cognitive development. For example, **scaffolding** is an important concept developed from Vygotsky's theory where other people assist a child's cognitive development:

- **Scaffolding** is when a **teacher**, another **adult** or a **more cognitively advanced child** acts as an **expert** to guide the child.
- They do this by making suggestions or doing demonstrations to provide a **framework** by which the child learns to do a task.
- At first the child might need lots of help, but as they learn **less help** is needed and they can carry on learning **independently**.
- For scaffolding to work it needs to take place within the child's **zone of proximal development** (**ZPD**) (see page 162).

Prof. Telfer's trainee teachers suddenly realised he didn't know what he was talking about.

	Wood et al (1976) studied scaffolding
Method:	**Thirty** children aged 3–5 were given the task of building a model and were **observed**. A **tutor** gave help to each child according to how well they were doing — the help was either in the form of showing or telling.
Results:	Scaffolding allowed the children to complete a task they **wouldn't** have been able to do alone. The **effectiveness** of the scaffolding was influenced by various factors, e.g. how the tutor **simplified** the task, and how they helped them **identify important steps**. **Showing** was used most when helping **younger** children, whilst **telling** was used more with the **older** children. Also, the **older** the child was the **less** scaffolding was needed for them to complete the task.
Conclusion:	Scaffolding **can** be helpful but consideration needs to be given to **maximise** its effectiveness.
Evaluation:	This study had fairly **good ecological validity**, but there was less control over variables, **reducing reliability**.

Applying the Theories to Education

Bruner Proposed a **Spiral Curriculum**

Bruner (1966) agreed with Vygotsky that **social interaction** is important for cognitive development, and he made some important suggestions for education:

1) **The Spiral Curriculum** — although a child's age and level of development will **limit** what they can learn, Bruner argued that even difficult concepts can be introduced at an appropriate level from an **early age**. As the child grows the concept can be **repeatedly revisited**, each time in more depth — this will achieve a more complete and in-depth understanding. In this way, children can **build up** their knowledge, and the earlier learning should make the later learning **easier**.

2) **Motivation** — Bruner argued that children are more motivated to learn if they have an **intrinsic interest** in what they're studying. This is **more of an incentive** than external motivations like getting good marks. So teachers should encourage an **active interest** in topics and aim to come up with engaging ways to teach them.

3) **Language** — by **discussions** in class, children can learn about **other perspectives**, and achieve **deeper understanding**.

4) **Discovery Learning** — Bruner emphasised that children should not just learn facts, but should learn by **exploring** and **discovering** facts. This also helps them to learn about the **process** of acquiring knowledge.

Bruner's ideas have been very influential — for example the use of a spiral curriculum is now quite common.

Application of Theories to Education May Need to Be **Reviewed**

1) Although theories of cognitive development have been **usefully applied** to education, there are often **practical difficulties** involved. For example, it can be very time-consuming to continually assess the ZPD of all the children in a class. Also, providing enough appropriate challenges and finding appropriate expert peer tutors can be a problem.
2) As **more research** is done and **theories develop**, the implications for education need to be regularly reviewed. For example, **Sylva** (**1987**) has suggested that Piaget's learning by discovery is **not** actually always the most effective approach and that his theory should not be relied on so heavily.

Archie suspected that his peer tutors were neither expert nor appropriate. He was no fool.

Practice Questions

Q1 What is meant by 'discovery learning'?

Q2 How is Vygotsky's approach to education different from Piaget's 'child-centred approach'?

Q3 What is involved in 'scaffolding'?

Q4 What is meant by a 'spiral curriculum'?

Q5 Why might applications of cognitive theories to education need to be regularly reviewed?

Exam Question

Q1 Outline and evaluate the application of theories of cognitive development to education. [24 marks]

A spiral curriculum — just going round and round in circles...

I'm pretty sure I experienced a spiral curriculum when I was at school. About twice a year in biology lessons they'd make us put a piece of pondweed in a beaker of water and count the bubbles. I never actually found out why though, so I'm guessing something went a bit wrong there. They should probably think about reviewing that approach, in my opinion.

Development of Moral Understanding

Hmmm, moral development. Being good, being bad, it's not always simple and clear cut which is which. For example, would it be morally wrong to skip these pages and go watch TV instead? Well, you'll never know unless you read them...

Kohlberg Thought That **Moral Understanding** Progresses in **Stages**

1) Kohlberg argued that your **moral understanding increases** as you grow older because at each stage you take more and more of the **social** world into account.
2) He investigated this idea using a series of ten **moral dilemma** stories. An example of the type of dilemma he used is the **'Heinz dilemma'**. In the story, Heinz chose to break into a shop to steal expensive drugs to cure his dying wife.
3) The participants had to decide whether these actions were **justified**. Kohlberg was interested in the participants' **reasons** for their decision.

Fred had been waiting for help for hours. He wouldn't be volunteering for any more studies.

	Kohlberg (1963) — Study of moral understanding
Method:	A sample of **72 boys** aged 10, 13 and 16 were each **interviewed** for approximately 2 hours. Each child was asked to think about a selection of **moral dilemmas** and **comment** on the actions taken by the characters. They were then asked to **justify** their reasoning. Kohlberg **recorded** their answers.
Results:	Kohlberg classified the children's responses into three groups. He used these to come up with three levels of moral understanding — **preconventional morality**, **conventional morality** and **postconventional morality**. Each of these levels is made up of **two stages** (see below). The answers of the **younger** children tended to fit into the preconventional level, whereas the answers of the **older** children tended to reflect the conventional stage. Few participants showed postconventional morality. The participants appeared to be **consistent** in their thinking and presented similar answers to different moral dilemmas.
Conclusion:	Children **progress** from a state of preconventional morality into a state of conventional morality. Only **much later**, if at all, do they show postconventional morality.
Evaluation:	Participants had to come up with the responses themselves, rather than choosing from a list of possible responses. This meant that the responses were not influenced by any **pre-existing ideas** that Kohlberg may have had. However, in sorting the participants' responses into levels, Kohlberg may have shown some **investigator bias**. This study **lacked ecological validity** as the dilemmas were hypothetical, and showed **gender bias** as all the participants were boys. Also, the results of this study cannot be generalised to more **collectivist cultures** where the **rights of the individual** are more likely to come second to **social obligations**. Finally, as Kohlberg himself later pointed out, his study was **limited** as it did not allow for emotions such as **guilt** and **empathy**.

Kohlberg Described **Three Levels** of **Moral Understanding**

Kohlberg used his findings to come up with **three levels** of moral understanding — preconventional, conventional and postconventional. Each of these levels is made up of **two stages**.

Level 1 — ***Preconventional Morality***

Stage 1 — Punishment and obedience orientation

Reasons for behaviour aren't taken into account. The only reason for not doing something is because you'll be **punished**. For example, Heinz shouldn't steal the drugs because he'll go to jail.

Stage 2 — Instrumental purpose orientation

Morality is based on meeting your **own interests** and getting what you **want**. For example, Heinz should steal the drugs because otherwise his wife will die and he'll be upset.

Development of Moral Understanding

Level 2 — Conventional Morality

Stage 3 — Morality of interpersonal cooperation

You try to live up to the **expectations** of people who are **important** to you. Behaviour that improves your relationship with these people is seen as moral. For example, Heinz should steal the drugs as his family and friends would expect him to do everything he can to save his wife.

Stage 4 — Social-order orientation

Moral behaviour is behaviour that fits in with **social norms**, **obligations** and **rules**, e.g. following the law. Morality is seen in the context of society as a whole. For example, Heinz shouldn't steal the drugs because it's against the law, and laws should always be followed.

Level 3 — Postconventional Morality

Stage 5 — Social-contract orientation

Laws are seen as **flexible** in certain situations, and not all of **equal importance**. Laws are only followed if they contribute towards the welfare of others. For example, Heinz should steal the drugs — although stealing is against the law, it's better to steal than to let his wife die.

Stage 6 — Universal ethical principles

You've developed your own set of **abstract moral principles** that you follow above those laid down by the law. For example, Heinz should steal the drugs as human life has a higher value than personal property.

Other Researchers Have Studied Kohlberg's Findings

Other researchers have reviewed and evaluated Kohlberg's work:

1) **Sobesky (1983)** found that using **different versions** of Heinz's dilemma (i.e. different consequences for Heinz and his wife of Heinz stealing or not stealing) **changes the response** of the reader. So an individual's response **isn't fixed** depending on the stage of moral development they're at, but changes according to the **situation**.
2) The theory is **sex-biased**. Most of Kohlberg's work was carried out on **US males**, so his findings may not apply to other groups. Gilligan claimed that the theory was **androcentric** and focused too much on male-oriented ideas about **justice** rather than also taking into account **other moral approaches** that might appeal more to women.
3) **Hart and Fegley (1995)** found that some morally-driven people are **not** motivated by duty or by right and wrong, as Kohlberg suggested — some people are motivated to behave morally because it makes them **feel good**.

Practice Questions

Q1 Give two problems with Kohlberg's (1963) study of moral understanding.

Q2 List Kohlberg's six stages of moral understanding.

Q3 What did Sobesky (1983) find when he studied Kohlberg's dilemmas?

Q4 What did Hart and Fegley (1995) discover about the motivation of morally-driven people?

Exam Question

Q1 a) Outline one theory of moral understanding. [8 marks]

b) Evaluate the theory of moral understanding outlined in (a). [16 marks]

The Heinz dilemma — baked beans or ketchup?

So the little kid who hangs around on the street corner nicking bikes can just blame it all on not having progressed through Kohlberg's different levels of moral understanding. Great. Anyway, whether you agree with it or not, you need to learn about Kohlberg's theory of moral understanding before you move on. Go on — you know it's the right thing to do...

Development of Social Cognition

Social cognition is about understanding about yourself and others, and being able to see things from other people's perspective. So, for example, I know that I'm awesome and that you're probably not having much fun right now...

A Sense of Self Develops During Childhood

Having a **sense of self** includes things like:

- being able to **distinguish** between self and others, and referring to each with **appropriate language**
- having knowledge of our **experiences**, **abilities**, **motivations**, etc.
- having ideas about **body image**

Important stages during development include:

1) **Existential self** — from about three months old we learn to **distinguish** self from non-self, and find out that we exist separately from other things. The development of **object permanence** (see p.160) may help this.
2) **Categorical self** — from about two years old we start to use language to **describe ourselves**, using culturally defined categories, e.g. age, male/female, tall/short, etc. We are also described by **other people** in this way, which can influence our idea of ourself. For example, describing a child as 'clever' or 'naughty' could influence their **self-esteem**.
3) **Identity crisis** — **Erikson (1968)** claimed that during **adolescence**, when going through body changes and starting to make plans for the future, we may **try out** different roles until we find our true identity.

Having a sense of self also involves being able to see yourself as **others** see you. This requires some understanding of the minds of others, and being able to see things from **their perspective**.

Theory of Mind (ToM) is About Understanding Other People's Minds

Humans have a unique ability to **cooperate** and carry out **complex interactions**. It's thought this is possible because we have a **theory of mind**. This involves **understanding that we and others have minds** with knowledge, feelings, beliefs, motivations, intentions, etc. We can **explain** and **predict** other people's behaviour by making inferences about their mental states. This includes the knowledge that others may have **false beliefs** about the world.

	Baron-Cohen et al (1985) — theory of mind in autistic children
Method:	Three groups of children were studied — children with autism with an average age of 12 years, children with Down's Syndrome with an average age of 11 years, and 'normal' children with an average age of 4 years. The experiment used two dolls — Sally had a basket, Anne a box. Children were asked to name the dolls (the **naming question**). Then Sally was seen to hide a marble in her basket and leave the room. Anne took the marble and put it in her box. Sally returned and the child was asked, 'Where will Sally look for her marble?' (**belief question**). The correct response is to point to the basket, where Sally believes the marble to be. They were also asked, 'Where is the marble really?' (**reality question**) and 'Where was the marble in the beginning?' (**memory question**). Each child was tested twice, with the marble in a different place the second time.
Results:	**All** of the children got the **naming**, **reality** and **memory** questions correct. In the **belief** question, the children with Down's Syndrome scored **86%**, the 'normal' children **85%**, but the children with autism scored **20%**.
Conclusion:	The findings suggest that autistic children have an **under-developed theory of mind**, sometimes called **mind-blindness**. They seem unable to predict or understand the beliefs of others.
Evaluation:	Dolls were used throughout the study, causing it to lack **ecological validity**. Also, children with autism may in fact have a more highly developed theory of mind and understand that dolls don't have beliefs. Repeating the study by acting out the scenes with **humans** might show an increase in ability on the tasks. However, **Leslie and Frith (1988)** did a similar study with real people and not dolls and found the same pattern of results.

Most children develop ToM at around **four** years old. However, the kind of questions asked in Baron-Cohen et al's false belief task may be difficult for younger children to understand. It seems that **three-year-old** children can pass some versions of the test, so theory of mind may actually develop **earlier**.

There's also disagreement about the **development** of ToM. It may have an **innate** basis, but **nurture** and **experience** are also likely to be important in its development.

Development of Social Cognition

Understanding Others Involves **Perspective-taking**

One aspect of having a ToM is understanding that other people's **perspectives** can differ from your own. Children gradually become more skilful in their **perspective-taking ability**. **Selman (1980)** studied children's perspective-taking ability by analysing their responses to stories presenting dilemmas. For example:

> Selman told children a story about a girl who could rescue a friend's cat by climbing a tree. However, she'd promised her father that she wouldn't climb trees. Selman asked the children if she should be punished if she did climb the tree.

Like all little girls, Molly had perfected the "who, me?" look. She knew Daddy wouldn't mind about the tree.

From the children's answers, Selman identified **five** kinds of **perspective-taking**:

1) **Undifferentiated and Egocentric** — up to about six years of age, children can separate **self** and **other**, but in a physical sense only. They don't perceive any psychological differences, seeing the other person in the same way they see an object.

2) **Differentiated and Subjective** — from five to nine, children understand that other people have **different perspectives** because they have access to **different information** (i.e. know different things). However, only their own perspective is seen as important and they can't take the perspective of the other person.

3) **Second-Person and Reciprocal** — between seven and twelve, children can put themselves in someone else's shoes and view a situation from **another's perspective**. They also realise that other people can do the same.

4) **Third-Person and Mutual** — between ten and fifteen years old, children develop the ability to take the perspective of a **third impartial person** who's viewing an interaction between other people.

5) **In-Depth and Societal-Symbolic** — from about fourteen, children understand that **third-party perspectives** can be influenced by factors such as **social or cultural values.** They can see a situation from a variety of different perspectives, e.g. moral, legal, etc.

As children go through these stages they become better able to understand that other people have different perspectives, and can use information to put themselves in other people's shoes.

Selman's ideas about perspective-taking can have **practical applications** in **education**. For example, using **multi-cultural** materials and having **class discussions** can expose children to different perspectives. This may help to promote their perspective-taking ability.

Practice Questions

Q1 Explain what is meant by 'existential self', 'categorical self' and 'identity crisis'.

Q2 How does Baron-Cohen et al's false belief task show whether or not a child has a theory of mind?

Q3 How did Selman study perspective-taking ability?

Q4 Name Selman's five stages of perspective-taking.

Exam Question

Q1 a) Describe theories of the development of a child's sense of self. [8 marks]

b) Discuss the development of children's understanding of others, including perspective-taking. [16 marks]

Actually, I took the marble while your back was turned and swallowed it...

One of my friends at school definitely went through that identity crisis thing. He started out as an emo kid, suddenly went really sporty and obsessed with football, and then for a term or two he seemed to think he was a rapper. He also spent nearly a whole year dressing like a cowboy. I think he's settled down now though — last I heard he was an accountant.

The Mirror Neuron System

Here comes the science bit — all about the biological basis for social cognition. I knew you'd be thrilled. Enjoy.

Social Cognition Has a Biological Basis

1) **Neurons** (**cells**) in the cerebral cortex are organised into **four** main areas: the **frontal**, **temporal**, **parietal** and **occipital** lobes.
2) Different processes, such as **visual perception**, involve one or more of these lobes. Some areas of the brain seem to have very specialised roles in **cognition**.
3) It seems likely that many of our sophisticated **social** abilities, such as **theory of mind**, also involve complex brain mechanisms — these may have **evolved** as our brains and intelligence grew. Abilities like this could have been stimulated by our complex **social living** (see page 158).
4) Attempts have been made to **connect** findings from neuroscience and social psychology and combine them into more complete theories — this is known as **social neuroscience**.

Mirror Neurons Respond to the Actions of Others

Mirror neurons are brain cells that are involved in **performing** an action, such as holding a cup. However, they're **also** active when you **observe** someone else doing the same action. So, whether you're actually holding a cup, or only observing someone else holding a cup, particular mirror neurons will be **active**.

	Di Pellegrino et al (1992) — recording neuron activity
Method:	**Electrodes** were inserted into individual neurons in the **premotor cortex** of macaque monkeys. When the monkeys reached for food, the **activity** in the neurons was recorded.
Results:	The neurons were **active** when the monkeys reached for food, but also, unexpectedly, active when they observed **someone else** reach for food.
Conclusion:	This was the **first** study to provide evidence for the existence of **mirror neurons**. Although the function of mirror neurons is not yet clear, they may help in understanding observed behaviour.
Evaluation:	The experiment was **not** designed to study mirror neurons, so the information gathered about them was **limited**. Also, this experiment involved inserting electrodes into animals' brains, which raises **ethical issues**.

It's hard to record the activity of individual neurons in the brains of **humans**. So, studies have been done using brain scanning techniques such as **functional Magnetic Resonance Imaging** (fMRI), which analyse **brain activity** during particular kinds of behaviours. For example, Iacoboni et al (1999) found that there are areas of the **frontal** and **parietal cortex** that are active when people carry out and observe actions.

Mirror Neurons May Be Important for Social Cognition

Neurons that are active both when **you** do something and when you see **other people** do the same thing may help you **understand** the behaviour of others.

	Fogassi et al (2005) — Mirror neurons and intentions
Method:	The activity of **41 mirror neurons** in 2 macaque monkeys were recorded as they observed a person pick up an apple as if to eat it, or pick up the apple and place it in a cup.
Results:	**Different** groups of neurons responded to the two outcomes (eat or place). Also, some neurons fired after the apple was picked up but before the second action (eat or place) was carried out.
Conclusion:	Different patterns of response link with different **behavioural objectives** and some neurons seem to predict the **intention** of actions. So, mirror neurons may help to **understand** and **predict** the behaviour of others.
Evaluation:	Animals may behave differently under lab conditions, meaning the experiment has **low ecological validity**. Also, the experiment was carried out on monkeys so it's difficult to **generalise** the results to humans — neurons in humans may not respond in the same way.

Experiments with **humans** using **fMRI** show that brain areas that are active when we feel particular emotions (e.g. happiness or pain) are also active when we see others feel the same emotion. This supports suggestions that mirror neurons may be involved in **empathy**.

The Mirror Neuron System

There's a Lot of **Debate** About the **Role** of Mirror Neurons

1) The **function** and **importance** of mirror neurons is not yet fully understood. For example, they may be involved in **imitation** — but macaque monkeys (which have mirror neurons) have a **limited ability** for imitation learning.
2) A connection between mirror neurons and **theory of mind** (**ToM**) has also been debated. However, mirror neurons are found in monkeys that **don't** seem to have ToM in the same way that humans do. Also, **fMRI research** shows that ToM tests activate brain regions that **aren't** generally thought to be part of the mirror neuron system. It may be that mirror neurons can be involved in **learning by imitation**, but that the development of ToM involves **more** than this.
3) More needs to be learnt about the **development** of mirror neurons. **Falck-Ytter** (**2006**) reckoned that mirror neurons start to develop during the **first year** of life. However, **Meltzoff and Moore** (**1977**) found that human infants can imitate facial expressions **soon after birth**. This could either suggest that mirror neurons have an **innate** basis, or else that imitation **doesn't** necessarily involve mirror neurons.

Social Neuroscience Has Raised **Important Issues**

Jake knew what went on in those labs and was holding Dr. Anwar's dog hostage until Maeve was returned to him safely.

1) **Social neuroscience** is **inter-disciplinary** — it involves both **biological** and **social** concepts and theories. These different types of theories may **mutually inform** each other — biological research can help understand social processes better, and vice versa. This means we can understand behaviour at different levels of explanation.
2) This approach may bring important **insights** into human **social cognition** (e.g. the basis of **empathy**). Also, some conditions associated with developmental problems (e.g. **autism**) might be better understood.
3) Animal experiments involve invasive methods, e.g. inserting electrodes into the brain — this raises **ethical issues**.

Practice Questions

Q1 What are mirror neurons?

Q2 How have mirror neurons been studied in animals and in humans?

Q3 Who first identified mirror neurons?

Q4 Outline a piece of evidence supporting the idea that mirror neurons may be involved in empathy.

Q5 Why is social neuroscience a particularly valuable new field of research?

Exam Questions

Q1 Discuss the development of social cognition, including the role of the mirror neuron system. [24 marks]

Q2 Outline and evaluate research on the role of the mirror neuron system. [24 marks]

OK, he's picking up the cup — ready neurons... aim... and fire...

This is an interesting little topic to end the section with — it's all fresh and new and nobody knows quite what's going on. There are new ideas springing up and being shot down all over the place. And to think, if a monkey hadn't happened to look over and see someone picking up some food, these pages might never have existed. What a loss that would've been.

Clinical Psychology

This section is quite a nice one really — clinical psychology is all about diagnosing mental disorders and then treating them, so the researchers here are actually trying to help people. Almost brings a tear to your eye, doesn't it...

Clinical Psychologists Explain and Treat Mental Illness

1) Clinical psychology focuses on studying, explaining and treating **emotional** or **behavioural disorders**.
2) Clinical psychologists assess patients using **interviews**, **observations** and **psychological tests**. They then help patients work through their problems, e.g. using talk therapies.
3) Researchers gather **primary** and **secondary data** to improve understanding of mental disorders. Clinicians then apply this to **individual cases** to help them establish a clear **diagnosis** and decide upon the correct **treatment** for each individual.

- **Primary data** — information collected during the researcher's direct observations of a patient, e.g. test results, answers to questionnaires, observation notes.
- **Secondary data** — information collected from other studies. This data can be used to check the validity of studies, or used to prove or disprove a new theory.

Clinical Psychology Uses Twin Studies

1) **Twin studies** are used to find out if **genetic factors** influence the development of mental disorders.
2) They involve looking at **concordance rates** — the **chance** that both twins will develop the mental disorder.
3) **Identical** (**MZ**) twins share all their genetic material, and **non-identical** (**DZ**) twins share around half. So, if both MZ twins are **more likely** to develop schizophrenia (a higher concordance rate) than both DZ twins, it can be assumed that schizophrenia has a **genetic** cause. However, it can't be the full story unless concordance rates are **100%** in MZ twins.

There's more on schizophrenia and twin studies on p.176.

Gottesman and Shields (1966) — schizophrenia in twins

Method:	Hospital records for the previous 16 years were examined to identify people with schizophrenia who had a **twin**. Around 40 sets of twins agreed to take part in the study, which was a **natural experiment** using **independent measures**.
Results:	The concordance rate was about **48%** for **MZ** twins and about **17%** for **DZ** twins. The exact figures vary depending on the type of schizophrenia, but overall, MZ twins had a much higher concordance rate than DZ twins.
Conclusion:	As the results for MZ twins are much higher, this suggests a **genetic cause** for schizophrenia.
Evaluation:	The results for MZ twins don't show 100% concordance, which means that there must be **other important factors** that influence schizophrenia. Although the researchers had a large amount of data covering a long period of time, it's unlikely the study could be **replicated** until new data existed.

Twin Studies Have Strengths and Weaknesses

Strengths

- **Rich data** — researchers have the opportunity to study **rare phenomena** in a lot of **detail**.
- **Unique cases** — existing theories can be challenged, and ideas for future research can be suggested.
- **High ecological validity** — the variables aren't manipulated so the findings should be **true to real life**.

Weaknesses

- **Causal relationships** — the researcher **doesn't** have much **control** over the variables, so the findings could be the result of an extraneous variable. This means that it's **difficult** to establish **cause and effect**.
- **Generalisation** — only using a **single case** means it's difficult to generalise the results to other people.
- **Ethics** — it can be difficult to get **informed consent** if the subjects have a **mental disorder**.
- **Opportunities** — identical twins are quite **rare**, so there aren't very many research opportunities, and sample sizes are usually pretty small.

Clinical Psychology

Clinical Psychology Uses Animal Studies

Animal studies are used in clinical psychology because they allow researchers to carry out tests that couldn't be done on humans. However, using animals for research raises ethical issues.

Lipska et al (1993) — schizophrenia in rats

Method: This was a **laboratory experiment** that involved making lesions in rats' brains to see if they developed schizophrenia-like symptoms. Areas of the hippocampus associated with schizophrenia were damaged using an injection of ibotenic acid a week after the rats were born.

Results: The rats with a damaged hippocampus developed schizophrenia-like symptoms as their brains matured, e.g. hyperactivity, memory problems and a lack of response to rewards.

Conclusion: Damage to the hippocampus can lead to the onset of schizophrenia-like symptoms, which suggests that the hippocampus plays a role in the development of schizophrenia.

Evaluation: The variables in this experiment were tightly controlled, which means that it should be possible to establish **cause and effect** — the rats wouldn't have developed these symptoms if their brains hadn't been damaged. However, it's difficult to know how many symptoms of schizophrenia the rats were actually experiencing, because you can't establish whether they were having hallucinations or delusions.

Animal Studies Have Strengths and Weaknesses

Strengths

- **Ethics** — researchers can conduct experiments on animals that they **couldn't** do on **humans** because of **ethical restraints**, e.g. lesion studies. This means that clinical psychologists can investigate the **causes** of **mental disorders**, e.g. the effects of particular chemicals or social deprivation. They also don't need to get the animal's informed consent or worry about deception.
- **Speed of reproduction** — most animals reproduce much more **quickly** than humans, so it's quicker and easier to carry out **longitudinal studies** of **genetic influence**, e.g. to see whether schizophrenia has a genetic cause.
- **Detachment** — it's easier for researchers to be **impartial** with animal participants than with humans, so the results are more likely to be **objective**.

Weaknesses

- **Qualitative differences** — humans and animals are qualitatively different, so there are **problems** with **generalising** the results from animal studies to humans. Substances can have different effects on different animals, e.g. **morphine** has a calming effect on humans, but it causes manic behaviour in cats.
- **Language** — animals don't have **language**, which is a vital part of human behaviour. In clinical psychology this means that animals **can't describe** their **symptoms**, so it's difficult to know whether they're experiencing any mental abnormalities.

Practice Questions

Q1 Outline the aims of clinical psychology.

Q2 What's the difference between primary and secondary data?

Q3 Outline one advantage of twin studies.

Exam Question

Q1 a) Describe two research methods used in clinical psychology. [8 marks]

b) Evaluate the research methods outlined in (a). [16 marks]

Twin study — like a normal study but with two desks...

Just when you thought there couldn't possibly be any more different types of psychology, clinical psychology had to go and rear its ugly head. Woe is you. Although, to be honest, I've got limited sympathy. If you really thought that there weren't any other types of psychology then you obviously haven't been paying much attention. And we can't have that, can we...

Schizophrenia

*A lot of people think that schizophrenia involves having multiple personalities, but it **really really doesn't**, so don't make this mistake in the exam else you'll look like a right plum duff. And nobody wants to look like a right plum duff.*

Schizophrenia Disrupts the Mind's Ability to Function

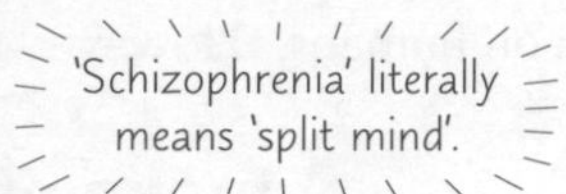

1) **Schizophrenia** is a **thought process disorder**. It's characterised by **disruption** to a person's **perceptions**, **emotions** and **beliefs**.
2) The onset of schizophrenia can be **acute** (a **sudden** onset, where behaviour changes within a few days), or **chronic** (a **gradual** deterioration in mental health that develops slowly over time).
3) **Males** and **females** are **equally** affected. In **males** schizophrenia usually develops in their **late teens** or **early 20s**, while **females** tend to develop it 4 or 5 years **later**. Overall, **0.5%** of the population is affected.
4) It's thought that schizophrenia **isn't** a **single disorder** but that there are various **subtypes** — however, there still **isn't** an agreed **definition**.

Schizophrenia has Lots of Different Clinical Characteristics

People with schizophrenia can experience a **range** of possible **symptoms**:

1 Perceptual symptoms

- **Auditory hallucinations** — **hearing** things that **aren't there**. People often hear **voices** saying **abusive** or **critical** things.
- Sometimes people **see**, **smell** or **taste** things that aren't there.

2 Social symptoms

- **Social withdrawal** — not **taking part** in or **enjoying** social situations.
- People might be **aloof** or **avoid eye contact**.

3 Cognitive symptoms

- **Delusions** — **believing** things that **aren't true**. People can have **delusions** of **grandeur** (where they believe they're more **important** than they are, e.g. that they're the king) or of **paranoia** and **persecution** (where they believe people are out to **get them**). Some schizophrenics also experience **delusions** of **control** — they believe that their **behaviour** is being **controlled** by **somebody else**.
- **Thought control** — believing that your **thoughts** are being **controlled**. For example, **thought insertion** is when people feel that someone's putting thoughts into their heads. **Withdrawal** is when they believe that someone is **removing** their thoughts. They might also believe that **people** can **read** their thoughts — this is **broadcasting**.
- **Language impairments** — **irrelevant** and **incoherent speech**. People often show signs of **cognitive distractibility**, where they **can't maintain** a **train** of **thought**. They might also **repeat sounds** (**echolalia**), **jumble** their **words** (**word salad**), make **nonsensical rhymes** (**clang associations**) and **invent words** (**neologisms**).

4 Affective / emotional symptoms

- **Depressive symptoms** — a **lack** of **energy** and **interest** in things, especially in **personal care** and **hygiene**.
- **Lack of emotion** — **not reacting** to typically emotional situations. This is also called **emotional blunting**.
- **Inappropriate emotions** — **reacting** in an **inappropriate** way, e.g. laughing at bad news.

5 Behavioural symptoms

- **Stereotyped behaviours** — continuously **repeating** actions, which are often **strange** and **don't** have a **purpose**.
- **Psychomotor disturbance** — **not** having **control** of your **muscles**. People may experience **catatonia**, where they sit in an **awkward position** for a **long time**. In this state people will sometimes **stay** in whatever position they're **put** in (so if you lift their arm over their head it'll stay like that **until** you move it **back**).
- **Catatonic stupor** — lying **rigidly** and **not moving** for **long** periods of **time**. People are **conscious** during these episodes and can **remember** what was going on **around** them, although they **don't** seem **aware** of it at the **time**.

Symptoms Can be Categorised into Two Types

The **symptoms** of schizophrenia are sometimes categorised as **Type 1** or **Type 2**:

1) **Type 1** symptoms are **positive** symptoms. This is where people **experience** something, feel that something is **happening** to them, or **display** certain **behaviours** — e.g. hallucinations, delusions, jumbled speech.
2) **Type 2** symptoms are **negative** symptoms. This is where people **don't** display 'normal' behaviours — e.g. they're withdrawn, unresponsive and show a lack of emotion.

Schizophrenia

The DSM-IV Classifies Mental Disorders

1) The **DSM-IV** is the fourth edition of the American Psychiatric Association's Diagnostic and Statistical Manual of Mental Disorders.
2) It contains a list of **mental health disorders**. Individuals are rated on **multiple axes / dimensions** and diagnostic **categories** are used, e.g. personality disorders and psychosocial problems.
3) It aims to give diagnosis of mental disorders **reliability** and **validity**:

For a person to be diagnosed as schizophrenic, the DSM-IV states that their symptoms must significantly impair reality testing — the ability to function in the real world. The symptoms have to have been present for at least six months.

Reliability

Reliability is how far the classification system produces the **same diagnosis** for a particular set of symptoms. In order for a classification system to be reliable the **same diagnosis** should be made **each time** it's used. This means that **different clinicians** should reach the **same diagnosis**.

Validity

Validity is whether the classification system is actually measuring what it **aims to measure**.

- **Descriptive validity** — how similar individuals diagnosed with the disorder are.
- **Aetiological validity** — how similar the cause of the disorder is for each sufferer.
- **Predictive validity** — how useful the diagnostic categories are for predicting the right treatment.

There can be Problems with the Reliability and Validity of Diagnoses

Problems with reliability

1) Schizophrenia diagnosis may be affected by **cultural bias**. For example, **Harrison et al (1984)** showed that there was an **over-diagnosis** of schizophrenia in **West Indian** psychiatric patients in Bristol.
2) No research has found any cause for this, so it suggests that the **symptoms** of **ethnic minority** patients are **misinterpreted**.
3) This questions the **reliability** of the diagnosis of schizophrenia — it suggests that patients can display the **same symptoms** but receive **different diagnoses** because of their ethnic background.

Problems with validity

1) **Rosenhan (1973)** conducted a study where people with no mental health problem got themselves admitted into a **psychiatric unit** by saying they heard voices — they became **pseudopatients**.
2) Once they'd been admitted they behaved 'normally'. However, their behaviour was still seen as a **symptom** of their **disorder** by the staff in the unit. For example, one pseudopatient who wrote in a diary was recorded as displaying 'writing behaviour'.
3) This questions the **validity** of the **diagnosis** of mental disorders — once people are **labelled** as having a disorder, all of their behaviour can be **interpreted** as being **caused** by the **disorder**.

Practice Questions

Q1 What are the differences between positive and negative symptoms of schizophrenia?

Q2 What is the DSM-IV?

Q3 Outline the clinical characteristics of schizophrenia.

Exam Question

Q1 Discuss the issues surrounding the classification and diagnosis of schizophrenia. [24 marks]

Word salad — like crunchy alphabet spaghetti...

Like so many things in psychology, schizophrenia is incredibly hard to define. People can show a variety of symptoms, which can be classified in different ways. Learning this is a bit of a pain now, but at least it means you should have loads to say in the exam, and you can't really ask for more than that. Well, apart from a holiday in the Caribbean, private jet, yacht...

Explanations of Schizophrenia

Different people have different ideas about what causes schizophrenia. This was mostly a sneaky little ploy dreamt up by psychologists and examiners to make your revision harder. OK, that's not strictly true, but it does feel like it sometimes.

Schizophrenia Could be Caused by **Biological Factors**

Concordance rates are the chance that someone will develop a disorder if they're related to someone who has it.

1) **Genetic** Factors (Inherited Tendencies)

Being **genetically related** to someone with schizophrenia can significantly **increase** a person's **chances** of developing it. **Family** and **twin** studies have looked at **concordance rates**:

Gottesman (1991) reviewed about 40 twin studies and found that with **identical** (**MZ**) **twins** there was about a **48%** chance of **both** being schizophrenic. With **non-identical** (**DZ**) **twins** there was about a **17%** chance.

Evidence for...

1) **Shields (1962)** found that **MZ twins** raised in **different families** still showed around **50%** concordance.
2) **Adoption studies** have found that when children are **adopted** because one or both of their **biological parents** has schizophrenia, the **chance** of them developing it is still the **same**. This suggests that **genetics** are more significant than the **environment**.

Evidence against...

1) No study has found a **100%** concordance rate, so schizophrenia **can't** just be caused by **genes**. **Shared environment** may cause higher concordance rates in **family** studies because children **imitate** 'schizophrenic' **behaviours** from their relatives.
2) This means **other factors** need to be considered, e.g. biochemical or psychological factors.

2) **Biochemical** Factors

Post-mortems and **PET scans** have shown that schizophrenics have abnormally high levels of the neurotransmitter **dopamine**. These findings led to the development of the **dopamine hypothesis**, which states that **synapses** that use **dopamine** as a **neurotransmitter** are **overactive** in the brains of people with schizophrenia.

Evidence for...

1) **Antipsychotic** drugs **reduce** the **symptoms** of schizophrenia by **blocking** dopamine receptors. This suggests that it's the **overactive** dopamine receptors **causing** the symptoms.
2) Drugs like **amphetamines**, which **increase dopamine function**, can sometimes cause **schizophrenia-like** symptoms in people without schizophrenia.

Evidence against...

1) **Antipsychotic** drugs only work on the **positive symptoms** of schizophrenia, e.g. hallucinations. This means that increased dopamine function **doesn't** explain **negative symptoms** like social withdrawal.
2) The **link** with dopamine is **correlational**, so it doesn't show **cause and effect**. It may be that increased dopamine function is a **symptom** of schizophrenia, rather than a cause of it.

3) **Neurological** Factors

Abnormal brain structure, caused by **abnormal development**, could be the cause of schizophrenia.

Evidence for...

1) **Johnstone et al (1976)** compared the **size** of the **ventricles** (hollow areas) in schizophrenics' brains with non-schizophrenics' brains. They found that the people with schizophrenia had **enlarged ventricles**, which suggests that **schizophrenia** is **linked** to a **loss** of **brain tissue**.
2) **Buchsbaum (1990)** carried out **MRI scans** on schizophrenics' brains and found **abnormalities** in the **prefrontal cortex**.

Evidence against...

1) **Non-schizophrenics** can also have **enlarged ventricles**, which goes against **Johnstone's** evidence.
2) These findings are **correlational**, so they don't show **cause and effect**. It may be that abnormal brain structure is a **symptom** of schizophrenia, rather than a cause of it.

Explanations of Schizophrenia

Schizophrenia Could be Caused by **Psychological Factors**

1) **Behavioural** Factors

Behaviourists argue that schizophrenia is **learnt** through **operant conditioning**. Someone may do something that gets a **positive reaction** or **reward** from others. This **encourages** the person to **repeat** the behaviour — it **reinforces** it.

Evidence for...	**Token economies**, which use **reinforcement** to encourage '**normal**' **behaviours**, can help **treat** schizophrenia (see next page). This suggests that some of the behaviour could be **learnt**.
Evidence against...	**Biological and psychological research** suggests that schizophrenia **isn't** just a **learnt behaviour**.

2) **Psychodynamic** Theory

Freud claimed that schizophrenia is caused by over-whelming **anxiety**. It's a **defence mechanism** involving **regression** into an **early stage** of **development**. **Hallucinations** are the **ego's** attempt to **restore contact** with **reality**.

Evidence for... **Laing (1967)** also argued that schizophrenics **lose contact** with **reality** as a way of **coping** with **social pressure**. He claimed that it was wrong to encourage schizophrenics to conform.

Evidence against... There **isn't** any **research evidence** to **support** Freud's theory. **Psychoanalysis isn't** an **effective treatment**, which suggests that psychodynamic theory **doesn't** explain what **causes** schizophrenia.

3) **Socio-cultural** Factors

The **social causation hypothesis** states that people with **low social status** are more likely to suffer from schizophrenia than people with higher social status. It's thought that factors like **poverty** and **discrimination** cause **high stress levels**, and that this can cause schizophrenia.

Evidence for...

Harrison et al (2001) found that people who were born in **deprived areas** were more likely to develop schizophrenia. This suggests that factors like **poverty**, **unemployment** and **crowding** have an **impact** on schizophrenia.

Evidence against...

These results are **correlational**, so they **don't** show **cause and effect**. The **social drift hypothesis** suggests that there are more people with schizophrenia in deprived areas because having schizophrenia gives them a **lower social status**, e.g. because they might be unemployed.

4) **Cognitive** Factors

Cognitive psychologists argue that schizophrenia is caused by **faulty information processing**. This leads to **delusions**, **thought interference**, **language impairment** and **memory problems**.

Evidence for...	**Neufeld (1978)** compared the cognitive processes of people with schizophrenia with a **control** group. The participants with schizophrenia took **longer** to **encode stimuli** and showed **short-term memory problems**. This suggests that their ability to process information was impaired.
Evidence against...	**Biochemical** research suggests that **cognitive** problems are **caused** by **increased dopamine function**, rather than faulty information processing.

Practice Questions

Q1 Outline the role that biochemical factors might have in causing schizophrenia.

Q2 Outline the socio-cultural factors that could explain schizophrenia.

Exam Question

Q1 Outline and evaluate explanations of schizophrenia [24 marks]

Explain schizophrenia — I can barely even spell it...

So there isn't just one definite idea about what causes schizophrenia — surprise surprise. At least these pages are quite useful though. When you're evaluating one explanation of schizophrenia, you can use all the other explanations as evidence against it — so you could use the evidence for social theory as evidence against genetic factors, or whatever. Not bad eh?

Treating Schizophrenia

There are a number of different treatments for schizophrenia, and most people benefit from having a combination of a few of them. After all, why just have one when you can have them all — the more the merrier I say...

Schizophrenia Can be **Treated** Using **Biological Therapy**

Therapy using drugs is also called chemotherapy.

1) The **biological** approach to treating schizophrenia involves **drug therapy**.
2) Treatment is based on the **dopamine hypothesis** (p.176) — the theory that schizophrenia is linked to increased dopamine activity in the brain. **Antipsychotic drugs** (**neuroleptics**) work by **blocking dopamine receptors**.

Advantages

- Drug therapy is effective at reducing **positive symptoms**, e.g. hallucinations.
- It's **successful** for a large number of schizophrenia patients, meaning that more people can live in the **community** rather than being institutionalised.
- It's the most **widely-used** and **effective** form of treatment for schizophrenia. Almost all other treatments are used **alongside** drug therapy.

When you're evaluating a treatment for schizophrenia, you can use the advantages of another treatment as a disadvantage of the one you're evaluating.

Disadvantages

- Drug therapy **isn't** very effective for treating **negative symptoms** like social withdrawal.
- It treats the **symptoms** of schizophrenia but **not** the **cause**. Symptoms often **come back** if people stop taking antipsychotic drugs. This leads to the '**revolving door phenomenon**', where patients are constantly being discharged and re-admitted to hospital.
- There are **ethical issues** surrounding the use of drug therapy. Some people argue that drug treatment is a '**chemical straitjacket**' — it **doesn't** really **help** the patient, it just **controls** their **behaviour** to make it more socially acceptable and easier to manage.
- Most people will experience some **short-term side effects** when taking antipsychotic drugs, e.g. drowsiness, blurred vision, dry mouth, constipation and weight gain.
- **Long-term side effects** include increased risk of **diabetes** and **tardive dyskinesia** (involuntary repetitive movements that continue even after they've stopped taking the medication).
- **Clinical trials** have shown that as many as **two-thirds** of people stop taking antipsychotic drugs because of the side-effects. However, **newer** antipsychotic drugs seem to have **fewer long-term side effects** than the **older** ones.

Schizophrenia Can be **Treated** Using **Psychological Therapies**

1 Behavioural Therapy

1) **Behavioural** treatment for schizophrenia is based on **operant conditioning** — learning through **reinforcement**.
2) **Token economies** can help encourage people in **psychiatric institutions** to perform **socially desirable behaviours**, e.g. getting dressed and making their beds. Patients are given **tokens** which reinforce these behaviours — they can then **exchange** these for something they want, like sweets or cigarettes.

Advantages

- Token economy programmes can produce **significant improvements** in **self care** and **desirable behaviour**, even with **chronic institutionalised schizophrenics**.
- For example, **Ayllon and Azrin (1968)** set up a token economy with schizophrenic patients in a **psychiatric institution**. They found that the amount of socially desirable behaviour **increased** — patients went from performing an average of **5** chores a day to around **40**.

Disadvantages

- Token economies don't have high **ecological validity** — they don't **transfer** into the **real world**. Once people are away from institutions they often don't continue showing desirable behaviour, because there's **nothing** to **reinforce** it.
- The patients' behaviour might be **superficial** — they might only produce desirable behaviour if they're going to receive a token.
- There are **ethical issues** surrounding the use of **behavioural therapy**. It could be argued that it **doesn't** really **help** the patient, it just makes their behaviour more acceptable to other people.

Treating Schizophrenia

2 Cognitive Behavioural Therapy

1) Cognitive behavioural therapy (CBT) is based on the assumption that patients can be helped by **identifying** and **changing** their '**faulty cognitions**'.
2) Schizophrenic patients are encouraged to **reality-test** their **hallucinations** and **delusions**, e.g. to question and try to control the voices they hear.
3) They do **role-play exercises** and **homework** to test out their 'faulty thinking' and are helped to see the **consequences** of thinking differently. Through this they can gradually realise where the 'faults' in their thought patterns are, and can begin to change them.

Advantages

- **Sensky et al (2000)** found that CBT was **effective** in treating schizophrenic patients who **hadn't responded** to **drug treatment**. It was helpful with **positive** and **negative** symptoms, and patients **continued** to **improve** 9 months after treatment had ended.
- CBT puts patients **in charge** of their own treatment by teaching them **self-help strategies**. This means there are **fewer ethical issues** than with other therapies (e.g. drug therapy).

Disadvantages

- CBT only treats the **symptoms** of schizophrenia — it **doesn't address** the **cause** of the disorder.
- It's difficult to **measure** the effectiveness of CBT because it relies on **self-report** from the patient, and the **therapist's opinions**. This makes it **less objective**.
- Patients can become **dependent** on their therapist.

3 Psychotherapy

1) Psychotherapy aims to identify the **underlying cause** of the mental disorder.
2) This is done using different therapeutic techniques, e.g. **dream analysis** and **free association**.
3) When the **unconscious conflicts** that are causing the problems are made **conscious**, the therapist and patient can discuss and try to resolve them. This will hopefully lead to the disorder being cured.

Advantages

- It aims to treat the **cause** of the disorder, not just the **symptoms**.
- Patients have **more control** over their treatment than with other therapies, e.g. drug therapy.

Disadvantages

- **Other forms** of treatment (e.g. CBT) have been found to be more **effective**.
- It's **difficult to prove** the effectiveness of psychotherapy — it's based on **subjective data** and the **unconscious mind**. There's also a risk that patients will develop **false memories**, e.g. of childhood abuse.

Practice Questions

Q1 Outline some disadvantages of drug therapy in the treatment of schizophrenia.

Q2 How can token economies benefit schizophrenia patients?

Q3 Outline one advantage of CBT in the treatment of schizophrenia.

Exam Question

Q1 Describe and evaluate treatments of schizophrenia. [24 marks]

Chemical straitjackets — might be a bit itchy...

Well, at least after reading about all the things that can go wrong with your brain it's nice to know there are some treatments. Not as nice as walks in the rain or cuddles or pink wafers, no, but quite nice all the same. I'd love a cuddle right about now. If you're in a similar predicament then take a moment to hold this book close to you and have a little snuggle. Ahh...

Depression

Everyone feels sad sometimes — it can be because a bad thing happens, or just be something you can't quite put your finger on. This is normal and nothing to worry about. It only becomes a problem when these feelings won't go away.

Depression is a Mood Disorder

Mood disorders are characterised by **strong emotions**, which can influence a person's ability to **function normally**. A mood disorder can affect a person's **perceptions**, **thinking** and **behaviour**. **Depression** is one of the most **common** mood disorders. There are many types, including:

1) **Major depression** (**unipolar disorder**) — an **episode** of depression that can occur **suddenly**.
   - Major depression can be **reactive** — caused by **external factors**, e.g. the death of a loved one.
   - Or, it can be **endogenous** — caused by **internal factors**, e.g. neurological factors.
2) **Manic depression** (**bipolar disorder**) — **alternation** between two **mood extremes** (**mania** and **depression**).
   - The change in mood often occurs in regular **cycles** of days or weeks.
   - Episodes of **mania** involve **over-activity**, **rapid speech** and feeling extremely **happy** or **agitated**.
   - Episodes of **depression** involve the symptoms covered below.

Depression has Lots of Clinical Characteristics

People with depression can experience a **range** of possible **symptoms**:

Physical / behavioural symptoms
- **Sleep disturbances** — **insomnia** (being unable to sleep) or **hypersomnia** (sleeping a lot more than usual).
- Change in **appetite** — people may eat **more** or **less** than **usual**, and gain or lose **weight**.
- **Pain** — especially **headaches**, **joint ache** and **muscle ache**.

Affective / emotional symptoms
- Extreme feelings of **sadness**, **hopelessness** and **despair**.
- **Diurnal mood variation** — changes in mood throughout the day, e.g. feeling worse in the morning.
- **Anhedonia** — no longer **enjoying** activities or hobbies that **used** to be **pleasurable**.

Cognitive symptoms
- Experiencing persistent **negative beliefs** about **themselves** and their **abilities**.
- **Suicidal** thoughts.
- **Slower** thought processes — **difficulty concentrating** and **making decisions**.

Social / motivational symptoms
- Lack of **activity** — **social withdrawal** and loss of **sex drive**.

The DSM-IV Classifies Mental Disorders

The **DSM-IV** is the fourth edition of the American Psychiatric Association's Diagnostic and Statistical Manual of Mental Disorders. It contains a list of **mental health disorders**. Individuals are rated on **multiple axes / dimensions** and diagnostic **categories** are used, e.g. personality disorders and psychosocial problems. It aims to give diagnosis of mental disorders **reliability** and **validity**:

Reliability

Reliability is how far the classification system produces the **same diagnosis** for a particular set of symptoms. In order for a classification system to be reliable the **same diagnosis** should be made **each time** it's used. This means that **different clinicians** should reach the **same diagnosis**.

Validity

Validity is whether the classification system is actually measuring what it **aims to measure**.
- **Descriptive validity** — how similar individuals diagnosed with the disorder are.
- **Aetiological validity** — how similar the cause of the disorder is for each sufferer.
- **Predictive validity** — how useful the diagnostic categories are for predicting the right treatment.

Depression

There can be **Problems** with the **Reliability** of **Diagnoses**

Both Dr. Jim and Dr. Bob would defend their diagnoses to the death.

1) For a person to be diagnosed with **major depression**, the DSM-IV states that at least **five symptoms** must have been present nearly every day for at least **two weeks**.
2) However, the diagnosis of depression isn't always **reliable** — people displaying the **same symptoms** don't always get the **same diagnosis**.
3) Also, women are **twice as likely** to be diagnosed with depression than men:

- There don't seem to be any clear reasons for why **women** would be **more likely** to suffer from depression than **men**.
- Some researchers have claimed that it's to do with **hormonal differences** between men and women. Others have said it's because of **socio-cultural** factors — the different ways that males and females are **socialised** means they react differently to stressful life events.
- However, it could be that clinicians **expect** more women to suffer from depression than men, so are more likely to diagnose a **woman** with depression than a **man** who displays the **same symptoms**.

There Can be **Problems** With the **Validity** of **Diagnoses**

Rosenhan (1973) conducted a classic study that questioned the **validity** of the diagnosis of mental disorders. He believed that psychiatrists **couldn't tell the difference** between **sane** people and people with **mental disorders**.

1) People who didn't have any kind of mental health problem got themselves admitted into a **psychiatric unit** by claiming they heard voices — they became **pseudopatients**.
2) Once they'd been admitted they behaved 'normally'. However, their behaviour was still seen as a **symptom** of their **disorder** by the staff in the unit. For example, one pseudopatient who wrote in a diary was recorded as displaying 'writing behaviour'.
3) This questions the **validity** of the **diagnosis** of mental disorders — once people are **labelled** as having a disorder, all of their behaviour can be **interpreted** as being **caused** by the **disorder**.

Practice Questions

Q1 What's the difference between major depression and manic depression?

Q2 What is anhedonia?

Q3 Outline the cognitive symptoms of depression.

Q4 What is the DSM-IV?

Q5 What does validity mean in terms of the diagnosis of mental disorders?

Q6 Outline a study that demonstrates problems with the validity of diagnoses.

Exam Question

Q1 a) Outline the clinical characteristics of depression. [8 marks]

b) Discuss issues surrounding the classification and diagnosis of depression. [16 marks]

I've got reactive depression just from reading this...

Yes, these pages are a touch on the gloomy side, but depression affects a lot of people, so it's really worth knowing about. And it's also in the exam... Make sure you can describe the different types of depression, outline the major symptoms, say what the DSM-IV is and have a bit of a chat about reliability and validity. By then you'll have probably cheered right up...

Explanations of Depression

These pages cover the possible causes of depression. And no, having to spend all your time revising won't go down well with the examiners as a valid cause of depression. It'll get you neither sympathy nor marks. Here's the stuff that will...

Depression Could be Caused by Biological Factors

1) Genetic Factors (Inherited Tendencies)

Being **biologically related** to someone who has depression seems to **increase** a person's **chance** of developing it.

Evidence for...

1) **McGuffin et al (1996)** found that if one **identical (MZ) twin** has **major depressive disorder**, then in about **46%** of cases their **twin** is **also** diagnosed with it. For **non-identical (DZ) twins** the **concordance rate** is about **20%**.
2) **Wender et al (1986)** studied the **biological parents** of **adopted** children who had **major depressive disorder**. The **biological** parents were **8 times** more likely to have depression than the children's **adoptive** parents.

Evidence against...

1) The **concordance rates** found in **family** and **twin** studies **aren't 100%**, so **genetics** can't be the whole story. **Environmental factors** could also play a role.
2) Genetic factors only seem to explain **endogenous depression** (depression caused by internal factors) — **psychological** factors seem to have more **influence** in the development of **reactive depression.**

2) Biochemical Factors

Low levels of **serotonin** have been linked to depression. **Kety (1975)** developed the **permissive amine theory**, which states that **serotonin** controls the **levels** of the neurotransmitter **noradrenaline**. A **low level** of **serotonin** causes the level of **noradrenaline** to **fluctuate** — **low** levels of **noradrenaline** then cause **depression**, while **high** levels cause **mania**.

Evidence for...

1) **Anti-depressant** drugs work by **increasing** the **availability** of **serotonin** at the synapses by preventing its reuptake or breakdown. This suggests that it's the **low levels** of serotonin that **lead** to **depressive disorders**.
2) **Post-mortems** carried out on people who committed **suicide** have shown abnormally **low levels** of **serotonin**, suggesting that this may have **caused** their depression.

Evidence against...

1) Just because **antidepressants** relieve the **symptoms**, it **doesn't** mean they treat the **cause**.
2) Low levels of serotonin could be a **result** of depression, not the cause.
3) **Psychological** research has found **alternative explanations** for the cause of depression.

Depression Could be Caused by Psychological Factors

1) Socio-cultural Factors

Social psychologists focus on how depression can be **triggered** by something **external**, e.g. a bereavement or divorce.

Evidence for...

Brown and Harris (1978) studied depression by **interviewing** housewives in London. They found that **61%** of the subjects **with depression** had recently experienced a **stressful life event**, compared with only **19%** of the **non-depressed** subjects. Of the subjects who had experienced a stressful event but had a **close friend**, only **10%** had depression. This can be compared with the **37%** of depressed subjects who **didn't** have a **close friend**. These results suggest that **depression** is **influenced** by **stressful life events** and a **lack** of **emotional support**.

Evidence against...

1) Brown and Harris's study just shows a **correlation**, so you can't prove **cause and effect**. It could actually be that depression makes some stressful life events **more likely** to happen, e.g. someone might be more likely to lose their job or get divorced as a result of their depression.
2) The effect of social factors **doesn't** explain why some people experience **endogenous depression** (sudden depression that occurs because of internal factors). Other approaches might have better explanations.

Explanations of Depression

2) Behavioural Factors

Behaviourists reckon that depression develops when **stressors** (e.g. death of a loved one or being made redundant) lead to a **lack** of **positive reinforcement**. The attention that depressive behaviour then draws (e.g. sympathy from others) can then provide **positive reinforcement**, meaning the person **learns** to continue being depressed. It may also be influenced by **learned helplessness**. This occurs when people **learn not to try** because they believe they'll **never succeed**.

Evidence for...

Seligman (1975) restrained dogs so that they **couldn't avoid** receiving **electric shocks**. Later when they **could** actually avoid the shocks they **didn't** even **try** — they displayed **learned helplessness**. This can be **generalised** to humans — when people **aren't** in **control** of **stressful events** they eventually **learn not to try** and improve them, causing them to become **depressed**.

Evidence against...

Behaviourist theory **ignores** the influence of **biological** factors. It also only explains **reactive depression** (depression caused by external events). It may be that biological factors are responsible for causing **endogenous depression**.

3) Cognitive Factors

Abramson et al (1978) developed **Seligman's (1975)** theory of **learned helplessness** into a **cognitive theory**. They looked at people's **thought processes** in response to **failure** and stated that failure can be interpreted as:

1) **Internal** (the person's fault) or **external** (caused by something else).
2) **Global** (applies to all situations) or **specific** (just applies to this situation).
3) **Stable** (likely to continue) or **unstable** (could easily change).

Depressed people may see failure as **internal**, **global** and **stable** (it's their fault, happens in all situations and won't change).

This is just one example of a model of faulty cognitions — there are other models (see page 185).

Evidence for...

Beck et al (1979) found that depressed people had **negative** thought processes — they **exaggerated** their **weaknesses** and **played down** their **strengths**.

Evidence against...

This is just a **correlation** — it doesn't prove cause and effect. It may be that **negative thinking** is actually the **result** of depression, **not** the **cause** of it. Instead, **biological** or other **psychological** factors could be the cause.

4) Psychodynamic Theory

Freud claimed that if a child feels **unloved** by its **parents** it becomes **angry**. This creates **guilt**, so the anger is **redirected** towards the **self**. These feelings are **repressed**, but may later **return** following a **stressful life event**, causing **depression**.

Evidence for...

Brown and Harris (1978) found that the women they interviewed were **more likely** to have depression if they experienced **disrupted** childhood attachments, especially if their **mother** had **died**.

Evidence against...

There **isn't** any **research evidence** to **support** Freud's theory, so it's **unfalsifiable** (impossible to prove right or wrong). It also **ignores** the significance of **other factors** in causing depression, e.g. biological factors.

Practice Questions

Q1 Outline research evidence that supports the theory that genetic factors can cause depression.

Q2 Outline the role that serotonin might have in causing depression.

Q3 What evidence is there to suggest that depression is caused by stressful life events?

Exam Question

Q1 a) Outline biological explanations for depression. [8 marks]

b) Outline and evaluate a psychological explanation for depression. [16 marks]

Genes can make you depressed — especially if the fly comes undone...

It's the usual drill here — learn an explanation of depression, then learn another one so you can use it to tear the first one apart. It's a wonder the psychologists who come up with these theories don't get more depressed themselves. You'd think having thousands of A-level students telling them they're wrong would upset them a bit. But no, they're as happy as Larry.

Treating Depression

Depression is horrible, so you'll be pleased to know that there are loads of treatments available for it. You may be less pleased to know that you have to learn them all, but you shouldn't really be surprised, so try to keep your chin up.

Depression Can be Treated Using Biological Therapy

Therapy using drugs is also called chemotherapy.

1) The **biological** approach to treating depression involves **drug therapy**.
2) Treatment is based on altering the levels of **serotonin** and **noradrenaline** in the brain. These **neurotransmitters** regulate things like emotions, sleep patterns, sex drive and reaction to stress.
3) There are **four** main types of antidepressant drugs:

- **Selective serotonin reuptake inhibitors (SSRIs)** increase the availability of **serotonin** by preventing its reuptake.
- **Tricyclic antidepressants (TCAs)** increase the availability of **serotonin** and **noradrenaline** by preventing their reuptake.
- **Monoamine oxidase inhibitors (MAOIs)** increase the availability of **serotonin** and **noradrenaline** by preventing their breakdown.
- **Serotonin and noradrenaline reuptake inhibitors** (**SNRIs**) prevent the reuptake of **serotonin** and **noradrenaline**, so increase their availability.

Ashley and George's sleep patterns were perfectly in sync.

Advantages

- Studies have shown that antidepressants are successful in **reducing** the **symptoms** of depression for **more than half** of patients.
- It's the most **widely-used** and **effective** form of treatment for depression. Psychological treatments are often used **alongside** drug therapy because antidepressants can remove some of the **symptoms**, allowing **other therapies** to focus on the **cause** of the depression.

Disadvantages

- Antidepressants only treat the **symptoms** of depression. **Other therapies** are needed to try and tackle the **cause** of it.
- There are **ethical issues** surrounding the use of drug therapy. Some people argue that drug treatment is a **'chemical straitjacket'** — it **doesn't** really **help** the patient, it just **controls** their **behaviour** to make it more socially acceptable and easier to manage.
- Antidepressants can have **side effects**, e.g. drowsiness, dry mouth, indigestion and nausea.

Depression Can be Treated using Psychological Therapies

1 Psychotherapy

1) Psychotherapy aims to identify the **underlying cause** of the mental disorder.
2) This is done using different therapeutic techniques, e.g. **dream analysis** and **free association**.
3) When the **unconscious conflicts** that are causing the problems are made **conscious**, the therapist and patient can discuss and try to resolve them. This will hopefully lead to the disorder being cured.

Advantages

- It aims to treat the **cause** of the disorder, not just the **symptoms**.
- Patients have **more control** over their treatment than with other therapies, e.g. drug therapy.

Disadvantages

- Psychotherapy can be **distressing** for people because they're encouraged to **recall traumatic events**. This can sometimes be more difficult to deal with than the original symptoms.
- It's **difficult to prove** the effectiveness of psychotherapy because it's based on **subjective data** and the **unconscious mind**. There's also a risk that patients will develop **false memories**.
- **Other forms** of treatment, e.g. cognitive behavioural therapies (see opposite page) and drug therapy have been found to be **more effective**.

Treating Depression

2 Cognitive Behavioural Therapies

There are several models that explain how **faulty cognitions** can lead to depression. For example:

Ellis (1962) — The **ABC model** claims that disorders begin with an **activating event (A)** (e.g. a failed exam), leading to a **belief (B)** about why this happened. This may be rational (e.g. 'I didn't prepare well enough'), or irrational (e.g. 'I'm too stupid to pass exams'). The belief leads to a **consequence (C)**. Rational beliefs produce adaptive (appropriate) consequences (e.g. more revision). Irrational beliefs produce maladaptive (bad and inappropriate) consequences (e.g. getting depressed).

Beck (1963) — Beck identified a **cognitive triad** of negative, automatic thoughts linked to **depression**: negative views about **themselves** (e.g. that they can't succeed at anything), about the **world** (e.g. that they must be successful to be a good person) and about the **future** (e.g. that nothing will change).

Cognitive behavioural therapy (CBT) aims to **identify** and **change** the patient's **faulty cognitions**.
This is generally what happens during CBT:

1) The therapist and client **identify** the client's **faulty cognitions**.
2) Therapists sometimes encourage their clients to keep a **diary** so they can record their thought patterns, feelings and actions.
3) The therapist tries to show that the cognitions **aren't true**, e.g. the client doesn't always fail at what they do.
4) Together, they set **goals** to think in more positive or adaptive ways, e.g. focusing on things the client has succeeded at and trying to build on them.
5) Although the client may occasionally need to look back to past experiences, the treatment mainly focuses on the **present situation**.

Advantages of CBT

- **Brandsma et al (1978)** found that **CBT** is particularly effective for people who put a lot of **pressure** on themselves and feel **guilty** about being **inadequate**.
- CBT **empowers** patients — it puts them in charge of their own treatment by teaching them **self-help strategies**. This means there are **fewer ethical issues** than with other therapies like drug therapy.

Disadvantages of CBT

- Faulty cognitions might be the **consequence** of a disorder rather than its cause. For example, depression may be caused by a chemical imbalance in the brain, which causes people to think very negatively.
- Cognitive therapies may take a long **time** and may be more effective when **combined** with other approaches, e.g. drug therapy.

Practice Questions

Q1 Outline the biological approach to the treatment of depression.

Q2 Give one advantage of drug therapy in the treatment of depression.

Q3 Outline what happens in cognitive behavioural therapy.

Exam Question

Q1 a) Outline one or more approaches to the treatment of depression. [16 marks]

b) Evaluate one approach to the treatment of depression. [8 marks]

This depression stuff is really getting me down...

...but not to worry, these are the last two pages on depression. And they are all about treatment — which is surely the least depressing aspect of depression. Anyway, best learn these pages pretty sharpish, before you sink into a murky mire of miserableness. Then you can move on to the much more cheerful topic of... phobic disorders. Well, it's a bit more cheerful...

Phobic Disorders

Anxiety isn't always a problem — it can help to motivate you to perform your best. Like to revise before an exam, for example. It's only when you start feeling anxious all the time, or about slightly odd things, that it becomes a disorder.

A Phobia is an Irrational Fear

1) A phobia is an example of an **anxiety disorder**.
2) A phobia is an **extreme**, **irrational fear** of a particular **object** or **situation**.
3) There are **three** types of phobia classified by the **DSM-IV**:

1 Specific phobias

This is a fear of specific **objects** or **situations**. There are **five** subtypes:

1) **Animal** type (also called **zoophobia**, e.g. fear of spiders)
2) **Environmental dangers** type (e.g. fear of water)
3) **Blood-injection-injury** type (e.g. fear of needles)
4) **Situational** type (e.g. fear of enclosed spaces or heights)
5) **'Other'** (any phobia that isn't covered in the categories above)

2 Social phobia

This is the fear of **being in social situations** (e.g. eating in public or talking in front of a group of people). It's usually down to the possibility of being **judged** or being **embarrassed**.

3 Agoraphobia

1) This is a fear of **open spaces**.
2) It's specifically linked to the **fear** of having a **panic attack** in a public place and **not** being able to **get away**.
3) It often develops as a **result** of **other phobias**, because the sufferer's afraid that they'll come across the **source** of their **fear** if they leave the house.

Phobias have Several Clinical Characteristics

The different types of phobia all have very **similar** clinical characteristics.

Cognitive symptoms	**Irrational beliefs** about the **stimulus** that causes fear. People often find it **hard** to **concentrate** because they're **preoccupied** by **anxious thoughts**.
Social symptoms	**Avoiding** social situations because they cause **anxiety**. This happens especially if someone has **social phobia** or **agoraphobia**.
Behavioural symptoms	Altering behaviour to **avoid** the feared object or situation, and trying to **escape** if it's encountered. People are often generally **restless** and **easily startled**.
Physical symptoms	Activation of the **fight or flight** response when the feared object or situation is encountered or thought about. This involves release of **adrenaline**, **increased heart rate** and **breathing**, and **muscle tension**.
Emotional symptoms	**Anxiety** and a feeling of **dread**.

There are Various Diagnostic Criteria for Phobias

The **DSM-IV** (see next page) classifies a fear as a phobia if you can put a tick next to these criteria:

1) There's **significant prolonged fear** of an object or situation.
2) People experience an **anxiety response** (e.g. increased heart rate) if they're exposed to the phobic stimulus.
3) Sufferers **realise** that their phobia is **irrational** and **out of proportion** to any actual danger. They may try to **hide** their phobia from other people, which can cause more anxiety.
4) Sufferers go out of their way to **avoid** the phobic stimulus.
5) The phobia **disrupts** their **lives**, e.g. they avoid social situations.

Sophie did everything she could to hide her parrotophobia.

Phobic Disorders

The DSM-IV Classifies Mental Disorders

1) The **DSM-IV** is the fourth edition of the American Psychiatric Association's Diagnostic and Statistical Manual of Mental Disorders.
2) It contains a list of **mental health disorders**. Individuals are rated on **multiple axes / dimensions** and diagnostic **categories** are used, e.g. personality disorders and psychosocial problems.
3) It aims to give diagnosis of mental disorders **reliability** and **validity**:

Dr. Bale could pretend to read the DSM-IV all he liked — everyone knew he kept a comic inside it.

Reliability

Reliability is how far the classification system produces the **same diagnosis** for a particular set of symptoms. In order for a classification system to be reliable the **same diagnosis** should be made **each time** it's used. This means that **different clinicians** should reach the **same diagnosis**.

Validity

Validity is whether the classification system is actually measuring what it **aims to measure**.
- **Descriptive validity** — how similar individuals diagnosed with the disorder are.
- **Aetiological validity** — how similar the cause of the disorder is for each sufferer.
- **Predictive validity** — how useful the diagnostic categories are for predicting the right treatment.

There can be Problems with the Validity and Reliability of Diagnoses

Problems with validity

1) **Rosenhan (1973)** conducted a study where people who didn't have any kind of mental health problem got themselves admitted into a **psychiatric unit** — they became **pseudopatients**.
2) Once they'd been admitted they behaved 'normally'. However, their behaviour was still seen as a **symptom** of their **disorder** by the staff in the unit. For example, one pseudopatient who wrote in a diary was recorded as displaying 'writing behaviour'.
3) This questions the **validity** of the **diagnosis** of mental disorders — once people are **labelled** as having a disorder, all of their behaviour can be **interpreted** as being **caused** by the **disorder**.

Problems with reliability

1) Clinicians can show **bias** when they're diagnosing mental disorders.
2) For example, **Johnstone (1989)** found that patients from **lower social classes** tended to be given more **serious diagnoses** than patients from **higher social classes**.
3) This questions the **reliability** of the diagnosis of mental disorders — it suggests that patients can display the **same symptoms** but receive **different diagnoses** because of their social background.

Practice Questions

Q1 What are the five subtypes of specific phobias?

Q2 List some of the physical symptoms of phobias.

Q3 Outline the diagnostic criteria for phobias.

Exam Question

Q1 a) Outline the clinical characteristics of phobias. [8 marks]

b) Discuss the issues of validity and reliability in the diagnosis of phobias. [16 marks]

Keep calm keep calm keep calm keep calm keep calm keep calm...

These pages don't exactly make for relaxing bedtime reading do they — anyone else got a sweat on? On a lighter note, writing out 'keep calm' so many times has meant I've got that weird thing where the words have lost all their meaning and look really strange. It looks more like 'keep clam' now, which I suppose is actually quite sound advice...

Explanations of Phobias

There are lots of possible causes of phobias, and they won't learn themselves. 'Tis a pity, but that lovely job is left to you.

Phobias Could be Caused by **Biological Factors...**

1) **Genetic** Factors (Inherited Tendencies)

1) Some phobias are much more **common** than others, and many of these are of things that can be **dangerous** to humans, e.g. snakes, spiders, heights.
2) This suggests that humans have **evolved** a **genetic predisposition** to fear these things because it has **survival value**. This is **preparedness theory**.
3) The assumption is that phobias have a **genetic** cause, so they should run in families, or be shared by identical twins who will have the same genes.

Mark's fear of heights was manageable, as long as Julie kept holding the bridge up.

Evidence for...

Using a family interview method, **Reich and Yates (1988)** found a **higher** rate of social phobias amongst **relatives** than other disorders. **6.6%** of those with phobias had a relative with it too, compared to **0.4%** of those with panic disorders.

Evidence against...

Torgerson (1983) found that identical (MZ) twins **don't** always share phobias. This suggests that **other factors** are also involved in causing phobias, e.g. psychological factors.

2) **Neurological** Factors

Biological theories explain why people can develop phobias without having had an associated bad experience.

Evidence for...

1) **Gray (1982)** identified the **behavioural inhibition system** — a circuit in the **limbic system** in the brain that's linked to **anxiety**. When something unexpected and possibly dangerous happens, signals are sent to this area from the **cortex**. This causes **anxiety** which may make the person 'freeze'. How **susceptible** someone is to anxiety and panic may depend on how **sensitive** this circuit is.
2) **Johnson et al (2000)** did a **longitudinal study** showing that adolescents who **smoked** were **15** times more likely to develop **anxiety disorders** later in life, especially if they were heavy smokers. This may be due to the effects of **nicotine**, which may make areas of the **brain** more **sensitive**.

Evidence against...

1) **Johnson et al's (2000)** research is **correlational** — it doesn't prove that smoking **caused** the anxiety.
2) This research **doesn't** take other factors into account. For example, **behavioural** research has shown that some phobias, especially specific phobias, can be **learnt**.

...or **Psychological Factors** (surprise surprise)

1) **Behavioural** Factors

Behaviourists believe that phobias are **learnt** through **classical** or **operant conditioning**.

Classical conditioning — This especially explains **specific phobias**. A previously **neutral** thing starts to trigger anxiety because it becomes **associated** with something **frightening**. **Watson and Rayner (1920)** conducted a study on an 11-month-old boy called **Little Albert**. A loud noise was made every time he played with a **white rat**. He then began to **associate** the **rat** with the **frightening noise**, and showed fear when he saw it.

Operant conditioning — This especially explains **social phobia** and **agoraphobia**. A person's fear goes when they **get away** from the situation that causes **fear**. This is **negative reinforcement** — they **learn** to avoid the stimulus that causes anxiety because they feel **better** when they **escape** it.

Evidence for... Behavioural **therapies** are very **effective** at treating phobias by getting the person to **change** their **response** to the **stimulus** (see p.188). This suggests that they're treating the **cause** of the problem.

Evidence against... **Davey (1992)** found that only 7% of spider phobics recalled having a **traumatic experience** with a spider. This suggests that there could be **other explanations**, e.g. biological factors. (But just because they couldn't remember the experience, this doesn't mean it didn't happen.)

Explanations of Phobias

2) **Socio-cultural** Factors

It's thought that **upbringing** could affect the development of **phobias**.

Evidence for...

1) **Arrindell et al (1989)** reported that people with **social phobia** claimed that their parents were **controlling**, **over-protective** and **didn't** show much **affection**. This suggests that **upbringing** can cause social phobia.
2) **Social learning theory** states that behaviour is influenced by your **environment** and the people you grow up with. Children may see that a parent or older sibling is afraid of something and **imitate** their **response**.

Evidence against...

1) The research on upbringing is **correlational**, and it relies on people's **memory**, which can be **inaccurate**.
2) **Other factors** may be responsible, e.g. some people may have a biological pre-disposition that makes them more likely to develop phobias.

3) **Psychodynamic** Theory

Freud argued that phobias **hide** an **unconscious fear**. The real fear creates so much **anxiety** that it's **displaced** onto something less frightening or embarrassing.

Evidence for...

Freud used the case study of **Little Hans** to support his theory. Little Hans had a **fear** of **horses**, which Freud thought was caused by **Oedipal conflict**. Freud claimed that Hans was **attracted** to his mother and frightened that his father would **punish** him for being his rival. This fear created so much **anxiety** and guilt that it was **displaced** onto horses, which were like Hans' father because they wore bridles (which looked like his beard) and had big penises. Right...

Evidence against...

1) Freud's theories are **unfalsifiable** — they're **unscientific** because they can't be proved wrong.
2) Hans had been very frightened by seeing a horse fall down in the street. It could be that this produced a phobia of horses through **classical conditioning**.

4) **Cognitive** Factors

Beck and Emery (1985) proposed that interactions between an anxious person's **cognitive processes** and their belief in their **vulnerability** makes them more likely to interpret stimuli as being threatening.

Evidence for...

Hope et al (1990) showed participants words written in different colours. Participants with social phobia took **longer** to name the colour of **social threat words** (e.g. 'failure'). This suggests that they **processed** them in a different way.

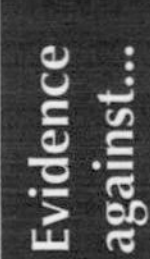

Evidence against...

- This **doesn't** show **cause and effect** — it could be that feeling vulnerable is a **symptom** of anxiety, not the **cause** of it.
- Phobias could be caused by other factors, e.g. **biological factors**.

Practice Questions

Q1 Outline evidence to support the genetic explanation of phobias.

Q2 How can phobias be explained by classical conditioning?

Q3 Outline evidence against the Oedipus conflict being the cause of Little Hans' phobia.

Exam Question

Q1 Describe and evaluate psychological explanations for one anxiety disorder. [24 marks]

What was Little Hans' brother called? — Tiny Feet...

You've got to feel for Little Hans — somehow it's a bit more socially acceptable to be scared of horses than it is to be in love with your mum and scared of your dad's penis. In fact, these 'Little' chaps have had quite a raw deal overall — poor Little Albert's fear ended up being generalised to all white fluffy things, until he was afraid of Santa's white fluffy beard. Sob...

Treating Phobic Disorders

If, like me, you've completely lost concentration and started chewing your fingers off and staring at the wall, the ceiling or anything else in view, then these are just the pages to pick you up and give you a good shake. Just what you wanted.

Phobic Disorders Can be Treated Using Biological Therapy

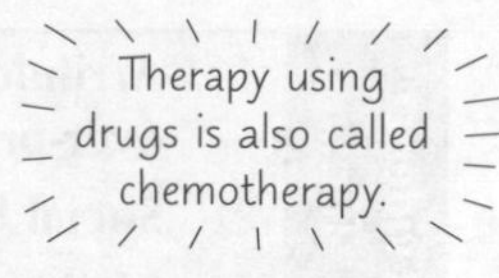

1) The **biological** approach to treating phobic disorders involves **drug therapy**.
2) **Anxiolytic drugs** (e.g. tranquillisers) such as benzodiazepines, **reduce anxiety** by increasing the activity of the neurotransmitter **GABA**. GABA produces a feeling of **calmness**.

Advantages

- **Benzodiazepines** take effect very **quickly**. This means that they're good for treating **phobias** in the **short term**, e.g. before stressful events like exams.
- **Davidson et al (1993)** compared the effects of **benzodiazepines** with a **placebo**, and found that benzodiazepines were **more effective** at reducing the symptoms of social phobia.

Disadvantages

- **Benzodiazepines** can cause side effects like **drowsiness**. They also cause physical and psychological **dependency**, so they **can't** be used **long-term**.
- The **symptoms** of phobias often **return** when people come off medication.
- Drug therapy only treats the **symptoms** of the disorder. Other therapies are needed to try and tackle the **cause** of it, e.g. behavioural therapies.

Phobic Disorders Can be Treated Using Psychological Therapies

1 Behavioural Therapies

Behavioural treatment for **specific phobias** is based on **classical conditioning** (learning through **association**). There are **two techniques** for treating specific phobias:

Systematic desensitisation — Wolpe (1958)

1) Systematic desensitisation works by using **counter-conditioning** so that the person learns to **associate** the **phobic stimulus** with **relaxation** rather than **fear**.
2) Patients **rank feared situations**, from the **least stressful** (e.g. saying the word *spider*) to the **most stressful** (e.g. holding a spider). They are then taught **relaxation techniques** like deep breathing.
3) The patient then **imagines** the anxiety-provoking situations, starting with the least stressful. They're encouraged to use the **relaxation techniques** and the process stops if they feel anxious.
4) Patients will gradually be able to work through the feared situations on the list without feeling **anxious**.

Exposure therapy

1) This involves exposing the patient to the phobic stimulus **straight away**, without any relaxation or gradual build-up. This can be done in **real life**, or the patient can be asked to **visualise** it. For example, someone who was afraid of heights might imagine standing on top of a skyscraper.
2) The patient is kept in this situation until the **anxiety** they feel at first has **warn off**. They realise that nothing bad has happened to them in this time, and their fear should be **extinguished**.

Advantages

- **Behavioural therapy** is very effective for treating **specific phobias**. **Zinbarg et al (1992)** found that **systematic desensitisation** was the **most effective** of the currently known methods for treating phobias.
- It works very **quickly**, e.g. **Ost et al (1991)** found that anxiety was reduced in **90%** of patients with a specific phobia after just **one session** of **therapy**.

Disadvantages

- There are **ethical issues** surrounding behavioural therapy — especially **exposure therapy**, as it causes patients a lot of anxiety. If patients **drop out** of the therapy **before** the fear has been extinguished, then it can end up causing **more anxiety** than before therapy started.
- **Behavioural therapy** only treats the **symptoms** of the disorder. **Other therapies** are needed to try and tackle the **cause** of it, e.g. cognitive behavioural therapy.

Treating Phobic Disorders

2 Cognitive Behavioural Therapy

Cognitive behavioural therapy (CBT) helps patients by **identifying** and **changing** their **faulty cognitions**. For example, many people with **social phobia** assume that they'll **embarrass themselves** in social situations, so think it's best to avoid them. Here's what generally happens during CBT:

1) The therapist and client **identify** the client's **faulty cognitions**.
2) The therapist tries to show that the cognitions **aren't true**, e.g. the client doesn't always embarrass themselves.
3) Together, they set **goals** to think in more positive or adaptive ways, e.g. going to a party and talking to people they don't know. The aim is to prove to the client that their **negative thoughts** about what's going to happen are **wrong**, and so **reduce** their **anxiety**.

Advantages

- **CBT** is effective at treating phobias, e.g. **Thorpe and Salkovskis (1997)** found **reduced anxiety** in spider phobics after only **one session** of CBT.
- CBT **empowers** patients — it puts them in charge of their own treatment by teaching them **self-help strategies**. This means that it's a very **ethical** treatment.

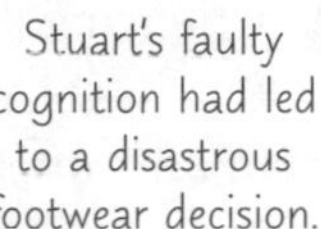

Stuart's faulty cognition had led to a disastrous footwear decision.

Disadvantages

- Faulty cognitions might be the **consequence** of the disorder rather than its cause. For example, phobias may be caused by a chemical imbalance in the brain which leads to faulty thought processes.
- Patients can become **dependent** on their therapist.

3 Psychotherapy

1) Psychotherapy aims to identify the **underlying cause** of the mental disorder.
2) This is done using different therapeutic techniques, e.g. **dream analysis** and **free association**.
3) When the **unconscious conflicts** that are causing the problems are made **conscious**, the therapist and patient can discuss and try to resolve them. This will hopefully lead to the disorder being cured.

Advantages

- It aims to treat the **cause** of the disorder, not just the **symptoms**.
- Patients have **more control** over their treatment than with other therapies, e.g. drug therapy.

Disadvantages

- Psychotherapy can be **distressing** for people because they're encouraged to **recall traumatic events**. This can sometimes be more difficult to deal with than the original symptoms.
- It's **difficult to prove** the effectiveness of psychotherapy — it's based on **subjective data** and the **unconscious mind**. There's also a risk that patients will develop **false memories**, e.g. of childhood abuse.

Practice Questions

Q1 Name a type of drug that can be used in the treatment of phobic disorders.

Q2 What is meant by exposure therapy?

Q3 Outline what happens in cognitive behavioural therapy.

Exam Question

Q1 Describe and evaluate one or more treatment for a phobic disorder. [24 marks]

I treat my phobic disorder really well...

Yesterday I took it to the pictures, then I bought it a choc ice and let it go on the swings for half an hour. You've got to show you care sometimes. And it doesn't have to be anything fancy, just a little token of your affection is often enough. The most important thing is to spend some quality time together, make each other laugh, and just show a little bit more love...

Obsessive-Compulsive Disorder

Obsessive-compulsive disorder (OCD) is a type of anxiety disorder. Most of us have the odd obsessive thought (like checking your phone's off ten times before the exam starts) — but in OCD it's taken to extremes and affects daily life.

OCD is an Anxiety Disorder with Two Parts

1) Obsessive-compulsive disorder is a type of **anxiety disorder** that has two parts — **obsessions** and **compulsions**. Most people with OCD experience obsessions and compulsions that are **linked** to each other. For example, excessive worrying about catching germs (an obsession) may lead to excessive hand washing (a compulsion).
2) Obsessive-compulsive disorder affects about **2%** of the world's population. Sufferers usually develop the disorder in their **late teens** or **early 20s**. The disorder occurs **equally in men and women** and in all **ethnic groups**.

Obsessions are the Cognitive Part of the Disorder

Obsessions are **intrusive** and **persistent thoughts**, **images** and **impulses**. They can range from worrying that you left the oven on to worrying that you might kill your parents. For thoughts like these to be **classified** as obsessions, the **DSM-IV** (see next page) states they must meet the following criteria:

- **Persistent** and **reoccurring** thoughts, images or impulses that are **unwanted** and cause **distress** to the person experiencing them. For example, imagining that you've left the door unlocked and burglars are rampaging through your house.
- The thoughts, images or impulses are **more serious** than just worrying too much. For example, continuing to focus mentally on the imaginary burglar, rather than dismissing it as an unlikely event.
- The person actively tries to **ignore** the thoughts, images or impulses but is **unable to**.
- The person is aware that the thoughts, images or impulses are **created by their own mind** and aren't the result of **thought insertion** (a symptom of some other disorders — see page 174).

Compulsions are Repetitive Actions

Compulsions are **physical** or **mental repetitive actions**. For example, **checking** the door is locked nine times or repeating a certain **phrase** or **prayer** to **neutralise** an unwanted thought. The problem is that the action only reduces the anxiety caused by an obsession for a **short time**, which means that the obsession starts up again. The **DSM-IV** uses the following diagnostic criteria:

1) The person **repeats physical behaviours** or **mental acts** that relate to an obsession. Sometimes the person has rules that they must follow strictly. For example, a rule that you must check the door is locked ten times before you can leave home.
2) The compulsions are meant to **reduce anxiety** or **prevent** a feared situation — in reality they're **excessive** or **wouldn't actually stop** a dreaded situation.

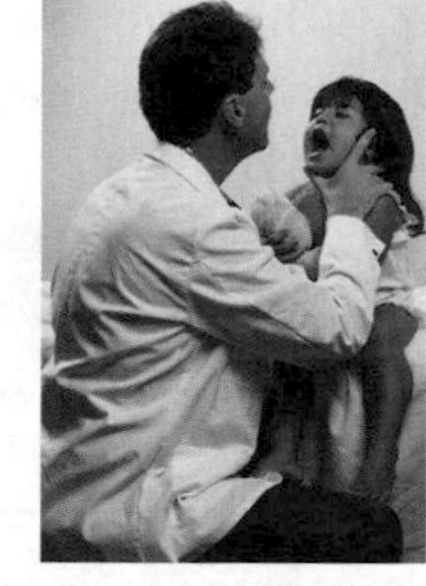

No matter how many times he checked, the doctor still couldn't prove who'd eaten his stash of lollipops.

The DSM-IV states that if the obsessions or compulsions last **more than an hour each day** this is an indication of a **clinical case** of OCD. An alternative indication of OCD is if the obsessions and compulsions **interfere** with a person's ability to maintain a relationship, hold down a job or take part in social activities.

There are Several Types of OCD Behaviours

There are several common types of OCD behaviours. Here are four:

1) **Checking** — includes checking that the lights are off or that you have your purse.
2) **Contamination** — this involves a fear of catching germs by, say, going to a restaurant, touching door handles, shaking hands or using public toilets.
3) **Hoarding** — keeping useless or worn-out objects, such as old newspapers or junk mail.
4) **Symmetry and orderliness** — getting objects lined up 'just right', such as having all the tins in your food cupboard facing forward in exactly the same way, or everything on your desk arranged in a neat order in the right places.

Obsessive-Compulsive Disorder

The DSM-IV Classifies Mental Disorders

1) The **DSM-IV** is the fourth edition of the American Psychiatric Association's Diagnostic and Statistical Manual of Mental Disorders.
2) It contains a list of **mental health disorders**. Individuals are rated on **multiple axes / dimensions** and diagnostic **categories** are used, e.g. personality disorders and psychosocial problems.
3) It aims to give diagnosis of mental disorders **reliability** and **validity**:

Bob didn't actually have OCD — he was just extremely adept at stationery management.

Reliability

Reliability is how far the classification system produces the **same diagnosis** for a particular set of symptoms. In order for a classification system to be reliable the **same diagnosis** should be made **each time** it's used. This means that **different clinicians** should reach the **same diagnosis**.

Validity

Validity is whether the classification system is actually measuring what it **aims to measure**.

- **Descriptive validity** — how similar individuals diagnosed with the disorder are.
- **Aetiological validity** — how similar the cause of the disorder is for each sufferer.
- **Predictive validity** — how useful the diagnostic categories are for predicting the right treatment.

There can be Problems with the Validity and Reliability of Diagnoses

Problems with validity

1) **Rosenhan (1973)** conducted a study where people who didn't have any kind of mental health problem got themselves admitted into a **psychiatric unit** — they became **pseudopatients**.
2) Once they'd been admitted they behaved 'normally'. However, their behaviour was still seen as a **symptom** of their **disorder** by the staff in the unit. For example, one pseudopatient who wrote in a diary was recorded as displaying 'writing behaviour'.
3) This questions the **validity** of the **diagnosis** of mental disorders — once people are **labelled** as having a disorder, all of their behaviour can be **interpreted** as being **caused** by the **disorder**.

Problems with reliability

1) The DSM criteria can cause **problems** in diagnosing OCD. How do you decide **objectively** when it is that worrying too much about something actually becomes an obsession? Is there a **clear point** when a physical behaviour or mental act becomes a compulsion?
2) People with **other disorders**, for example eating disorders, also experience obsessions and compulsions. This means that they could be **misdiagnosed** as having OCD.

Practice Questions

Q1 Give an example of an obsession.

Q2 Give an example of a compulsion.

Q3 List four common types of OCD behaviour.

Exam Question

Q1 a) Outline the clinical characteristics of OCD. [8 marks]

b) Discuss the issues surrounding the classification and diagnosis of OCD. [16 marks]

Doctor, Doctor, I'm having unwanted thoughts about revision...

OCD isn't always about checking and straightening rituals. Often the intrusive thoughts can be violent and upsetting. However, people suffering from OCD rarely act on these thoughts — but the thoughts do cause them considerable stress.

Explanations of OCD

There's more than one theory about what causes OCD and there's evidence for and against each of these theories. So basically nobody is really sure — but don't go thinking that gives you an excuse not to read about it.

OCD Could be Caused by Biological Factors

Concordance rates tell us how likely a person is to develop a disorder if their twin has it.

1 Genetic Factors (Inherited Tendencies)

Some researchers think that **genetics** plays a part in OCD. Studies have looked at **concordance rates** to see if being related to someone with OCD **significantly** increases your chances of developing the disorder.

Evidence for...

1) **Billet et al** (1998) did a **meta-analysis** of twin studies that had been carried out over a long period of time. They found that **identical (MZ) twins** had a concordance rate of **68%**, compared to **non-identical (DZ) twins** with a concordance rate of **31%**.
2) **Pauls et al** (2005) found that **10%** of people with an **immediate relative** (i.e. parents, offspring or siblings) with OCD also suffered from the disorder. This is compared to around **2%** of people in the general population.

Evidence against...

1) No study has found a **100%** concordance rate, so **genetics can't** be the full story in OCD. It's possible that children **imitate** the obsessive and compulsive behaviour of their relatives.
2) Concordance rates don't prove that OCD is **caused** by genetics. It may be that **general anxiety** is genetic and that going on to develop OCD itself has **other contributing factors**, e.g. biochemical or psychological factors.

2 Biochemical Factors

PET scans have shown that levels of the **neurotransmitter serotonin** are lower in OCD sufferers.

Evidence for...

1) **Insel** (1991) found that a class of drugs called **SSRIs**, which increase levels of serotonin, can reduce symptoms of OCD in **50 to 60%** of cases.
2) **Zohar et al** (1996) also found that **SSRIs alleviated symptoms in 60%** of patients with OCD.

Evidence against...

1) **SSRIs** appear to offer some relief to sufferers of OCD. However, as this is **not** true in **100%** of cases, there must be **more** to understanding OCD.
2) The **link** with serotonin is **correlational**, so it doesn't show **cause and effect**. It may be that decreased serotonin levels are a **symptom** of OCD, rather than a cause of it.

3 Neurological Factors

Some research using **PET scans** has found that **abnormality** in the **basal ganglia** within the brain may be linked to OCD.

Evidence for...

1) **Max et al** (1995) found **increased rates** of OCD in people after **head injuries** that caused brain damage to the **basal ganglia**.
2) Other researchers have found **increased activity** in this area during OCD-related thoughts and behaviours.
3) OCD is often found in people with **other diseases** which involve the basal ganglia, e.g. **Parkinson's** and **Huntington's chorea**.

Evidence against...

1) **Aylward et al** (1996) didn't find a significant difference in **basal ganglia impairment** between OCD patients and controls.
2) Basal ganglia damage **hasn't** been found in **100%** of people with OCD, so it can't be the full story.

Explanations of OCD

OCD Could be Caused by Psychological Factors

1 Behavioural Factors

1) Behaviourists use both **classical** and **operant conditioning** (see page 156) to explain OCD.
2) A person might behave in a certain way **by chance** when they are feeling anxious. When the anxiety goes away they unconsciously learn to **associate** the action with the removal of the anxiety. It becomes a reflex response. This is **classical conditioning**. They then **repeat** the action when they next feel anxious because they've learnt that it removes anxiety. This is **operant conditioning**.

Evidence for... **Baxter et al (1992)** and **Schwartz et al (1996)** found that **behavioural therapy** can reduce the **symptoms** of OCD and change the **biochemical factors** associated with it.

Evidence against... Both these behaviourist explanations **only** explain the **compulsive behaviour** and **not** the **obsessional thoughts**, which are an important aspect of OCD.

2 Psychodynamic Theory

Freud claimed that **potty training** causes **conflict** and **anger** in the child when their parents teach them how to use a toilet properly. This is **repressed** because the parents are more powerful. In adulthood this **can resurface**, causing anxiety, which is **displaced** into obsessions and compulsions.

Evidence for...

- Research into **stress** supports the idea that feeling **unimportant** and **out of control** may increase the likelihood of developing a mental disorder.
- **Adler** (1931) suggested a **link** between developing OCD and having had **overbearing parents**. In adulthood, engaging in **ritualistic behaviours** gives the person an opportunity to be very good at something (like hand washing) and so feel an increased level of **control**.

Evidence against...

Milby and Weber (1991) found **no link** between potty training conflicts and developing OCD.

3 Cognitive Factors

1) The cognitive-behavioural approach to OCD was put forward by **Rachman and Hodgson** (1980). It suggests that people with OCD **process thoughts** differently. As a result they're **unable** to easily dismiss any unwanted thoughts and impulses. This can be made worse if they're feeling **stressed** or **depressed**.
2) These unwanted thoughts and impulses cause **anxiety**, and the sufferer uses compulsive behaviours to **remove** this. This is the **behavioural** part of the cognitive-behavioural approach.

Evidence for...

1) There is a **link** between **depression** and **OCD**. This supports **Rachman and Hodgson's** idea that feeling stressed or depressed may make people more vulnerable to OCD.
2) **Salkovskis and Kirk** (1997) asked OCD sufferers to try to **suppress** their obsessional thoughts on some days and allow them to surface on others. They reported **more** distressing thoughts on the days they were deliberately trying to suppress them compared to the other days.

Evidence against... The cognitive-behavioural explanation **describes** the difficulty OCD sufferers have in suppressing unwanted thoughts but it **doesn't really explain** why they have this difficulty.

Practice Questions

Q1 What differences in concordance rates for OCD did Billet et al (1998) find in MZ and DZ twins?

Q2 What were the findings of the Salkovskis and Kirk (1997) study?

Exam Question

Q1 Compare and contrast two or more explanations for OCD.
Refer to psychological evidence in your answer. [24 marks]

That Freud was potty...

There's not a single bit of evidence for potty training disasters triggering OCD — but old Freud said it so it must be true... The other theories hold a bit more water though (sorry). Anyway, just make sure you know them really well.

Treating OCD

Choosing the right treatment can be difficult — one man's meat is another man's poison and all that. However, some treatments for OCD do appear to be more effective than others. Sadly we still haven't found the magic solution.

OCD Can be Treated Using Biological Therapy

Therapy using drugs is also called chemotherapy.

1) The **biological** approach to treating OCD involves **drug therapy**.
2) Drug treatments usually work by increasing levels of **serotonin** in the brain using **selective serotonin reuptake inhibitors (SSRIs)**. These are a type of **antidepressant** drug that **increase** the availability of **serotonin**.
3) SSRIs **prevent the reuptake** of serotonin in the gap between two neurons. This allows the nervous system to get **more benefit** from the serotonin as it passes across.

Advantages

- Several researchers have found SSRIs to be **effective** in treating OCD. **Thoren et al** (1980) found that use of an SSRI was significantly better at **reducing obsessional thoughts** than a placebo.
- Research has found that using **other antidepressants** that don't affect serotonin levels is **ineffective** at reducing OCD symptoms.

Disadvantages

- Up to **50%** of patients with OCD **don't** experience any improvement in their symptoms when taking SSRIs. Out of those that do improve, up to **90%** have a **relapse** when they stop taking them.
- SSRIs have to be taken for **several weeks** before the patient experiences an improvement in their symptoms.
- **Side effects** of using these types of drugs include **nausea** and **headaches**, and sometimes increased levels of **anxiety**. This can cause people to **stop taking** their medication.

OCD Can be Treated Using Psychological Therapies

1 Cognitive Behavioural Therapies

Cognitive behavioural therapy (CBT) can be used as a psychological treatment for OCD.

1) CBT **challenges the obsessions** by making the person **test** or **question** the accuracy of some of their unwanted thoughts. For example, if a person believes they have to check that their front door is locked 10 times, they could be encouraged to test this by only checking the door once and then going out. When they come back and see that they haven't been burgled, and that the door is still locked, they may **question their need** to check the door 10 times.
2) CBT also uses **thought stopping**, which means shouting "Stop!" when the patient indicates that they are having the **obsessional thoughts or impulses**. They then **refocus** their mind on a more appropriate thought. The idea is that over time the patient will be able to do this by themselves **without support**.
3) By giving the sufferer **information** to challenge their obsessions, CBT can help **prevent the compulsions**.

Advantages of CBT

- CBT can be used to treat both the **obsessions** and the **compulsions**.
- **Franklin et al** (2002) found that CBT can be **combined with ERP** (see next page) to create a treatment that's **more effective** than either on its own.
- The patient is more **active** if they use CBT than if they use drugs. Encouraging people to be active in their treatment might be a more **positive** way to treat patients.

Disadvantages of CBT

- CBT can be **very challenging** for patients — they have to be willing to cope with the **increased anxiety** that is caused by the treatment. This might be **too distressing** for some and so drug treatments might be a better option for these patients.

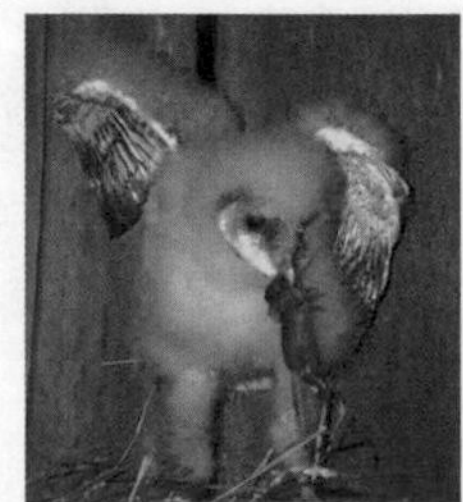

The mouse had shouted "Stop!" several times, but it didn't seem to have stopped the owl's obsessional thoughts about eating him.

Treating OCD

2 Behavioural Therapies

Exposure and response prevention (ERP) is commonly used as a behavioural treatment for OCD. Here's how it could go:

1) With support from a therapist the OCD patient **identifies** some **situations** that cause them anxiety. They then **rank** these situations in order of the anxiety they produce. For example, if the OCD is to do with germs the patient's list might include touching a doorknob, using a communal toilet and shaking hands.
2) The patient is then exposed to the **first situation** and encouraged **not to use the compulsions** they usually use in this situation (e.g. using elbows to operate a door handle). Although this causes an **increase in anxiety**, after a time the **anxiety drops** as it can't stay high for long periods of time.
3) At the same time the patient is taught to use **relaxation techniques**, is **reassured** and is encouraged to take part in **different behaviours**. Once this is successful they then move on to the **next exposure task** that they listed.

Advantages

- It's been found in studies that ERP was **effective** in treating around **75%** of patients with OCD.
- For people with **mild OCD** it's possible to use ERP **without a therapist** as a **self-help** technique.
- Behavioural therapies only take around **3 to 8 weeks**.

Disadvantages

- Behavioural treatment is much **less successful** in patients who have obsessional thoughts but **don't** carry out **compulsive behaviour**.
- The **distress** caused by **resisting** compulsions can cause patients to **drop out** of therapy.

3 Psychotherapy

1) Psychotherapy aims to identify the **underlying cause** of the mental disorder.
2) This is done using different therapeutic techniques, e.g. **dream analysis** and **free association**.
3) When the **unconscious conflicts** that are causing the problems are made **conscious**, the therapist and patient can discuss and try to resolve them. This will hopefully lead to the disorder being cured.

Advantages

- It aims to understand the **underlying cause** of the disorder, rather than just focusing on the **symptoms**.

Disadvantages

- Psychotherapy **ignores the biological cause** of OCD.
- There's **no controlled study** that supports the **effectiveness** of psychoanalysis in the treatment of OCD.
- **Other treatments** such as the use of drugs or ERP have much **higher success** rates.

Practice Questions

Q1 What does SSRI stand for?

Q2 What is meant by 'thought stopping', used in CBT?

Q3 Give an example of an exposure task for a person using ERP to treat OCD related to germs.

Q4 Give two therapeutic techniques used in psychotherapy.

Exam Questions

Q1 Compare and contrast at least two treatments for OCD. Refer to psychological evidence in your answer. [24 marks]

Q2 Tony has been offered a choice of a drug prescription or a course of ERP to treat his OCD.
Give him advice and information based on psychological research. [24 marks]

Exposure and response prevention — an end to the joys of skinny dipping...

No treatment is without its problems. Some ethical problems apply to any kind of mental health treatment. For example, patients should be able to withdraw from treatment at any time. However, health care professionals sometimes encourage them to continue even when the side effects of drugs are uncomfortable or the therapies are causing increases in anxiety.

The Influence of Media on Social Behaviour

Violent television shows and video games are all over the place these days and they get blamed for all kinds of problems — mostly for corrupting young people. Psychologists are interested in what effect they actually have on viewers...

*The **Media** May Influence Our **Behaviour***

1) **Social learning theory** suggests that we **model** our behaviour on behaviour that we **observe** — whether it's anti-social or pro-social behaviour.
2) There's much **debate** about whether the media influences our behaviour in this way. A central point to this debate is the effect of observing violence in TV programmes and video games — particularly on children's behaviour.
3) **Bandura's Bobo Doll experiments** (1961) showed that children who'd watched an adult behaving aggressively towards a doll were **more likely** to behave **aggressively** than those who hadn't seen the aggressive behaviour.
4) If the observed behaviour has a **positive outcome** we are **more likely** to copy it than if the outcome is negative.
5) Social learning theory also claims that if the model is **high status** or **admired** they are **more influential**.

*Violent Media May be Used as a **Justification** for **Anti-social Behaviour***

1) Aggressive behaviour falls **outside the social norm** — it's considered to be **anti-social**.
2) Knowing this and still displaying aggressive behaviour can cause someone to feel **psychologically uncomfortable**.
3) **Justification theory** suggests violent media can be used to **reduce** this psychological discomfort.
4) If someone watches violent programmes or plays violent video games, they will become used to seeing aggressive behaviour — they may begin to think that it's **normal** and **acceptable**.
5) This helps them **justify** their own anti-social behaviour and feel **less guilty** about it.
6) This justification of their anti-social behaviour means that they're **more likely** to behave that way **again**.

*There Have Been Many **Studies** Into the Effect of **Television** on **Behaviour***

Loads of studies have examined the **link** between **violence on TV** and **aggression**.

Huesmann et al (1984) conducted **longitudinal studies** which found a relationship between **exposure to TV violence** at a young age and the number of **criminal convictions** at the age of 30. They claimed it showed the development of anti-social behaviour and aggression.

Paik and **Comstock** (1991) conducted a **meta-analysis** that summarised the findings of over a thousand studies examining the link between **TV violence** and **aggressive behaviour**. The results suggested a **strong link** between exposure to violent programmes and aggressive behaviour.

The results of these studies show a **correlation** between exposure to violent TV programmes and aggressive behaviour, but they don't show **cause and effect**. This means we can't say for sure that watching violence on TV causes aggressive behaviour — it could be that **aggressive** children are **more likely** to **watch violent programmes**.

There have also been studies examining the effect that observing **pro-social behaviour** on TV has on **behaviour**.

Sprafkin et al (1975) showed 3 groups of children different TV programmes. Group 1 watched a programme where a boy **saves a puppy**. Group 2 watched a similar programme but with **no helping behaviour**. Group 3 watched a programme with **no interaction** between animals and humans. The children could hear the sounds of some distressed puppies and were placed in front of two buttons. They were told that each time they pressed one button they would be given **points** — the more points they got the bigger the prize they would be given. Pressing the other button wouldn't give them any points but it would alert someone to **help** the puppies. Group 1 children were the **most likely** to spend their time **calling for help** rather than collecting points.

Many studies **don't measure** whether pro-social behaviour is a **long-term** or **short-term effect** of exposure to such programmes. **Sagotsky et al** (1981) found that 6 and 8 year olds modelled cooperative behaviour **immediately after** they witnessed it. However, **7 weeks** later, **only the older children** were still showing the behavioural effects.

The Influence of Media on Social Behaviour

Video Games and Computers May Also Affect Behaviour

1) The popularity of **video games** has stimulated new research into the influence that media has on behaviour.
2) Like other media (e.g. films), games receive **age ratings** depending on their content. Ratings are determined by things like violence, sexual themes, drug use, criminal behaviour or bad language.
3) It's thought that games may have **greater potential** to **influence behaviour** than other types of media due to their **interactive nature**.
4) Some people believe that violent video games can be held **directly responsible** for influencing some specific crimes.

Example

The use of violent video games by the **Columbine High School shooters** has been cited by some people as a reason for the 1999 massacre that killed 13 people and injured 24 others. The families of some of the victims took **legal action** against the companies that produced them but were **unsuccessful**.

5) However, many people **don't believe** that video games can be blamed for crimes. They point out that most people who use the games don't go on to imitate the violent behaviour that they see in them.
6) **Greitemeyer and Osswald** (2010) found that playing games with a **pro-social** theme (e.g. saving a city or fighting crime) leads to an **increase** in pro-social behaviours. Other research has found that playing **action** video games can help **improve speed, accuracy** and even the ability to see **contrast**.

A **meta-analysis** of early research by **Anderson and Bushman** (2001) suggests that playing violent video games does **increase aggression** and **decrease pro-social behaviour** in young people.
Studies have been carried out on the effect that violent video games have on the **emotions** of people playing them.

Anderson and Bushman (2002) — Video games and emotions

Method: This study was a **lab experiment** involving 224 participants in **two independent groups**. Participants played either a violent or non-violent video game and were then asked to 'finish off' three stories from a variety of 'story stems', e.g. one started with a minor car accident. Each participant was asked to describe what the main character would do, say and feel.

Results: Participants who had played the violent game described the main character as being **more aggressive** than those who'd played the non-violent game, e.g. shouting at, starting a fight with or stabbing the other driver.

Conclusion: Playing video games produces **aggressive thoughts** and **emotions** in players.

Evaluation: **Low ecological validity** may have led the participants to give responses which didn't reflect the way they would react in real life. Participants might have shown **demand characteristics** (see page 221) due to their recent exposure to violent scenarios. This was a lab study so there was good **control of variables** and the results are therefore **reliable**.

Practice Questions

Q1 What does justification theory say about violent media?
Q2 List two positive effects that some video games could have on the player.
Q3 Describe Anderson and Bushman's (2002) study.

Exam Question

Q1 a) Describe and evaluate at least one explanation of media influences on behaviour. [8 marks]

b) "Violent video games have a more harmful effect than any other form of media." Discuss this statement. [16 marks]

You know what else is anti-social? Staying in to revise. Grrrrr.

Nothing to stress you out here — you do need to learn all the different studies though. General waffling that the media can affect behaviour won't cut any mustard in the exam. Funny saying that, why would you want to cut mustard...

Persuasion and Attitude Change

Love, hate, approval, disapproval… attitudes we hold on many different things. If attitudes predict behaviour it'd be pretty nifty to know how to shape the attitudes of other people. Pretty manipulative as well, but that's how things go.

Persuasion *is the Art of Changing Someone's* ***Attitude***

Our **attitudes** are our feelings towards something — they can be **positive** or **negative** views.
Persuasion is **changing an attitude**, usually using **messages** about the object, person or concept in question.

1 *The* ***Hovland-Yale Model*** *Identifies the* ***Key Elements*** *of Persuasion*

1) **Carl Hovland** researched **effective persuasion techniques** at Yale University.
2) Hovland argued that a person's change in attitude was a **sequential process**:

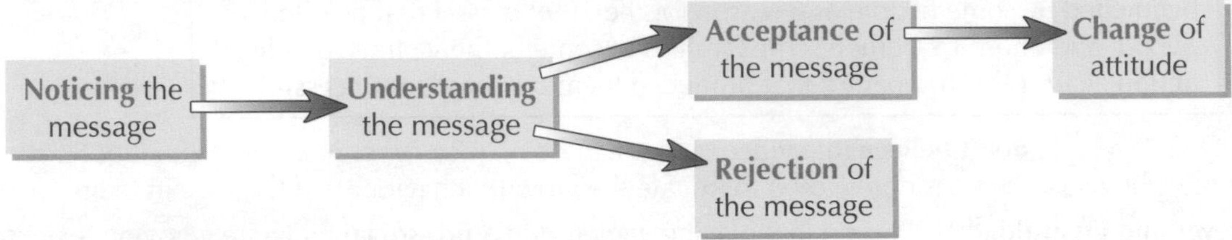

3) Hovland wanted to find out what factors affect the likelihood that a change in attitude will take place. To do this, his team took an **experimental approach** to studying persuasion, systematically **changing one variable** at a time.
4) The results of his research became known as the **Hovland-Yale model** (1953) and identified **four important components** of persuasion:
   - **The source of the message** — e.g. the **trustworthiness**, **expertise** and **attractiveness** of the persuader.
   - **The message content** — e.g. the **number**, **strength**, **order** and **emotional appeal** of the arguments.
   - **The recipient** — e.g. the **age**, **IQ** and **personality traits** of the person being persuaded.
   - **The situation** — e.g. whether given **formally** or **informally**, and whether the message is **relevant**.
5) The Hovland-Yale model suggests the key factors involved in creating a change in attitude but **doesn't address why** these factors are important.
6) The Hovland-Yale model assumes that we always carry out a **very careful thought process**. More recently, other psychologists have found evidence to suggest that we **don't** always carry out such a thorough process.

2 *The* ***Elaboration-Likelihood Model*** *Identifies the* ***Processing Routes*** *of Persuasion*

1) **Petty and Cacioppo (1986)** agreed with Hovland that if you try and persuade someone about something, they **consider** the argument. However, they believed that people **don't always** consider all of the information available, such as the credibility of the source, as this takes up too much **cognitive effort**.
2) Petty and Cacioppo (1986) reckoned that a persuasion message can take effect through **two processing routes**:
   - **The Peripheral Route** — low-level mechanisms such as **conditioning**, use of quick **decision-making rules** (e.g. 'experts are always right') and **attractiveness** of the message determine our attitudes. The peripheral route **doesn't involve much analysis** of the merits of the message itself.
   - **The Central Route** — high-level mechanisms, such as **evaluation of the source** and **content** of the message, determine our attitudes. Persuasion via the central route occurs when someone has the **time**, **motivation** and **ability** to **analyse** the message. When this happens, the likelihood that they'll elaborate on the information that they have increases.

   This is known as the **elaboration-likelihood model** (ELM).
3) The elaboration-likelihood model is comprehensive and can explain particular experimental findings, but it can't be used to predict them beforehand — it **lacks the predictive power** which a useful model should have.

Persuasion and Attitude Change

The **Media** are Pretty **Good** at **Persuading** Us

Martin knew those porridge adverts he watched were getting at something, but he just couldn't quite put his finger on it.

1) Both the **Hovland-Yale model** and the **ELM model** (see previous page) attempt to explain the process that can lead us to **change our attitude** about something. It's something that **advertisers** and the **media** are pretty keen to understand (for obvious reasons).
2) Television is used by **advertisers**, **political parties** and **health organisations** to persuade their audience.
3) TV is a really popular way of delivering a persuasion message because of the double whammy of **audio** and **visual information** which is delivered, and the potentially **huge audience**.
4) **Different techniques** based on models of persuasion are used to make TV persuasion as effective as possible. Here are a few to think about:

- **Pleasant associations** — products being sold are often teamed with things the audience will automatically feel positive about, such as **humour**, **success** and **sex**. Through **classical conditioning**, the product may become associated with these things — the audience may be persuaded through the **peripheral route** that they need to buy it.
- **Making the message bizarre** — many TV adverts are 'off the wall' and totally **unconnected** to the product they're advertising. This encourages **deep processing** of the persuasion message and accesses the **central route** of persuasion.
- **Using familiar figures** — **celebrities** are often used to advertise products and they're usually **matched up** to the product they're selling, e.g. models advertising beauty products. People delivering the message don't actually need to be famous — just **recognisable figures**. A man in a white coat spouting long words will give an image of scientific credibility, for example. In this way, advertisers can tap into the **peripheral or central route** of persuasion by activating **mental associations** with the personalities used, or increasing motivation to **process** the message more deeply.
- **Fear** — adverts often tap into the **emotion** of fear. For example, NHS **anti-smoking adverts** have shown children breathing out cigarette smoke to emphasise the **dangers** of passive smoking. Researchers like **Meyerowitz and Chaiken** (1987) have found that adverts like these, which arouse fear in the viewer, can act as a **peripheral cue** for persuasion. However, according to **Witte et al** (1998), if a message creates **too much fear**, there is a point at which the audience will just **switch off**.
- **Repetition** — most adverts are repeated more than once. One reason for this is that **peripheral emotional cues** (e.g. the Andrex puppy) only last as long as they are **memorable** — repetition makes them more memorable and eventually **automatic**. Repeating a message enough also leads to **familiarity** with it. Researchers have found that, more often than not, familiarity leads to **trust** and **persuasion**.

Practice Questions

Q1 List the four factors in persuasion identified by the Hovland-Yale model.

Q2 Explain the difference between the peripheral and central routes of persuasion.

Q3 Describe a technique used in TV for persuasion.

Exam Question

Q1 a) Describe and evaluate at least one model explaining how attitudes can be changed. [16 marks]

b) Discuss the effectiveness of television in persuasion. [8 marks]

The lots-of-revision model has one key element of persuasion — fear...

So there you have it — you should be able to persuade anyone of anything now. Just make sure that the source, content, recipient and situation of the model are correct, go at them via the peripheral and central routes, make them feel afraid (mwah ha ha) until they don't know what they think anymore — and do it all through their telly. You can't go wrong.

The Psychology of 'Celebrity'

"When I grow up, I wanna be famous" trill countless starry-eyed children. As an outcome of the relatively new mass media, we've only just begun to look for ways to explain 'celebrity', but there are already a few different theories...

Audiences Can Develop **Relationships** With **Celebrities**

1) The relationships that audiences develop with celebrities are very **different** from the relationships formed within **normal social networks**.
2) They are **one-sided**, with one person knowing lots and the other usually knowing nothing about the other party.
3) The term used to describe this type of relationship is **parasocial**.
4) The **study** of parasocial relationships between audiences and celebrities has become a branch of **social relationship research** in its own right.
5) As well as audiences developing relationships with celebrities, many people are **attracted** to the **concept of celebrity** and want to be one themselves.

Their relationship was distinctly one sided but that didn't discourage Molly.

The **Attraction** of Celebrity Can be Explained in an **Evolutionary Context**...

1) The **evolutionary explanation** for the attraction of celebrity is based on the idea that everyone has a basic selfish drive to ensure their **genes** have the best possible chance of being **passed on**.
2) Celebrity is seen as a way to achieve this and can be looked at from **two different perspectives**:
   - **Becoming a celebrity makes a person more desirable.** In evolutionary terms, it may result in gaining **economic advantage**, which may make a person **more attractive** to others. This then increases their chances of **passing on their genes**.
   - **Desirable people become celebrities.** Celebrities may be seen as individuals who are hugely popular due to their **personality traits**. So becoming famous acts as confirmation of having characteristics that others find attractive. **Hartup** (1992) researched the characteristics of people who became popular in their own social circles from an early age. The characteristics that were valued included **social dominance** and **athletic ability** in boys and **prettiness** in girls.

...or in a **Social Psychological Context**

1) Wann (1995) studied the **active role** that audiences play as **fans** — a **social psychological explanation** for the attraction of celebrity.
2) This has led to the creation of the term **fandom** — used to describe **a group of fans** of a particular celebrity. Fandom can provide individuals with:
   - **Enhanced self-esteem.**
   - **Escape, entertainment** and **excitement**.
   - **Enhanced family** and **group affiliation**.
3) The extent to which fandom provides these **varies** between individuals and contributes to how **likely** someone is to be a fan. For example, someone whose self-esteem is greatly increased and who finds high levels of entertainment and escape in fandom is likely to find the concept of celebrity more attractive than someone whose self-esteem is only slightly enhanced.
4) Several aspects of fandom are **very social in nature**, providing a group of people with a **shared focus of interest**. Some people believe that 'being a fan' of something can play an important role in adolescence — it might help young people make the **transition** from **parental** to **peer attachments** by providing a **common source** of gossip.

The Psychology of 'Celebrity'

There are Three Stages of Fandom

Explanations of fandom suggest that celebrity worship can be a result of **normal instincts** and **motivations**. However, sometimes fandom can take on a **more intense form** and becomes something which is **pathological**. **Three stages of fandom** have been identified:

1) **Entertainment-Social** — where the relationship with the celebrity exists as a source of fun, shared with others in a social group.
2) **Intense-Personal** — obsessive thoughts begin to arise in relation to the celebrity, (e.g. "Justin Timberlake is my soul mate").
3) **Borderline-Pathological** — obsessive thoughts begin to give rise to fully-fledged fantasies (e.g. "Justin Timberlake is my boyfriend") and behaviours (e.g. sending love letters to Justin Timberlake). It is at this stage that stalking may begin, which involves a level of pursuit that is intimidating.

Stalkers Don't Always Conform to the Stereotypical Image

The word '**stalker**' immediately conjures up images of an unattractive and obsessive loner-type, whose walls are decorated with news clippings and photographs of the star who has become the object of their fixation. This image is largely created by the media and contains several **misconceptions**, which **Spitzberg** is largely credited with de-bunking:

Myth: Stalking mainly affects celebrities

Stalking involving a well-known person is more likely to be reported in the media than stalking involving a member of the public — so it's clear why this would be assumed. However, it's estimated that around **21% of the population** will be pursued at some point.

Myth: Stalkers are strangers

In fact, in most cases stalkers have been involved in an **intimate relationship** with the person they're pursuing.

Myth: Stalking ends in violence

News reporting usually focuses on cases where there has been some dramatic ending, and films which portray a sensational account of stalking draw the most attention. However, stalking **doesn't usually involve violence**.

Practice Questions

Q1 What is meant by a parasocial relationship?

Q2 What are the three stages of fandom?

Q3 Give two misconceptions about stalking.

Exam Question

Q1 a) Discuss research into intense fandom. [8 marks]

b) Outline the social explanation of the attraction to celebrity. [16 marks]

Celeb worship is harmless. My fiancé Justin Timberlake totally agrees...

So in summary, it's normal to be interested in celebrities and what they do, unless you take it too far and become a stalker. But even if you do you'll still look normal, so no-one will know you're a stalker. Now just learn all the details and technical terms and you'll be all set for the exam. And whilst you do that I'll just nip out and grab my favourite glossy magazine...

Models of Addictive Behaviour

Alcohol, smoking, gambling, chocolate, shopping... examples of things people claim to be addicted to. So what is it that makes them all so darn irresistible? Guess what... no one's quite sure yet so there are several different theories.

Addiction often involves three stages — **initiation** (e.g. taking up smoking), **maintenance** (e.g. carrying on smoking even when you have to go outside in the rain) and **relapse** (e.g. having a cigarette when you'd given up). There are three models that attempt to explain addiction — biological, cognitive and learning.

Addictive Behaviour Can be Explained by the Biological Model of Addiction...

The **biological approach** includes **neurological** and **genetic explanations** for addictions.

1 The Neurological Approach

Both the highs and lows of addiction can be explained at the level of **neurons**...

1) The neurotransmitter **dopamine** is released at particular synapses in the brain and affects **motivation** and **pleasure** (amongst other things).
2) Some substances (e.g. food and addictive drugs), **increase the release** of dopamine or **prevent its reuptake** at synapses.
3) These both **increase dopamine levels** in the brain and so **dopamine receptors** on neurons are **stimulated** — this gives the person a feeling of pleasure or satisfaction.
4) Once the dopamine has been removed from the synapses (reuptake), this feeling **disappears**. In order to regain it, the person wants to take **more** of the substance.
5) If the substance is used **repeatedly**, the body becomes **used** to the **higher levels** of dopamine. The rate at which it's broken down increases and its **reuptake** also **increases**. This means that **more** of the substance is needed to produce the **same effect**. This is known as **tolerance**.
6) If the addict then **stops** taking the substance, they experience effects which are the **opposite** of the drug's effects. These are called **withdrawal symptoms** and can be removed by taking **more** of the substance.

2 The Genetic Approach

1) It's been suggested that some addictions are **inherited**.
2) A review of studies by Sayette and Hufford (1997) concluded that **identical (MZ) twins** showed a **higher rate of concordance** for **alcoholism** than **non-identical (DZ) twins**, suggesting that alcoholism is controlled to **some extent** by **genes**.
3) This can explain why, despite the fact that many people drink alcohol on a regular basis, only a **small proportion** develop an **addiction** to it.
4) However, there must be an **environmental aspect** to alcoholism as the MZ twins didn't show 100% concordance. It's also not clear whether the result is just **specific to alcoholism**, or can be generalised to addiction as a whole.

The true cost of his addiction only hit Andy when he was asked to settle his tab.

However, the biological model of addiction doesn't take **psychological** and **social influences** into account.

...by the Cognitive Model of Addiction...

The **cognitive approach** looks at the **thought processes** behind an addiction. These could be shaped by a person's...

1) **attitude towards the behaviour** — e.g. 'alcohol helps me to feel confident and relaxed'.
2) **perception of others' opinions** — e.g. 'I need to drink to fit in'.
3) **perception of their ability to control their own behaviour** — e.g. 'I can't cope in social situations if I don't drink'.

The cognitive model can be used in therapy sessions to **reduce addictive behaviour**. Cognitive therapists help the addict to **identify** the **thoughts** that **trigger** their addictive behaviour. They're then taught **strategies** to **change** their behaviour, e.g. avoiding certain situations, and practicing new thought patterns. Cognitive therapy usually contains a **behavioural component** which teaches the addict **new skills**, e.g. alternative relaxation techniques.

Models of Addictive Behaviour

...and by the **Learning Model** of Addiction

The **learning approach** explains addiction by looking at the role the **environment** plays in the **maintenance** and **relapse** of **addictive behaviour**.

1) **Repeatedly** using a substance, e.g. heroin, in the **same environment** will lead to **associations** forming between the substance and the **stimuli** in the environment, e.g. needles, other addicts.
2) When these stimuli are present the body **expects** to receive the substance and will **compensate in advance** for certain **effects** of the drug. For example, heroin addicts feel anxious without the drug, because their body anticipates the increased relaxation that will follow its use.
3) This is known as **classical conditioning**, and is one of the factors that leads to the **initiation** of **addiction**, **tolerance** and **withdrawal effects**.
   - **Addiction** — The environmental stimuli lead to compensatory effects which are often the opposite of the drug effects. The user then wants the substance in order to remove these effects.
   - **Tolerance** — Compensatory effects oppose the effect that the substance has on the body, so larger quantities of the substance are needed to create the same effect.
   - **Withdrawal symptoms** — If the body experiences compensatory effects but doesn't receive the substance, the person will feel the opposite of how they would if they took the substance.

There is research evidence for this model of addiction.

Siegel et al (1982) — The effect of context on overdose likelihood

Method: This was a **lab experiment** using **independent groups** of rats. Two groups of rats were given heroin until they developed a **tolerance** to it. After 30 days the heroin dose was **doubled**. For half of the rats, this dose was given in the **usual room**. For the other half, it was given in a **different room**.

Results: 32% of the rats that had the double dose in the usual room died, compared to 64% of the rats in the new room.

Conclusion: **Tolerance** and **withdrawal symptoms** are a **conditioned response** to drug-related stimuli. When there's no familiar stimuli to allow anticipation of the drug, compensatory effects aren't triggered and the body is less prepared to deal with a larger quantity of the drug than usual. This increases the risk of death.

Evaluation: This result can explain **unusual cases** of overdose where addicts have died after taking an amount of drugs which they had coped with in the past. Also, it can explain why many ex-addicts, having 'got clean', go back to taking drugs when they return home — there they are surrounded by stimuli that are **associated** with drugs. Studies like this have **real-life applications**. As a result of findings that drug-related stimuli can increase cravings, anti-drug campaigns no longer use posters which show drug paraphernalia, e.g. syringes and spoons.

Practice Questions

Q1 What is tolerance?

Q2 What are the three cognitive factors underlying addiction?

Q3 Describe the results of the study by Siegel et al (1982).

Exam Question

Q1 a) Outline and evaluate at least one biological explanation of addiction. [16 marks]

b) Discuss another explanation for the initiation, maintenance and relapse of addiction. [8 marks]

My tolerance for this topic is rapidly reducing...

There you have it — nice explanations for any sneaky little addictions you've got. I think the cognitive model explains my peanut butter on toast addiction pretty well — I can't get through the working day without it. But then again, it could be the dopamine hit that has me reaching for the toaster, or the sight of the toaster itself... which, now I think about it... mmm, toast.

Explaining Smoking and Gambling

As the pastimes of gangsters and cowboys, you can understand why so many people think that smoking and gambling must be cool. But they'd be wrong — addictions are so last century, and can cause a fair number of problems.

*Many People Are **Addicted** to Smoking*

The chemicals in cigarettes can cause diseases such as **cancer**, **emphysema** and **bronchitis**. Despite this, many people smoke and some continue to smoke after being diagnosed with one of these conditions — this is because smoking is **addictive**. Even though many smokers want to quit, the **success rate** of those who attempt it is **very low**.
Addiction to smoking can be explained in more than one way:

*1 The **Biological Approach** Explains Smoking as an **Addiction to Nicotine***

1) There are many chemicals in cigarettes but it's the **nicotine** that causes **addiction**.
2) Nicotine stimulates the release of **dopamine**, increasing the level of dopamine in the brain and providing feelings of **pleasure** and **relaxation** (see page 204).
3) If nicotine's taken **regularly** the body **expects it** and **reduces** the amount of dopamine that's released naturally.
4) In order to maintain **normal dopamine levels** and the effect that they have on the body, nicotine needs to be taken regularly. This **reinforces smoking behaviour**, leading to more frequent smoking and **addiction**.
5) **Quitting** smoking is very difficult as the body becomes used to nicotine and **relies** on it to stimulate dopamine release. Quitting deprives the body of nicotine, leading to **low dopamine levels** until the body readjusts.
6) This causes unpleasant **withdrawal symptoms** such as anxiety, restlessness, sleep disturbance and weight gain.

*2 The **Social Learning Approach** Explains Why People **Start** Smoking*

1) **Social learning theory** states that new behaviour (in this case smoking), is learned through **observation**, or **modelling**. Whether the behaviour is imitated depends on the perceived **consequences**.
2) If smoking is **positively reinforced**, e.g. by **benefits** such as fitting in with peers, then it's likely to be **copied**. Seeing **role models** (e.g. parents or celebrities) smoking also encourages people to smoke.
3) Once someone has started smoking they will experience withdrawal symptoms if they stop. These encourage people to start smoking again (to remove the symptoms). This is known as **negative reinforcement**.
4) Often, smoking becomes **associated** with other activities and objects, e.g. alcohol — this is classical conditioning and it makes it difficult to not smoke in certain environments (see page 205).

	Akers and Lee (1996) — the effects of social learning over time
Method:	A five year **longitudinal study** of 454 secondary school students was conducted using **self-report questionnaire surveys**. These measured how frequently the students smoked and 'social learning variables'. These were things like whether friends smoked, how often friends smoked, and perceived attitudes of friends and parents towards smoking.
Results:	Significant **positive correlations** were found between the social learning variables and smoking.
Conclusion:	Social learning can partly account for whether smoking begins in adolescence.
Evaluation:	Methods relying on self report may be **unreliable**, and correlation doesn't prove that social learning causes smoking to begin. Also, the effect of social learning wasn't analysed to show the relative influence of different **variables**, e.g. gender or parental vs. peer influence.

*There's Been **Debate** Over Whether Smoking is an **Addiction** or a **Habit***

For a long time cigarette companies claimed that people smoked for **psychological** reasons (smoking for pleasure, which becomes part of a routine), rather than **physiological** reasons (smoking to avoid the unpleasant withdrawal symptoms caused by changes in the brain). They argued that this meant smoking was a **habit** rather than an **addiction**. However, **both** the physiological and psychological aspects are important in smoking. The physiological impact of withdrawal symptoms are well documented but the effects of psychological dependence shouldn't be underestimated.

Explaining Smoking and Gambling

Gambling Doesn't Involve Any Substance Use But Can Still Be **Addictive**

Addiction to gambling can also be explained by many approaches:

1 The **Biological Approach** Explains Gambling as an **Addiction to Adrenaline**

1) The **stress** of awaiting the outcome of a bet triggers the release of the hormone **adrenaline**.
2) This induces an **adrenaline rush**, making the person more alert and experiencing a 'natural high'.
3) In order to regain this rush, gamblers will place **more bets** and a **physiological addiction** may develop.
4) **Repeated gambling** can cause the body to develop a **tolerance** to adrenaline. This can lead to more frequent gambling or bets involving more money in order to get the same rush.
5) **Other chemicals** triggered by stress could also be responsible for gambling addictions. There's some evidence that gambling releases **endorphins**, chemicals that block pain and negative effects of stress.

2 The **Psychodynamic Approach** Suggests Gambling is Driven By **Masochism**

1) **Bergler** (1958) proposed that gamblers gamble to **lose**, in order to **punish** themselves.
2) This **reduces** the **guilt** they feel from rebelling against their parents during childhood. He suggests that gamblers **identify** with the casino dealer or roulette wheel, etc. as **parental figures**.
3) Bergler presented **case studies** where treatment relevant to his theory was successful in curing some gamblers of their addiction but **scientific evidence** is still lacking at the moment.

3 The **Cognitive Approach** Suggests Gambling is Driven By **Faulty Reasoning Mechanisms**

1) **Decision making** can be based on **rational consideration** or **quick** (**sometimes faulty**) **rules**.
2) **Wagenaar** (1988) identified 16 rules that gamblers commonly use when making decisions. These include:

- **The illusion of control** — gamblers think of gambling as **skill-based**. This creates superficially high expectations when in reality the outcomes are often determined by chance alone.
- **Representative bias** — gamblers believe that **random events** should **look random**, e.g. 'tails' seems increasingly likely the longer a run of consecutive 'heads' lasts. Many gamblers believe that the longer a losing streak lasts the more likely a win will follow. This is known as the **gambler's fallacy**.
- **Illusory correlations** — gamblers have **superstitions** which they believe help them succeed, e.g. blowing the dice for a 6.
- **Fixation on the absolute frequency of successes** — gamblers can **recall many past wins**, just because they gamble so much. This creates a false image of how often they win.

Practice Questions

Q1 Describe the study by Akers and Lee (1996).

Q2 Define 'physiological' and 'psychological' dependence to smoking.

Q3 List the faulty reasoning mechanisms that can lead to gambling addiction.

Exam Question

Q1 a) Outline a biological explanation for addiction to smoking. [8 marks]

b) Outline an alternative approach to explaining this addiction. [8 marks]

c) Discuss the difference between smoking as a habit and as an addiction. [8 marks]

Exams = stress = adrenaline = addiction to exams. Something's not right...

There are a lot of people out there who think that smoking and gambling are evil addictions that ruin lives — and I'm one of them. If they didn't exist you wouldn't have to learn about them, the examiners couldn't ask you about them and we'd all be much happier. Unfortunately that's not the case, so you'd best get down to business and learn these pages. Enjoy.

Vulnerability to Addiction

Not everybody becomes an addict. Behaviours such as drinking and gambling remain controllable pastimes for many people, so there must be individual differences at work. And, surprise surprise, you need to know what they are.

Stress Could be a Factor in the Development of Addiction

I'm stressed just looking at them — pass the chocolate.

1) **Sinha** (2007) used **brain imaging** to investigate the relationship between **stress** and **drug addiction**. She found that the **same part of the brain** was activated during stress as during drug craving.
2) Sinha suggests that stress makes people more **vulnerable** to reacting to **cues** associated with drugs. This could make them **more likely** to develop an addiction.
3) This research shows an **association** between stress and addiction — but it **doesn't explain** it. Drug use might cause altered brain function, or altered brain function might encourage drug use — or there may be **another cause**, and drug use and altered brain function are both results of this.
4) **Operant conditioning** (learning through reinforcement — see page 156) could explain why stress might make people more vulnerable to addiction if the pleasurable effects of the substance **reduce the symptoms** of stress. For example, alcohol is a **depressant** so it can make a stressed person feel **more relaxed**. This acts as a **positive reinforcement** and so they're more likely to **repeat** the drinking behaviour.

Age and Peers are Factors that Seem to be Linked in Addiction

1) **Zucker** (2008) found that the **age of onset** of drinking was important. The **earlier** people start drinking the more likely they are to have drinking problems.
2) **Martino et al** (2006) carried out a **longitudinal study** to look at the social factors that affect the **drinking habits** of adolescents. They concluded that the norms for drinking behaviour are learned through **social observations** and **interactions**. The **perceived approval** or **use** of alcohol by **parents**, other important adults and **peers** **increased the likelihood** of future decisions to drink and get drunk.
3) Research has shown that although being **socially withdrawn** can be negative for other reasons, such as loneliness, it actually **protects** young people from the **influence** of their **peers** in relation to addiction:

- **Fergusson and Horwood** (1999) found that children who were **socially isolated** from their peer group at the age of **10** because of **social anxiety** were **less likely** to use drugs or drink alcohol when they were **15**.
- **Shedler and Block** (1990) found that **18-year-olds** who hadn't tried drugs were more likely to be **socially isolated**, **over-controlled** by others and **anxious**.

Younger People are More Affected by Peer Pressure

Sumter et al (2009) found that a person's **age** affects their ability to **resist peer pressure**.

Sumter et al (2009) — age differences in resisting peer pressure

Method:	**464 children and adolescents** were given a questionnaire that assessed their ability to resist **pressure** from their **peer group**. The questionnaire was written in a **style** suitable for all ages and used hypothetical **everyday situations**.
Results:	The participants' answers showed that they were **more vulnerable** to being influenced by their friends when they were **younger**. The participants became **more resistant** as they got **older**.
Conclusion:	As adolescents become **more mature** they are **less influenced** by others. This could explain why early experiences with substances have **long-term effects**.
Evaluation:	This was a **cross-sectional study** so individual differences could have affected the results. Carrying out longitudinal research avoids this design flaw, but it takes longer to collect the data. Peer pressure can be both **positive** or **negative** when it comes to abusing substances. You're less likely to do it if your friends aren't — but more likely if they are.

Vulnerability to Addiction

Personality Can Affect *Addictive Behaviour*

1) **Eysenck and Eysenck (1976)** outlined three main personality dimensions:

- **P** for **psychoticism**, which includes being egocentric, aggressive and impulsive.
- **E** for **extroversion**, which includes being outgoing, happy and sociable.
- **N** for **neuroticism**, which includes being anxious, moody and irritable.

Eysenck suggested that some personality characteristics make a person **more prone** to addiction.

2) **Francis (1996)** found that people with nicotine, heroin and alcohol addictions scored **more highly** on **N** and **P** scales on psychometric tests compared to the E scales.
3) The exact relationship between addiction and personality is **unclear**. Being irritable and impulsive could mean you are **more likely to use** substances such as alcohol or drugs. Or it could be that these personality characteristics make you **less able to control** your use of the substances.
4) Alternatively it could be that **having an addiction** leads a person to be moody and impulsive, and makes them less likely to be happy and outgoing.

Some *Personality Disorders* are Associated with *Substance Abuse*

1) **Rounsaville et al (1998)** found that people diagnosed with **antisocial personality disorder** were more likely to be alcoholics compared to those without the disorder.
2) Other research suggests a link between **attention deficit disorder** and alcohol abuse.
3) Substance abuse is a problem for some people with **mental health problems** as they may use alcohol and drugs to **self-medicate**. This makes it difficult to work out where the **causal relationship** lies. A person with mental health problems might drink or use drugs to help them **cope**, or using these substances might make them more **vulnerable** to mental health problems. It's **difficult to test** this as ethics is a major issue in this area.

Practice Questions

Q1 What technique did Sinha use when investigating the relationship between stress and addiction?

Q2 What was concluded from Martino et al's (2006) study?

Q3 Identify the relationship that has been established between age and resistance to peer influence.

Q4 Give the personality characteristics that P, E and N stand for.

Q5 Give two personality disorders that are more common in people with alcohol addiction.

Exam Questions

Q1 Describe and discuss research into risk factors associated with the development of addiction. [24 marks]

Q2 "Some people are more likely to develop alcohol addiction than others."
Evaluate the accuracy of this statement and refer to psychological evidence in your answer. [24 marks]

We can blame our parents? That's a relief. I knew it wasn't my fault...

It looks like the great mystery of why some people never know when to grab some cheesy chips and call it a night remains unsolved for the moment. It's likely that a combination of factors including stress, peer influence, age and personality explain why some people are more at risk of developing addictions than others — but I'm just going to blame my parents.

Reducing Addictive Behaviour

The old adage is true, prevention certainly is better than cure. That's why health psychologists are trying to figure out how to stop addictive behaviour before it starts. And how to stop it once it has started, just in case.

The Theory of Reasoned Action Explains How We Decide How We'll Behave

1) **Fishbein** and **Ajzen** (1975) developed the **theory of reasoned action** (**TRA**) model of behaviour.
2) It states that an individual's behaviour, e.g. whether they will give up alcohol, can be **predicted** by their **intention** to perform it. Intention is determined by two factors:

- The person's **attitude to the behaviour** — this is shaped by their **beliefs** about the **outcome** of the behaviour, e.g. 'I'll save money', and their **judgement** of whether the outcome is **positive or negative, likely or unlikely**.
- **Subjective norms** — this describes their **expectations** of the **social consequences** of the behaviour, e.g. 'My friends will think I'm boring', and their **motivation** to **follow these norms**, e.g. 'I want to be popular'.

3) Sheppard et al (1988) carried out a meta-analysis and found that the TRA had a **strong predictive use** — it was pretty good at predicting intentions and behaviour. It's also a useful model for knowing how to **alter** an individual's intentions and behaviour. However, it's been criticised for **neglecting factors** such as **habits** and **emotional aspects**, which are also important when intentions are being formed.

The Theory of Planned Behaviour is a Modification of the TRA

1) **Ajzen** (1991) added a third factor to the TRA — a person's **perceived behavioural control**, e.g. 'I don't have the will power to give up alcohol'. This factor **increases** the model's **predictive power**.
2) This theory is known as the **theory of planned behaviour** (**TPB**). It suggests behaviour is influenced in two ways:

- **Indirectly** — if a person believes that the behaviour is **too difficult** they don't form the initial intention to carry out the behaviour.
- **Directly** — if the **perception** of their own level of control is **accurate**, e.g. they don't have sufficient willpower, they won't succeed.

3) In contrast to the TRA, the TPB takes into account the fact that people **don't always have complete control** over their behaviour, as there may be obstacles that stand in their way.
4) Norman et al's (1998) study found that **perceived behavioural control** was a strong predictor of binge-drinking. The TPB could therefore be used to develop **intervention strategies** and **prevention programmes**.
5) Both models ignore the fact that there may be **discrepancies** between **attitude** and **behaviour** and that a person's behaviour is not always a reflection of their **intentions**. People's actions aren't always rational and based on deliberate decision making processes. This is especially true for **addictive behaviour**, which is often **irrational**.

The Health Belief Model Can be Used To Predict Behaviour

1) The factors that the **health belief model** uses as predictors of behaviour include someone's:

- **Perception of susceptibility and severity** — their belief of how **likely** and **serious** the threat to their own health is if they don't carry out the preventative health behaviour, e.g. the danger of developing lung cancer as a result of smoking.
- **Perception of cost-benefit** — they weigh the **benefits** of the behaviour (e.g. reduces cancer risk) against its **costs** (e.g. suffering withdrawal symptoms).

2) The health belief model takes into account factors that **encourage** people to break their addictive behaviour. These factors are known as **cues to action** and include experiencing **symptoms** of health problems or exposure to **media campaigns**.
3) The model also considers the influence that **personal variables**, e.g. age, sex, social class and personality traits have on a person's perceptions.
4) The comprehensive nature of the model means that it's an ideal tool for designing **individual intervention strategies** and highlights the importance of **tailoring interventions** to an individual's personal profile.

Reducing Addictive Behaviour

*A Range of **Interventions** Are Used to **Reduce Addictive Behaviours***

Biological Interventions

1) The biological approach to reducing drug and alcohol addictions involves a **gradual detox**, where the **quantity** of the substance used is **reduced over time**.
2) **Medication** may be prescribed to stop addictive behaviour, e.g. Antabuse® is prescribed to alcoholics. It causes nausea if it's combined with alcohol, discouraging alcoholics from drinking. The addict will form an **association** between drinking and nausea — this will continue even when they stop taking Antabuse®. This is known as **aversion therapy**.

   Meyer and Chesser (1970) carried out a **repeated measures experiment**. A group of alcoholics who were prescribed Antabuse® were compared to a **control group**. Around **50%** of those taking Antabuse® stayed **teetotal** for at least a year — significantly more than in the control group. From this study they concluded that an **unpleasant response** can be **conditioned** to an **addictive behaviour**.

3) However, any medication prescribed has to be **carefully controlled** so it doesn't become an addiction itself.

Psychological Interventions

1) The psychological approach consists of a range of therapies that aim to change the way an addict **behaves** by changing their thought processes.
2) **Cognitive behavioural therapy** identifies the thoughts that cause the behaviour, e.g. 'I can't cope without cigarettes', and then changes this thought process. This is known as **cognitive restructuring**.
3) Cognitive behavioural therapy has had some **success**, e.g. it has enhanced the effectiveness of nicotine replacement treatment for quitting smoking.

Public Health Interventions

1) Public health interventions address addictive behaviours on a **wide scale** to **reduce** their **impact on society**.
2) For example, to reduce smoking the government **banned adverts** for cigarettes. They also ran **anti-smoking campaigns**, placed **warning messages** on cigarette packs and **increased prices**. More recently, they've made it **illegal** to smoke in **enclosed public places**.
3) Some public health interventions **aren't** as **straightforward** as they sound. It was once proposed in America that the amount of **nicotine** in cigarettes could be **reduced gradually** until smokers were no longer addicted. However, in reality smokers might just end up **smoking more** to get the same effect. The measure would also meet with **opposition** from smokers.
4) It's **difficult** to prove the **efficacy** of public health interventions. One study found **5.1%** of smokers gave up smoking after asking their **GP** for advice — but there's no way of telling if they'd have done that without help.

Practice Questions

Q1 According to the theory of reasoned action, what factors determine attitudes to addictive behaviour?

Q2 Describe the main findings of the study by Meyer and Chesser (1970).

Q3 How has the government tried to reduce smoking?

Exam Question

Q1 a) Outline the theory of planned behaviour. [4 marks]

b) Discuss some different interventions used to reduce addictive behaviours. [20 marks]

I need an intervention to sort out my TRA — tremendous revision anger...

Phew, that's a whopping amount of information on reducing addictive behaviour. You need to learn all the models of prevention and all the types of intervention that are so carefully described for you on these two pages. Lovely jubbly.

Studying Anomalous Experience

It may make entertaining TV, but lots of people just aren't convinced that paranormal abilities like telepathy and out-of-body experiences really exist. And there's a very good reason for their doubt — a serious lack of evidence.

Anomalous Experiences** Can't Currently be Explained by **Science

1) Something that **can't be explained by science** is called an **anomalous experience**. There are many different types:
   - **Out-of-body experience** — a sensation of **floating** around **outside** of your own body.
   - **Near-death experience** — sensations experienced when you're **close to death**, often interpreted as a glimpse into the 'afterlife'.
   - **Spontaneous psychic ability** (**psi**) — **extra-sensory perception**, e.g. telepathy, clairvoyance or psychokinesis (altering an object, e.g. moving, bending or softening it using the mind).
   - **Past-life experience** — remembering events from a **previous existence**.
   - **Anomalous healing** — healing through **unexplainable methods**, e.g. by a spiritual healer or through prayer.
2) Anomalous experiences **can't just be immediately rejected** — many things that were once considered mysterious, e.g. thunder and lightning, can now be explained scientifically.
3) So it's important that all anomalous experiences are **investigated thoroughly** — they may one day be explainable, either by what we **already know** about human behaviour, or accepted as something **completely new**.

Pseudoscience** and **Fraud** Can be Mistaken For **Anomalous Experiences

Pseudoscience

Explanations based on evidence that's been collected through **faulty scientific processes** are known as **pseudoscience**. The results of many demonstrations of so-called anomalous experiences turn out to be caused by methodological issues such as **cognitive bias** and **experimenter effects**.

Cognitive biases

Spontaneous events, such as having a dream come true, are the main reasons why people believe in anomalous experiences. People who believe in such things have been shown to be **more susceptible** to the **illusion of control** than people who don't. The illusion of control is a **cognitive bias** (a faulty judgement) which causes people to believe that they're able to **control** or **influence** the outcome of an event over which, in reality, they have no control.

Experimenter effects

The **outcome** of any psychological experiment can be affected by the **expectations of the experimenter** and how this manifests itself in their **behaviour**. Certain researchers consistently find significant results using the same methods whilst others consistently fail. This is known as **experimenter effects**. As a result of this, it's been suggested that only people who **don't believe** in that particular anomalous experience should be allowed to replicate the experiments. Experimenter effects exist in **both directions** though, and the expectations of sceptics could affect the experiment **just as strongly** in the **other direction**.

Fraud

Research has also been blighted by cases of **fraud**, where scientists have **deliberately deceived people**, invalidating observations and results. Researchers who believe in the anomalous experience are **more likely** to **miss the tricks** of fraudsters as they are biased towards results that are **consistent with their existing beliefs**.

People claiming to have **psychic abilities** usually demonstrate them **most successfully** when they have some **control** over how they show them and the way they are observed. In order to reduce the chances of pseudoscience and fraud being passed off as anomalous experiences, **Wiseman and Morris** (1995) developed a set of **methodological guidelines** for research into this area. They include advice on issues such as **randomisation of stimuli** and **preventing 'sensory leakage'** (soundproofing rooms, etc.).

Studying Anomalous Experience

Studies into Psi Often Provoke Controversy

There's a high degree of skepticism about psi among scientists and psychologists.

1 Ganzfeld Studies Have Shown Mixed Results for ESP

1) **Ganzfeld studies** test participants for **extra-sensory perception** (**ESP**).
2) One participant, known as the **receiver**, is in a state of mild sensory deprivation. This is usually done by covering their eyes with halved ping pong balls, playing white noise through headphones and sitting them in a soundproof room lit with red light.
3) A participant in another room, the **sender**, then concentrates on a visual stimulus in an attempt to transfer it to the receiver.
4) The receiver is then shown **four stimuli** — one is the stimulus the sender attempted to transfer by ESP. If the receiver correctly identifies this stimulus it's called a **hit**.
5) The results and interpretation of Ganzfeld experiments vary:

Suddenly the idea of sensory deprivation seemed a lot more appealing...

A review of 28 Ganzfeld studies by **Honorton** (1985) showed a **38% hit rate**, significantly above the 25% rate of chance. He claimed that this provided **evidence for ESP**. **Hyman** (1985) disagreed, **criticising** the studies for a **lack of randomised stimuli**, **inconsistent judging procedures** and **selective reporting**. After consideration, Honorton and Hyman jointly agreed on suitable conditions to address these flaws and **autoganzfeld studies** were designed to take these into account. The results of autoganzfeld studies **still produced significant results**.

A **meta-analysis** by **Milton and Wiseman** (1999) of 30 autoganzfeld studies showed **no significant evidence for ESP**. This analysis was criticised for including studies which **deviated** from the conventional technique. When the ten studies closest to the original technique were analysed by **Bem et al** (2001), a **significant hit rate was found**.

2 Little Evidence Has Been Found for Psychokinetic Ability

1) Some people claim to have **psychokinetic ability**, which allows them to move objects using their mind alone.
2) Many people dispute these claims — they believe that **tricks** are used to make it appear that objects have been altered by psychokinesis. Several **magicians** have demonstrated how this can be done.
3) Belief in psychokinesis is often explained by cognitive biases such as the **illusion of control** (see opposite page).
4) To establish whether psychokinesis is possible researchers have searched for evidence in **laboratory conditions**:

One common method is to ask participants to **alter the outcome** of a computerised **random number generator**. This allows a lot of data to be collected in **controlled conditions**. **Holger et al** (2006) conducted a **meta-analysis** on the results of 380 such studies. They did find an effect but it was extremely small — it was probably only reported because of its **interesting** and **controversial nature**.

Practice Questions

Q1 What is pseudoscience?

Q2 Name two methodological issues which could explain so-called anomalous experiences.

Q3 Summarise the method used in Ganzfeld studies.

Exam Question

Q1 a) Explain the term anomalous experience, using examples. [8 marks]

b) Describe how pseudoscience can influence research into anomalous experiences. [8 marks]

c) Outline and evaluate the evidence for the existence of ESP. [8 marks]

I don't condone cheating — but telepathy would be a mighty useful skill...

This is all getting a bit odd now — what with past life and out-of-body experiences. If you're not too spooked out you need to learn about pseudoscience, fraud and the controversy around Ganzfeld studies. If you are too spooked out you need to learn about pseudoscience, fraud and the controversy around Ganzfeld studies as well. There's no getting away from it.

Explanations for Anomalous Experience

When it comes to the paranormal most people fall into one of two groups — skeptics and believers. Skeptics explain weird and untoward stuff as anything from a hoax to a misunderstanding, whereas believers, well, they believe...

Coincidence Could Explain *Anomalous Experience*

1) A **coincidence** is when events **appear to be linked** (e.g. dreaming about a car crash and then being involved in one) when in fact the two events are unconnected and occurred closely together purely by **chance**.
2) **Marks (2000)** suggests that coincidence can be explained by **subjective validation**.

Subjective validation is a **cognitive bias** (an error of judgement caused by faulty thought processes) that means we are more likely to believe in and pay attention to information that has **personal relevance**. As we concentrate on this personally relevant information (e.g. a dream we had), we don't pay attention to information that **feels less relevant** to us but is actually more relevant (e.g. the fact that a car pulled out in front of us). So we only see evidence that **reinforces** our belief in a **psychic reason** for the coincidence.

Probability Judgements Could Explain *Anomalous Experience*

1) Making a **probability judgement** involves assessing **how likely** it is that something will happen. This is usually **subjective**, so the judgment may differ widely from the actual true statistical probability.
2) According to **Wiseman and Watt (2006)**, **probability misjudgements** mean that we may believe in a psychic reason for something happening rather than the real reason.
3) An example of this would be believing that destiny is at play just because you find out that you have the same birthday as the person you fancy. However, the **statistical likelihood** of them being born on that particular date is the same regardless of whether or not it has personal relevance to you.

Magical Thinking and Superstition Involve Cognitive Bias

1) A **superstition** is a belief that an object or action will affect outcomes when there is **no logical reason** for it to do so. For example, believing that wearing your lucky green underpants will mean you pass your driving test — even though passing this test is down to your driving skill and what you wear is irrelevant.
2) Superstitions are the result of **cognitive biases** such as the **illusion of control** (see page 212).

- **Lorenz (1963)** suggests that superstition is a **response** we have adapted as a way to cope in some situations where we don't know or don't understand the **true causality**. It is better for us psychologically to believe in a false relationship rather than not to know what the relationship is at all.
- **Vyse (2000)** suggests that in some situations (e.g. job interviews, weddings or sports events), even if people have prepared as much as they could have, there are still some aspects which are **out of their control**. This means it's difficult to predict the outcome. Using superstition allows people to **feel more in control** than they actually are.

Karl's flock of ducks worked like a lucky charm — he had yet to be hit whilst crossing the road.

3) Superstitions can be **negative** (e.g. believing that breaking a mirror brings bad luck) or **positive** (e.g. believing that lucky charms bring good luck).
4) Positive superstitions may promote **optimism** and **self-efficacy** (belief in your ability to do something). This increased belief may increase the chances of the person influencing the situation themselves. This is known as the **placebo effect**, and it **reinforces** the initial superstition.
5) However, positive superstitions can still have a **negative effect** if the person is very **dependent** on them. E.g. putting your red underpants on by mistake on the day of a test might cause **anxiety** that impairs performance.
6) **Magical thinking** is believing that if you **think** about something happening, or **say** that it will happen, it's **more likely** to actually happen. For example, you might think that wishing that you will win the lottery will make it more likely that you will win. This shows an **incorrect understanding of causality**. **Cognitive bias** means you **ignore** the actual cause (which is **pure chance**) and believe that your wish manipulates the outcome.

Explanations for Anomalous Experience

Some **Personality Factors** are Related to **Anomalous Experience**

1) **Ramakrishna (2001)** used students as participants in his research and tested them for their **extra-sensory perception** (**ESP**) ability.
2) He reported a **positive correlation** between scores in ESP tests and some personality traits, including being **relaxed**, **assertive**, **sociable** and **talkative**. He found a **negative correlation** between ESP scores and other personality traits, including being **withdrawn**, **suspicious** and **impatient**.
3) Ramakrishna's study is supported by **other research** that has found a similar relationship between personality and anomalous experience. However, we can't assume that certain personality factors make anomalous experience more likely (or vice versa). This research only suggests a relationship and **doesn't show causality** — other variables besides personality could also be involved.

Bob might not have scored highly on the ESP test but he still had a hunch that it was time to move house.

Extroversion Might Be Linked to **ESP**

Evidence for...

- **Honorton et al (1998)** did a **meta-analysis** of **38 studies** testing **ESP** and **extroversion**.
- The experiments included **Ganzfeld studies** that **limit** the choice of possible answers, and tests that allowed **free choice** in the answers. They found that overall extroverts scored more highly than introverts on ESP tests in 77% of the studies.
- Other research also supports the possibility of a **causal relationship** between anomalous experiences and extroversion.

Evidence against...

- When ESP is tested in an **experimental setting** the situation is very **artificial**. Introverts may feel less comfortable and less able to focus on the task. Extroverts are **less likely** to feel uncomfortable and so their performance isn't affected. If this is true then the **anxiety** of taking part in an unfamiliar task could be an **extraneous variable** that affects **introverts** more than extroverts.
- **Haight (1979)** conducted **spontaneous ESP tests** in a social situation so that all participants would feel **relaxed** whatever their personality type. Introverts and extroverts **didn't score differently** on these tests.

Practice Questions

Q1 What is a coincidence? Give an example.
Q2 What is a superstition? Give an example.
Q3 Describe the cognitive bias involved in magical thinking.
Q4 Outline the correlations found by Ramakrishna (2001) between performance in ESP tests and personality traits.
Q5 How many studies did Honorton et al (1998) use in their meta-analysis?

Exam Question

Q1 a) Outline the role of coincidence and probability judgements in anomalous experience. [8 marks]

b) Discuss explanations for superstitious behaviour. [8 marks]

c) Discuss the findings of research investigating personality and anomalous experience. [8 marks]

Magical thinking — an effective revision spell...

If you're a skeptic you're probably scoffing at all this anomalous experience malarkey by now. But chances are you've indulged in some superstitious behaviour in your time — touching wood, not walking under ladders, crossing your fingers — they all fall under paranormal belief. We've all dabbled in it, whether truly skeptical or out there giving the evil eye.

Research into Exceptional Experience

Whether you believe in anomalous experiences or not, the paranormal can't be dismissed as hokum unless it's been researched properly. The big problem with this is that paranormal experiences are really quite hard to study...

There's Been **Research** Into **Psychic Healing...**

Psychic healers claim they can treat illness and injury **without any physical intervention**. Instead, the healer moves their hands over the patient's body without making contact. The aim is to transfer a force and restore **balance** in the patient. Some studies have been done to try to determine whether psychic healing actually works.

Attevelt (1988) — Evidence for the psychic healing of asthma

Method:	In an **independent groups design**, 96 asthma patients were allocated to one of 3 groups — an **optimal group**, a **distance group** and a **control group**. Patients in the optimal group received treatment from a psychic healer in the usual way. The distance group patients were also treated by a healer, but this time from behind a screen. The control group didn't receive any treatment but the screen was present. Distance group and control group patients didn't know which group they belonged to as their physical experiences were the same. **Physical** and **subjective** measures of asthma symptoms were taken.
Results:	The **physical symptoms** of asthma (measured by peak flow) improved significantly in **all patients**. The **optimal group** improved significantly more than the other groups on **subjective measures** of well-being (i.e. they 'felt' an improvement).
Conclusion:	The lack of difference between **physical symptoms** of patients in the different groups shows that improvement was **not down to paranormal effects**. The **subjective improvement** in the optimal group patients but not distance group patients shows the influence of **psychological** rather than paranormal factors.
Evaluation:	Participants were **randomly allocated** to groups after being stratified (see page 220) according to the severity of their asthma. This prevented **bias** in the groups. The people who took the patients' peak flow measurements didn't know which group each patient belonged to. This also prevented **bias**. The use of a **control group** distinguished the psychological effects of visiting a healer from the physiological effects.

...Out-of-Body Experiences...

An **out-of-body experience** (**OBE**) is a sensation of floating **outside the body**, seeing the world from a different perspective. They're **spontaneous** and **rare** events so researching them is difficult. Most evidence is based on **case studies**.

Many people remain skeptical about OBEs and much of the research into them has been heavily criticised.

Tart (1968) — The Case of Miss Z

Method:	This **case study** was based on a young woman (Miss Z) who reported experiencing OBEs in her sleep since childhood. Tart brought her into a sleep lab for 4 nights to **compare** her reports of OBEs with **physiological data** collected from an EEG that monitored her brain activity. Also, numbers were written down and placed where they couldn't be seen from the bed (e.g. lying on top of high shelves). Miss Z was asked to find these target numbers during her OBE, whilst she was physically still in bed.
Results:	Miss Z's OBEs **correlated** with a particular pattern of non-dreaming, non-awake brain waves. On one occasion, she also correctly identified a 5 digit target number.
Conclusion:	OBEs have a **physiological** basis.
Evaluation:	The study had to rely on Miss Z's own reports of when and for how long she had left her body. These reports were **retrospective** and **subjective**. Tart couldn't be sure that Miss Z hadn't found out the target number conventionally, e.g. from seeing its reflection in the nearby clock face. This study isn't accepted as reliable psychological research by the wider scientific community.

Some recent studies have **induced** states similar to OBEs through brain stimulation of participants. This suggests that OBEs could be explained by **physiological mechanisms** causing a kind of 'waking dream'.

Research into Exceptional Experience

...Near-Death-Experiences...

Like OBEs, NDEs are hard to prove and many psychologists question whether they actually occur or not.

There are obviously **ethical issues** involved in creating states of near death for the purposes of studying **near-death-experiences** (**NDEs**). So, like OBEs, most research has to be taken from **case studies**. From an accumulation of 102 case studies, Kenneth Ring (1980) determined that:

1) Individuals reporting NDEs **don't fit** a particular **gender**, **age**, or **religious profile**.
2) There also appears to be **no link** between the reporting of a **NDE** and a person's **attitude** towards the paranormal.
3) Individuals who came close to death or were clinically dead for a period of time report experiences such as moving through a tunnel towards a **light**, **OBEs**, **reuniting** with **dead loved ones** and feeling total **contentment**. These experiences were found even when the moments leading up to near-death were particularly nasty.
4) **Medication** at the time of death **did not predict** the experience of NDE.
5) Reports of NDEs are more **coherent** than reports of hallucinations.
6) Individuals who report experiencing a NDE also report **life-changing shifts of attitudes**, often developing a newly found appreciation of life and loved ones.

...And *Psychic Mediumship*

Psychic mediumship is the ability to **communicate with spirits** and transmit messages from the dead to the living. There are a range of methods with which mediums claim they can communicate with the dead, including **telepathy** and being **possessed by spirits** that then talk through them. Studies of psychic mediumship are usually based on **séances** — intentional attempts to communicate with spirits. One of the most famous studies into psychic mediumship is the **Scole Experiment**.

> The **Scole Experiment** took place in Norfolk between **1993** and **1998**. Researchers including Fontana, Ellison and Keen witnessed 37 séances in rooms that were thoroughly **searched** beforehand to try to **prevent any trickery**. A professional magician was also present to identify any attempts at **fraud**. During the séances a number of paranormal occurrences were reported. These included the **materialisation** of objects, **levitation**, patterns of **light**, **voices** and the appearance of **whole people** or **body parts**.

Some people believe that the Scole Experiment provides **evidence** of life after death and mediumship. No fraud was identified at any time during the experiment and the professional magician present confirmed that **no currently known trickery** could have produced the effects that were observed. However, the experiment has been **heavily criticised** and isn't widely accepted as evidence for mediumship. The **experimental conditions** were unreliable — to some extent they were controlled by the mediums. For example, the researchers wanted to use infra-red imaging (as most of the séances took place in darkness) but this was rejected by the mediums as they claimed it would distract them. Also, all the experimenters believed in the paranormal so may have shown **experimenter effects** (see p.212).

Practice Questions

Q1 Describe the findings of the study by Attevelt (1988).

Q2 Describe the case study of Miss Z.

Q3 Outline some typical features of a near-death-experience.

Exam Question

Q1 a) Outline the difficulties of studying paranormal experiences scientifically. [8 marks]

b) Discuss the effectiveness of psychic healing. [16 marks]

Revision — definitely a near death experience...

And that's the end of the section — yay. Once you've learnt these two pages that is. Then you'd best go back through the whole section to check you still remember all the fascinating stuff you've learnt on the way. Yep, back through the spooky bits, the addictions and the celeb worship, all the way to attitudes and persuasion. What a strange journey you've been on.

Is Psychology a Science?

Whether psychology is a science or not is a real slippery rogue of a topic. Before you can decide, you need to know what science is — and no-one seems to have quite agreed on that either. It's like they're trying to make life difficult...

Science is about Establishing Truths

1) Scientific research should be **objective** — independent of **beliefs** or **opinions**.
2) So, the methods used should be **empirical** — based on **experimental data**, not just theory. The best way to make sure of this is to carry out an experiment that collects **quantitative data** and has strictly **controlled variables**.
3) This means that you should be able to establish **cause** and **effect**.

However, it's **hard** to make an experiment completely **objective**. **Rosenthal and Fode (1963)** showed this in an experiment on psychology undergraduates. They were told to train some **rats** to run a maze, and that some of the rats were **genetically pre-disposed** to be **better** at **learning** than others. Actually there was **no difference** between any of the rats, but the students' **results** showed that the supposedly more **intelligent** rats did **better** in the maze task. This shows how researchers can bring their own **biases** and **expectations** to an experiment.

Scientific Theories Should Have Validity and Reliability

1) All scientific work must undergo **peer review** before it's published — it's sent to **experts** in the field (**peers**) so they can assess its **quality**.
2) Poor research **won't pass** peer review so it won't get published. This helps to **validate conclusions** — it means published theories, data and conclusions are more trustworthy.
3) Other scientists then read the published research, and try to **repeat** it. This tests whether the theory is **reliable**. If it is, then the results should be **replicated** every time the experiment is done — this shows that the findings **aren't affected** by **time** or **place**.
4) If the replica experiments provide evidence to back it up, the theory is thought of as scientific 'fact' (**for now**).
5) If **new evidence** comes to light that **conflicts** with the current evidence the theory is questioned again. More rounds of **testing** will be carried out to see which evidence, and so which theory, **prevails**.

There are Problems With Doing Research on Humans

Psychological research is very **different** to the research in **other sciences** — humans are **complex**, so it's **hard** to find **general laws** for their behaviour.

1) **Sampling** — scientists can't study every occurrence of something, so they need to use samples that represent what they're looking at. This is fine if it's something like carbon or gravity. The problem in psychology is that humans vary a lot, and in different ways — e.g. age, gender, culture or class could all be explanations for a person's behaviour. This makes it really difficult to generalise to the whole population from small samples.
2) **Operationalisation** — operationalising variables means defining them in measurable terms. However, **human behaviour** is often hard to define, so it's questionable whether things like motivation or love can be operationalised accurately. This means that human behaviour is a very **difficult variable to control**.
3) **Procedures** — experiments focus on just a few specific variables, so they're simplistic compared to real life. The lack of **ecological validity** means you might never see genuine behaviour in a controlled experiment.
4) **Participant variables** — people bring their **past learning and experiences** to experiments. They may try to figure out what the experiment's about and change their behaviour — **demand characteristics**. People's behaviour also changes if they know they're being watched — the **Hawthorne Effect**. **Social desirability bias** is when people change their behaviour to make themselves look better, e.g. more generous.
5) **Experimenter effects** — the experimenter can **influence** participants without meaning to, by giving out subtle **clues** about how they should behave. This means you can never know for sure if behaviour is genuine.

Is Psychology a Science?

Some Psychological Approaches are More Scientific than Others

Very scientific ↕ Not very scientific

Biological

Empirical methods are used which get quantitative data, e.g. brain scans. This means results can be replicated and aren't affected by participant variables such as past experience. The theories are falsifiable.

Falsifiable means that they can be proved wrong.

Timmy wondered if giving the tortoise a push would prove that it could run.

Behaviourist

Only looks at observable behaviour, not thought processes or emotions, so the methods are empirical. E.g. animal studies get quantitative data and falsifiable theories. However, participant variables can have an impact on results.

Cognitive

Empirical methods are used, e.g. memory tests, so findings can be replicated and the theories are falsifiable. But, it's hard to isolate the variables because it's hard to separate cognitive processes. Also, participant variables can affect results.

Social

Some experimental methods are used which get quantitative data, e.g. Milgram's (1963) study. Other methods are based on observation and get qualitative data, e.g. studies that look at prejudice. This means the variables can be difficult to operationalise and control.

Psychodynamic

Psychodynamic theories are based on abstract concepts that can't be tested, e.g. the unconscious mind. This means they're non-falsifiable. The non-experimental research methods (e.g. dream analysis) produce qualitative data and are unreliable, so the findings can't be replicated or generalised.

Practice Questions

Q1 Describe the role of peer review in validating new knowledge.

Q2 Give three problems with doing research on humans.

Q3 Describe one psychological approach that can be said to be scientific.

Exam Question

Q1 Discuss the extent to which psychology is a science. [24 marks]

Is psychology a science — it's a bit late in the book to bring this up...

So, you might have to answer the question of whether psychology is a science or not. Trouble is, the answer isn't a simple 'yes' or 'no'. Instead, you'd have to give a selection of arguments for and against, demonstrating how carefully you've revised this topic and how clever you are. So unless you've a particular desire to look like a plonker — I'd learn these pages.

Designing Psychological Investigations

Before you can study something, you need to design your investigation. In order to do this you need to have a clear idea about exactly what information you need to collect, and what the most appropriate method for this might be.

*Research Takes **Samples** From a **Target Population***

It's really important that the sample is **representative** of the population. It should include the **variety of characteristics** that are found in the group, e.g. the group '**student**' includes both **males** and **females**. If the sample is **biased** in any way, it's hard to **generalise** any findings to the whole population.

There are many different ways to select a sample:

1) **Random sample** Everyone in the target group has an **equal chance** of being selected. Although this is **fair** and will probably provide a **good variety** of people, it doesn't guarantee that the sample will be **representative** — some subgroups could be **missed**.
2) **Systematic sample** Taking every *n*th name from a **sampling frame** (a record of all the names in a population), e.g. every 3rd name from a register, or every 50th name from a phone book. This is useful if there is a sampling frame available, but it isn't **truly random** or **representative**, and subgroups may be missed.
3) **Opportunity sample** Studying **whoever is available** at the time, e.g. students. This is **quick**, **easy** and **cheap**, but it's very unlikely that the sample will be **representative**.
4) **Self-selected sample** Participants **volunteer**, e.g. by responding to a newspaper advertisement. This can **save time** and there may be many replies, producing a **large sample**. However, it's unlikely to be representative as only certain types of people are likely to volunteer.
5) **Stratified sample** All of the **important subgroups** in the population (e.g. different age or ethnic groups) are identified and a **proportionate number** are **randomly obtained**. This can produce a fairly representative sample, but it takes a lot of **time/money** to do and subgroups may be **missed**.

Here's a reminder of some of the different **research methods** used for psychological studies, and their advantages and drawbacks. Most of this should be familiar to you from AS, but you can never have too much information...

***Questionnaires** — Face-to-Face, on the Phone, or via the Internet*

Questionnaires are a **self-report** method.
Self-report methods involve asking participants about their feelings, beliefs and attitudes, etc.

Advantages **Practical** — can collect a large amount of information quickly and relatively cheaply.

Disadvantages

Bad questions — leading questions (questions that suggest a desired answer) or unclear questions can be a problem.
Biased samples — some people are more likely to respond to a questionnaire, which might make a sample unrepresentative.
Social desirability bias — people sometimes want to present themselves in a good light.
What they say and what they actually think could be different, making any results unreliable.
Ethics — confidentiality can be a problem, especially around sensitive issues which people might not want to discuss.

Other self-report methods include **interviews** and **case studies** (see page 232).
Self-report methods often provide **qualitative data**.

***Correlational Research** Looks for **Relationships** Between Variables*

Correlation means that two variables appear to be **connected** — they rise and fall together, or one rises as the other falls.

BUT it **doesn't** always mean that one variable **causes** a change in the other, e.g. as age increases so might stress, but ageing doesn't necessarily **cause** stress.

Advantages

Causal relationships — these can be ruled out if no correlation exists.
Ethics — can study variables that would be unethical to manipulate, e.g. is there a relationship between the number of cigarettes smoked and incidences of ill health?

Disadvantages

Causal relationships — these cannot be assumed from a correlation, which may be caused by a third, unknown variable. Sometimes the media (and researchers) infer causality from a correlation.

Designing Psychological Investigations

Experiments can be done in a laboratory or in the natural environment.

Laboratory Experiments are Controlled and Scientific

1) The aim is to **control** all relevant variables except for **one key variable**, which is altered to see what its effect is. The variable that you alter is called the **independent variable**.
2) Laboratory experiments are conducted in an **artificial setting**.

Advantages

Control — the effects of extraneous variables (those that have an effect in addition to the key variable) are minimised.
Replication — you can run the study again to check the findings.
Causal relationships — it should be possible to establish whether one variable actually causes change in another.

Disadvantages

Ecological validity — experiments are artificial and might not measure real-life behaviour.
Demand characteristics — participants' behaviour changes when they know they're being studied. They may respond according to what they think is being investigated, which can bias the results.
Ethics — deception is often used, making informed consent (see p.224) difficult.

*Field Experiments are Conducted **Outside** the Laboratory*

In **field experiments**, behaviour is measured in a **natural environment** — like a school, the street or on a train. A **key variable** is still altered so that its effect can be measured.

Advantages

Causal relationships — you can still establish causal relationships by manipulating the key variable and measuring its effect. However it's very difficult to control all the variables in a field experiment.
Ecological validity — field experiments are less artificial than those done in a laboratory, so they reflect real life better.
Demand characteristics — these can be avoided if participants don't know they're in a study. They will behave as they usually do in real life.

Disadvantages

Less control — extraneous variables are often much more likely in a natural environment.
Ethics — often can't give informed consent and can't be debriefed. Observation must respect privacy.

*Natural Experiments Measure but **Don't Control** Variables*

A **natural experiment** is a study where the independent variables **aren't** directly manipulated by the experimenter. In other words, things are left as they naturally would be.

Advantages

Ethics — it's possible to study variables that it would be unethical to manipulate, e.g. you can compare a community that has TV with a community that doesn't to see which is more aggressive.

Disadvantages

Participant allocation — you can't randomly allocate participants to each condition, and so extraneous variables (e.g. what area the participants live in) may affect results. Let's face it — you've got no control over the variables so it's ridiculously hard to say what's caused by what.
Rare events — some groups of interest are hard to find, e.g. a community that doesn't have TV.
Ethics — deception is often used, making informed consent difficult. Also, confidentiality may be compromised if the community is identifiable.

Practice Questions

Q1 Why might you get an unrepresentative sample when carrying out questionnaire-based research?

Q2 Describe a disadvantage of correlational research.

Q3 What are the main advantages of laboratory experiments?

Exam Questions

Q1 Outline three methods that could be used to selected a sample. [6 marks]

Q2 Outline the advantages that field experiments have over laboratory experiments. [4 marks]

Designing Psychological Investigations

All research studies involve testing or measuring participants. If you want the results to be meaningful, the tests need to be reliable and valid. And if you want to pass your exam you need to know what reliability and validity mean.

Reliable *Tests Give* ***Consistent Results***

Reliability refers to how **consistent** or **dependable** a test is. A reliable test carried out in the **same circumstances**, on the **same participants** should always give the **same results**. There are different types of reliability:

Internal reliability — different parts of the test should give **consistent results**. For example, if an IQ test contains sections of supposedly equal difficulty, participants should achieve similar scores on all sections.

The internal reliability of a test can be assessed using the **split-half method**. This splits the test into two halves, e.g. odd and even numbered questions, and the results from each half should produce a **high positive correlation**.

External reliability — the test should produce **consistent results** regardless of **when** it's used. For example, if you took the same IQ test on two different days you should achieve the same score.

The external reliability of a test can be assessed using the **test-retest method**. This involves **repeating** the test using the **same participants**. A reliable test should produce a **high positive correlation** between the two scores. A problem with this is that the participants may have changed in some way since the first test, e.g. they may have learnt more. To avoid this, external reliability can be checked using the **equivalent forms test**. This compares participants' scores on two different, but equivalent (equally hard), versions of the test.

Inter-rater reliability — the test should give **consistent results** regardless of **who** administers it. For example, if two researchers give the same person the same IQ test they should both record the same score.

This can be assessed by **correlating** the scores that **each researcher** produces for **each participant**. A **high positive correlation** should be found.

Valid *Tests Give* ***Accurate Results***

Validity refers to how well a test measures what it **claims to**. For example, an IQ test with only **maths questions** would not be a valid measure of **general intelligence**. There are different types of validity:

1) **Internal validity** — the extent to which the results of the test are caused by the variable being measured, rather than extraneous variables.
2) **External validity** — the extent to which the results of the test can be generalised, e.g. to a larger population.
3) **Ecological validity** — the extent to which the results of the test reflect real-life.

Validity can be **assessed** in different ways:

- A quick (but not very thorough) way of assessing validity is to simply **look** at the test and make a judgement on whether it **appears** to measure what it claims to. For example, an IQ test that just consisted of maths questions could be identified as having low validity by this method.
- **Comparing** the results of the test with the results of an **existing measure** (that's already accepted as valid) can help to determine the validity of the test.
- The results of the test can be used to **predict** results of **future tests**. If the **initial** results **correlate** with the **later** results it suggests that the test has some validity and can continue to be used.

Designing Psychological Investigations

Reliability and Validity Can Both be Improved

There are several ways that the **reliability** and **validity** of tests can be **improved**:

Standardising research

Standardising research involves creating **specific procedures** which are followed every time the test is carried out. This ensures that all the researchers will test all the participants in **exactly the same way**, e.g. in the same sequence, at the same time of day, in the same environment, with all participants receiving exactly the same instructions. This reduces the possibility of extraneous variables affecting the research. Therefore it will help to improve **internal validity, external reliability** and **inter-rater reliability**.

Mark had spent all morning standardising the procedure and was feeling pretty smug about the end result.

Operationalising variables

1) **Operationalising variables** involves **clearly defining** all of the research **variables**.
2) For example, in a study of whether watching aggressive TV influences aggressive behaviour, the terms '**aggressive TV**' and '**aggressive behaviour**' need to be defined.
3) 'Aggressive TV' could include cartoons or human actors. One of these might influence human behaviour and the other might not — this needs to be taken into account when planning, carrying out and drawing conclusions from the investigation.
4) Similarly, 'aggressive behaviour' could refer to physical and verbal aggression, or just physical aggression.
5) Clarifying this from the start improves the **reliability** and **internal validity** of the test.

Pilot studies

Pilot studies are small scale **trial runs** of the test. They're used to check for any problems before the test is carried out for real. They also give researchers practice at following the procedures. Pilot studies allow the **validity** and **reliability** of the test to be **assessed in advance**, which then gives the opportunity for **improvements** to be made.

Practice Questions

Q1 Explain the difference between internal reliability and external reliability.

Q2 How does the split-half method test for internal reliability?

Q3 Why does standardisation help to improve the reliability and validity of research?

Q4 What is a pilot study?

Exam Questions

Q1 Describe how validity could be assessed in any two pieces of psychological research that you've studied. [6 marks]

Q2 Describe how reliability could be improved in any two pieces of psychological research that you've studied. [6 marks]

Reliable tests? Who cares. Reliable results are what you need right now.

So, it turns out that 'reliable' and 'valid' are more than just terms to bandy around and throw into answers with some sort of vague idea that they're good things for studies to be. They've got specific meanings and you need to know them. These examiner types are so demanding — it's like they've got nothing better to do than sit around thinking up stuff for you to learn.

Ethics

Remember Milgram's obedience research from AS? The one that made participants think they were giving lethal electric shocks to others. It was a bit... "unethical", some might say. If you're not sure what that means, worry not, just read on...

Ethics are an Important Issue in Psychology

1) Psychological research and practice should aim to improve our **self-understanding**, be **beneficial** to people and try to **improve the quality of life** for individuals.
2) As professionals, psychologists are expected to do their work in an **ethical manner**.
3) **Ethical guidelines** are **formal principles** for what is considered to be acceptable or unacceptable.
4) In the UK these are produced by the **British Psychological Society (BPS)**. However, questions are raised about whether the guidelines are **adequate** and **appropriately applied**.

Ethical Guidelines Must Be Followed During Research

Informed Consent

- BPS guidelines state that participants should always give **informed consent**.
- They should be told the aims and nature of the study before agreeing to it.
- They should also know that they have the **right to withdraw** at any time.

1) **BUT** if the participant is under 16 years of age they **can't give consent** (although a parent can).
2) In **naturalistic observation** studies, consent is not obtained. In this case the research is acceptable provided that it is done in a **public location** where people would expect to be observed by others.
3) Even when informed consent is supposedly obtained, issues may be raised. **Menges (1973)** reviewed about 1000 American studies and found that **97%** had not given people all the information about the research.

Deception

- If participants have been deceived then they cannot have given **informed consent**.
- However, sometimes researchers must **withhold information** about the study because the participants wouldn't behave **naturally** if they knew what the aim was.

1) The BPS guidelines state that deception is only acceptable if there is strong **scientific justification** for the research and there's **no alternative procedure** available to obtain the data.
2) Researchers can also ask **independent people** if they would object to the study. If they wouldn't, then the study may be done with naïve participants (although the naïve participants **may not agree** with others' opinions).
3) Participants could just be given **general** details — although if too little is said they may feel **deceived**, but if participants know too much then they may not behave naturally.
4) The **severity** of deception differs, e.g. research on memory may involve **unexpected** memory tests (that participants weren't informed about). This is **less objectionable** than the deception involved in Milgram's study.

Protection from harm

- The BPS guidelines say that the risk of harm to participants should be **no greater** than they would face in their normal lives. It's hard to **accurately assess** this.

1) Research procedures can involve physical and psychological discomfort, e.g. **Glass and Singer (1972)** exposed participants to noise to make them stressed, and participants in **Milgram's** research suffered extreme distress.
2) Some people face **risks** in their work (e.g. soldiers) but that doesn't mean they can be exposed to risks in research.
3) Researchers don't always **know in advance** what might be distressing for participants.

Debriefing

- Debriefing is supposed to return participants to the state they were in **before the research**.
- It's especially important if **deception** has been used.

1) Researchers must fully explain what the research involved and what the results might show.
2) Participants are given the **right to withdraw their data**.

Ethics

5 Confidentiality

- None of the participants in a psychological study should be **identifiable** from any reports that are produced.

1) Data collected during research must be **confidential** — researchers can't use people's **names** in reports.
2) Participants must be **warned** if their data is not going to be completely anonymous.
3) However, some groups or people might be **easily identifiable** from their **characteristics** — more so if the report says where and when the study was carried out, etc.

*Some Research Raises **Sensitive Social Issues***

1) Findings from psychological research may highlight **social issues** and create negative effects or reactions in society.
2) Socially sensitive research can be defined as research that may have implications for the individuals in the research, or for groups in society — e.g. the participants' families, or particular cultural groups.

e.g. Research into **genetics** raises many issues:

1) Research into whether there are genetic influences on **criminal behaviour** raises important questions, e.g. whether genetics could be used as a **defence** against being convicted for a crime.
2) Also, there's the possibility of **compulsory genetic testing** to identify people with a particular gene.
3) Such **screening** could also identify genes linked to psychological disorders such as **schizophrenia**.
4) Although this may potentially help people it could also lead to **anxiety** and **social stigma**, especially as people may have a **genetic vulnerability** for a disorder but not actually **develop it**.

e.g. Using a factor like **race** as an **independent variable** is a very sensitive issue:

1) Some studies using **IQ tests** have shown possible **racial differences** in **intelligence**.
2) The issue is whether this is an **appropriate topic** for research because of **social tensions** that the results and conclusions may produce.
3) Such research is often **discredited** because of **methodological problems** with the IQ tests that were used. For example, they may have been **biased** towards some social-cultural groups — this shows that we need to be careful about the **conclusions** that we draw from research methods.

Practice Questions

Q1 What are 'ethical guidelines' and why are they needed in psychology?

Q2 Why is it sometimes impossible to obtain informed consent from participants?

Q3 When is it permissible to deceive participants?

Q4 What is the purpose of debriefing?

Exam Question

Q1 a) Outline three BPS guidelines for psychological research with human participants. [8 marks]

b) Discuss why ethical guidelines are important in psychological research with humans. [16 marks]

It's the debriefing part that bothers me — I'd rather stay clothed, thanks...

There's absolutely no getting around it — ethics and psychological research are inextricably linked. So you really can't blame those pesky examiners for making you learn about it. Well, you probably could, but it would be a bit harsh. Anyway — learn it, then if anyone tries any nasty research on you at least you know your rights. Knowledge is power, my friend.

Probability and Significance

Inferential statistics let you make an 'inference' (or educated guess) about whether your results show something significant, or if they're due to chance. "Marvellous", I hear you cry. "Just what I've always wanted to learn about..."

Inferential Statistics** are about Ruling Out **Chance

1) You can never be 100% certain that results aren't all down to chance. So instead of 'proving' a hypothesis, you have to be content with finding out whether it's **likely** to be true. This is called **statistical significance**.
2) If your results are statistically significant, it means that you can **read something into them** — they're unlikely to be just down to chance.
3) If your results are **not statistically significant**, it means they could have happened by chance rather than being the effect of changes in your independent variable, so you can't really read anything into them.

*Use **Statistical Tests** to Find Out if Your Results **Mean** Anything*

OK, it's not easy, this bit — so stop texting people and concentrate...

1
- The first thing you do is write out your **null hypothesis** — this is the theory you want to **test**.
- In a statistical test, you assume your null hypothesis is **true** (for the time being, at least).
- (So a null hypothesis might be *"rats that eat poison and rats that eat sugar pellets are equally likely to be ill"*.)

2
- Next you choose a **significance level** — this is a **'level of proof'** that you're looking for before you read anything into your results.
- The smaller the significance level, the stronger the evidence you're looking for that your results aren't just down to chance.
- A significance level is a **probability**, and so is a number between 0 and 1.
- (Probabilities near 1 mean things are very **likely**, and probabilities near 0 mean things are very **unlikely**.)
- Significance levels are always **very small** — usually 0.05 (5%) or less. (Because a significance level is very **small**, events with probabilities smaller than the significance level are very **unlikely** to happen.)

I didn't inhale, honest.

3
- You then turn all your experimental results into a single **test statistic** (p.228-231).
- Then you can find out how likely this test statistic is (and so how likely your results are), **assuming the null hypothesis is true.**

4
- If the probability of getting your results (assuming the null hypothesis is true) is **less than the significance level**, then they must be **really unlikely** — and so it's pretty safe to say that your null hypothesis **wasn't true** after all.
- This is what stats-folk mean when they talk about 'rejecting the null hypothesis'. (If you reject your null hypothesis, you assume your **alternative hypothesis** is true instead.)

5
- If you reject your null hypothesis, you can proudly shout out that your results are **statistically significant**.
- (So rejecting the null hypothesis above would mean that *"rats that eat poison and rats that eat sugar pellets are not equally likely to be ill"*.)

6
- If you **don't reject** the null hypothesis, it means that your results could have occurred **by chance**, rather than because your null hypothesis was wrong.
- If this happens, you've proved **nothing** — not rejecting the null hypothesis doesn't mean it **must be true**.

7
- Using a significance level of **0.05** (5%) is okay for most tests.
- If the probability of your results is **less** than this ($p \leq 0.05$), then it's **pretty good evidence** that the null hypothesis **wasn't true** after all.
- If you use a significance level of **0.01** (1%), then you're looking for **really strong evidence** that the null hypothesis is untrue before you're going to reject it.

Probability and Significance

There are Two Types of *Potential Error*

It's possible to make errors when you're deciding whether or not to reject the null hypothesis.

A **Type 1 error** is when you **reject** the null hypothesis when it was **actually true.**
The significance level gives you the **probability** of this happening.
This is why significance levels are **small**.

A very small significance level (e.g. 0.01 or 1%) is used when you need to be very confident in your results, like when testing new theories.

A **Type 2 error** is when you **don't reject** the null hypothesis when it was **actually false.**
This can happen if your significance level is **too small** (e.g. if you want very strong evidence of the need to reject a null hypothesis and so use a 0.01 significance level).

Choosing significance levels is a **compromise** — if the level you choose is **too big** you risk making a Type 1 error.
If the significance level you choose is **too small**, you could make a Type 2 error.

There are *Various Ways* to *Test Significance*

1) Remember that you can never be 100% sure that a hypothesis is correct — it's always possible that results are just due to **chance**.
2) Significance levels are assigned to establish the **probability** of the result being due to chance, and if this is acceptably low (e.g. 5%), then you can reject the **null hypothesis**.
3) **Inferential statistical tests** help to decide whether to accept or reject the null hypothesis. However, there are many **different tests** and it is crucial that you use the **correct one** for your data. We'll get to the specific tests over the next few pages.
4) You use inferential tests to calculate what's called an **observed value** (the value you get when you carry out the test on your results). The observed value is then **compared** against a **critical value**, which is provided for each test in a **critical value table**. This indicates whether or not the results are significant.
5) In some tests, if the observed value is **more than** the critical value, the results are considered to **be significant**. In others, the observed value must be **equal to or less than** the critical value to **show significance**.

Her date's significant lack of arms, legs and head was no matter to Julie, who just needed someone to lean on.

Practice Questions

Q1 What does it mean if the results of an experiment or study are not statistically significant?
Q2 What two significance levels are commonly used in statistical tests?
Q3 Name the two types of error that can be made.

Exam Questions

Q1 Outline what is meant by $p \leq 0.05$. [2 marks]

Q2 Outline the two types of errors that can be made when deciding whether to reject the null hypothesis. [4 marks]

Q3 Describe the role of a critical value table in interpreting the results of an investigation. [2 marks]

There's a high probability that you'll be able to infer this stuff is important...

So, got all that? If not, have a read back over the pages again until it sinks in. In a very small nutshell, you can't ever rule out the fact that your results are down to chance, but you can ensure that the likelihood of that is as small as possible. And, joy of joys, there are some lovely statistical tests over the page to show you how it's done. I know, I know, I'm spoiling you.

Inferential Statistics

If the thought of maths in general, and statistics in particular, makes you want to run for the hills, then take a ticket and get in line. Unfortunately the hills aren't an option, but really, the stats bit isn't so bad if you stick with it. Honest.

Several Things *Determine Which* ***Inferential Test*** *Should be Used*

Inferential statistics allow you to make an educated guess about whether or not a hypothesis is correct. Deciding which inferential test you use for your data is determined by the following factors:

Research Design

Research may have either **related measures** (if a repeated measures or matched participants design was used), or **unrelated measures** (if an independent measures design was used).

Research Aims

Some inferential statistics test whether there is a **significant difference** between two (or more) groups of scores:

- For example, 'did the participants in group A have significantly higher average scores than those in group B?'.
- This is what happens in an **experiment**. The IV is manipulated to see if it produces **changes** in the DV that are significantly different from the **control condition** (or other experimental conditions).
- Some inferential statistics test to see if there is a **significant association** between two (or more) variables:
- For example, whether they occur together more than would be expected by chance.
- This is what we look for in **correlation studies** — to see if two variables are positively or negatively associated, more than would be expected by chance factors alone. If they are, a **significant** correlation has been shown.

Level of measurement / type of data

The results of a study can be collected in different ways, which affect how they can be analysed.

- **Nominal data** — This is the most basic level of measurement — a **frequency count** for completely **distinct categories**. For example, in a study where a confederate pretends to need help, you could assign each passer-by to either an 'altruistic' category (if they helped) or a 'non-altruistic' category (if they did nothing).
- **Ordinal data** — All of the measurements relate to the **same variable**, and measurements can be placed in ascending or descending **rank order**, e.g. on a **rating scale** for aggression where 1 = 'not aggressive' and 10 = 'extremely aggressive'. But you can't say a person with a score of 10 is twice as aggressive as a person with a score of 5, just which one was **more** or **less** aggressive.
- **Interval data** — Measurements are taken on a scale where **each unit is the same size**, e.g. length in centimetres. Interval data places participants in rank order **according to the differences** between them, e.g. in a race, participant 'F' was quickest, in 15.8 seconds and participant 'B' was second, in 16.5 seconds. Technically, an **absolute zero point** is needed to make judgements about whether one score is twice that of another. When we have this (e.g. 0 seconds, 0 centimetres, etc.) then we call it a **ratio scale**.

Spearman's Rho is a ***Correlation Coefficient***

To work out (and then test the significance of) **Spearman's rho** correlation coefficient, you need values for two different variables (e.g. hours of revision and average test scores for 10 students).

a) The values for each variable are placed into **rank order** (each variable is ranked separately). The lowest value for each variable gets rank 1 (and in the above example, the biggest value will get rank 10).

b) The **difference** (**d**) in ranks for each student's variables is calculated. (So a particular student may have done the most revision, but got the 3rd best results, in which case the difference in ranks will be d = 3 – 1 = 2.)

c) The value of d for each student is **squared**, then the results are added together (to get $\sum d^2$).

d) Then the special **Spearman's correlation coefficient** calculation is done, which is $r_s = 1 - \frac{6 \times \sum d^2}{N \times (N^2 - 1)}$

(where N is the number of students, or whatever).

e) To find out whether the result is **significant** (and so whether the variables are linked), you compare the outcome of that nightmarish calculation with a **critical value** that you look up in a **statistics table**.

Inferential Statistics

The **Wilcoxon Signed Ranks** Test — A Test of Difference for **Related** Data

The Wilcoxon Signed Ranks test is used when a hypothesis states that there'll be a difference between two sets of data, when the data is ordinal, and when the experiment is a repeated measures or matched pairs design.

Example: A group does a memory test with two methods of memorising, in a **repeated measures** design:

	Participant no.	1	2	3	4	5	6	7	8
No. words recalled	Method 1	6	5	10	6	8	5	9	8
	Method 2	7	7	8	8	7	6	9	9

1) The **difference** between each participant's two scores is calculated:

Participant no.	1	2	3	4	5	6	7	8
Difference	1	2	2	2	1	1	0	1
Sign (+/-)	-	-	+	-	+	-		-

Always subtract in the same direction, noting if the result is a positive or negative value. Any differences of zero are removed from the results.

2) The differences are given a **rank** to show their **order** — the lowest gets rank one. Ignore +/- signs.

Difference	1	2	2	2	1	1	0	1
Rank	2.5	6	6	6	2.5	2.5		2.5
Sign (+/-)	-	-	+	-	+	-		-

When there are a few of the same number, calculate their mean rank. e.g. Here, there are four 1s, which should be rank 1, 2, 3 and 4, so they all get the mean rank 2.5.

3) **Total** the **ranks** for the positive differences and for the negative differences. The smallest is the **observed value of 'T'**.

Total negative differences = 2.5 + 6 + 6 + 2.5 + 2.5 = **19.5**
Total positive differences = 6 + 2.5 = **8.5**
So, the **observed value of T = 8.5**.

4) The observed value must be **less than or equal to** the **critical value** to be significant.

- Critical values for each number of participants can be found in a **special table** that you'll be given.
- The number of participants is the actual number of people **taking part** in the trial, so 8 in this case.

Sarah wanted to work out the observed value but had totally forgotten which bottle was which.

Practice Questions

Q1 Why do differences in research aims determine which inferential test to use?

Q2 Name the three different types of data.

Q3 What do you need to be able to work out Spearman's Rho?

Exam Questions

Q1 Discuss the factors that need to be considered when deciding which statistical test should be used. [12 marks]

Q2 Outline when the Wilcoxon Signed Ranks test would be appropriate. [2 marks]

I guess stats why they call it the blues...

Actually, that's a bit unfair. I'm sorry. All this stats stuff is dead useful — a good understanding of research methods and how they can affect your results is really important for this course as a whole. And even better than that, there's only a few more pages to go to the end of the section, after which point you can have a lie down until you recover. See, it's not so bad.

Inferential Statistics

Just two more inferential tests to learn on these pages and then you can move on, I promise. To make it a bit easier, there's a worked example for each. Breathe in, breathe out, breathe in, breathe out, rank, significance, data, easy.

The **Mann-Whitney U Test** is Used with **Ordinal Data**

The **Mann-Whitney U Test** is a test of difference (or of similarity) for **unrelated data**.
It focuses on **ranks** and is used when you have **ordinal** data.
Take a look at the following example:

> Two groups took part in a study investigating whether drinking a **vitamin drink** once a day for 4 weeks improved performance on a **verbal memory** test compared to a group who had not had any vitamin drinks.

Number of words recalled								
	Vitamin group	19	13	9	12	21	15	14
	No vitamin group	7	5	10	8	6	11	18

Firstly, the Data Needs to be **Ranked**

The data is ranked regardless of the group each score is in. Start with the **lowest score** (in the example it's 5) and give it a rank of '**1**'. Then the next lowest score gets a rank of '2' and so on.

Number of words recalled								
	Vitamin group (A) (rank)	19 (13)	13 (9)	9 (5)	12 (8)	21 (14)	15 (11)	14 (10)
	No vitamin group (B) (rank)	7 (3)	5 (1)	10 (6)	8 (4)	6 (2)	11 (7)	18 (12)

If some of the data values are the **same** then you have to use an **average** rank. E.g. if the 3rd and 4th values are the same then you'll use 3.5.

The **Ranks** for **Each Group** are then **Added Up**

Look at the **ranks** associated with the vitamin group's scores and **add** them up.
Then do exactly the same for the no vitamin group.

- Sum of ranks in **vitamin group** (R_A) = 13 + 9 + 5 + 8 + 14 + 11 + 10 = 70
- Sum of ranks in **no vitamin group** (R_B) = 3 + 1 + 6 + 4 + 2 + 7 + 12 = 35

When you think about it, if the vitamin group really did show **better** verbal recall then their scores will be **higher** than the no vitamin group. This means that the **ranks** of the scores in the vitamin group will also be **higher**.
The Mann-Whitney U test then uses the following scary-looking formulas:

$$U_A = N_A N_B + \frac{N_A(N_A + 1)}{2} - R_A$$

$$U_A = (7 \times 7) + \frac{7(7 + 1)}{2} - 70$$

$U_A = \mathbf{7}$

$$U_B = N_A N_B + \frac{N_B(N_B + 1)}{2} - R_B$$

$$U_B = (7 \times 7) + \frac{7(7 + 1)}{2} - 35$$

$U_B = \mathbf{42}$

N_A is the number of people in group A
N_B is the number of people in group B
R_A is the sum of the ranks for scores in group A
R_B is the sum of the ranks for scores in group B

You need to select the **smaller** of these, 7, and call it '**U**'.
The observed U must be **less than or equal to** the **critical value** to be **significant**.
Critical values can be found in a table that you'll be given in the exam. In this case, the critical value is **6**, so there's **no significant difference** between the two groups.

Inferential Statistics

The **Chi-square Test** is Used with **Nominal Data** and **Independent Samples**

There's no better way of explaining this than showing you an example. So, hey presto...

> A student is interested in seeing whether finding reality TV programmes **entertaining** is related to being either **male** or **female**. His results are shown in the table below.

The **chi-square test** tests the **null hypothesis**. In this example, the null hypothesis would be that there's **no association** between finding reality TV entertaining and being male or female — this is shown by the **expected frequencies**. Under the null hypothesis, the expected frequencies show that **equal amounts** of men and women find reality TV entertaining, and equal amounts do not.

	Men	Women	Totals
Finds reality TV entertaining	19	35	54
(expected frequency)	(27)	(27)	
Does not find reality TV entertaining	41	25	66
(expected frequency)	(33)	(33)	
Totals	60	60	120

The expected frequencies are worked out using the following formula:

$$E = \frac{\text{row total} \times \text{column total}}{\text{overall total}}$$

John was stunned that the "chai test" involved more than just "add boiling water and brew for 4 minutes".

You Then Just Have to Put the Numbers into a **Formula**

The chi-square (χ^2) is calculated using yet another scary-looking equation:

$$\chi^2 = \Sigma \frac{(O - E)^2}{E}$$

O is the observed frequency
E is the expected frequency

So, for each pair of observed and expected frequencies, take the expected score away from the observed score, square this and then divide by the expected score. Do this for all the observed and expected pairs — then add up all your answers (that's what the Σ means).

If you work through this example, χ^2 turns out to be **8.62**.
You can then use a critical value table to see if this is significant (it is, so the null hypothesis is **false**).

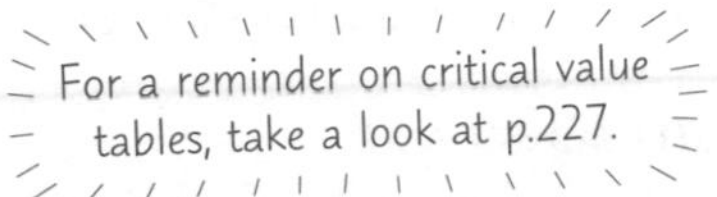
For a reminder on critical value tables, take a look at p.227.

Practice Questions

Q1 What type of data is a Mann-Whitney U test used on?

Q2 When would a researcher use a chi-square test?

Q3 How do you calculate an expected frequency?

Exam Question

Q1 Ian is interested in whether there is an association between being an only child and having a pet. Suggest a null hypothesis and a suitable inferential test for this study. [4 marks]

Just to throw another spanner in the works, you say "kai", not "chi"...

...but this isn't an inferential statistical test speaking exam (and thank goodness for that, by the way), so that's useless info. What will help, though, is knowing what each statistical test is used for. So, the Mann-Whitney U test is for ordinal data and the chi-square test is for nominal data. Mann-Whitney, ordinal, chi-square, nominal. Breathe in, breathe out, easy.

Analysis of Qualitative Data

Qualitative data is data that involves anything other than numbers. It could be words, sounds or pictures, for example.

Observational Methods *Can Provide Qualitative Data*

1. NATURALISTIC OBSERVATION Participants are observed in their **natural environment**, normally without their knowledge.

Several design issues are involved:

1) **Sampling of Behaviour**. Researchers may use **event sampling**, where they only observe and record the particular events of interest. **Time-interval** sampling is used if the observation is over a long period of time.
2) **Recording Behaviour**. Researchers may make notes, or complete pre-made forms to record how often something happens. A problem with this method is that researchers may **miss** some behaviours or **disagree** over behaviours, so video or audio recordings may be made.
3) **Rating Behaviour**. Behaviours need to be described and placed into **categories**, e.g. solitary play, cooperative play, etc. Researchers can do a **frequency count** of how many times each behaviour is observed.

ADVANTAGES / DISADVANTAGES

a) The observation is in the participants' natural environment so there is **ecological validity**.
b) Participants don't know they're being observed so should behave naturally and not show **demand characteristics**.
c) There is **no control** over any of the variables so **cause and effect relationships** cannot be established.
d) Observers may be biased in how they interpret behaviours. So, it's important to establish **inter-observer reliability** by comparing two or more observers' recordings to ensure that they're similar.
e) For **ethical reasons** naturalistic observations can only be done where people would **expect to be observed**.

2. PARTICIPANT OBSERVATION An observer **joins the group** they are studying. They may be known to the group or hidden.

ADVANTAGES/DISADVANTAGES

a) Insights about groups may be found that other methods couldn't show, but it can be more difficult to record data.
b) However, 'hidden' observation raises **ethical issues**.
c) If the researcher is known to the group then they won't **behave naturally**.
d) Equally the researcher may get emotionally **attached** to the group, and become **biased**.

3. INTERVIEWS The structure of an interview can vary.

1) **Fully structured** — a set sequence of questions with **closed answers**, i.e. multiple-choice (this is quantitative).
2) **Informal/Unstructured** interviews — the interviewer asks questions with no set structure and answers are **open**, i.e. the person being interviewed can respond in any way.

ADVANTAGES/DISADVANTAGES

a) Fully structured interviews are **quick** and **easily analysed**, but the structure **limits** how the interviewee responds.
b) Unstructured interviews can provide lots of **detailed**, **insightful** qualitative data, but this is **hard to analyse**.
c) To **compromise**, both open and closed questions can be used.
d) Researchers must make sure that questions are not **ambiguous**, **double-barrelled** (combining more than one issue in a single question) or **leading**.

4. CASE STUDIES These involve the **detailed study** of an individual, or small group using many different methods*.

ADVANTAGES/DISADVANTAGES

a) Lots of **data** may be obtained, providing detail that other methods can't give.
b) This may give insight into unique cases and **unusual situations** which may help to develop theories, e.g. case studies on children who were **socially privated** have shown its **effects on their development**.
c) Researchers have very **little control** over variables in the study and can mistakenly identify **causal relationships**.
d) Results can't be **generalised** to the rest of the population.

*E.g. interviews (structured and/or unstructured), observations, psychometric tests (e.g. intelligence tests), experiments, etc.

Analysis of Qualitative Data

*It's Difficult to **Objectively Analyse** Qualitative Data*

1) Once **quantitative data** is collected it can be **easily** and **objectively** analysed.
2) However, **qualitative data** (such as an interview transcript) is much more difficult to analyse **objectively**.

Qualitative Analysis Involves Subjective Decisions

Qualitative analysis can involve making **summaries** and identifying key **themes** and **categories**. For example:

1) Analysis of a transcript or video involves identifying statements — e.g. feelings, jokes, criticisms, etc. Different researchers may read different things into the statements.
2) Such analysis may give the basis for **hypotheses**, e.g. about what may be found in other sources / other things the participant may say — the hypothesis formation is therefore **grounded in the data** (but could still be subjective).

Criticisms

1) How do you decide **which categories to use** and whether a statement fits a particular category?
2) How do you decide what to **leave out** of the summary, or which quotations to use?

These are **subjective** decisions and researchers may be **biased**, possibly showing statements or events **out of context**.

Strengths

1) Qualitative analysis preserves the **detail** in the data.
2) Creating hypotheses during the analysis allows for new **insights** to be developed.
3) Some **objectivity** can be established by using **triangulation** — other sources of data are used to check conclusions (e.g. previous interviews). With more sources researchers can cross-check their interpretations.

Content Analysis** is a Way to **Quantify Qualitative Data

1) When analysing a transcript, **coding units** can be established, e.g. 'references to cultural stereotypes'. These phrases are given **operationalised definitions**, e.g. 'defining a cultural stereotype'.
2) A **frequency count** of how many times each coding unit occurs in the transcript can be done, producing **quantitative data**, which can then be **statistically analysed** — this is known as **content analysis**.

Strengths — A **clear summary** of the patterns in the data may be established. Statistics provide a more **objective basis** for comparisons and statistical tests may show, for example, that a coding unit is **significantly** more frequent in one source of data than in another.

Criticisms — Subjective judgements are still made to define coding units. Also, reducing the data to particular coding units removes detail, and the true meaning of things may be lost when taken **out of context**.

Practice Questions

Q1 What is naturalistic observation?

Q2 Explain the difference between structured and informal/unstructured interviews.

Q3 What are the advantages and disadvantages of case studies?

Q4 What is content analysis?

Exam Questions

Q1 Explain why the analysis of qualitative data can be subjective. [2 marks]

Q2 Give one advantage and one disadvantage of content analysis. [4 marks]

Case study — leather, brown, handle, wheels... but thinks it's still a cow...

Phew, that's a whole lot of stuff on analysis of qualitative data. Which makes me think it must be important. It shouldn't be too bad to learn — four observational methods, a little bit on objectively analysing the results and an even littler bit on quantifying them. Learn that and it's job done. For now that is — there are still a few pages left before you can totally relax.

Presenting Data

It's all very well investigating the effects of the 'sarcastic clap' on a live interpretive dance show, but you also need to be able to present the results clearly. Results can be presented in different ways and you need to know what they are...

Data Can Be Presented in Various Ways

1) **Qualitative** data from observations, interviews, surveys, etc. (see pages 232-233) can be presented in a **report** as a '**verbal summary**'.
2) The report will contain **summaries** of what was seen or said, possibly using **categories** to group data together. Also **quotations** from participants can be used, and any **research hypotheses** that developed during the study or data analysis may be discussed.
3) When **quantitative** data is **collected** (or **produced** from qualitative data, e.g. by a **content analysis** — see p.233), it can be **summarised** and presented in various ways. Read on...

Tables are a Good Way to Summarise Quantitative Data

Tables can be used to clearly present the data and show any **patterns** in the scores.

Tables of '**raw data**' show the scores **before** any **analysis** has been done on them.

Other tables may show **descriptive statistics** such as the mean, range and standard deviation.

Table To Show the Qualities of Different Types of Ice Cream

	Quality (score out of 10)		
Type of ice cream	Tastiness	Thickness	Throwability
Chocolate	9	7	6
Toffee	8	6	7
Strawberry	8	5	4
Earwax	2	9	8

Bar Charts Can be Used for Non-continuous Data

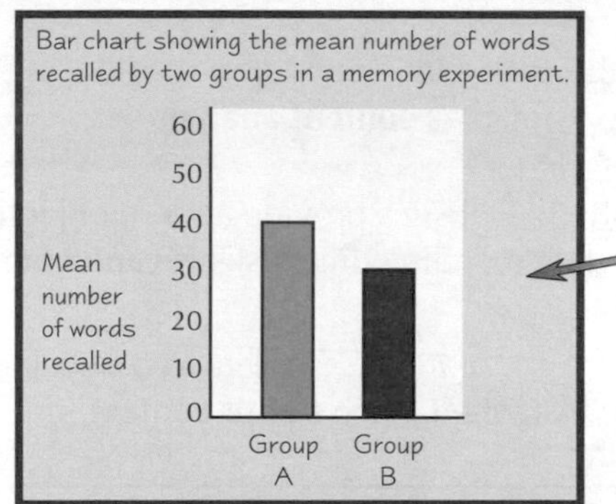

Bar charts (bar graphs) are usually used to present '**non-continuous data**' — when a variable falls into **categories** rather than being measured on a numbered scale.

This bar chart shows the number of words recalled by two different groups in a memory experiment.

Note that the columns in bar charts **don't touch** each other. Also, it's preferable to always show the **full vertical scale**, or **clearly indicate** when it isn't all shown (otherwise it can be **misleading**).

Histograms are for When You Have Continuous Data

Histograms show data measured on a '**continuous**' scale of measurement.

This histogram shows the time different participants took to complete a task.

Each column shows a **class interval** (here, each class interval is 10 seconds), and the columns **touch** each other.

All intervals are shown, even if there are **no scores** within them.

It's the **height** of the column that shows the number of values in that interval.

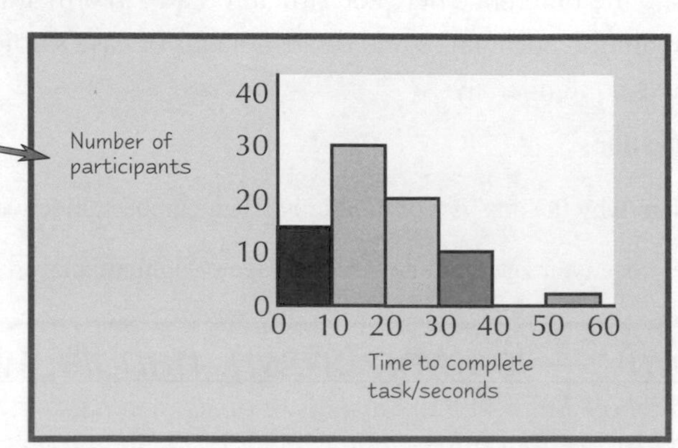

Presenting Data

Frequency Polygons are Good for Showing More Than One Set of Data

Frequency polygons are similar to histograms, but use **lines** to show where the top of each column would reach.

It can be useful to combine **two or more** frequency polygons on the same set of axes — then it's easy to **make comparisons** between groups.

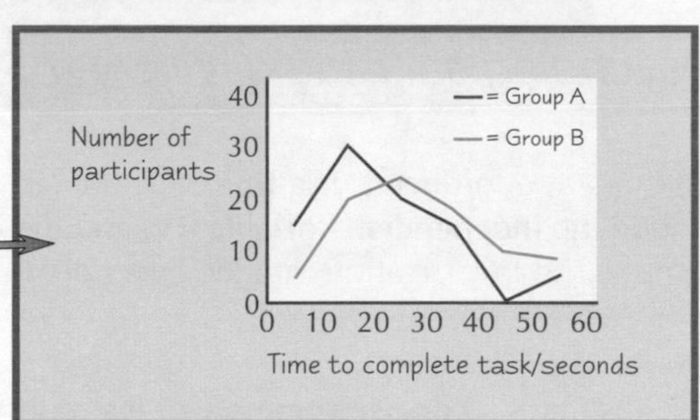

Scattergraphs Show Relationships Between Co-variables

Correlation is a measure of the relationship between **two variables**, e.g. how closely **exam grades** are related to **amount of revision**. A correlational coefficient is produced — these range from **–1** (a perfect linear **negative** relationship) to **+1** (the same, but **positive**). In a **correlational study** data can be displayed in scattergraphs.

1) **Positive correlation** — this means that as one variable rises, so does the other (and likewise, if one falls, so does the other).
   Example: hours of study and average test score.
   The correlation coefficient is roughly **0.75** (close to +1).

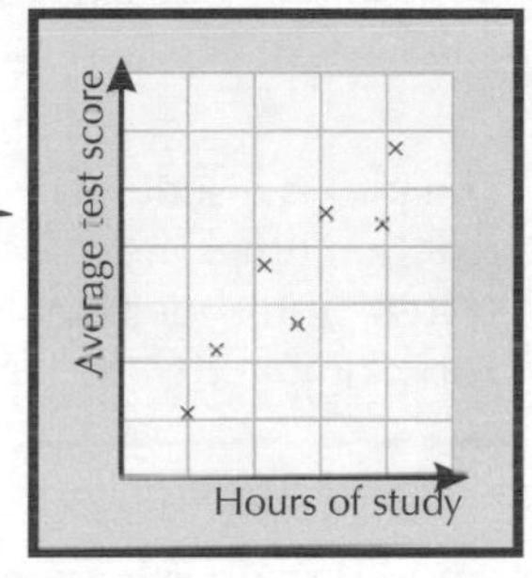

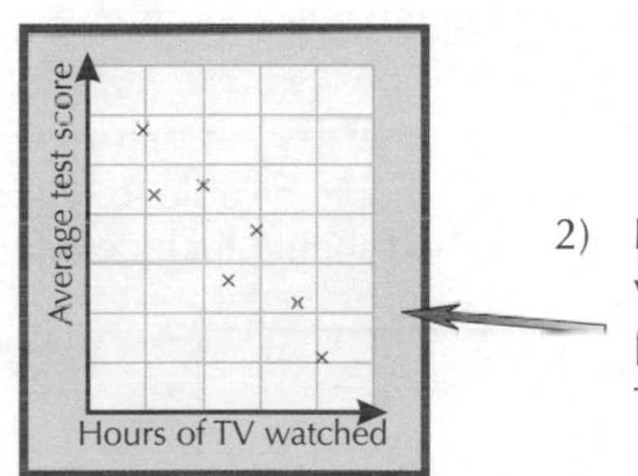

2) **Negative correlation** — this means that as one variable rises, the other one falls (and vice versa).
   Example: hours of TV watched each week and average test score.
   The correlation coefficient is roughly **–0.75** (close to -1).

3) **No correlation** — if the correlation coefficient is 0 (or close to 0), then the two variables aren't linked.
   Example: a student's height and their average test score.
   The correlation coefficient is roughly **0.01** (close to 0).

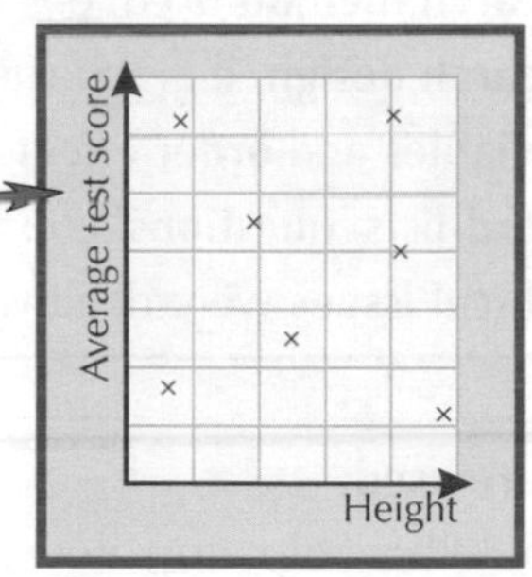

Practice Questions

Q1 What kind of data is shown on bar charts?

Q2 What type of data do histograms represent?

Q3 What is the difference between a negative correlation and no correlation?

Exam Question

Q1 Describe three ways of summarising quantitative data. [6 marks]

What? They want numbers and charts as well? Are you having a graph?

Producing a graphical representation of results means that you can identify trends and correlations without having to trawl through endless reams of numbers. There's nothing worse than trying to work out 'what it all means' when all you really want to do is go downstairs and have a bowl of soup. But if you pop it on a graph, you can be at your saucepan in seconds.

Reporting on Psychological Investigations

Once the research study has been done you'd think that'd be the end of it and the poor overworked psychologist could have a break. But no — the study has to be written up and it has to be done in a certain way. Some people are so picky.

Reports on Psychological Studies Have a **Specific Structure**

Title

The first thing a report needs is a **title**. It should say what the study's **about** and include the **independent variable** (**IV**) and the **dependent variable** (**DV**). For example, 'An Investigation into the Effect of Hunger on Reaction Times'.

Abstract

The abstract's a **concise summary** of the report (often no more than 120 words), telling the reader about the research and findings without them having to read the **whole report**. It should include brief descriptions of the **aims** and **hypotheses** of the study, the **method**, and a summary of the **results**. The abstract should also contain interpretations of the findings and any significant **flaws** in the study. A lot to fit into a small space...

Introduction

The introduction is a general **overview** of the **area** being studied, including **existing theories**. It should also discuss a few **studies closely related** to the current study.

Aim and Hypotheses

The aim is a sentence stating the **purpose** of the study. For example, 'To investigate whether reaction times are affected by hunger levels'. The hypothesis is what's actually going to be **tested**, and should include the **independent variable** and the **dependent variable**. For example, 'There is no relationship between hunger levels and reaction time'.

Method

The method describes **how** the research was **carried out**. Someone should be able to **replicate** the study by following the method, so it needs to be **detailed**. The method should include information on:

The **design of the investigation**, for example:
- The **research method** used, e.g. field experiment, interview.
- The **research design**, e.g. repeated measures, and any potential problems with the design.
- How **variables** and **order effects** were **controlled**, e.g. counterbalancing, randomisation.
- How **word-lists**, **questions**, etc. were chosen.
- How **ethical issues** were dealt with.

The **procedure used**:
- This should be a blow-by-blow account of **what happened** each time a participant took part.
- It should start with **how** the researcher and the investigation were **introduced** to the participant and how **informed consent** was obtained.
- It needs to include what was **said** to the participants (the standardised instructions), how the study was **carried out** and how the participants were **debriefed**.
- The method should also contain details of how the **data** was **recorded**.

The **use of participants**, for example:

The **number** of participants used.

The **demographics** of the participants, e.g. age, employment, gender, etc.

The **sampling method** used (see p.220).

How participants were **allocated** to **conditions**.

The **resources used**, for example:

The **materials** used, e.g. questionnaires, pictures, word lists, etc.

Any **apparatus** used — it's often useful to include diagrams or photographs of these.

Reporting on Psychological Investigations

Results

The results of the study can be reported as **descriptive** or **inferential** statistics. Descriptive statistics include **tables**, **graphs** and **charts** (see p.234-235). Inferential statistics (see pages 228-231) involve doing **statistical tests** on the data. The results section needs to include explanations of **why** certain tests were chosen, e.g. because the study was looking for a correlation. The **results** of the test — including the observed value, the critical value and level of significance should also be included.

Discussion

The discussion covers a range of things including:

- **An explanation of the findings** — **summarising** the results and **relating** them to the **aim** and **hypothesis**. The null hypothesis should be accepted or rejected in the discussion. Any **unexpected** findings should also be addressed and explained here.
- **The implications of the study** — for example, whether the study relates to **real-life situations**, e.g. interviews, exams, etc.
- **The limitations and modifications of the study** — any **problems** or **limitations** need to be explained, along with modifications that could **improve** the study.
- **The relationship to background research** — the results need to be related to the **background research** covered in the introduction. The data should be compared to other data and comments made on whether or not the findings of the study support the findings of other studies.
- **Suggestions for further research** — at least two ideas for further research should be included.

References

The references section contains a list of all the books, articles and websites that have been used for **information** during the study. It allows the reader to see where the information on the **research** and **theories** mentioned in the report (e.g. in the introduction) came from. References should be presented in **alphabetical order** of first author's surname.

Appendices

Any **materials** used, e.g. questionnaires or diagrams, can be put in the appendix. **Raw data** and **statistical test calculations** also go here.

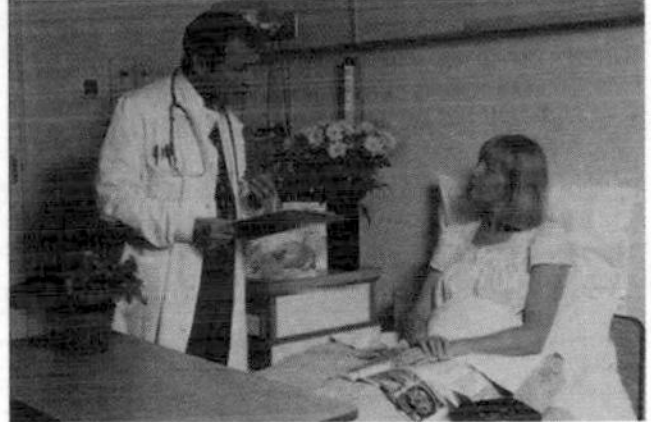

When Ellie said she needed help with her appendix, a hospital trip wasn't what she had in mind.

General Tips

The report should be written in the **third person**, e.g. 'the participants were asked to recall numbers' rather than 'I asked the participants to recall numbers'. The language used should be **formal**, e.g. 'the participants in the study were an opportunity sample', rather than 'the participants were basically anyone we could get hold of.'

Practice Questions

Q1 What should be included in an abstract?

Q2 In which section of a report would you find an overview of the research area?

Q3 List six things that should be included in a method.

Q4 Name two types of statistics that could be included in the results section of a report.

Q5 In which section should materials such as questionnaires be included?

You've achieved your aim and reached the end of the section — result...

If you're the kind of person that has their own special celebratory dance for moments of crowning glory or achievement, I suggest you perform it now — because this is the end of the book. If you've made it this far and learned everything in between then you are now (unofficially) an unstoppable psychological research machine. And very smart, too.

Do Well in Your AQA Exam

These pages are about how to ace the exam. Which is, after all, the name of the game. And what a fun game it's been.

There are **Two Units** in AQA A2 Psychology

The Unit 3 (Topics in Psychology) exam has eight questions

1) There'll be **one question** on each of the following topics — Biological Rhythms and Sleep, Perception, Gender, Relationships, Aggression, Eating Behaviour, Intelligence and Learning, and Cognition and Development.
2) Don't worry though — you just need to choose **three** of these questions to answer. Each one is worth **24 marks** and could be either a **single question** or a **two-part question**.
3) The exam lasts for an **hour and a half**.

You'll be marked on the quality of your written communication in all three answers.

The Unit 4 (Psychopathology, Psychology in Action and Research Methods) exam is split into three sections

1) **Section A** is on **Psychopathology** and you'll have to answer **one 24 mark question** out of a choice of **three**.
2) **Section B** is on **Psychology in Action** — again, you need to answer **one 24 mark question** out of **three**.
3) **Section C** has one **compulsory** question on **Research Methods**. It's worth **35 marks** and is split into **several parts**.
4) The exam lasts for **two hours**.

You'll only be marked on the quality of your written communication in section A.

The **Number of Marks** Tells You **How Much to Write**

1) The number of marks that a question is worth gives you a pretty good clue of **how much to write**.
2) You get **one mark per correct point** made, so if a question's worth four marks, you need to write four decent points.
3) In the Research Methods Section (Unit 4) there's no point writing a huge answer for a question that's only worth a few marks — it's just a **waste of your time**.
4) For the longer essay-style questions, make sure that you've written **enough** to get good marks, but don't waffle.

You Need to Meet Certain **Assessment Objectives**

Just as in AS, there are three assessment objectives covered by the two units — **AO1**, **AO2** and **AO3**. The way that a question is **worded** can give away which assessment objective is being tested.

AO1 is about the facts and theories

These questions test your **knowledge and understanding of science**. You get marks by **recalling** and **describing** psychological knowledge, such as theories, studies and methods. For example, you might get asked to **describe a theory** of depression. To get the marks, you'd simply need to describe what the theory proposed and describe its key features. What you don't need to do is evaluate the theory — that'd just be a waste of time that you could use elsewhere, and you wouldn't get any extra marks.

AO2 gets you to apply your knowledge

AO2 questions are slightly different in that they get you to **apply your knowledge and understanding** of science. It's likely that these questions will begin with '**discuss**' or '**evaluate**'. Rather than just recalling stuff, e.g. listing relevant experiments, you've got to **apply your knowledge** to the situation in these questions. So, you'd need to use the experiments you've come up with to **support your argument**. You also might have to apply your knowledge to situations you've not come across before. For example, you could be asked to assess the **validity**, **reliability** or **credibility** of a study that's new to you.

AO3 is about 'How Science Works'

'**How Science Works**' focuses on how scientific experiments are carried out. You need to be able to suggest appropriate **methodology** and know how to make sure measurements and observations are **valid** and **reliable**. You could also be asked to **analyse** and **evaluate** the **methodology** and **results** of a study described in the exam. When you're doing this, don't forget about things like **ethics** and **safety**.

Do Well in Your AQA Exam

An *Example Answer* to Show You What to Aim for...

See pages 122-123 "Development of Perception" for more about this answer.

1 (a) Outline one cross-cultural study into the development of perceptual abilities. *(8 marks)*

(b) Outline the nature-nurture debate in relation to explanations of perceptual development. *(16 marks)*

(a) Segall et al (1966) investigated whether the Müller-Lyer illusion has a cross-cultural effect. They showed the Müller-Lyer illusion to a group of South Africans and a group of rural Zulus, and asked them which line was the longest. Most of the urban South Africans identified the line with the inwardly pointing arrows as being longer than the line with the outwardly pointing arrows, even though the lines were actually the same length. Segall et al believed this was because they were used to an environment dominated by straight lines (e.g. in their buildings) and interpreted the diagram in 3D. In other words, they saw one line as a corner receding away from them, and the other as a corner projecting towards them. The brain interprets the line receding away as being further away, so interprets it as being larger than the image it forms on the retina.

The Zulus were less susceptible to the Müller-Lyer illusion than the urban South Africans — a large proportion of them identified the lines as being the same length. Segall et al believed this was because they were less familiar with an environment made heavily from straight lines (e.g. their huts were circular) so didn't apply size constancy in the same way as the urban South Africans. This meant that they didn't perceive any difference in the length of the lines. Segall et al saw this cross-cultural difference in perception as evidence that perceptual abilities are developed in response to the environment. In other words, perception is the result of nurture.

Get straight into gaining marks by introducing the study you're going to outline.

This question is worth 8 marks so make sure you write enough — a couple of sentences won't do.

(b) Some psychologists believe that the development of perceptual abilities such as depth perception and visual constancies are the result of nature — they're innate abilities. Others believe that they are the result of nurture — we learn them through interaction with our environment. There are studies to support both sides of this debate.

For example, Gibson and Walk (1960) investigated the development of depth perception in babies. They created a 'visual cliff' and investigated whether six-month old babies would crawl over the 'deep' side. They found that babies were reluctant to crawl over the deep side, and concluded that babies could perceive this as a drop. From this, they concluded that depth perception is the result of nature. However, the babies that Gibson and Walk tested were 6 months old so could have learnt depth perception by this age.

Campos (1970) addressed this problem by using a different measure of depth perception. He measured the heart rate of babies who could and couldn't crawl on both sides of the cliff. He found that the heart rate of babies who couldn't crawl didn't change on either side of the cliff, suggesting that they are not aware of the depth. However, the heart rate of babies who could crawl dropped on the deep side, suggesting that older babies are aware of the change in depth. Campos concluded that as only the older babies appeared to be aware of depth this shows that depth perception is learned and therefore down to nurture.

The conflicting findings of these studies and many more (e.g. Segall et al (1966) suggests perceptual development is the result of nurture, Bower (1985) suggests it's the result of nature) mean that no conclusion can yet be drawn on whether perceptual development is the result of nature or nurture. In fact, many psychologists now believe that perceptual abilities could come about by a combination of the two.

The question's about the nature-nurture debate so include evidence for nature **and** for nurture.

Sum up your answer with a brief conclusion — but don't just repeat everything you've said.

... And Some Pointers About What to *Avoid*...

1) It's important to remember that it's not just a case of blindly scribbling down **everything** you can think of that's related to the subject. Doing this just **wastes time**, and it doesn't exactly impress the examiner.
2) You only get marks for stuff that's **relevant** and **answers the question**.
3) So, read the question a couple of times before you start writing so that you really understand what it's asking.
4) Try to **structure** your answer in an **organised** way. If there's one thing that examiners find worse than a load of pointless information, it's being unable to make head or tail of an answer. So, before you start, jot down a **plan** of what you want to write so you don't end up with a really jumbled answer.

Index

Index

Index

Index

Index